WHAT IS BEING SAID ABOUT *FACES OF FOUNDERS: HIRAM, MAINE*

As a Maine historian I highly recommend Sally Williams's *Faces of Founders: Hiram, Maine.* Though the author states, "It is not a complete history or genealogy of the early settlement," it provides the flavor and salient details necessary to arrive at an understanding of the early place and the people who settled and shaped Hiram. I have written a history of Maine, histories of L.L.Bean and Sweetser Children's Home, as well as numerous biographical pieces, and writing a town history, even with a top coauthor, was the hardest thing for me to manage. Sally Williams is a first-rate historian who knows her subject intimately and presents it clearly and honestly.

—William David Barry, author of *Maine: The Wilder Half of New England* (2012)

Faces of Founders will surprise even lifelong residents of Hiram with its newfound stories and facts thanks to Sally Williams's intrepid search for the town's hidden past. One of my particular interests as a cultural historian is the people earlier historians left out, so it's a pleasure to read a town history that tells of Native Molly Ockett and other women whose struggles to "make do, or do without" are so often neglected. The life of Mary Jane Barker is one of my favorites to ponder. Raised in a genteel household, orphaned, wed at sixteen, she died at forty-four. She followed her husband to frontier Michigan, where she no doubt set aside her fancy needlework to scrub the dairy, tend the chickens, and get done what needed to be done to raise her nine children. *Faces of Founders* helps us know and remember a past that is otherwise virtually impossible to comprehend in today's world.

—Jan Eakins, Maine historian, writer, instructor

Town accounts are often notoriously dry, but in the right hands, they can be remarkable. Sally Williams moves deftly between the traditional establishment of Hiram and the rich social fabric of those who settled there. Smoothly written and generously illustrated, *Faces of Founders* shows insightful connection between the past and the present.

—Deborah Gould, author of *The Eastern, Book One: The Early Years* and *The Eastern, Book Two: Later On*

Through a persistent search for Hiram's story, Sally Williams has compiled a beautifully and carefully constructed history not only of events but of the human condition. *Faces of Founders: Hiram, Maine* transcends the past and propels you into a present that still endures in the architecture, the landscape, and the people that make up our shared experience.

—Bradford Fuller, author of *Brownfield, Maine: An Illustrated History*

Curious people want to know how things used to be in their hometowns. We wonder how the strong and adventurous people who arrived here centuries ago made the spot livable. We try to imagine how they kept themselves safe, what food they found and produced, how they related to Native people. How did they build things, get from place to place, make tools, use money, raise children, treat illness, share resources, and keep order for the common good? How did women routinely constrained by societal norms in a rugged "man's world" remain strong and inventive, even into widowhood?

In her thoroughly engaging book of history *Faces of Founders: Hiram, Maine* author Sally Williams lays out in colorful detail what life was like in early Hiram and surrounding towns, from 1774 through the 1830s. Williams has done the meticulous scholarly research. We get the prize: educational and fascinating stories of the courage, mistakes, and ingenuity of those who lived here long ago.

In this modern era we bemoan our "busy-ness." Williams's book is a terrific tutorial and reminder: Early settlers did well nearly all things essential.

—Ellie Stein, Wards Hill, Hiram

Faces *of* Founders

Hiram, Maine

SALLY WILLIAMS
HIRAM HISTORICAL SOCIETY

Faces of Founders: Hiram, Maine
Copyright © 2021 Sally Williams

ISBN: 978-1-63381-271-0

On the cover:
Survey of Saco River by Bracey Banks, 1788,
Massachusetts Land Office Planbook 2:7

Designed and produced by:
Maine Authors Publishing
12 High Street, Thomaston, Maine
www.maineauthorspublishing.com

Printed in the United States of America

*This book is dedicated to Hubert W. Clemons (1929–2019),
without whose research this book would not have been written.*

THIS BOOK EXPLAINED

For many years it was thought that records of Hiram before its incorporation as a town in 1814 were lost or destroyed. Recently, however, we discovered that the Maine State Archives holds many Hiram documents, chiefly financial records, but also records of the militia and schools, town clerk, and Overseers of the Poor, along with warrants of the selectmen and constables. The Maine Historical Society also holds many letters of the Wadsworth family, early founders of the town, as well as some tax and voting records. The Massachusetts State Archives preserves legislative records before 1820, at which time Maine separated from Massachusetts to become a state, and the Massachusetts Judicial Archives does the same for its documents. This is a rich if incomplete record of the government of Hiram, or Great Ossipee, from early settlement in 1774 to incorporation, and it inspired the writing of this book.

Receipts, bills for services rendered, tallies of school children, inventories of property for highway taxes and poll taxes and school taxes, supplies given to paupers, formation of committees, summons of drills for the militia, and lists of voters all provide the details that formed the basis for official summarized reports—the backup, so to speak. They add flesh to the founders, as do the secondary histories and family genealogies consulted, and help fill gaps left by the lack of a U.S. federal census of Hiram for 1810, which was lost.

This book focuses on early life in the years before "Hyram" or "Great Ossapee," as it was frequently spelled, became a legal town, and it follows some settlers and traces some family connections through 1830 and beyond. Above all, it is a tribute to those founders who made Hiram a viable community surrounded by "a forest primeval with towering pines and hemlocks.[1]

Extensive research, much of which was conducted using technology not available to earlier historians, refutes some past misunderstandings about Hiram history. The book provides new insights into the power of settlers in town, county, and state governance. It sheds light on some of the scurrilous land deals. It overturns the idea that settlers were always self-sufficient. It reconfirms settlers' close relationship to the environment, their dependence on animals and neighbors, and the devastating power of nature. It reveals the flaws of individuals and the strength of families amid the energy and adventurous nature of the times.

Part 1 sums up what life was like in this pioneer settlement in southwestern Maine in the period 1774 to 1830. Part 2 focuses on forty-five founding families, some of whose stories have not been told. It is especially difficult to trace the lives of women, so it was thrilling to locate an account of Mary Jane Barker, who attended a Portland finishing school, married at age 16, and followed her physician husband to the western wilderness of Michigan. It was doubly exciting to ferret out the letter written by Rebecca Baston, newly widowed by the suicide of her kind and affectionate husband, leaving her with six young children, his debts, her unforgiving father-in-law, and her prospective poverty. More stories can be found throughout the book.

What the book is not: a complete history or genealogy of the early settlement.

There is much more to learn. If you can fill in some of the gaps in Hiram's history, please get in touch.

Sally Williams

President, Hiram Historical Society

PO Box 105

1593 Pequawket Trail

Hiram, ME 04041

207-615-4390 or gardenlit@gmail.com

---

1 Raymond C. Cotton, *Hog Reaves, Fields Drivers and Tything Men* (Hiram, ME: Hiram Historical Society, 1983), 6. Also a shortened phrase in Ridlon, *Saco Valley Settlements and Families*,145. Attributed to Llewellyn A. Wadsworth's address at the family reunion in Duxbury, MA, in 1882.

IN APPRECIATION

This book could not have been written without the aid of Hubert Clemons, who, over many years of meticulous research in a field we know to be fraught with ambiguities and contradictions, laid the groundwork of the genealogical connections of the people of Hiram. I am also indebted to the institutions of Maine and Massachusetts that preserved records of the plantation of Hiram or Great Ossipee and answered endless queries: Maine Historical Society, Maine State Archives, Massachusetts State Archives, Massachusetts State Library, Dyer Library and Saco Museum, McArthur Public Library, and the Maine historical societies of the towns with which Hiram shares its history: Baldwin, Biddeford, Brownfield, Cornish, Denmark, Fryeburg, Gorham, Parsonsfield, Porter, Scarborough, Sebago, Standish, Wells, Library of Michigan (MDE), Monadnock Center for History and Culture, Peterborough, New Hampshire, and others. I thank Soldiers Memorial Library for pointing to historical files collected before Hiram Historical Society was founded in 1978 and moved into quarters in the Great Ossipee Museum (former Mt. Cutler School). I thank the staff of the Hiram Town Office for help in accessing and copying town records and for their encouraging interest in the project to tell the history of the District of Hiram before its incorporation as a legal town in 1814, and also the Town Offices of Cornish, Porter and Standish. Thank you Conrad Hartford, Del and Grace Gilpatrick, Bruce Nason, Jim Hannaford, Jack and Diane Barnes, Charles Gilmor, Ruth McLucas Knight, Sue Moulton, Jack Wadsworth, Ken Kimball, and others who shared their knowledge of the town and granted permission to digitize their photographs. I appreciate that medical historian Dr. Richard Kahn kindly commented on Peleg Wadsworth's illness and death. I thank many readers, namely, John Babin, Bill Barry, Joyce Bibber, Patricia Brown, Jan Eakins, Charlotte Fullam, Janet Gunn, Grace and Del Gilpatrick, Jim Hannaford, Sylvia Pease, Jan Iler, Tilly Laskey, Tiffany Link, Jackie Moore, Nick Noyes, Ellie Stein, and others, such as Charles Gilmor, who steered me toward a better path. And additionally, my many thanks to Sue Moulton for her patience with my questions and for her research into Wadsworth family history.

Not least, my husband, Jan, who put up with it all.

CONTENTS

～ The Setting ～

INTRODUCTION TO HIRAM, MAINE

The town of Hiram is situated thirty-five miles northwest of Portland, Maine, in southern Oxford County. By car it is a one-hour drive from Portland along Routes 25, 113 (Pequawket Trail Scenic Byway), and 117. In its thirty-nine square miles, geographical features include Mt. Cutler, named for founder Timothy Cutler, two rivers—the Saco and the Ossipee—scenic hills and forests, and numerous streams and ponds, in particular Barker Pond, Middle Pond, Southeast Pond, Stanley Pond, Clemons Pond, Trafton Pond, and Jaybird.

It is surrounded by the towns of Baldwin, Cornish, Parsonsfield, Porter, Brownfield, Denmark, and Sebago.

The earliest surveys for settlement were in 1773 by Benjamin Prescott, on the east side of the Saco River. In 1774, Lt. Benjamin Ingalls surveyed the west side. Major land grants were awarded to Josiah Waters (c. 1790), Benjamin Prescott (c. 1794), and Timothy Cutler (1788). Brigadier General Peleg Wadsworth purchased seventy-eight hundred acres for settlement in 1790. Peleg Wadsworth and Timothy Cutler are considered the principal founders of the town. Hiram was part of York County until 1805, when it was ceded to the newly formed Oxford County. It was incorporated as a town in 1814 when the population was about four hundred. The population grew until about 1880. In 2018 it was 1,731, about five hundred more than the population in 1850 before the Civil War, migration to the west, and the two World Wars lowered the number. Prominent neighborhoods were Hiram Bridge, East Hiram, Durgintown, Tripptown, South Hiram Village (later included in the Kezar Falls association), and, lastly, New Settlement.

Abundant water power attracted industries in the late eighteenth and nineteenth centuries. In the mid-nineteenth century Hiram was a thriving agricultural town supporting eighteen school districts, two hotels, two Grange halls, fraternal organizations, more than twenty shops, and mills for lumber and planing, grinding grain, and carding. It had factories for men's clothing, slate blackboards, ax handles, and furniture—ten thousand chairs were made in 1832. Logging and ice cutting were prominent, along with tourism, and principal crops of hay and corn and apples. Two railroads—the Portland & Ogdensburg Railroad in 1871 and the narrow gauge Bridgton & Saco River Railroad in 1883—brought economic prosperity for agricultural and wood products. In the nineteenth and early twentieth centuries, Hiram was a nearly self-sustaining community supported by farming, logging, ice cutting, clothing manufacturing, retail shops, and tourism. Residents earned supplemental income as blacksmiths, coopers, cordwainers, millers, milliners, tailors, lawyers, preachers, and teachers.

Hiram's early history was similar to that of other New England farming towns, but it differed in significant ways. Its proprietors were benevolent. Its principal patriarch was a Revolutionary War hero. It was enriched with natural resources. It was not isolated—it was less than a day's horse ride from Bartlett, New Hampshire, and to Portland, Maine—thus it lured industry, some of it innovative, such as silk. It did not escape from national realities, however, such as indentured servitude and poverty. These are what make Hiram's history both common and special. The book *Faces of Founders: Hiram, Maine* tells the stories of some of these industrious people.

Today's businesses are in food production (Grandy Oats), agriculture (Apple Acres orchard and restaurant, Good Buddy Farm, Old Homestead Farm, and Avella), retail (Paisley Pines Quilt Shop, Left Antler Gunsmithing, and Hiram Village Store collectibles), solar installation (SunVersion), metal fabrication (Eastman Welding), and woodworking (Tear Cap Workshops). Residents work at home in technological services. Hiram is also home to Four Corners general store, Maine Teen Camp, three consolidated schools (School Administrative District 55), and historic buildings: the Arts Center at 8 Hancock Avenue, Hiram Community Center, and Great Ossipee Museum of Hiram Historical Society. On the National Register of Historic Places are John Watson Intervale Farm, Lemuel Cotton Store, Soldiers Memorial Library, and Wadsworth Hall. Hiram is a pleasant place to live.

TIMELINE OF EVENTS—INTERNATIONAL, NATIONAL, AND LOCAL

1661—Native American Captain Sunday deeds land north of Ossipee River where it joins Saco River

1763—Treaty of Paris ends French and Indian Wars. Interior lands of Maine are safer

1773—Boston Tea Party

1773—Benjamin Prescott surveys land east of the Saco River in **Hiram**

1774—Continental Congress meets to organize opposition to Britain's Intolerable Acts

1774 August—Lt. Benjamin Ingalls surveys land west of Saco River around Hancock Brook in **Hiram**

1774—John Wilkinson invents his boring machine, considered by some to be the first machine tool

1775 April—Battle of Lexington and Concord, Massachusetts

1775 October—The British burn Portland, Maine, including Timothy Cutler's bakery

1779—Massachusetts creates the District of Maine

1779—Revolutionary War Penobscot Expedition retreat is led by Gen. Peleg Wadsworth

1779—Capt. John Lane and family share hospitality with John Clemons family in **Hiram**

1780—John and Abigail Clemons settle between Clemons and Little Clemons ponds in **Hiram**

1783 September—Treaty of Paris ends the Revolutionary War

1787 May—American Constitution adopted

1787 November—Timothy Cutler awarded six thousand acres in **Hiram** and Porter

1790 March—Gen. Peleg Wadsworth purchases seventy-eight hundred acres in **Hiram** at 12.5 cents per acre

1790—Thomas Saint invents the sewing machine in England

1790—First U.S. census shows eighteen families living in **Hiram**

1793—England and France at war

1801—Cutler petitions to incorporate **Hiram** as a town, General Wadsworth opposes, petition is denied

1802—Bach's sonatas and partitas for solo violin are published

1803—France sells the Louisiana Purchase to the U.S.

1804—Richard Trevithick invents the steam locomotive—first ferry, New York to Hoboken, New Jersey

1805—Battle of Trafalgar; Lewis and Clark expedition begins

1807—**Hiram** is incorporated as a district (plantation), gains part of Brownfield

1807—Congress bans importation of African slaves

1808—Beethoven completes Sixth Symphony

1814 June 14—**Hiram** is incorporated as a town; first Town Meeting held November 7, 1814

1814 December 24—Treaty of Ghent ends the War of 1812

1816—Move for separation of Maine from Massachusetts grows from lack of support in the War of 1812

1817—Baron Karl von Drais invents the dandy horse, early velocipede, precursor to the modern bicycle

1822—Connecticut bans property ownership as a requirement for voting

1822—Cotton mills in Lowell, Massachusetts, begin production with women workers

1822—Charles Babbage begins building the first programmable mechanical computer

1825—Erie Canal is completed

1829 November 12—Gen. Peleg Wadsworth, founder of **Hiram**, dies

1830—Fifth U.S. census: population totals thirteen million, including 2.3 million African Americans, of whom two million are enslaved. Population west of the Appalachian Mountains is three million, more than 25 percent of the U.S. population

Great Falls on the Saco River was an important place to Native Americans. This view is looking upstream toward Mt. Misery. In the center lie Emery's Mills, built in the late nineteenth century. The east-bank portion of the Mills washed away in the great freshet of March 1895, the west bank in April 1896. Mills such as Emery's blocked the free flow of the river that Native Americans depended upon for fishing and critical sustenance. Passage was a source of contention.

NATIVE AMERICANS

many misunderstandings

Native Americans lived along the Saco and Ossipee rivers for centuries before the arrival of white men, the first of whom were hunters and trappers who did not settle. The tribes inhabiting the Saco River on contact were the Sokokis, or Pequawkets, one of the subdivisions of the Abenakis.

In 1666, long before settlers arrived, Native American Captain Sunday, a chief of the Sokokis tribe, deeded to Major William Phillips of Saco several tracts of land above Great Ossipee River the tribe called "Three Hills of Rocks." In 1807 the town taxed Phillips' heirs for a tract of fifteen hundred acres in Hiram above the falls,[2] which convinced historian Gideon T. Ridlon that this property was in Hiram.[3]

The precise location of this property is unknown,

---

2 In the Highway Tax compilation for 1806 under "Nonverified" entries is written "1500 acres of Phillips Grant, present owners unknown," taxed $4.36. Maine State Archives, Hiram, Box 14.

3 Gideon T. Ridlon, *Saco Valley Settlements and Families* (Portland, ME: G. T. Ridlon, facsimile of the 1895 edition, 1984), 145.

Map of York County, Maine, 1791.[4]

but there are three prominences in Hiram above the falls it could be: Mt. Cutler, Falls Mountain, and Gould Mountain or Peaked Mountain.

Over thousands of years, Native Americans had developed an effective agriculture of corn, beans, squash, and tobacco, which they shared with the early settlers, who eagerly adopted the techniques. Corn, the principal crop, was planted in May when alewives migrated up fresh water rivers. Four to six of the best corn seeds and two to three Brazilian beans[5] were grouped over a fish and mounded with earth. The beans twined around the stalks and kept the ground free of weeds. Surrounding both were pumpkins and squash, and the whole garden was enclosed to ward off herbivores. This system, known as "the three sisters," proved more successful than the settlers' methods learned in the old country and is still practiced. The Natives likewise benefited from the settlers' more efficient tools.

Mary Harris, captured in Deerfield, Massachusetts, and marched north, described her memories of tribes growing corn in the intervale above the great falls in Hiram.[6] This is near where Gen. Peleg Wadsworth, c. 1795, set up Daniel Hickey's farm, which is unrecognizable in today's forest. In the 1950s, a farmer plowing his field of corn in this intervale downstream from Hiawatha Campground struck a carved-stone digging tool, certainly used by Native Americans.

Prior to white people arriving, the digging, planting, weeding, harvesting, and dressing tools of the Native Americans were wooden spades, horseshoe crab shells, clam shells, hands, and Stone-Age stone tools.[7]

Felling trees with primitive carved stone axes to clear land was arduous, and Natives preferred to set trees on fire or girdle them and wait for them to die. Ash from burning brush also enriched the soil.

Settlers brought iron hoes and cast-iron kettles that greatly alleviated the work of women and

---

4   Lora Altine Woodbury Underhill, *Descendants of Edward Small of New England and the Allied Families, with Tracings of English Ancestry*, Vol. 1 (Cambridge: Privately printed at the Riverside Press, 1910), 62.

5   Similar to Pinto beans.

6   Joseph Keller, interpreter, to the governor of Massachusetts, account October 24, 1744, letter December 3, 1744, detailing information regarding the Eastern Indians told to him by two of the sons of the kidnapped Mary Harris. Massachusetts State Archives Collection Vol. 31, 510–511, 518–520.

7   Stone tools are pictured in Ridlon, *Saco Valley Settlements and Families*, following p. 20.

A digging tool found by a farmer in the intervale above the great falls in Hiram. About seven inches long, it is small enough to fit comfortably in one's hand. Scraping marks from the plow are visible. It is privately owned.

children who toiled in the fields and cooked and/ or preserved the harvest. Corn and beans were harvested in September, dried and stored in "Indian barns," holes in the ground on slopes to shed water and lined with bark. Men cultivated tobacco.[8] The settlers' unwieldy wooden plows were unnecessary in the no-till gardens of Native Americans.

The friendly beginnings of relations between settlers and Native Americans soon dissolved into hostilities. One of the causes was misunderstandings about property rights. Native Americans had a culture

of communal land stewardship that was diametrically opposed to the European concept of private use and ownership. Natives believed they were allowing settlers to pass through their shared places, and gave deeds to the same land to several people, whereas white settlers believed they were buying ownership when they exchanged money or goods for property rights. Settlers thus offended Natives when they built dams on the Saco River to run mills, interfering with passage of the tribe's seasonal migrations south to plant corn in spring, to fish and gather berries in summer in Saco, and to harvest corn on the journey back to their homeland of Pequawket (Fryeburg) in fall. Clashes ensued as each believed the other was violating their terms.

Tensions between settlers and Native Americans became high when Squandro was sachem in 1675. Settlers enraged him enough that he put a curse on the Saco River. The story has several similar versions. In one, three drunken sailors from an English ship set out in a rowboat up the Saco River and decided to test their belief that Native American babies knew how to swim instinctively because the Native way of swimming was to dog paddle instead of doing the breaststroke, which, in Europe, was learned. They upended the canoe of Squandro's wife and her infant son, Menewee. Though the mother saved the baby from drowning, he died later. Squandro, normally a dignified and solemn man friendly to settlers, went into a rage and laid a curse that each year the river would take three white men until all white men fled.

Violence between the tribe and white settlers followed and led to the First Abenaki War, also known as the northern theater of King Philip's War. Squandro influenced a band of Androscoggins to attack whites in Saco in 1675, killing or capturing men and women. With the coming of settlers at the mouth of the Saco, many Native Americans retreated upstream and joined the Pequawkets or fled to Canada. After Captain Lovewell's murderous mission in 1725 to attack Abenakis in Pequawket (Fryeburg), the Pequawkets were reduced to two dozen fighting men.

---

8   Principal sources used about agriculture were Clarence A. Day, *A History of Maine Agriculture 1604–1860* (Orono, ME: University Press, 1954), and Richard W. Judd et al., editors, *Maine: The Pine Tree State from Prehistory to the Present* (Orono, ME: University of Maine Press, 1995).

Despite hostilities between Native Americans and whites in the seventeenth and early eighteenth centuries, when the first settlers arrived in Hiram in 1774, most of the Natives had succumbed to disease and there was no fighting. After the fall of Quebec during the French and Indian Wars, a few members of the tribe returned to Pequawket. "The last mention of the tribe living at Pequawket was in a petition to the General Court of Massachusetts dated at Fryeburg, in which the able bodied men asked for guns, ammunition and blankets for 'fourteen Native warriors" who became soldiers on the patriot side.[9] Among those Natives who fought in the Revolution and returned to Fryeburg were Old Philip and Captain Swarson (sometimes written Swanson). Philip was the last-known chief of the Pequawkets in this period. Abenaki peoples live in western Maine today.

A settler described Tom Hegon, or Tumtumhegan, another Native American soldier, as "a surly, ugly fellow and among the foremost in instigating the Indians against the whites." It is not known how his tribe viewed him. He participated in a raid upon Bethel and led captives, including Colonel Clark and Segar, to Canada in 1781.[10] Tom Hegon and his wife lived near Clemons Pond in Hiram and befriended John and Abigail Clemons, who settled there in 1780, along what is now called the Notch Road.

Abenakis, a woman (left) and a man. Courtesy of the City of Montreal, Records Management and Archives.

Mollyockett (Marie Agathe) c. 1740–42 to August 2, 1816 Pequawket Abenaki

Mollyockett was a legend in her time, for healing both settlers and Natives. Born in Saco, she was baptized Marie Agathe by French Catholic priests, but her Native name, meaning Singing Bird, was pronounced Mali Agit, and sounded like Mollyockett to English ears. In her long, hard life she experienced huge changes—the wars of the French and English and an intrusive wave of settlers after the Revolution, which eroded the tribe's hunter-gatherer way of life.

Striking with a large frame, erect posture, and pointed cap, Mollyockett became a familiar figure as she walked the region gathering herbs. Pequawket was the center of her life and, like others of her tribe, she migrated with the seasons. But she also traveled alone through northern New England, healing whoever needed it, asking little in return, and earning the gratitude of settlers. Some, however, were troubled by her strange, "savage" ways. Though a converted Methodist, she did not observe the Lord's day and was berated by a white woman for picking blueberries on a pleasant Sunday.[11]

Anecdotes abound.[12] One especially harsh winter

---

9 Ridlon, *Saco Valley Settlements and Families*, 16.

10 Dr. Nathaniel Tuckerman True, *The History of Bethel, Maine* (Bowie, MD: Heritage Books, Inc., 1994), 75–76. Segar's first name is unknown.

11 Ibid, 68-69.

12 Bunny McBride, *Women of the Dawn* (Lincoln: University of Nebraska Press, 1999), 43–67.

in Paris, Maine, she was refused shelter by three families until taken in by the Hamlins. While there, she healed two-year-old Hannibal Hamlin, later to become vice-president under Abraham Lincoln. Another patient cured was Henry Tufts, an infamous thief and autobiographer, who lived with Mollyockett's tribe for three years and wrote about it.[13]

Mollyockett was more than a healer and gatherer of herbs; she was a mother of four and the wife of Sabitus, whom she left because of his "intemperate habits and quarrelsome disposition."[14] Described as pretty and gentle, she had skills of her tribe. She wove a purse and created a bark box now in the Collections of Maine Historical Society. She shot moose and bears and collected duck feathers to make a bed, which she presented to Mrs. Swan of Bethel. She was loquacious and entertained residents with stories. She was fond of rum and beer. Though she slept in her camp, she took her meals with settlers.

Mollyockett saved the life of Colonel Clark of Boston, a trader of furs, by walking hours to warn him that Tom Hegon intended to kill him, as he

Mollyockett wove this purse c. 1785.
Collections of Maine Historical Society.

had two of Clark's compatriots. Clark showed his gratitude by bringing her to live with his family in Boston, but after a year she returned to her beloved Bethel, where he built her a wigwam and tended her in her old age.[15] Mollyockett was said to be older than one hundred when she died on August 2, 1816,[16] the cold "year without a summer." She is buried in Andover, Maine.

A Third Generation's Record of Stories

Llewellyn A. Wadsworth (1838–1922), Hiram's town historian, recorded many stories. The following accounts are from an undated unpublished manuscript, pages 2 and 4 (pages 1 and 3 are missing).[17]

> Page 2:
> I will note another point. In June 1777, Capt. John Lane, one of three brothers who were Captains in the Revolution, settled on the bank of Saco river, about a mile from my present home, and some two miles from the place where Gen. Wadsworth settled in Hiram. I have heard his grand-son Wm. H. Lane, now deceased, relate that his father, grand-father Wm Lane told him that when he was a boy he used to go down by the river to the camp or wigwam of Vinsen, two Indian hunters and they would put corn into a kettle with bear's grease and parch it for him. There may have been many little incidents that I have not heard of and Longfellow[18] may have. I throw in here a funny little incident. One day Capt. Francis, the Indian mentioned on previous page, came to my father's house and my mother got him some dinner. We lived three miles from a gristmill and were out of

13 Edmund Pearson, editor, *The Autobiography of a Criminal: Henry Tufts,* (New York City: Duffield and Company, 1930). Original edition, *A Narrative of the Life, Adventures, Travels and Sufferings of Henry Tufts,* now residing at Lemington, in the District of Maine (Dover, NH: Printed by Samuel Bragg Jr., 1807), 59–68.

14 Dr. Nathaniel Tuckerman True, *The History of Bethel,* 67.

15 True, 68–69. The same account is given in *History of the Town of Bethel, Maine* by William B. Lapham, a facsimile of the 1891 edition, 1994.

16 To be one hundred when she died, she would have had to be born earlier than stated.

17 In the collection of Hiram Historical Society.

18 Henry Wadsworth Longfellow.

wheat flour. Mother had some Indian meal[19] and she made some bread. She apologized by saying that she was out of flour and her bread was all Indian. Instantly she was shocked at her careless remark but the old man looked up with a twinkle in his eyes and said: "Me all Indian too." Doubtless scores of incidents and traditions have passed into oblivion. I will mention one or two more facts to sustain your claim that there were enough of Indian legends in Hiram to sustain your theory.

page 4

P.S. It is about 10 P.M. and I subside. Llewellyn A. Wadsworth

My father resided on a farm some three miles from Gen. Wadsworth's. We always supposed that the Indians once had a Settlement on it. On the south side of "Bill Merrill Mountain" one of our highest (1730 feet) there was a place of some six acres of poplar growth. There was not an old growth tree, log, or stump on it. It was about twice as long as it was wide with square corners and regular sides. Father[20] told me that in 1824, the year he came to his lot to live, this spot was burnt over, and the poplar all killed but it grew up again. Persons seeing this growth in the Spring with leaves before any other trees; (and in Autumn the leaves fell before any other leaves) asked the reason, and was told of the Theory of an Indian clearing. The adjacent forest was mainly oak. There were perhaps a dozen trees on this plot besides poplar. There is no history or record of any white persons living there. In Aug. 12, 1914 at our Town Centennial of Incorporation, I had prepared a pamphlet of the first half century mainly and I quoted from Williams History[21] that in 1660 ancestors of the Pequawket Indians of the Saco Valley who fought at Lovell's Pond employed carpenters from some of the white settlements to build a fort to protect them against the Mohawk Indians. This was built at the junction of Saco & Ossipee rivers, probably on the high land between the rivers. This historic fort may have added to Longfellow's inspiration and also in the viewing of the magnificent Hiram Falls. The site of the first being some four miles below the General Wadsworth place.

---

19 Indian meal was coarsely ground cornmeal.

20 His father was Col. Charles Wadsworth.

21 Possibly William D. Williamson, *The History of the State of Maine: From Its First Discovery, A.D. 1602, to the Separation, A.D. 1820, Inclusive* (Hallowell, ME: Glazier, Masters & Co., 1832).

LIFE AS AN EARLY SETTLER

a hard row to hoe

Life was physically strenuous for settlers when the first lots were surveyed in 1774. Whether they lumbered, milled, or farmed, men, women, and children labored from dawn to dusk performing tasks differentiated mainly by gender. Women and children kept the home, garden, and small animals and men kept the fields and large animals.

Before rude huts could be built, men had to clear heavily forested land of trees and rocks. Men felled trees with ax and saw, then hewed and hauled them into place using levers to roll logs and chains to pull them. The more prosperous men owned oxen for this heavy work and rented them out for much-needed coin. Others borrowed oxen in exchange for labor. After a log house and barn were built, a settler could attend to building a one-story or one-and-a-half-story timber house. Settlers built mills on brooks, harnessing the plentiful water power for sawmills to cut logs into lumber and for gristmills to grind grain into flour.

Men spent much time making roads. The average farm lot was one hundred acres, which meant farms were isolated and there were long distances to traverse. After farmers built private roads, they petitioned the town to accept them as town roads supported by taxes. On the agenda at the first Town Meeting after Hiram became incorporated in 1814 was a vote on whether to accept Stephen and Ephraim Tibbetts' road (the voters agreed to do so).

Roads were dirt and rutted, and turned to mud after rain or thaw. Logs and other heavy loads were more easily transported in winter, when they could be pulled on sleds. Men elected as surveyors of highways ensured that snow was packed on roads to allow safe passage of sleighs. Ax, saw, shovel, crowbar, rake, and scythe were the primitive hand tools available— farmers made them from wood and blacksmiths forged blades for them. Early wagon beds were built directly upon axles, which produced a very uncomfortable and jarring ride over the rough roads. Elliptical springs, which eased the passenger's ride, were not introduced until the Civil War. Horseback was the preferred mode of transportation, if it was not necessary to carry a heavy load. Horses were so important that Peleg Wadsworth became enraged when one of his was stolen.[22]

People walked to do routine errands. They walked miles to the Post Office (opened in 1801), to the store at the "Bridge" (opened in 1816), to church, and to schools. They walked to Wadsworth Hall for boot repairs and new boots, and to neighboring homes to arrange labor for roads and fields and raising houses and barns. Women were called to administer medical aid and they gathered in groups to sew and share news. People communicated in person or by writing letters. The constable posted public notices at prescribed places. Beginning in 1803, these were published three consecutive times in the Portland weekly newspaper, *Eastern Argus*.

People were sweaty and dirty after so much toil, and keeping clean was work. Making the all-important soap fell to the women. One type of soap suited all purposes: household cleaning, dishes, laundry, and hygiene. To make it, water was added to hardwood ashes in one wooden bucket[23] that dripped into a larger wooden container; the result was left to settle a few days to produce concentrated lye water that was boiled and stirred with tallow until the material began to harden. A little salt hastened the hardening time, after which it was ladled into smaller containers, such as old dishes or gourds. Before it was fully hardened, the soap was cut into squares and left in the sun to finish. This process took days. In some neighborhoods it became a community event to produce a large batch.

To take a bath or wash clothes, water had to be brought bucket by bucket from the spring, stream, or well to the hearth for heating. Bath water was shared.

Money was scarce. Coins were the preferred currency (settlers were skeptical of paper money) and were counted in the English system of pounds, shillings, and pence well after 1785, when the new

---

22 Peleg Wadsworth letter written June 4, 1809. Maine Historical Society, Coll. 16/2 Vol. 2, CLIX, 44.

23 Buckets were wooden and made by coopers because metal was scarce.

Congress authorized the dollar. Goods were expensive; hence, households produced as much as possible. Women cleaned, dyed, and spun wool and flax fibers, wove them into cloth, and created the outer and undergarments settlers wore, which were few. Luxuries, such as ribbons and lace, could be purchased in town only after 1816, when Whitten Pike and Simeon Chadbourne opened their stores. Not many families could afford such things.

Music played an important role. Though instruments were rare, people used their voices. Women and children eased the dull tedium of churning milk into butter and spinning wool into yarn by singing old English ditties and spirituals handed down orally through generations. One such ballad was "Pretty Polly," a song about a perfidious suitor.

Young women were encouraged to marry by age eighteen and to produce large families; hence, children outnumbered adults. Songs for children were meant to be fun, but often hid an industrial or political joke. "Here we go 'round the mulberry bush on a cold and frosty morning" may have referenced the difficulty of raising silkworms in a cold climate.[24] Other versions taught children how to perform chores, as in "This is the way we wash our clothes so early Monday morning," or comport themselves: "This is the way we comb our hair...." Early in life, children received instruction in farming via songs such as "Oats, Peas, Beans, and Barley Grow." When they gathered in taverns, men chanted the old lyrics of sailors. Both men and women soothed their souls with hymns sung in church.

Families spent much of Sunday in church. Until the first church was built in 1826, services were conducted in people's homes. John Ayer, the first recorded religious leader in Hiram, "exhorted" his listeners with strong and stirring arguments in his home. To make sure that people attended services and behaved on the Sabbath and during the week, voters elected upstanding citizens to the office of tithingmen to police behavior. Idleness and play were sins on the Sabbath. Billiards, games of chance, theatrical performances, and dancing were unlawful on all days.[25] By 1823, the culture was beginning to change. A young Hiram man, Daniel Small, wrote in his diary of his excitement at attending his first dance in Fryeburg, at which he may have met his future wife, Susan Abbott, the daughter of a preacher.[26]

Men joined the militia out of social duty to provide defense and safety for the community. They organized into companies and chose their captains. By 1827, Hiram had two light infantries commanded by Charles L. Wadsworth and Peleg Wadsworth Jr. Musters were held in Brownfield, Denmark, and Fryeburg, and in Hiram at Wadsworth Hall in inclement weather. Town taxes supported the militia at $.50 per soldier plus supplies such as ammunition (gun powder and cartridges). Benjamin Swett sometimes filled the cartridges. Selectmen ensured that the town stock of ammunition was adequate: sixty-four pounds of good gun powder, one hundred pounds of musket balls, one hundred flints, and three tin or iron camp kettles for every sixty-four soldiers.[27] At the annual Town Meeting of Hiram in April 1825, townspeople voted to raise $20 for the militia.

Militias fought in the French and Indian Wars and the Revolutionary War. In the War of 1812, militias were called up by the governor to supplement the federal army. Though opposing the War of 1812, Hiram nevertheless sent seventy-seven men to serve. Most Hiram men saw service in Portland for short terms of two weeks or less. Men called to the U.S. Army fought in New York, and three local men died because of it.[28]

Men made most decisions for households and the town. Only men could vote, though women owned property and paid taxes. Marriage was expected. Girls of marriageable age—by 18—sometimes traveled to visit kin to increase their acquaintances. The unmarried were thought to be eccentric or mentally unfit.

---

24 One of the agricultural crazes of the period was a mulberry mania or silk mania.

25 Freeman, *The Town Officer*, 1808, 234.

26 Maine Historical Society, Papers, Coll. 1449.

27 Ibid, 234.

28 Marshall Lewis was killed at the battle of Oswego; His brother Joseph died on the way home to Baldwin. James Gilmor succumbed at Sackets Harbor.

A decent farm living was difficult to achieve for single people, hence the large family unit. A household often consisted of the immediate family, visiting kinfolk, and extra laborers, who were sometimes paupers. Young women, kin or poor girls, were called into the family to care for the many children; young men labored for other farmers.

The population grew rapidly after 1800 and was welcome in the nascent settlement. Later, it contributed to over-farming and soil depletion with accompanying diminished opportunity, causing men to consider migrating to other parts of the country.

Almost all settlers were farmers, but very few farms were entirely self-sustainable. Plants and produce were selected for home use—surplus was sold for much needed cash. Principal crops were corn and hay. Mowing hay was a battle against time and preempted other labor, hence the pay scales for building roads and bridges were lower before and after haying season. Haying invited competition. The quickest with scythes were revered; slower men jumped out of the way or were injured by those behind them.

In their off hours, farmers earned cash in other occupations, and were coopers, blacksmiths, cordwainers, magistrates, millers, milliners, tanners, teachers, preachers, weavers, tailors, lawyers, and shopkeepers.

Animals were vital for food and transportation. Chores for caring for them were divided along gender—women tended chickens, milked cows, made butter and cheese, cooked and preserved food, and cleaned up. Men tended cattle, sheep, horses, and goats, and mucked out stalls. Livestock was important enough to be taxed along with buildings. Oxen pulled loads and plows and transported goods and settlers. Horses were prized and rented out to carry people and pull hay wagons. Pleasure carriages were rare, noted in inventories and taxed heavily.

Pound keepers and farmers collected stray animals, which were identified by color and marks, and registered with the town. Thomas Lord registered his sheep. "The mark of Thomas Lords sheep is a half crop on the underside of the right ear and the top of left ear cut off."[29] If the owners were unknown or didn't claim them after a fine was posted, the pound keepers could keep the strays Thus it was prudent to contain livestock with fencing so as to prevent damage they might inflict on gardens and crops when they strayed and for their monetary value. Hence, some roads were gated.

Nearly every family raised chickens for eggs and meat. Cows and goats and sheep produced milk for drinking, butter and cheese, and some meat. Gardens produced medicinal and culinary herbs and vegetables. Grains were needed for bread and porridge, and for cash. Fresh water, essential to life, was hauled in wooden buckets from streams, springs, and dug wells. Necessary knowledge included skills of preserving food and minimizing waste.

Chief crops were taxed. Hiram tax documents include a list of agricultural products grown in 1811. Corn topped the list, with 1,847 acres in one section of town. This incomplete list shows that bushels of corn far exceeded wheat, rye, oats, and barley. Interestingly, the records indicate this group of farmers preferred English hay and did not grow hops, cider, or meadow hay, though cider was a staple crop of the region.

Pests, shortages, and spoilage of stored crops proved an ever-present concern. In a letter of May 1, 1801, General Wadsworth urged his son Charles Lee Wadsworth to secure corn quickly. "Strout[30] considers to let you take the Corn at Hickey's[31] at 5/ [32] & desires you to measure it soon as possible to save the waste of mice & squirrels."[33] On April 4, 1815, townspeople voted to continue the bounty on crows until the authorized money ran out.[34]

Justices of the peace settled local disputes, such as in 1813 when tenant farmer Samuel Jelerson cheated Josiah Mayberry (Mabry) of his share of crops, and

29 Hiram Town Clerk records, April 5, 1830, 288.

30 Eleazer Strout.

31 Daniel Hickey had his own farm and was employed by General Wadsworth.

32 5 shillings.

33 Maine Historical Society, Coll. 16 Box 1/3.

34 Maine Historical Society, Coll. 1 Warrants.

in another case, in which Benjamin Swett accused Josiah of trading spoiled hay.

Life on a farm was full of perils. Accidental death was ever present. The long skirts worn by women and girls meant constant danger of catching fire while cooking at the hearth or making candles or soap. Nights were cold and dark. A settler did not heat or light the entire house—people came to the wood fire in the open hearth for warmth, and to a candle to light the way or to read. Books were scarce. The most widely read book was the Bible, but almanacs were popular for guiding plowing, planting, cultivating, harvesting, and flailing crops by phases of the moon and astrology. Fires in barns and houses were common due to incidents with lighted candles, oil lamps, and spilled embers. Travelers waited for the moon to rise to light the way on roads.

Numerous accidents occurred to people driving teams of oxen in the field or riding in wagons on the hills and rutted roads. A falling tree killed a brother of John Clemons in 1799 when he was working on General Wadsworth's land. Women bore many children, as birth control was unknown and labor on the farm was needed. Death from disease and childbirth and the accompanying sorrow was prevalent, as illustrated in an 1811 letter from Mehitable Bucknell to her sister.

> Hiram June 28th 1811
> My Dear sister
> Having an opportunity to write you a few lines & improve it with pleasure we are all in good health and want to see you very much, the time seems longer since I saw you than it did before you came home. We have heard from ???. Mr Gideon Merrill is dead Lydia[35] is very sick, I am very lonesome. I do not enjoy such a share of happiness as I have in times past. I no [sic] not the reason but I think your company would abdicate those dejected feelings from my mind and I should again retain my former happiness. I was this afternoon at the generals[36] and saw Mrs longfellow[37] and Miss lutia[38] Mrs Baton [Baston?] is just gone I watch with her as often as I can. it looks very alarming to see a person in the bloom of youth falling a victim of the king of terrors[39]
> From your sister
> Mehitable Bucknell[40]

Most likely Mehitable, age 24, wrote this letter to her older sister, Sarah Bucknell, age 28, both unmarried, older than 18, the age young women were expected to marry. This, as well as the lack of nearby girl friends to confide in, and the ever-present threat of disease and death contributed to her unusual expression of poignant loneliness.

What helped settlers overcome the hardships, restrictions, and isolation was the relief of occasional festive social gatherings, a safety net of town aid to the indigent, and neighbors helping neighbors.

---

35   Lydia may be Lydia Hill of Cornish, b. 1784, or Lydia Merrill of Cornish, b. 1789, married in 1807 to John Wedgewood of Parsonsfield.

36   General Peleg Wadsworth.

37   Zilpha Wadsworth, wife of Stephen Longfellow.

38   Lucia Wadsworth was Zilpha's sister.

39   King of Terrors was the personification of death, ever present in settlers' lives.

40   Mehitable Bucknell, b. 1787, was the daughter of Simeon and Hannah Burbank Bucknell. Mehitable had two sisters and four brothers: Sarah, b. 1783, was four years older; Mary, b. 1798, was 11 years younger. Her brothers were John (b. 1785), Benjamin (b. 1790), Andrew R. (b. 1792), and Simeon, Jr. (b. 1795). Sarah wed Asa Burbank of Hiram in July 1814, when he was a lieutenant in the War of 1812; she was 31, he was 28, and they had six children together. Mehitable married John Kimball of Hiram, his second wife, in 1818; she was 31, he was 22, and they had three children.

LAND SURVEY OF 1774

earliest settlers

The first white settler probably was Lt. Benjamin Ingalls. He journeyed up the Saco River in a party of five in August and September of 1774.

In his own words:

Sept. 5th 1774 then Daniel Foster and Abial Messer and John Curtis and Ebenezer Herrick and Benjamin Ingalls came up to the Great Falls Saco Rivor the west sid and Laid out a Tract of Land for each of ous as follows viz: —

Beginning [at] a maple Tree on ye Rivor Bank against Bryants Pond So Called Running West 160 Rods then Runing Sowth 80 Rods then Running East to Saco River Ebenezer Herricks Loot N 1 Pine tree then By the Side of Herricks Loot & one for John Curtis N 2 Pine tree 80 Rods down ye Rivor to a Read Oak Tree markt 2/3 then 80 Rods own the Rivor to a White Pine Tree markt 3/4.

Sept. 6th then Daniel Foster Abial Messer John Curtis and Ebenezer Herrick Layed out a Loot for Benja. Ingalls then Begun att a Pine Tree on the Bank of Sawco Rivor about 60 rods above Hancock Brook Runing west 100 Polls[41] to a maple tree markt IIII then Runing Sowth 600 Polls to a hemlock tree IIII then Runing East to a Pine on the Bank of Saco Rivor att the mouth of a Littell Brook which Runs out of the medow Cald Woodsoms medow Laied out and Bownded as above for Benjamin Ingalls & we markt it IIII.

Sept. 10th 1786 Mr Joshua Davis of flintstown[42] went with me and Preambed the Lines and Bownds of my Lott as above.

July 15 1786 Mess Joshua Davis and Jess Walker went with me and Vewed the Bownds of the Land that I Laied owt in agust and Sept. 1774[43]

White men had obviously been here before Ingalls and named features he described—"Hancock brook," "Bryants pond," and "Woodsoms meadow." Hancock was John Hancock, son of William, who came from Londonderry, Ireland, to Buxton. He was a hunter and trapper, and his story goes like this: "He had built a hunting camp near the large pond and retired to that sylvan retreat to hunt and trap for the winter. Tradition, well supported by several reliable persons who lived at the time, makes one John Brown, a native of Scarborough, come to Buxton with a hand-sled loaded with valuable furs and wearing a coat known to have belonged to Hancock. He immediately went to Portland, where he disposed of his peltry, and disappeared to be seen no more. Search revealed the vacant camp and a spoon bearing Hancock's name, but neither his body, gun, nor traps were ever discovered."[44]

Other white men involved before 1774 were Maj. William Phillips of Saco, Maine, who "purchased" land on the west side of the Saco River from the Native American Captain Sunday in 1666, and Benjamin Prescott, who surveyed a grant on the east side of the Saco River in 1773.

Who Were These Men?

Lt. Benjamin Ingalls, described as "the first pioneer," was the son of Moses and Maria Ingalls, of Andover, Massachusetts, born August 1, 1728.

He entered the British army and was captured at Louisburg by Sir William Pepperell in 1745. In 1761 he was commissioned as lieutenant. About 1765 he left the army and made voyages to sea. In 1774 he

---

41 Pole, a unit of length equal to one rod.

42 Flintstown was an early name for Baldwin.

43 Ridlon, *Saco Valley Settlements*, 146.

44 Ibid., 146. Hancock's name is mentioned in the inventory of his father's estate in 1770.

came to Great Falls on the Saco river, where he surveyed several lots of land, one of which he settled on; this was at the bend of the river, and the cellar was to be seen not many years back. While living here his nearest neighbors were James Howard, in Brownfield, and Mr. Cookson, in Standish.[45] In October 1785, the "great freshet" swept away his house, hovel, and blacksmith shop. He then removed to Flintstown, now Baldwin, and settled near "Ingalls pond.[46]

Benjamin and his first wife, Rebecca Pearsons, had three children: Benjamin Pearsons; Micajah, who became a Revolutionary War soldier under Captain Lovejoy; and William. His second wife was Mary White. Their daughter Mary, born November 25, 1779, was the first white child born in Hiram. They had six other children: William, David, Jane, Dolly, Loammi, and Ruth. Ingalls operated a ferry across the Saco River. Later in life, the couple lived with their daughter Jane, who married Capt. Charles Lee Wadsworth after his first wife died. The Ingalls died in Hiram and are buried in West Baldwin. Ingalls also has the distinction of being a founder of two towns, Hiram and Baldwin.

Daniel Foster, the second settler, from Massachusetts, was the brother-in-law of Lt. Benjamin Ingalls, having married Benjamin's sister Anna.

He settled on a part of the Ingalls' lot, soon after 1774. He took cold and died in the spring of 1782, it being the first death in the settlement. He left no children and his wife returned to Massachusetts. On Thanksgiving Day, 1874, the centennial of the settlement was observed at the Congregational Church. Hon. Walter F. Watson presided, and Llewellyn A. Wadsworth served as secretary. The pastor, Rev. Albert Cole, of Cornish, made a historical address.

Daniel Foster's marker on the River Road, 2019.

Capt. Samuel Wadsworth and Christopher Allen were chosen a committee to mark Mr. Foster's grave with a suitable memorial. In 1875 the town granted $100 for that purpose, and a marble tablet was erected at this grave on a little knoll east of the road above Hiram Falls. The hill nearby is still called Foster Hill.[47]

The inscription on the stone reads:

This stone was erected in 1875 by the Town of Hiram in memory of Daniel Foster who was born in Andover, Mass. on Jan. 7, 1726 to Moses & Eliza B. Foster. He settled in Hiram in the Autumn of 1774 and died of Fever in the Spring of 1782, being the second settler and the first person who died in Hiram.

John Curtis built a house and barn on his one hundred acres, which extended from Red Mill Brook

---

45 Ingalls or Ridlon may not have been aware of neighbors in Cornish: two sons of Henry Pendexter, who farmed spring to fall beginning 1773, and James Holmes, who settled in 1774. Leola C. Ellis and Kera C. Millard, *Early Cornish (1666-1916)*, (Cornish, ME, 1972).

46 Ridlon, *Saco Valley Settlements and Families*, 146.

47 Llewellyn A. Wadsworth, *Centennial, Hiram, Maine, 1814-1914* (Cornish, ME: Webb-Smith Printing Co., 1914), 10.

to Hancock Brook along the Saco River.[48] He sold the property in April 1782 to John Ayer of Pearsontown (Standish), with the exception of one acre that he reserved for himself. In the deed he is described as a cordwainer (shoemaker). Curtis's wife, Moley (Molly), was illiterate and signed the deed "X her mark," as did Ayer's wife, Elizabeth, when they sold to their son Humphrey Ayer in 1797.

The facts known about John Curtis are few. He married the widow Ann Miller of Fryeburg on October 12, 1785. He sold land in Conway, New Hampshire, in 1798 and died in Fryeburg March 8, 1800.

Ebenezer Herrick. There are three Ebenezer Herricks from Massachusetts who could have come to Hiram in September 1774. It may have been the sergeant major in Col. James Frye's regiment who enlisted May 14, 1775, and was killed on June 17, 1775, at the battle of Bunker Hill, where he had lost a gun and cartridge box. Perhaps it was the private who served with Col. John Mosely's regiment September 21, 1777, to October 1780. Or he may have been the private serving in Capt. Amos Upton's company, Capt. John Dix's company in General Lovewell's brigade, and Capt. William Green's company off and on from April 21, 1775, to November 1, 1780.[49] There is no deed in his name. In the 1790 census, an Ebenezer Herrick is listed in Sedgewick, Maine, along with many other Herricks.

Abiel Messer was an ensign who served in Canada from 1755 to 1758 under Capt. Edmund Mooers, the same officer Benjamin Ingalls served under, but he was discharged three years before Ingalls enlisted. He was from Methuen, Massachusetts, and married there in June 1775. There is no record of a property transfer, nor any other mention of him.

---

48 Llewellyn A. Wadsworth, *Centennial, Hiram, Maine, 1814-1914,* 1914), 9. This property is Brookside Farm, 6 Hiram Hill Road.

49 Office of the Secretary of the Commonwealth, *Massachusetts Soldiers and Sailors of the Revolutionary War* (Boston: The Office, 1896–1908), 756.

SETTLERS BEFORE JANUARY 1, 1784

rightful claim to land

To replenish the treasury after the Revolution, Massachusetts set up a committee of three men in Boston and began a massive sale of "unappropriated lands."[50] Timothy Cutler's grants and that of Gen. Peleg Wadsworth were awarded during this time. Prior settlement on land sold as unappropriated complicated ownership. Some settlers were squatters unknown to owners and thus illegal, but some owned the land legally, paid for and deeded. To settle this controversial matter, the Massachusetts Legislature passed a law in 1786 that would give title to one hundred acres to any settler who could prove that he was living on it prior to January 1, 1784, and had improved the land by fulfilling certain requirements, in particular, building a house and barn.

Seventeen settlers in Hiram made claims.[51]

To the Hon Samuel Phillips Jr. Esq. & others: A Com. [committee] on the sale of lands in the Co. of York. The petition of the subscribers humbly showeth that prior to the 1st day of January 1784 your petitioners entered on lands belonging to the Government, lying between Brownfield, New Hampshire [sic], and the Great Ossapee River, and some of us have made considerable improvements. That being informed that the General Court have granted one hundred acres of land to each, on certain conditions and as most of your petitioners have sons,[52] we therefore request your favors to make each of us a Grant of so much as we severely subscribe for, upon such conditions as you in your wisdom shall seem reasonable, and your petitioners as in duty bound shall we pray. Hiram, May 7th, 1788.

Benjamin Burbank, Jr.	100 acres
John Clemons	100
John Clemons, Jr.	100
Bena. Bickford	100
Phillip Corey	100
Daniel Baston	
Benjamin Burbank	100
John Ayer	100
Michael Floyd	100
Sim. Bucknell	100
George Whales his mark X	200
Benjamin Ingalls	300 (in 1774)
John Bucknell Jr.	100
Curtis Bean	100
Wm. Richardson	200
Meshack Libby	100
Stephen Libby	100

John Ayer purchased his 400 of 3 settlers before 1784. He gave $550 for 100 acres.[53]

Who Were These Men? Did They Stay in Hiram?

Of these seventeen settlers, eight remained in Hiram for an extended period, as did their children.

John Ayer sold to his second son Humphrey in 1797 after fifteen years and removed to Cornish to join him. Their daughter and son-in-law, Sarah and Thomas Barker, remained in Hiram, having bought their house from Humphrey. Ayer owned land awarded to the Cutler Grant.

Daniel Baston, Simeon Bucknell, and John Bucknell Jr. were also long-term residents of Hiram, settling on the Cutler Grant.

---

50 "Unappropriated" land sold by the Committee for the Sale of Eastern Lands in Hiram was land formerly occupied by Native Americans who were decimated by disease and driven out by development.

51 Massachusetts State Archives.

52 It was important to fathers to own land to pass down to their sons.

53 Deeds to three hundred acres are recorded in Oxford County Registry of Deeds, Fryeburg, totaling 312 pounds. The pound was the currency of the Commonwealth of Massachusetts and its Colonial predecessors until 1792, but continued in use for many years. Like the British pound sterling of that era, the Massachusetts pound was subdivided into 20 shillings, each of 12 pence, but the Massachusetts pounds had less value.

Benjamin Burbank, born about 1725, a teacher in 1770 in Arundel, Maine (now Kennebunkport), settled on the Cutler Grant. On the same day Cutler wrote the deed to him, June 18, 1791, Burbank deeded his property to Thomas Spring of Grafton, New Hampshire. Burbank lived in Brownfield in 1800, signing Timothy Cutler's petition for incorporation in 1801 as a resident of Brown's Addition, ceded to Hiram in 1806.

Benjamin Burbank Jr. was drafted for war service in Cambridge July 4, 1778, when he was twelve, probably serving as a drummer or errand boy.[54] Where he went after he signed the petition in 1801 is not known. Another son of Benjamin Burbank, Israel, who also served at Cambridge, remained in Hiram and was the second U.S. postmaster in 1803. He was active in local government.

John Clemons died in 1790 but had lived in Hiram ten years. John Clemons Jr. departed westward in 1804 after twenty-four years in Hiram, but other Clemonses stayed. Clemons settled on the Wadsworth Grant.

George Whales was a Revolutionary soldier who settled in Hiram near the lower bridge on the Ossipee River. The Whales family was reputed to have Native American blood, according to Llewellyn A. Wadsworth, Hiram historian.[55] His funeral was held at the old Union Meeting House on January 21, 1841. Daniel Small attended and noted it in his diary. George was the father of John Whales Sr., who married Miriam Day. His son and grandson were supported by the town in 1821 and 1824. These are

the only records found of this illiterate man, who never held office or voted. John's son John Jr. married Eunice Fly on April 29, 1820, and settled near the Tripp Schoolhouse at Oak Hill in South Hiram. Whales Hill and Whales Brook are named for him. Their children were George, Lois, Delilah, Benjamin, Tamar, Solomon, and Miriam. Benjamin, John Jr., and Solomon voted in 1822. The name is also spelled "Wales" and "Whale."[56] Other Whaleses purchased property on the Wadsworth Grant. No deed to George Whales was found on Wadsworth or Waters grants.

The following settlers left Hiram before 1800:

Curtis Bean was in Brownfield in 1787. Benjamin Bickford was in Porterfield in 1790, as was Michael Floyd. Stephen and Meshack Libby were still in Hiram in 1790, but by 1792, when their deed from Cutler was finalized, they were in Porterfield.

Phillip Corey and his wife, Patience, who settled on the Waters Grant, sold in 1790, but were still in Hiram in June 1791, when he assisted in the appraisal of the estate of John Clemons. In 1800 the Coreys were in New Grantham, New Hampshire. Of William Richardson there is no more information.

Benjamin Ingalls moved to Baldwin after his house was washed away in the Great Freshet of 1785. It is interesting to note that he started with one hundred acres but is listed as having three hundred. It is possible he received the additional two hundred acres from Herrick and Messer, whose two hundred acres are unaccounted for. Presumably he settled on the Cutler Grant, but there is no deed from Cutler.

---

54 George Burbank Sedgley, *Genealogy of the Burbank Family and the Families of Bray, Wellcome, Sedgley (Sedgeley) and Welch* (Farmington, ME: Printed by the Knowlton & McLeary Co., 1928), 48.

55 Hubert Clemons, "The Whales/Wales Family of Hiram and Denmark, Maine," *Downeast Ancestry*, June 1985, 19:1,7.

56 Ibid.

SETTLERS IN THE 1790 U.S. CENSUS OF "HIRAM TOWN"

There were eighteen male heads of households in Hiram in 1790. What happened to them?

Ayer, John
> John Ayer, who built the first mill and was the first religious leader, moved to Cornish by 1800 with his son Humphrey Ayer, but his eldest daughter, married to Thomas Barker, remained in Hiram until they moved to Portland.

Barker, Thomas
> Thomas Barker remained in Hiram, married John Ayer's daughter Sarah, and built a dam in 1807 at the pond named after him. He also owned other property in Hiram and a sawmill in Baldwin. Before 1815 he moved to Portland, where he and his family were friends and neighbors of the family of Henry Wadsworth Longfellow.

Baston (Boston), Daniel
> Daniel Baston settled on Hiram Hill on one hundred acres on Cutler's Lower Grant, as did his sons.

Bucknell, John
> John Bucknell remained in Hiram, as did his father (Simeon) and son (John Jr.).

Burbank, Benjamin
> Benjamin Burbank sold his Hiram property in 1791 to Thomas Spring, but his descendants remained in Hiram. He was also listed in the Brownfield census.

Clements (Clemons), John
> John Clemons, for whom Clemons Ponds are named, lived in Hiram until his death in 1790. Descendants still live in Hiram.

Dyer, Bickford
> A Bickford Dyer was listed both in Porterfield and in Hiram in the same 1790 census, with identical family configurations. Perhaps there were two identical families; perhaps he moved between census counts (the census was nine months in the making, ending August 9); perhaps he lived close to the border and was counted by a census taker in each town configuration. Regardless, in 1800 he was living in Flintstown (Baldwin) and he was still there in 1820.

Eastman, Solomon
> Solomon Eastman did not appear in the Hiram census of 1800, but showed up in Fryeburg in the 1820 census.

Gould, Aaron
> Moses and Aaron Gould settled on Gould Mountain in Hiram. They had left by 1800, but other Goulds moved to Hiram after 1820.

Haywood (Howard), Lemuel
> Lemuel Howard settled in Hiram near Clemons Pond and married John Clemons's daughter, Hannah, in 1780.

Libby, John
> John Libby and Stephen Libby were living in Porterfield by 1792.

Libby, Jonathan
> There is no further information about Jonathan Libby.

Libby, Stephen
> Stephen Libby and John Libby were living in Porterfield by 1792.

McLucas, John
> John McLucas remained in Hiram until his death in 1813, after which his family fell into poverty.

Midget (Mudget), David
> David Mudget signed the petition to incorporate Parsonsfield in 1785. He was living in Parsonsfield in 1800 and 1820 with a household of five, including three "Foreigners" (most likely Irish). Descendants of David Mudget live in Parsonsfield today.

Ryan, Curtis
> There is no further information about Curtis Ryan.

1790 Brownfield Census of the Area that Became Hiram in 1806–07

Burbank, Benjamin
> Benjamin Burbank sold his Hiram property in 1791 to Thomas Spring.

Burbank, Israel
> Israel Burbank remained in Hiram.

Lane, John

    Capt. John Lane died in Buxton in 1822. Other Lanes remained in Hiram.

Osgood, Asa

    Asa Osgood remained in Hiram until his death in 1833, and was active in town affairs, as was his son Asa Osgood Jr.

Veasey, Thomas

    Thomas Veasey sold his property in 1805 and left Brownfield before it was ceded to Hiram.

Watson, John

    John Watson remained in Hiram, as did many of his descendants.

LAND GRANTS

a remote Massachusetts committee

After the Revolutionary War, the treasury of the Commonwealth of Massachusetts was depleted. In an effort to build its coffers, it sold public lands in Maine. Under successive authorizations, the Committee for the Sale of Eastern Lands (1780–1801) and the Land Office were the primary agencies responsible for the management and sale of public lands in Maine. Sales were slow during its first twelve years, but during this period two major grants in Hiram were sold—to Wadsworth and Waters.

There were four principal land grants in Hiram (listed in the sequence they were granted): Prescott, Cutler, Wadsworth, and Waters. Foster's Gore (two thousand acres) was added to Hiram from Denmark in 1806 as part of a town incorporation plan, but was not treated as a grant. A plan that accompanied the unsuccessful petition for incorporation in 1801 showed the four grants that would later compose much of the town of Hiram.[57]

Grants were made to buyers with the understanding they would settle them with families as quickly as possible after being surveyed.

All grants had to be surveyed and plans submitted. Surveys could be general outlines or lot plans. Lot plans for grants in Hiram have not been found, although some deeds mention lot numbers. Two tracts comprising the southerly part of the town were surveyed by Vere Royse[58] in 1783, at the request of Nathaniel Merrill and others.[59] The Wadsworth Grant was surveyed by Samuel Titcomb, January 1790, and submitted by Peleg Wadsworth in 1795.[60]

Prescott's Grant. Prescott's Grant was first surveyed by Benjamin Prescott in 1773 and resurveyed by Lothrop Lewis in 1809.[61] When Lewis surveyed it the land was covered in pine and oak trees and he valued it at $2 to $3 per acre because of the potential timber. Another plan of Prescott's Grant is dated November 25, 1816.[62]

Prescott's grant contained eight hundred acres east of the Saco River south of the Bridge. It was bounded on the north by Brownfield, east and south by Flints Town (Baldwin), and west by Saco River. In 1794 it was known as "Prescott's Location" and "Prescott's Patent." After the decease of Benjamin Prescott, the first surveyor, it was divided in half between Henry Prescott, Esq., and others: heir Daniel Epps and other heirs represented by Joshua Heath and James Osgood of Conway, New Hampshire, and Nathaniel Merrill, a surveyor from Fryeburg. In 1800, three Hiram families totaling twenty people lived there: John Bucknall (Bucknell) in a household of nine; the James Gilman (Gilmor) family of four; and seven in the family of Samuel Sloper.[63]

In 1809, Henry Prescott sold six hundred acres to Thomas Barker of Hiram and Thomas Cutts, a wealthy merchant of Saco, to be divided equally.[64] In the same year, Daniel Smith of Durham, New Hampshire, sold 348 acres to Ephraim Kimball and Benjamin Furber, both of Farmington, New Hampshire, which they divided the same day.[65] One of the boundaries was a "Beach tree" marked "BP 1773,"[66] a year earlier than the Ingalls survey across the river in August 1774.

---

57 Massachusetts Land Office, Planbook 25:25.

58 Vere Royce, who served under George Washington, was surveyor in North Conway, NH, and Fryeburg, ME. He died in Fryeburg in 1811. Ancestry.com/Message Board, January 11, 2020.

59 Massachusetts Land Office, Planbook 2:11.

60 Massachusetts Land Office, Planbook 21:16.

61 Massachusetts Land Office, Planbook 2:4.

62 Massachusetts Land Office, Planbook 25:60.

63 U.S. Census 1800, Prescott's Grant, York County.

64 York County Registry of Deeds, Alfred, Book 5, page 112 from copy in Oxford County Registry of Deeds, Fryeburg, now in Paris.

65 Ibid., 122.

66 BP stood for Benjamin Prescott.

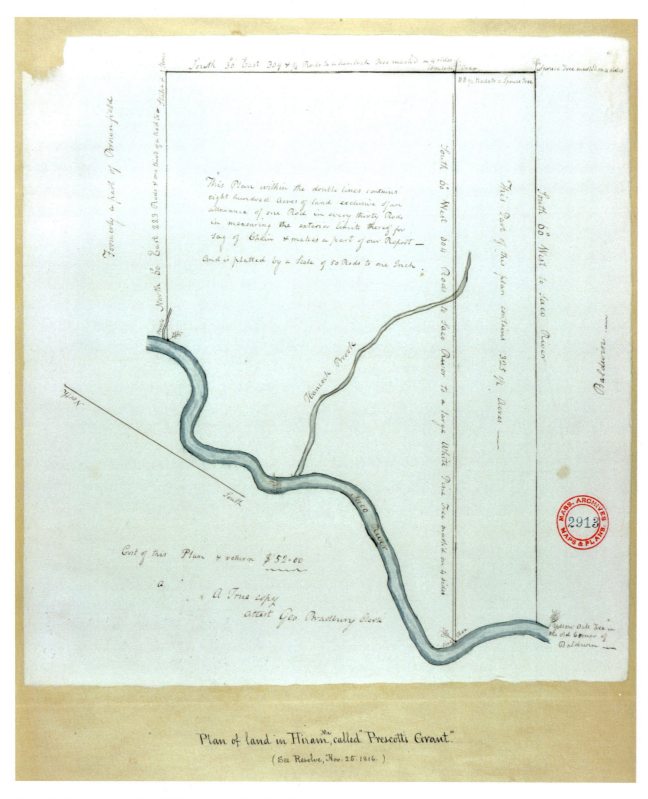

Prescott's Grant, surveyed in 1773 and mapped in 1816.[67]

On February 24, 1814, 193.75 acres were sold to Seth Spring of Biddeford, Maine,[68] and the whole was incorporated into Hiram in 1814.

Cutler's Grants. In 1787 the Massachusetts Legislature resolved to award Timothy Cutler damages as compensation for five hundred acres in

---

67   Massachusetts State Archives, SCI 50X 3rd Series, v. 36, p. 3.
68   Massachusetts State Archives, Deed 6:279.

Cumberland, purchased of John Wiswall, of which Cutler was "disseized."[69]

Timothy Cutler had very bad luck with ownership of his Cumberland land. The five hundred acres he purchased of John Wiswall had been granted to Wiswall's grandfather, Ichabod Wiswall, when Massachusetts was known as the Province of the Massachusetts Bay. It was inherited by John's father, Peleg Wiswall. Before the paperwork was completed, which took several weeks, John Wiswall sold it to Cutler.

In the transition from Province to Commonwealth, Massachusetts sold the land to other people. The General Court agreed Cutler had been wronged. The Committee for the Sale of Eastern Lands, a committee of three men in Boston, appraised Cutler's five hundred acres in Cumberland at 150 pounds and 50 pounds for damages, for a total of 200 pounds owed to Cutler. The Committee reported on December 12, 1788, that Cutler was entitled "to lay out two tracts of unappropriated lands belonging to this Commonwealth containing in the whole six thousand acres including ponds, bogs, rocks, mountains, and waters, excepting and reserving one hundred acres of land for each settler thereon prior to the first day of January, 1784, to be laid out as will best include his improvements and be least injurious" to his neighbors. Bracey Banks surveyed the land in 1788.[70] Nathaniel Merrill of Fryeburg made a plan from this survey in 1795.[71]

The deed was signed on January 27, 1789.[72]

The grant in Hiram was known as Cutler's Lower Grant, and measured twenty-two hundred acres. Cutler's Upper Grant of thirty-eight hundred acres was in Porterfield, partially annexed to Brownfield in an attempt to incorporate as towns, which was successful for Porter in 1807.

The Lower Grant in Hiram was enclosed in the area defined by the Hiram/Brownfield line running southwesterly from the Saco River about two miles, then southeasterly about two and a half miles, then northeasterly about two and a quarter miles to the Saco River, and then up the Saco to the starting point.

Before Massachusetts signed the deed to Cutler on January 22, 1789, Cutler gave assurance that settlers who had petitioned for their land would be deeded. Seventeen settlers had petitioned in 1788. Six settlers had claims on Cutler's Lower Grant along the Saco River; six lots were set off for them as "Settler's Lots." The six were John Ayer (he claimed four hundred acres and was awarded two hundred for a fee of three pounds two shillings), Simeon Bucknell (awarded one hundred acres for a fee of one pound eleven shillings six pence),[73] John Bucknell Jr. (awarded seventy-five acres "in consideration for good services"),[74] Benjamin Burbank (awarded one hundred acres for a fee of "six pounds and other good services,"[75] Benjamin Burbank Jr. and Benjamin Ingalls (he claimed three hundred from the 1774 survey). Hiram settlers claimed twenty-one hundred acres in the petition, but not all was on the Cutler Grant. John Clemons and possibly George Whales settled on the Wadsworth Grant. Philip Corey settled on the Waters Grant. Recorded deeds were not found for all seventeen settlers.

Lots sold quickly.

In June 1789, Cutler sold two lots to Thomas Barker of Hiram (two hundred acres, 60 pounds), two lots to Abraham Tyler of Scarborough (two hundred acres, 60 pounds), and Jonathan Fogg of Scarborough (one hundred acres, 40 pounds). Others following before 1800 were Winthrop Eldridge (acreage and fee illegible); Abner Fogg of Scarborough, who bought one lot on the Lower Grant called "Happy

69 Massachusetts State Archives, Resolves of 1787, Chapter 91, Approved Nov. 20, 1787.

70 Massachusetts Land Office, Planbook 2:7.

71 Massachusetts Land Office, Planbook 21:12.

72 York County Registry of Deeds, Alfred, Book 51, page 218A, from copy in Oxford County Registry of Deeds, Fryeburg, now in Paris.

73 York County Registry of Deeds, Alfred, February 20, 1792, Book 54, 229A. From copy in Oxford County Registry of Deeds, Fryeburg, now in Paris.

74 Ibid., September 27,. 1790, Book 53, 185B, now in Paris.

75 Ibid., June 18, 1791, Book 55, 10A. Bucknell's deed contains a lot plan, the only one found.

Valley" (one hundred acres, 45 pounds); Abijah Lewis of Hiram (fifty acres, 22 pounds 10 shillings); John Pierce of Hiram (six lots, Lower and Upper Grants, $250); Simon Harding of Flintstown (260 acres, Lower and Upper, 200 pounds).

Cutler settled with Daniel Wiswall with acreage in both Upper and Lower Grants in 1805.[76] Daniel, as an heir of Peleg Wiswall, entangled Cutler's situation. Unknown to Cutler, when John Wiswall sold land in Cumberland to Cutler, he owned only half the property because he shared the inheritance from his father, Peleg Wiswall, with his brother Daniel. This led to negotiations that resulted in Daniel receiving thirteen hundred acres in Cutler's Grants as compensation, and his lawyer sharing one lot with Cutler, over 13 percent of the original grant of six thousand acres.

In a further irony, Peleg Wiswall's land in Cumberland, sold to Timothy Cutler, had been granted there because the original grant in 1767 by the Province of Massachusetts Bay to Peleg's father Ichabod Wiswall, for services to the "late Colony of Plimouth," was found to be in New Hampshire, and outside the jurisdiction of Massachusetts.[77]

Wadsworth's Grant. Gen. Peleg Wadsworth was in an entirely different situation from Cutler. Wadsworth purchased land in Hiram in 1790 with thought to his retirement. He paid one hundred and ninety-four pounds five shillings for 7800 acres (widely cited later as 12.5 cents per acre) in the western part of town, March 10, 1790.[78] Samuel Titcomb had surveyed it in January 1790, thus Peleg was familiar with its properties.[79]

Peleg reserved five hundred acres for his son Charles Lee Wadsworth and eight hundred acres for himself, and began to sell the remainder at reasonable prices. Some early owners on the Wadsworth Grant who bought directly from Peleg Wadsworth were John Clammons (Clemons) (1790, two hundred acres) of which 100 acres was claimed as a settler and deeded to John's widow, Abigail; in

1794: Thomas Baker Waite of Portland (1797, one thousand acres); James Eastman, John Bucknell, Jacob McLucas, Joseph Howard, James Fly Jr., David Trafton, Benjamin McLellan, Peleg C. Wadsworth, Charles Wadsworth, Peleg Wadsworth Jr., Thomas Trippe, Jacob Graffam, Artemas Richardson, John Wadsworth (Peleg's grandson), William Cotton, Edmund Butterfield, Lemuel Haywood (Howard), Jonathan Lowell, Samuel Tappan, Benjamin Baston, Moses Palmer, and Joshua Robins.

Waters Grant. About 1790, Daniel Waters (1731–1816), a captain in the Continental Navy, and others, purchased a triangular parcel of three thousand acres in the southeastern part of town, at the junction of the Saco and Great Ossipee rivers in South Hiram. In 1795, Col. Josiah Waters of Boston claimed one quarter as agent for the heirs of William Phillips. Maj. William Phillips of Saco had been deeded "three hills of rock" from the Native American Captain Sunday in 1666. The Massachusetts Supreme Judicial Court granted the partition, and on December 27, 1798, awarded him six hundred acres adjoining the Wadsworth Grant and the Ossipee River.[80] It was surveyed by Andrew Sherborn into six one hundred–acre lots and sold between 1798 and 1814. The day the land was surveyed, Waters sold lots one and two to Andrew Dunlap of Boston, brewer, for $400. The next day, Samuel Merrifield of Cornish bought lot four for $150 and the day after that Joseph Miller Thompson of Cornish paid $95.25 for lot three. In 1809, Samuel Merrifield turned his lot over to Simeon Merrifield of Wells for $200, and in 1812 bought two more, lots five and six, for $310, and sold part to John McLucas in 1813.

At times, nonresident land investors could not be found by Hiram tax agents. In the highway tax of 1806, four hundred acres owned by Josiah Waters was classed as "Present Owners Unknown" and taxed a total of $1.16. Also, fifteen hundred acres of the "Phillips Grant" was taxed $4.36 as "Present Owners Unknown." This was the Waters Grant.

---

76 Ibid., October 5, 1792, Book 59. 144.

77 Massachusetts State Archives, Province Laws, Resolves 1765–66, Chapter 86.

78 Massachusetts State Archives, Deed 6:355. Also Oxford County Registry of Deeds, March 10, 1790, Book 4, 207.

79 Massachusetts Land Office, Planbook 21:16.

80 Massachusetts State Archives, Supreme Judicial Court, December 27, 1798, 94.

Other settlers on the Waters Grant were Joseph Adams, who stayed, and Philip and Patience Corey, who did not.

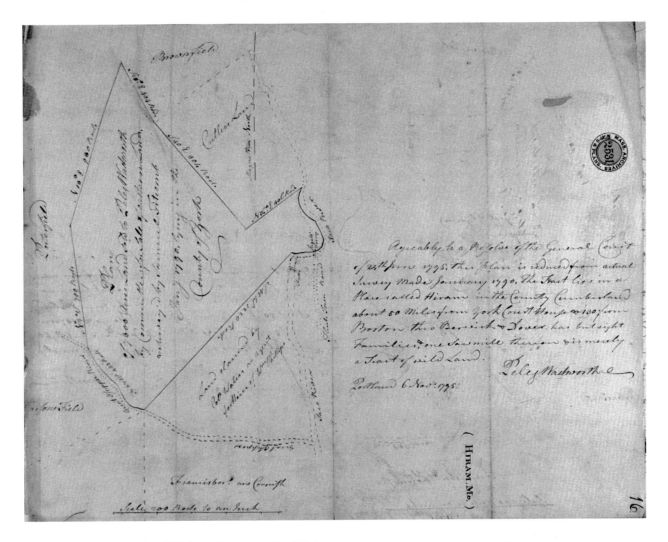

Grants to Waters, Cutler, and Wadsworth, surveyed in 1794 in Hiram, Maine.[81]

---

81   Massachusetts State Archives, SCI 47X 1794 Series, v. 9, 16.

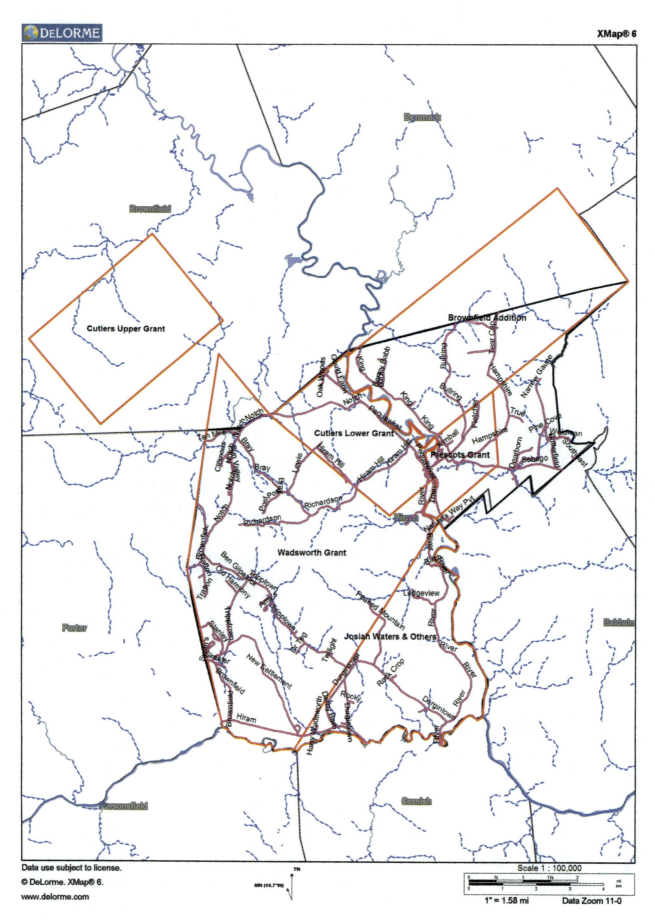

Map of land grants in Hiram. Courtesy of Delorme.

POWER AND DUTY OF TOWNS
Massachusetts laws

In this chapter the words "town," "district," and "plantation" are interchangeable. The word "town" is used for all.

Before 1820 when Maine became a state, Maine operated under the laws of Massachusetts. The duties of town officials were designated by law. To understand the founders of Hiram, it is necessary to first understand the duties of the officers and the responsibilities of towns and plantations. Although not all the founders of Hiram held office, many did. Furthermore, the duties of offices with quaint names such as fence viewer, field driver, pound keeper, overseer of the poor, and tithingman offer a useful insight into what life was like in the eighteenth and nineteenth centuries, when animals and religion were more prominent in people's lives and bound into the laws. The responsibilities set down here were taken from Samuel Freeman.[82]

Legal Inhabitants and Settlements

A high order of business of a town or district or plantation was to determine the legal inhabitants, both for the residents' rights of legal settlement, which obliged the town to support them in case they became poor and in need, and for their voting rights. It was complicated.

Women had the settlement of their husbands, and legitimate children had the settlement of their father, unless he had none, in which case they had the settlement of their mother. Illegitimate children had the settlement of their mother from birth, if the mother had legal settlement in the place they were born. Any citizen of the United States of twenty-one years of age with an estate of 60 pounds or annual income of 3 pounds 12 shillings for five years successively in the town or district of dwelling gained a settlement, as did any person who after the age of twenty-one years resided in and paid a town tax for five years successively. Any person chosen and serving one year in the office of clerk, treasurer,

selectman, overseer of the poor, assessor, constable, or collector of taxes gained a settlement. Male voters could be admitted as an inhabitant at any legal meeting if an article was submitted in the warrant for the meeting. An ordained minister of the gospel settled in the town where he preached was considered legally settled. A minor who served an apprenticeship to a lawful trade for four years and set up the same trade in the same town within one year after the expiration of the term and was twenty-one years of age and continued the trade for five years gained a settlement. But being hired as a journeyman was not considered as setting up a trade. The settlement in one town continued until a new one was established in another town.

All settlements were contingent on a person not having been warned to depart the town. The time frame varied from one to five years. The warning was incumbent upon the selectmen, who were also overseers of the poor.

In 1794 the law was expanded to allow persons of twenty-one years of age who were U.S. citizens with an estate of inheritance or freehold in the town where they dwelt, and an annual income of three pounds and took rents and profits thereof for three years successively, whether or not they lived on the land, to gain a settlement.

Preemptive strikes were also lawful. "All persons actually chargeable, or who through age or infirmity, idleness or dissoluteness, are likely to become chargeable to the places wherein they are found, but in which they have no lawful settlement, may be removed to the places of their lawful settlement, if they have any within the commonwealth." No person could have more than one legal settlement at a time.

And there were penalties. Any person who brought and left any poor or indigent person in any town or district wherein such pauper was not lawfully settled, knowing that person to be poor and indigent, was fined twenty pounds for every offense and could be sued in court. The fine was even more

---

82 Freeman, *The Town Officer*, 1808.

steep—one hundred pounds—for bringing into the commonwealth any person convicted in any other state or in any foreign country of any infamous crime or any for which said person had been sentenced to transportation.[83]

The power and duty of towns were described in twenty-six articles. These were arranged in alphabetical order as follows.

1. **Actions.** Power to begin a lawsuit and defend itself in a court of law (law passed 1786).
2. **By-Laws.** Power to make bylaws for directing, managing, and ordering its affairs, and to fix penalties for its observance, not to exceed thirty shillings for one offense. Such fines and forfeitures for the breach of any bylaw were prosecuted by the justice of the peace (law passed 1786).
3. **County Register.** Townsmen could vote for county register of deeds every five years at the annual meeting in March or any time there was a vacancy (law passed 1784).[84]
4. **County Treasurer.** Voted in annually in the month of March or April. Voters had to be qualified to vote for representatives.
5. **Ferries.** Wherever the Court of General Sessions of the Peace deemed necessary, towns were required to set up a ferry and provide a licensed ferryman to run it. The boat had to be in good repair on penalty of $20 for each neglect, and give "ready and due attendance on all passengers" on penalty of $1 for each neglect, one moiety[85] to the town, and one moiety to the informer. The general sessions of the peace granted such licenses. The penalty for operating without a license was $20, of which half went to the informer and half to the Commonwealth of Massachusetts. Towns neglecting to provide a ferryman were fined $40 per month (law passed in 1797).
6. **Fire.** Firewards or selectmen could pull down a building or remove furniture to prevent the spreading of a fire; towns would compensate the owner.

7. **Governour, Lieutenant Governour, Senators, and Counsellors.** These state officers were elected annually on the first Monday in April.
8. **Guide Posts.** It was the duty of the town or plantation to erect and keep in repair guide posts on all public roads, determined by the selectmen, on penalty of twenty shillings per month, to be recovered by indictment of the grand jury. The fine for defacing a guide post was between twenty and forty shillings, half to the complainer and half to the town or plantation (law passed in 1795).
9. **Horses.** It could be voted at the annual March or April meeting to grant liberty for horses to go at large without fetters within the town between April 15 and November 1, provided that no ungelded male horses more than one year old were permitted to go at large on the common or highways without fetters. The fine for a male horse was three shillings and an ungelded horse twenty shillings, to be paid to the field driver or anyone who sued (law passed in 1789). In 1793, the regulation was extended to asses and mules.
10. **Jurors, Grand.** The town was obligated to appoint grand jurors to serve either in the Supreme Judicial Court or the Court of General Sessions of the Peace. The penalty for not appointing jurors was forty pounds for the supreme court and twenty pounds for the general sessions court. (Law passed 1784, 1794)
11. **Jurors, Petit.** Townspeople had to assemble to appoint petit jurors, with the same penalties for not doing so. To select jurors, selectmen drew up a list of qualified men of good moral character. One-third of qualified jurors had their names written by the town clerk on separate pieces of paper and put into one jury box for the Supreme Judicial Court and one-half of the remainder of the list put into another box. Inhabitants had the right to restore to the box any name withdrawn by the selectmen for conviction of scandalous crime

---

83 Refers to penal transportation. England transported prisoners to its colonies. Georgia was a penal colony before the Revolution.

84 "Males qualified to vote were twenty-one years of age and resident in said Plantation for the space of one year next preceding having a freehold estate in said Plantation of the annual income of three pounds or any Estate of the Value of sixty pounds." From the Hiram warrant of 1806.

85 A moiety is one of two equal parts.

or gross immorality. Jurors had to be picked at least six days before the court sat (law passed in 1784). A photo of a jury box appears on page 89 in the chapter on Peleg Wadsworth.

12. **Militia.** Every town "shall be constantly provided with sixty-four pounds of good gun powder, one hundred pounds of musket balls, one hundred flints, and three tin or iron camp kettles for every sixty-four soldiers in the militia" on penalty of 6 pounds (law passed in 1793).

13. **Poor.** "Every town and district is obliged by law to relieve and support all poor and indigent persons, lawfully settled therein, whenever they shall stand in need thereof; and may raise monies therefor, and for their employment, as monies for other charges are raised [law passed 1794]. It is also 'holden' to pay any expense which shall be necessarily incurred for the relief of any pauper by any inhabitant not liable by law for his or her support, upon notice and request made to the overseers, and until provision shall be made by them [law passed in 1793]."

14. **Pounds.** Every town had to keep and maintain a sufficient pound for stray animals on penalty of ten pounds for every six months (law passed in 1789).

15. **Raising Money.** Towns were empowered to raise money for maintenance and support of the ministry, roads, schools, the poor, and other necessary charges arising within the town (law passed in 1786).

16. **Representatives.** Selectmen called meetings to elect state and federal representatives ten days before the annual vote.

17. **Senators.** The Commonwealth was divided into fifteen districts to elect "counsellors" and senators. Four districts were allowed for Maine—York; Cumberland; Lincoln, "Hancok," and Washington; and "Kennebeck"—which were allocated seven of the forty seats (act passed 1802).

18. **Schools.** Towns were to provide schoolmasters "of good morals, to teach children to read and write, and to instruct them in the English language, as well as in arithmetic, orthography, and decent behavior." Inhabitants were to be taxed for such. It was the duty of the assessors to determine in which district the lands

should be taxed and to certify it in writing to the clerk of the town. Residents had thirty days to pay the school taxes to the town treasurer. The money was at the disposal of the school committee of each district and each district chose an agent to oversee operations. Schools had to be in session for six months in towns of fifty families, on penalty of ten pounds, and twelve months for towns containing one hundred families, on penalty of twenty pounds. Any three freeholders of the school district qualified to vote in town affairs could call a meeting of the district. Much attention was paid to building new schoolhouses. If the school district could not agree on where to build a new schoolhouse, selectmen decided (act passed in 1800).

19. **Small Pox.** Inhabitants of a town could meet, with legal advance warning of eight days, and agree to erect, establish, or appoint a hospital for inoculation with small pox, by a majority vote. Selectmen or a committee could decide the regulations and restrictions and could also discontinue such a hospital. No hospital could be built within one hundred rods of any inhabited dwelling or situated in any adjacent town without the consent of the adjoining town. All inoculations had to occur in a licensed hospital on pain of forfeiting a fine not exceeding forty pounds, half to the county and half to the town.

20. **Suits,** see **Actions**

21. **Swine.** It could be voted to permit swine to roam at large within the town for the whole year or part of a year, under certain restrictions (law passed in 1789).

22. **Taxes.** Taxes were assessed based on the number of polls (headcount of eligible voters) plus real and personal property valued by the assessors and compiled into Lists of Rateables.

23. **Town Officers.** Officers were elected at annual meetings in March or April.

24. **Ways.** Money was to be raised at public meetings by vote for labor and materials to be expended on building and repairing the highways and townways. The rates were set for labor of men and of oxen, horses, cart, and plough (law passed 1786). Towns could also authorize their surveyors to enter into contracts and could empower

them to collect taxes not paid in labor (law passed in 1797). Towns could allow and approve of any town or private way laid out by the selectmen, or alter any, and record it in the town books (law passed in 1786). However, the Court of General Sessions could lay out roads that passed through towns, for which the towns had one year to raise and pay state or county taxes for their maintenance and repair on penalty of being served a "warrant of distress" from said court (law passed in 1797).

25. **Weights and Measures.** It was the duty of the Town Treasurer to procure before January 1, 1803, and preserve as standards at the expense of the town the following measures: one half bushel, one peck, one half peck, one ale quart, one wine gallon, one wine half gallon, one wine quart, one wine pint, one wine half pint, one wine gill (one quarter of a pint, four ounces). Specifications followed on size and materials. The half bushel, peck, and half peck may be made of wood; the other measures must be made of copper or pewter. Among other measures were one ell (one cubit, 18 inches), one yard, one set of brass weights to four pounds computed at sixteen ounces to the pound, a good beam, scales, and a set of troy weights.

Penalties for nonconformance were listed. The treasurer was required to have the troy weight compared, proved, and sealed every ten years by the commonwealth or county treasurer or some person authorized. It was also his duty to procure a proper town seal for the use of the sealer, under penalty of one hundred dollars. Measurers in Hiram were elected, not appointed by selectmen as stated in Freeman, 1808.[86]

26. **Workhouses.** Any town "may erect and provide a house for the employment of idle persons, who neglect and refuse to exercise any lawful calling or business to support themselves and families, and for the poor and indigent who want means to employ themselves." Towns could also join together to provide such a house, to purchase land to erect one, and to choose overseers (law passed in 1789).

Hiram chose to auction able-bodied paupers and their children to the lowest bidder until, at the Town Meeting of April 5, 1830, it was voted out. Hiram continued to board them with residents rather than in a designated workhouse, until 1879 when Hiram purchased a farm on Hampshire Street for this purpose.

---

86 Freeman, *The Town Officer*, 118–119, 192–194.

POWER AND DUTY OF OFFICERS[87]

social good and conscience

Officers were elected for annual terms at the annual Town Meeting held in March or April.

Assessor established the value of real property, a great proportion of which was livestock. The office was combined with that of selectman and overseer of the poor.

Clerk was a very important position that prepared the agenda and recorded the proceedings of Town Meetings, maintained town records, provided information for issuing licenses (such as liquor licenses), conducted elections, and maintained records of births, deaths, and marriages.

Collector of Taxes collected taxes and made a list of delinquents. The office was often combined with that of constable.

Constable served all warrants and other processes directed to him by the selectmen for notifying the townspeople of Town Meetings or for other purposes, such as criminal warrants. "He shall take due notice of and prosecute all violations of law respecting the observance of the Lord's day, profane swearing and gaming." Constables had the power of a sheriff.

Culler of Hoops and Staves: a disinterested party who determined the quality of hoops that were split and staves that were riven to be sold to the cooper, who made them into barrels. Riving was done with a froe, a heavy steel blade.

Fence Viewer looked at the line between neighbors to decide who took care of his half of the fence. The rule was that a line fence must be "hog tight and horse high." Good fences made good neighbors, and good neighbors made good fences, and back when everybody had livestock it was equally important for all.

Field Driver captured stray horses or cows and drove them to the town pound.

Hog Reeve: Hogs didn't drive easily. They had to be "reeved," removed forcibly to the town pound. Apparently it was the custom in some towns to appoint newly married men as hog reeves. Ralph Waldo Emerson was once hog reeve of Concord, Massachusetts.

Justice of the Peace settled minor criminal matters and disputes.

Overseer of the Poor administered relief of the poor, including food, clothing, and money raised through taxes, auctioning off indigents able to work, and approved payments for indigent Hiram residents found in "distress" in other towns.

Pound Keeper held the animal in the town pound until the owner came to recover it by paying for feed and fees. If the owner did not claim it within the specified time limit, the pound keeper could dispose of it as he saw fit.

Sealer of Leather had authority to see that all sales of leather were made honestly as to quality and quantity. The sealer of leather was authorized to put his "seal" or stamp of approval on items he inspected, tested, and certified.

Selectmen had overall responsibility for town government, convened Town Meetings which were frequent, and required the attendance of all eligible voters, meaning men with property. Duties were assessing property for taxes, supplying ammunition for the militia, taking care of the poor, holding elections, surveying roads, and providing jurors for the county.

Surveyor of Highways was responsible for seeing that the residents of his neighborhood road district labored to improve roads. Most men chose to reduce their highway tax by their labor. There were over twenty road districts in Hiram in 1820.

Surveyor of Lumber measured and approved lumber for sale according to standard lengths and widths for each type of wood.

Surveyor of Wood & Bark measured and approved logs for sale.

Tithingman in Colonial America were the moral police, responsible for maintaining order in the church and in the community on the Sabbath and other days, and did not collect ten percent of income as done in early England. The selectmen of every town chose "some sober and discrete persons to be authorized from the County Court, each of

---

87 Definitions are taken from various editions of Freeman, *The Town Officer*, as they applied to Hiram.

whom shall take charge of ten or twelve families of his neighborhood, and shall diligently inspect them, and present the names of such persons as transgressed the law, receiving as compensation for their services one third of the fines allowed." It was their duty to seize liquors sold without license, and also "to present the names of all single persons that live under family government, stubborn and disorderly children & servants, night walkers, typlers, saboath breakers, by night or by day, & such as absent themselves from the public worship of God on the Lords dayes, or whatever the course or practise of any person or persons whatsoeuer tending to debauchery, irreligion, prophaness, & atheisme among us, wherein by omission of family government, nurture, & religious duties, & instruction of children & servants, or idleness, profligat, uncivill, or rude practises of any sort."

Treasurer: Chief financial officer collected and dispensed funds, often with the assistance of the tax collector and a Committee on Accounts.

Most officers carried out their duties satisfactorily. A few, however, abused their office or were incompetent.

INCORPORATION

a long road

1801 to 1814

On the third attempt to incorporate Hiram as a town, the Massachusetts Legislature granted the request.

The first attempt was a petition led by Timothy Cutler in 1801. It was signed by twenty-four men in the Hiram settlement plus seven men in Brownfield's Addition and three in Prescott's Grant adjacent to Hiram.[88] Peleg Wadsworth, who was representing Maine in the U.S. Congress, heard of it from his son, Charles Lee Wadsworth, and opposed it, spelling out his reasons in a letter to his son dated February 13, 1801.[89] He pledged to stop it as it respected his land until he could see to it himself. As a result, Charles Lee filed a counter petition opposing incorporation as a town, which was signed by some of the same men who signed Timothy Cutler's petition to incorporate. Cutler's petition was denied. Transcriptions of the original documents appear in Appendix 23.

Peleg Wadsworth's Letter to His Son Charles Lee Wadsworth, February 13, 1801

Brigadier General Peleg Wadsworth, serving as U.S. congressman, wrote the following letter to his eldest son, Charles Lee Wadsworth, in Hiram detailing reasons he was opposed to incorporation, and, as was his custom, included political news, instructions for his farm, and advice on farming.

> City of Washington 13th Feby 1801
> Dear Sir
> I have just received yours of 22d January & am very glad to see in your conclusion that your family are all well; as Bertha was not so when last you wrote. I think it very fortunate that you have got Mr. Howard to work for you; I do not begrudge his wages at all. He will be an excellent Assistant to you besides he will make us some long shingles or short ones or other Lumber in the Evenings which will all help.

> I by no means wish to be incorporated with any town at present. It would be very inconvenient to all on my Grant & very needless at present. Nature has designed, in some future time when we become sufficiently numerous that my Grant with Cutlers lower Grant, the lower part of Brownfield & the upper end of Flints Town taking in the Gore to Great Ossipee River should be made into one town. This I take to be nearly your Idea. But there is no occasion for it at present. Who suffers as it is? On my Grant there are but Six families or eight & certainly we are much better off now than we should be to be worked up with the parts of other Towns. I am very glad you did not sign any Petition on the business & I am sure it will not be for the advantage of any of my Neighbours to go at a distance to make roads, as we have enough of our own to make—or to attend a Town meeting where we should have but very little influence.

> At present let Brownfield, Porterfield, Friburg [Fryeburg], Flintstown [Baldwin] & Cornish all stand as they are. If Cutlers Lower Grant wish to be annexed to Brownfield, let them do it; but for my part I shall oppose all incorporation of my Land to any Town whatever.

> You need not mention it, but I shall write to Daniel Davis of the Senate now at Boston & desire him to put a Stopper on the Business, as far as it respect my Land till I can have an opportunity of seeing to it myself. If they leave out my Land, I am willing they should suit themselves as to the rest. I should prefer belonging to Cumberland County: but there will be an inland County ere long.

> I should like to have about Six Sows if they can be had easily. I hope Mr. Clemons will make you out some money or perhaps

---

88 Brown's Addition was ceded to Hiram in 1807 and Prescott's Grant in 1814.

89 Maine Historical Society, Coll. 16, Box 1/3.

he can help you to a Sow or two by getting them on Credit somehow or other.

I fear the Snow will be too deep for your logging Business. I should be sorry not to have your barn filled but would not have you spoil your Oxen; which I am glad to find you have procured. You did well to Settle as you did with Tyler. Am sorry that Fly disappointed us in the Corn. If you can engage it handily it may be well to Secure a Supply. if you have not the money to pay down— pay a part & give your Note till I come; but have the Corn Secured at home or abroad if you purchase.

Am glad to hear your hay Spends so well; I think you will be able to give some browse as you get your wood & perhaps you can wood & logg at the same time. But this will be over before you receive this & I shall soon follow.

Congress have been three days in attempting to Chuse a President but have not effected that Business. Thirty Ballots have been taken in the House of Representatives & the result has been the same each time. 8 States for Jefferson. 6 for Burr & 2 divided. This makes no choice. The House has not been adjourned for three days.

Written in the margin: '14th 3 Oclock PM. No president—Votes still the same. The next ballot is to be taken on Monday next at 12 Oclock.'

[Editor's note: The letter is not signed. A letter Peleg wrote to his younger son George the same day makes no mention of the potential town incorporation.]

Committee for Incorporation, 1805

In 1805 a Committee for Incorporation was formed; whether elected or appointed is not known. Thomas Spring was the "committee man" to meet with the "other committees at Brownfield." The strategy was to collaborate with other towns to make more even the populations of the districts. In this plan Porter set off to Brownfield a portion of land including Cutler's Upper Grant and Brownfield gave Brown's Addition to Hiram. The committee was to draw up a plan to submit to the Massachusetts General Court, which it did by hiring surveyor Nathaniel Merrill. Esq. Joseph L. Howard went to Boston to submit it.

Petition to Incorporate Three Towns, 1806[90]

This petition of 1806 asked that three new towns be incorporated from plantations (districts) and tracts south of Fryeburg, with an adjustment to the bounds of Brownfield, which had been incorporated in 1802. As a result, Denmark and Porter were incorporated as towns on February 27, 1807, and Hiram was made a plantation, also called a district, having all the privileges of a town save representation in the General Court. So it was that John Watson, Thomas Veasey, Asa Osgood, and the Burbanks who had settled in Brownfield ended up in Hiram, changing towns without moving house.

On the day the legislature approved Hiram as a district, it also considered a petition to settle a dispute in the Plantation of Hiram regarding payment of taxes. Some landowners had refused to pay, believing the vote to raise taxes was illegal because of ineligible voters. It was noted that complaints of bad roads in Hiram had necessitated raising taxes.[91]

1814[92]

There were additional acts to pass in 1814 when the legislature, for the third time, considered incorporating Hiram. In order to change the status of Hiram from district to town, the act to incorporate Hiram as a district and unite with Brownfield in choosing a representative had to be repealed. When that was accomplished, the act to incorporate Hiram as a town could proceed

---

90 Massachusetts Legislature Acts 1806, Chap. 84, Massachusetts State Archives.

91 Massachusetts Legislature Resolves 1807, Chap. 23, Massachusetts State Archives.

92 Massachusetts Legislature Acts 1814, Chap. 41, Massachusetts State Archives.

Map of Brownfield showing boundaries with Hiram, Denmark, Fryeburg, and Porter, including lot plans before 1807. Copied by William Wentworth on December 19, 1832, from a map drawn by A. McMillan. Collections of Maine Historical Society.[93]

93 Maine Historical Society, Coll. 261, Box 1, William Wentworth papers.

if the town of Brownfield approved. Brownfield remonstrated, was assured that its right of representation was guaranteed, and the legislature approved incorporation of Hiram as a town on June 14, 1814. Transcriptions of original documents appear in the Appendix 23.

MILITIA

rally for the common defense

The predecessors of the Army National Guard were militias, important social institutions for defense and public safety. Voluntary militias served in the French and Indian Wars and the Revolution, but the men were irregularly trained and lacked discipline. The Militia Act of 1792, passed by the U.S. Congress, required every free and able-bodied white male citizen of a state between the ages of 18 and 45 to enroll in the militia. Each militia was commanded by a captain or commanding officer and mustered regularly. Town selectmen were responsible for equipping soldiers, at the request of the commanding officer.

The Militia Act of 1792 required a militia man to keep himself constantly provided with a good musket, an iron or steel rod, a sufficient bayonet and belt, two spare flints, a priming wire and brush, and a knapsack; a cartridge box or pouch to contain not less than 24 cartridges suited to the bore of his musket—each cartridge to contain a proper quantity of powder and ball; or with a good rifle, knapsack, shot-pouch, powderhorn, twenty balls suited to the bore of his rifle, and a quarter of a pound of powder. Appearing with full equipment was required, but if to exercise only, the knapsack and cartridges loaded with balls could be omitted.[94]

Most of the Hiram men who served in the War of 1812 were called up by the governor late in the war to serve in the state militia, not the federal army. Hiram men defended Portland for terms as short as one week, and they rarely saw action.

The earliest record of Hiram's militia is 1807 (below, in the original spelling).[95] A constitution was written in 1822, and by 1827 two light infantries in Hiram commanded by Charles Lee Wadsworth and Peleg Wadsworth Jr. were recorded.[96]

Following are some orders, bills, and receipts regarding Hiram's early militia.[97]

Revolutionary War Soldiers Who Settled in Hiram

Militias played a large role in the success of the Revolution. Many returning soldiers escaped the war-scarred coastal landscape by turning north and inland. Veterans who settled in Hiram were:

Names on the plaque at Soldiers Memorial Library:

Gen. Peleg Wadsworth
Maj. Nathaniel Warren
Capt. Thomas Spring
Capt. John Lane

Moody Brown
Jacob Brown
Daniel E. Cross
James Eastman
James Fly
John Gilpatrick
John Goodwin
Daniel Hickey
Daniel Lane
Abijah Lewis
Jonathan K. Lowell
John McLucas
Asa Osgood
John Robbins
Mastress Treadwell
William Storer
Dura Wadsworth
John Watson
Nathaniel Williams

Additionally:
David Durgin [98]
Stephen Tibbetts

---

94 Freeman, *The Town Officer*, 1808, 68.

95 Maine State Archives, Hiram Box 14.

96 Maine Historical Society, Coll. 1496.

97 Maine State Archives, Hiram Box 14.

98 Massachusetts. Office of the Secretary of State. *Massachusetts Soldiers and Sailors of the Revolutionary War* (Boston: The Office), 1896-1908.

September 21, 1807. Account of Peleg Wadsworth for ammunition bought at Portland.

Select Men of District of Hiram to Peleg Wadsworth Dr [Debit]

60# bullets at 9, Box for Do [Ditto]	$7.62
21 ½# powder at 3/	10.75
6 ½ Do at 3/9	4.06
60 flints at 14d [cents]	.84
Hauling the Above to Hiram	.50
	$23.77

Cr [Credit]	
by Cash paid of John Pierce	10.00
by Select Men order on Treasurer	13.77
	23.77

September 1, 1809. District of Hiram to Peleg Wadsworth

12# best Powder at 4/6#	$9.00
Box for Do [Ditto]	.34
	9.34

Received payment of Thos. Spring Esq. Treasurer. Peleg Wadsworth

October 18, 1811. "Mr John Watson Treasurer Please to Deliver to Josiah Mayberry Capt of the Company in the District ten Pounds of Powder from the town Stock in Your Possession. John Pierce, Asa Osgood, Selectmen of Hiram." This order was reviewed March 18, 1813, by Josiah Mayberry and Peleg Wadsworth.

September 19, 1812. "Mr John Watson Stockholder in the District of Hiram please to let Lt Marshall Spring have one and a half # of powder out the Town Stock. Signed by E. Kimball, Thomas Spring for the Selectmen."

Peleg Wadsworth's Account for Company utensils of Sept. 1814 asked for reimbursement of $28.77. It was submitted in 1815.

1814 Town of Hiram to Peleg Wadsworth:

Sept. 12 To 1 day attending to Rate Bills, Returns, Company Provisions & Ammunition	.67
4 Quires[99] Cartridge paper at 9	.50
Boy & Horse to Cornish to get the Same	.33
Sept. 13th paid Cash for making up Cartridges	1.00
Sept. 16th Ditto [Do] for 6 Large Tin Carry Kettles at 9/	9.00
Do for 6 Large Tin Mess pans at 6/	6.00
Do for 3 Small Do for _____3/8d	1.83
Do for 1 pt. Measure, 20, 2 ? Cups 16, 2 half Gill[100] Do 13. Tea 20 vol.	.69
To [??? name of] Steelyard 7/6	1.25
To 6 days attendance on Militia Company	2.50
To equip. & furnish them with Utensils & provisions	$28.77

---

99   Quire: English unit of measurement equal to 1/20 ream.

100   Gill, or teacup: English unit of measurement equal to 1/4 pint.

September 18, 1814. To one Half Day Delivering powder Bowls & flints to the Select men for the Company to go to Portland.

September 13th to Delivering powder twice	$.37
	.37
1815 going to Mr Burbanks three times for amunition	.75
Going to Capt Springs after Rattles & Pans & ammunicion	.50
1815 Commity on accounts one Day	1.00
To Laying out roads one Day	1.00
John Watson	3.99

The Committee are of Opinion that the above account Ought to be allowed with a Reduction of fifty Cents. Ephraim Kimball, Thos B. Watson, Charles L. Wadsworth.

September 17, 1819. "Mr John Watson Stockholder of the District of Hiram Sir, Please to let Capt. Mayberry have eight pounds of powder out of the Town Stock. Thomas Spring, Ephraim Kimball."

September 3, 1821. "To the Selectmen of the Town of Hiram. Gentlemen, you are hereby requested to furnish twenty pounds of Good Powder maid into Blank Cartridges for the use of Eighty men born on my Company roll and Deliver the Same at Fryburg on Fryday the fourteenth Day Sept ins [instant] in Front of John Bradleys Store at Six in the fore noon. Yours etc John Warren Capt."

April 25, 1821. "Received one dollar of Alpheus Spring for making cartridges for Hiram Company in the fall of AD 1819. Solomon Hartford."

May 3, 1824. "Dr [debit] Town of Hiram to B. [Benjamin] Bucknell

To 1 Gun & Equipment for Wm Gray $6.00."

August 30, 1824. "To the Gentlemen Select Men of Hiram you are requested to furnish powder for thirty men in the Company under my Command to be delivered to them on the ninth day of September next at eight o'clock AM, made into cartridges as the Law directs at the Dwelling House of Mr. Josiah Spring in Brownfield. Hiram, August 30th, 1824. Ephraim Kimball Capt."

September 1, 1824. "To the Select men of the Town of Hiram, Gentlemen, the number of Soldiers under my roll to be furnished with cartridges are eighty. I therefore request that one quarter of a pound of good Powder made into blank cartridges...as the law Directs to be delivered at the Dwelling house of Benjamin Swett, Hiram,[101] on Wednesday the eighth day of Sept. next at one o'clock in the afternoon. I also request that I may be furnished with money to the amount of twenty cents for each Soldier under my command, which will be eighteen dollars.[102] Charles Wadsworth Capt."

September 11, 1829. "Gent. Selectmen of Hiram, In compliance with the Law of this State I hereby inform you, that there are thirty men, viz. Peleg Wadsworth Jr., Andrew R. Bucknell, James Evans, William G. Burbank, William Pierce, Simeon Bucknell Jr., Joseph Butterfield, Peleg C. Wadsworth, Daniel Small, Aaron Williams, Daniel Pierce, Thomas Mayberry, Esrom [Ezrom] Kimball, Henry S. Burbank, Sewall Fly, John Clark, James Fly Jr., John Bucknell Jr., James Brazier, John Wadsworth, Henry Wadsworth, Uriah

---

101   Benjamin Swett sometimes filled the cartridges.
102   Capt. Wadsworth's arithmetic is incorrect. 80 men X $0.20 = $16.00, not the $18 he requested.

Wadsworth, Stephen Wentworth, Andrew Sloper, Noah McDonald, John McDonald, Edmund Butterfield, Jacob B. Rand, William P. Farnham, Abner McDonald, who live in Hiram, who are borne on the Roll of the Hiram Light Infantry & who are entitled to twenty-five cents each, which you are required to furnish them with on parade at the Town House in Brownfield on Tuesday the twenty-second day of Sept. at six O. clock PM.

I hereby certify the above named persons perform military duty (or rather are liable to perform military duty) in the company under my command. Peleg Wadsworth Jr. Capt. of the Hiram Light Infantry."

WAR OF 1812

unpopular and alienating

In 1812 President James Madison declared war on Great Britain for restricting trade and impressing American seamen into the Royal Navy. Washington, D.C., burned because of it. Maine was much affected. It was not a popular war in New England, especially on the coast, due to hardships of the U.S. trade embargo and the British occupation of Maine east of the Penobscot River. The war seemed farther away in Hiram, but the sentiment was similar: that the insults of the British did not warrant a war. Gen. Peleg Wadsworth opposed it, calling it neither "just, necessary or politic."[103] The war ended in 1815.

It was common practice to pay a substitute to take a draftee's place if one could afford it. The War of 1812 was no exception. Peleg Wadsworth Jr. wrote to his father about the prospect. The letter sheds light on the draft of militias in the late stage of the war. The summer of 1814 was a low point in the fighting. The British were poised to invade from Canada, and the U.S. appeared not to have enough troops to stop them. The British were inciting Native Americans against settlers farther west, and continuing coastal raids in the east. The White House in Washington, D.C., was burned in August. Luckily for townspeople, Congress passed the bill to incorporate Hiram as a town on June 14, 1814, before more chaos ensued.

> Portland Sept. 23, 1814[104]
>
> Dear Papa,
>
> Mr. Bucknell[105] is in town this morning & I think will set out for Hiram today. I will send a few lines by him to let you know I am one of the drafted ones. 19 were drafted from 39. Hartford[106] & Cross[107] are both drafted, Eastman[108] has enlisted during the war, he says he can have a furlough for 60 days & will take my place for thirty dollars besides the wage which is quite too much. Those who are drafted, I hear, are to stay forty days. I suppose I could get somebody to take my place for 10 or 15 dollars, besides the wages. I should like to know from you, whether that is too much; if not; how I should pay it. Perhaps I should have to leave my gun too for the person drafted. Bill Baston[109] has enlisted & signed his name, but not taken any pay yet & I think Mr. Baston would like to know of it. Those who are not drafted are not discharged; but will probably be, in a day or two. Peleg was not drafted.[110]
>
> Remember me to all the family. Your dutiful son, Peleg Wadsworth, Jr.
>
> If I can get a substitute before I hear from you for 10 $, I think I shall.

Another son of Peleg Wadsworth, Alexander Scammel, served in the War of 1812 as a lieutenant in the U.S. Navy on board the frigate *Constitution*. He served forty years on active duty and reached the rank of commodore.

After the war, New England flirted with secession, and Maine, disillusioned by the lack of support from Massachusetts, began organizing for separation. Hiram voted in favor of separation in the vote of 1816, held in Simeon Chadbourne's house, and again in 1819.

As disgruntled as townspeople were, Hiram responded patriotically. It raised soldiers for the U.S. Army, which was drastically underfunded, and raised seventy-seven men of the volunteer militia, under

---

103 Maine Historical Society, Coll. Box 16/6.

104 Ibid.

105 Most likely Simeon Bucknell.

106 Solomon Hartford, son of John and Hannah Fly Hartford.

107 Most likely one of the sons of Aaron and Sally Lewis Cross.

108 John Eastman [William J. Eastman].

109 William Baston, son of Benjamin and Martha Clark Baston.

110 Most likely cousin Peleg Wadsworth III, who is listed as serving under A. Spring's company.

the auspices of the state governor, to go to Portland to fight. There were no Hiram heroes in the war, and there was only one deserter, Robert McLucas. Robert's father, John, was exceptionally proud of his sons for enlisting and had accompanied four to their enlistment; he died traveling home to Hiram, and did not read about Robert's defection. Read more in the chapter Paupers, and John McLucas.

In the lists that follow, note that not all men recruited at Hiram were residents of Hiram, and that some Hiram residents signed up in different locations, serving under other commands. Nearby "Home Stations of Companies, Detachments, and Guards who responded to the Call of the Governor" were Bridgton, Brownfield, Denmark, Fryeburg, Hiram, and Porter, but not Baldwin, Cornish, or Parsonsfield. In the list below, reproduced from the original document, names of those known to be living in Hiram are marked with an asterisk (*). Note differences in spelling.

Records of the Massachusetts Volunteer Militia in the War of 1812, compiled by General Gardner W. Pearson, Adjutant General of Mass., 1913

Capt. A. Spring's Company, Maj. James Steele's[111] Battalion of Artillery. From Sept. 13 to Sept. 24, 1814. Raised at Hiram. Service at Portland.

Rank and Name
Alpheus Spring,* Captain
Asa Burbank,* Lieutenant

Thomas G. Watson,* Sergeant [Thomas B.]
John W. Chadbourn,* Sergeant
Ephraim Kimball,* Sergeant
John Bucknell,* Sergeant
Josiah Mabry,* Corporal
Benj Bucknell,* Corporal
Daniel Cram,* Corporal
Asa Osgood Jr., Corporal
J. Storer,* Musician
James McLucas,* Musician

Privates
Allen, Joseph*
Bickford, William
Boston, William* [Baston]
Bothwell, James
Brooks, William
Bucknell, Andrew R.*
Burbank, Israel, Jr.*
Chadbourn, Humphrey A.*
Chase, Gideon*
Clark, Jacob*
Coolrath, James
Cotton, William*
Cram, John*
Cross, Aaron*
Davis, Ephraim
Durgin, John*
Durgin, Joseph*
Eastman, John
Fillbrock, Jonathan
Fillbrock, Simon
Floyd, Michael
Fox, John, Jr.
Fox, Jonathan
French, Benjamin
French, Jacob
Gray, Abraham*
Gray, Joseph*
Hartford, Solomon*
Hayes, John
Howard, Henry
Jack, James
Lewis, Edward*
Lewis, Morgan*
Lewis, Noah*
Libby, Elisha
Libby, Hanson
Libby, John
Libby, Stephen, Jr.
Libby, Thomas
Libby, Tobias
Lord, Jacob*
Lord, Levi*
Lowell, Moses*

---

111   He married Jane Spring of Hiram.

Lowell, Reuben*
Lowell, Thomas*
McKissick, Aaron
McKissick, Moses
Merryfield, Richard*
Moulton, John
Nutter, Charles
Pearl, Dimon
Pierce, Benjamin I.*
Pierce, John, Jr.*
Pierce, Josiah*
Richardson, Aaron*
Robbins, Joshua*
Stanley, Elisha
Storer, John*
Thompson, Caleb
Tibbets, Ephraim*
Trafton, Jeremiah*
Truett, George
Vainey, Andrew [Varney?]
Wadsworth, Peleg, Jr.*
Wadsworth, Peleg 3rd*

Capt. W. Wheeler's Company, Lt. Co. W. Ryerson's Regiment. From Sept. 25 to Nov. 7, 1814. Raised at Rumford and vicinity. Service at Portland.
Known Hiram men:
Rank and Name
Asa Burbank,* Lieutenant
Thomas B. Watson,* Sergeant
Josiah Mayberry* [Mabry], Corporal

Privates
William Baston*
Stephen Burbank*
Humphrey A. Chadburn [Chadbourne]*
Noah Lewis*
Moses Lovell* [Lowell]
Thomas Lovell* [Lowell]
Asa Osgood*
Joshua Snow*[112]

Waiters
Samuel S. Burbank
Capt. E. Andrew's Detached Company, From July 4 to Sept. 2, 1814. Raised at Scarborough and vicinity. Service at Portland.

Abraham McLucas,* Musician

Llewellyn A. Wadsworth's journals noted additional soldiers from Hiram:

James Dyer*
Ensign John Howard,* was at Plattsburgh
Joseph Lewis*
Marshall Lewis,* enlisted at Fryeburg, mortally
      wounded at the Battle of Oswego
John McLucas,* mortally wounded at Portland
      [listed as soldier in error][113]
Robert McLucas*[114]
John P. Thompson*

Additional Names Noted on Soldiers Memorial Library Plaque:

James Gilmore* killed[115]
James McLucas*
Jeremiah McLucas*
John Watson*

---

112 Joshua Snow voted in Hiram in 1809. There is no later record.

113 John McLucas served in the Revolution, but not in the War of 1812. He died on March 27, 1813, at age sixty-nine, on the way home after bringing his sons to enlist in Portland. Death notice: *Eastern Argus*, April 1, 1813.

114 Robert McLucas deserted from Fort Scammel, Portland, *Eastern Argus*, February 18, 1813.

115 James Gilmore [Gilmor] was killed in the war, leaving a widow and seven children.

SEPARATION FROM MASSACHUSETTS

steady disaffection

Settlers in Maine had long wished to be free of the clutches of Massachusetts, petitioning Charles II with complaints.[116] There were whispers of separation from Massachusetts after the Revolution, but the first committee, headed by Peleg Wadsworth in 1785, died for lack of zeal, despite strong grievances. One perceived injustice was the Supreme Judicial Court's location in Boston, which necessitated long and costly journeys to conduct business. Others were reduced representation, inequitable taxes (on polls, estates, imports, and exports), and trade regulations that lowered the price of lumber to the detriment of Maine products, shippers, and boat builders. Coastal towns, disillusioned by the lack of support from Massachusetts in the War of 1812, joined with the sentiment on Maine's western frontier, seething since the Revolution, and began to organize for separation. Several votes were held.

Hiram was not a legal town so could not vote on separation in 1792, 1797, or 1807. After its 1814 incorporation, at a legal meeting of the Town of Hiram, held at the schoolhouse near Simeon Bucknell's on Saturday January 19, 1816, it was voted to petition the Legislature of Massachusetts for a separation of the District of Maine from Massachusetts proper. Alpheus Spring was elected moderator.

Asa Burbank, constable, called the next meeting of eligible voters for Monday, May 20, 1816, at one o'clock, to vote to request the legislators give their consent to the separation and to the erection of the District of Maine into an independent and separate state. Those eligible to vote were required to be at least twenty-one years of age, resident in the town for one year, and holding a freehold estate within the town of the annual means of $10 or an estate of the value of $200.[117] The vote was thirty-two in favor, thirteen against.[118]

On Monday, September 2, 1816, at three o'clock, the qualified inhabitants assembled at Simeon Chadbourn's house near the Saco River Bridge. The vote on whether it was expedient that the District of Maine be separated from Massachusetts and become an independent state was forty-three in favor, fourteen against.

On May 8, 1819, Constable Simeon Chadbourn called the eligible voters of the town to meet at two o'clock at his house to choose a representative to the General Court in Boston. Hiram chose Marshall Spring.

A final vote to separate was taken at the "new" Town House on Monday, July 26, 1819, at two o'clock. Fifty-three were in favor and nine against.

Another vote was held at the Town House on September 20, 1819, at two o'clock to choose a delegate to meet to form a "Constitution of frame of Government" at the Court House in Portland on the second Monday of October. Marshall Spring, Esq., was selected. The constitution was finalized in a vote on December 6, 1819, at one o'clock. Twenty-eight were in favor, one was against.

Congress then established Maine as the twenty-third state under the Missouri Compromise, in which Maine was admitted as a free state and Missouri as a slave state.

Hiram Town House, 14 Maple Street, where the final votes relating to separation were taken on July 26, 1819, as it appeared during Hiram's Centennial celebrations in 1914. It was built by July 1819 on land sold by Peleg Wadsworth to the town.

---

116 Coastal towns of Kittery, York, and Wells. Ronald F. Banks, *Maine Becomes a State* (New Hampshire Publishing Co. & Maine Historical Society, 1970), 11.

117 Hiram Town Clerk, Record 8, May 1819, 74.

118 Ronald E. Banks, *Maine Becomes a State*, 223.

TRANSPORTATION

*history littered with bad roads, broken
bridges, and fledgling canals*

Good roads were critical in a rural developing economy like Hiram's, which depended upon farming for survival and logging for income. Attention to roads was a high priority. There were thirty-four families in Hiram in 1800, and all men were kept busy laying out roads to their farms and reducing their taxes by working on them. There is no record of women reducing their taxes by working on roads.

Maintenance was a continuing problem, especially in wet weather. Modern paved roads can be bumpy and full of potholes, but imagine what it was like when all the roads were dirt and filled with deep ruts made by wagon wheels and the hooves of horses, oxen, and cattle. Farmers favored settling on the tops of mountains because of the "good" air, greater sunlight, and a longer frost-free growing season, but travel up and down mountain roads was often treacherous due to frequent washouts and other hazards. Tools available for repairs, such as removing rocks and filling ruts, were shovel, pick ax, crowbar, and oxen.

Roads preoccupied residents of the Plantation[119] of Hiram (1807–1814), as they would residents of the legally incorporated town (1814). The chief arguments against incorporating as a town that Peleg Wadsworth made in 1801 were that it would take away from time needed to build private roads on his grant and would require a great amount of time to attend meetings because of few roads and poor conditions.

Private roads were being built with great energy. Once built, owners emphasized getting them accepted as town roads so maintenance would be paid by town taxes. Highway surveyors for each district were elected to ensure that taxes were collected and labor secured for their maintenance. Men were obliged to work on roads and were paid in coin or in reduced taxes. Half the money allocated to each surveyor was to be spent by a specified day in July. From 1815 to 1830, a higher daily rate of $1.25 was paid during haying in July; pay was reduced to 75 cents after haying season.[120]

Useful Information in Tax Documents

Original highway and other tax documents are important sources of information about settlers' wealth. Frequently they show the valuation of real estate and personal property. In the original form they help to establish the neighborhoods where men lived because surveyors listed names in the neighborhoods they represented. To some extent they measure population growth. Districts were added and shuffled to reflect population in the neighborhoods.

For example, when Charles Lee Wadsworth was a surveyor of highways in 1807, there were only four names on his tax list, including his own, to keep his neighborhood roads in good repair. Four was not many men to cover the distance of over two miles, most of it on mountainous terrain. When he made the list for 1813 there were ten men assigned to him. The number of total surveyors also increased, from six in 1807 to seven in 1815, seventeen in 1825, and twenty-eight in 1830.

Nonresident property owners were identified as such and were also taxed, which aids in establishing dates of relocation of individuals as well as speculators.

There were three components to the highway tax: poll tax, real estate tax, and personal property tax. All households in Hiram, regardless of whether they were property owners, were taxed. Men without property paid only the poll tax. Women, who could not vote, paid only the real estate and personal property portions of the tax. Nonresident property owners paid less. Highway surveyors were responsible

---

119   Also known as "District of Hiram."

120   Maine State Archives, Hiram Box 14.

for collecting the highway tax and notifying the town of any delinquents.

Since roads were important for trade, the county also made demands. One of the items on the warrant of November 29, 1806 that necessitated a meeting was to see how Hiram would build a road recently laid out by the newly formed Oxford County.

Money for roads always surpassed amounts allocated to schools, the other high priority.

	Budget for Schools	Budget for Highways
1815	$100	$700
1820	$300	$1,000
1825	$350	$1,500
1830	$350	$2,000

Highway districts were more numerous than school districts as well. As many as thirty highway supervisors were noted in one undated document, whereas the most number of school districts was eighteen, and some of those were not always active.

Despite the diligence paid to maintenance, roads were bad, and complaints, disputes, and suits littered the history of Hiram. Rocks, mud, ruts, washouts, snow, and ice marred the dirt surfaces. Indeed, the poor layout and condition of roads into and through Hiram caused a petition for remedy, the Petition for a Turnpike Road to Hiram, 1801.[121]

Commonwealth of Massachusetts, 1801

To the Honorable General Court, now holden at Boston, in and for the Commonwealth of Massachusetts—Your petitioners humbly shew, That part of the road leading from Portland in the county of Cumberland, thro' Standish and Fryeburg to Coos, is bad and circuitous—That by reason of low lands, rocks and hills, the transportation of produce from the country to Portland and Saco markets, is rendered very expensive,

also merchandize carried into the country, is necessarily sold at a high rate in proportion to the price which the produce of the farms usually bears—That persons considerable removed in the country are reluctantly obliged to resort to some markets out of this Commonwealth, where the goodness of the road will admit of more easy and cheap transportation of their produce and merchandize than to and from said ports of Portland and Saco—That the present road is laid out principally through unincorporated places, whereby much difficulty and delay is occasioned in raising and appropriating money for the repairing of said road—That the inhabitants on said road are few in number and unable to keep in good repair the same as it is now improved, and altogether unable to open and support a road in the nearest direction towards said ports, which would greatly commode travelers—That in passing from the meeting-house in said town of Standish, to Capt. Thomas Spring's[122] in the plantation called Hiram, in the county of York (being a distance of about eighteen miles) more than three miles in distance, together with several bad hills, may be saved and avoided by having another road.[123]

Peleg Wadsworth found it necessary to direct the route and describe road conditions in a letter to his son Charles, who frequently traveled from Hiram to Portland. From Portland on April 12, 1801, Peleg wrote:

I found the Roads not so much work for the storm as I expected. There was no Snow below Ingal's Ferry & I had none below Standish—it was all rain. The roads will be good by Thursday if there is no more wet. Harding's Team is fully loaded down & start on Tuesday. I told him twas uncertain when

---

121 Massachusetts General Court, May 26, 1801. Massachusetts State Archives #3028, Senate unpassed legislative files, 1803.

122 Now called Old Homestead Farm, 1912 Pequawket Trail.

123 *Jenks' Portland Gazette*, December 13, 1802.

you would start. Take the new piece of road over the point of the hill before you come to Break Neck[124] as the Rocks in the old road round the point will probably break your wheels or axletrees. Also come by the way of Major Lewis',[125] the other is not passable.[126]

Even before the town was settled in 1774, the poor roads through Hiram were noted. Rev. Paul Coffin wrote of a journey from his home in Narragansett No. 1 (Buxton) to Piggwacket (Fryeburg) in the fall of 1768:[127]

> We passed great Ossipee[128] at two o'clock, then rode to Great Falls,[129] four miles from great Ossipee, and rested till three and a half of the clock, P. M. Great Falls are a considerable falls, steep and white and long.
>
> Great Falls, three and a half of clock, mount our steeds, having sixteen miles to ride. We rode over a long rocky hill, about two or three miles from Great Falls, called Johny Macks or Mc's hill, because John McMullin did not like it when clearing it. Thence rode till we found ten mile Brook, so called because about ten miles from Piggwacket. From thence to burnt meadow Brook,[130] eight miles from Piggwacket.
>
> Arrived there five and a half of clock. From thence set off about six of clock and rode three miles through rocky and muddy travelling and then through pitch pine Plains five miles, and reached cousin Samuel Osgood's at seven and a half of the clock, at Piggwacket.[131]
>
> We accomplished this ride in thirteen

Early roads may have looked like this one, a rural track up a hill, the center filled with weeds. Maggie Black Album 2, Collection of Hiram Historical Society.

> and a half hours, having begun at six in the morning and finished it at seven and a half in the evening—We were on our horses eleven hours. The road in general was remarkably good for so new a one. We did not walk our horses above three or four miles, the whole journey. A great deal of the road was pitch pine land, like a house floor.

But the Rev. Paul Coffin was not pleased in Hiram.

> From Great Ossipee to great Falls. pretty good riding—oak land and pitch pine. From great Falls to ten mile Brook something rough and bad riding. From ten mile Brook to burnt meadow Brook[132] pretty good riding.

---

124   Break Neck Brook, West Baldwin.

125   Major Abijah Lewis (1756–1830) lived on Hiram Hill. Peleg directed Charles to go northeast before turning south to Portland.

126   Maine Historical Society, Coll. 16/3.

127   Ride to Piggwacket, *Collections of the Maine Historical Society,* 1st Series, Vol. 4, Portland, ME, 1856.

128   Ossipee River.

129   In Hiram.

130   In Brownfield.

131   Now the home of Fryeburg Historical Society, Portland Road, Fryeburg village.

132   Both in Brownfield.

Dirt roads continued to be problematic in Hiram well into the mid-twentieth century. In this photo, ancient methods aid modern technology.

Roads continued to be a source of angst in Hiram. At the June 3, 1815, Town Meeting, Peleg Wadsworth was chosen agent to defend the town against an indictment for bad roads by the Circuit Court of Common Pleas at Paris, Maine. The town also received an indictment of the General Court for bad roads on December 6, 1819. In 1824, John Warren was chosen agent to defend a suit over the Denmark Road. In 1828, Benjamin Barker was chosen to defend the town against a court complaint

This accident on Richardson Road in the 1930s would have been a familiar scene for nearly 250 years in Hiram.

about the "new" county road on the south side of town. He was again called on in 1829 for a complaint about the Gilpatrick Road. In 1831, Artemas Richardson handled another indictment of the Court of Common Pleas in Paris.

Bridges

Another headache of town officials was attending to bridges. Early bridges were open (not covered) and made of wood, which needed frequent repair and rebuilding due to weathering and freshets (spring floods). Committees were elected at special meetings to investigate the best location, design, and materials of bridges and the piers they rested on. Agents were elected to fulfill roles of viewing condition, setting and collecting bridge taxes, and supervising the repair or building. Rates of pay and deadlines for completion were also voted at these meetings, as was approval of individual claims, such as the iron crowbar John Bucknell lost during the repair of the Saco River Bridge in 1812.[133]

Hiram had four major bridges to deal with before 1825: Saco River, Hancock Brook, and two on the

---

133 Maine State Archives, Hiram Box 4.Reimbursement was not approved, Hiram Town Clerk Record, January 16, 1815, 8.

Ossipee River that separated Hiram from Cornish. It was the negotiations with Cornish that caused the most consternation and delay, whether agreeing on the need for repair vs. a new bridge or design, cost, or labor. Major costs were shared equally and each town was responsible for its half of the bridge. Simple repairs could be made on each town's side, however, as occurred in 1814 when Hiram chose Joseph Durgin and Jacob Lord

> to nail that part of Cornish Bridge belonging to Hiram and make any other necessary repairs, and to put up a fence to prevent passengers from falling into the gully made by the Freshet and immediately that their Labours thereon should be accounted for in their future Highway Taxes.[134]

The first bridge over the Saco was built in 1805 by John Ayer, a "joiner" by trade, and Capt. Charles Lee Wadsworth. Though travelers were freed from the nuisance of calling for the ferryman, paying for, and riding the ferry, bridges were not free of problems. In winter, bridges had to be kept "snowed"; that is, enough snow had to be kept on the bridge to allow sleighs to pass. Sometimes snow had to be brought in, and it had to be "rolled" (packed by horses or oxen pulling a snow roller). Road accidents continued on bridges. In 1821, John Watson asked for replacement of twelve fathoms of cordage, bought in Portland for $2.50, that was damaged on the bridge.[135] Bridges were made of wood that was exposed to the weather and had a life span of about twenty years, and fewer if washed out in a flood.

The new bridge over the Saco was repaired in 1812, and by 1814 there was talk of replacing it. It was a lengthy business with many agents elected in various stages. Marshall Spring and Asa Burbank were to distribute subscription papers and obtain donations; John Pierce, Asa Burbank, and Isaac Gray were to view and ascertain the best place to erect the bridge; John Pierce, Asa Burbank, and Marshall Spring were to superintend the erecting of said bridge. Work was to be paid at $1.25 per day up to July 15, before haying, and 75 cents thereafter. It was voted that the town raise $300 on condition that enough money be obtained from other towns and by donations to erect and complete a permanent bridge. The tax list was made in March 1815. The list is in the Appendix.

Sometimes the agent's performance was subpar. Isaac Gray was elected agent to repair the Saco River bridge in April 1821 and dismissed in September. Agents were paid, but not always willing to take the job. Benjamin Barker tried to get out of it in 1827, but the town voted not to excuse him.

The new Saco River bridge was repaired in 1822, 1823, 1824, 1826, and 1827 before the town directed

The west end of the covered bridge over the Saco River, looking north, showing the fountain (center), c. 1890. Ella Butterfield's scrapbook in the collection of Hiram Historical Society.

---

134 Hiram Town Clerk, Record 7, November 1814, 5.

135 Maine State Archives, Hiram Box 4.

The west end of the covered bridge over the Saco River, looking east. Courtesy of Maine DOT.

the selectmen to examine the bridge, and named Benjamin Barker agent to superintend the repair under the direction of Selectman Ephraim Kimball. In 1828, it was decided to build a new bridge. This time the bridge had sharply pointed piers called "swords" or "heaters" to better deflect flowing ice.

The new bridge was accepted at the Town Meeting of October 3, 1829, when it was "Voted to accept the new Bridge as now stands under the covering."[136] The words "under the covering" indicate it was a covered bridge. This was possible, as the first covered bridge in Maine was built in Augusta in 1819, the cover being built over an uncovered bridge constructed by Timothy Palmer, who also built the first covered bridge in America in Philadelphia in 1805. Other covered bridges were also built in Maine in the 1820s.[137]

The two bridges across the Ossipee River and the Hancock Brook were also built and repaired repeatedly. Both bridges over the "great Ossipee river" were referred to in the same way, so there is confusion until 1830 when "upper" and "lower" bridges were distinguished.[138] But always there were controversial votes taken and reconsidered on such issues as which agent

was to be selected, whether the hemlock used was to be peeled or unpeeled, and what the shape and position of the piers was to be.

Burgeoning costs of frequent repairs caused the town to submit a petition to the legislature on January 2, 1826, requesting permission for a toll at the bridge over the Saco River.[139] Reasons cited were increased travel to Portland from Vermont and New Hampshire and other points that caused more repairs. Also new county roads imposed costs to the town. Furthermore, the town claimed that its expense, exclusive of the Saco River bridge, was greater than any of the towns in the vicinity, in proportion to the number of inhabitants and the amount of their valuations. Having to maintain two county roads running the entire length of the town, a county road across the northern corner, and a recent great addition by order of the Supreme Judicial Courts was another

The east end of the covered bridge over the Saco River, early twentieth century. Goodwin's Store is in the center. Courtesy of Maine DOT.

---

136 Hiram Town Clerk Record 3 Oct. 1829, page 286.

137 Maine Department of Economic Development, *Unique Me. The Great State of Maine Covered Bridges, 1-3-1970,* https://digitalmaine.com/cgi/viewcontent.cgi?article=1055&context=decd_docs.

138 The upper bridge is now called the Warren Bridge after John Warren, who was the agent in 1828. The lower bridge is now called the Cornish Bridge.

139 Maine State Archives, Hiram Box 14.

Cornish Bridge, the lower bridge over the Ossipee, before 1929 when it was replaced. Viewed from Cornish to Hiram. Courtesy of Maine DOT.

burden. Finally, the town argued that income from tolls would allow it to build a permanent bridge. The petition was signed by Selectmen Benjamin Bucknell, Alpheus Spring, and Ephraim Kimball. This petition suffered the same fate as the petition of 1801 for a private corporation toll road—it did not pass.

Today the town has little influence in the design and repair of the four state bridges over the Saco River and Ossipee River, and the culvert over Hancock Brook.

Canals

After the Revolution, the United States owned land from the East Coast to the Mississippi River. The country turned its attention to connecting to the

Warren Bridge, the upper bridge over the Ossipee River, before replacement in 1929. Viewed from Cornish to Hiram. Courtesy of Maine DOT.

Warren Bridge after replacement was flat and open as it was in the early nineteenth century. Note the unpaved roads. View from Cornish to Hiram. Courtesy of Maine DOT.

inland through turnpikes and canals, since coastal routes by river and sea were well developed. The success of the Erie Canal in 1816 prompted a surge of canal building in Maine.

Petitions to open canals in Buxton, Hiram, Brownfield, Fryeburg, and Denmark preceded the rush. They were: Moose Brook Canal, Brownfield (now Denmark), 1807; Hancock Brook Canal, Hiram and Denmark, 1811; Ten Mile Brook Canal, Hiram and Brownfield, 1813; Fryeburg Canal, 1815. Fryeburg Canal, begun in 1812, was unique in being built to control flooding rather than to float logs down to the Saco River. The promise of riches lured the Spring family to invest in Moose Brook Canal, Hancock Brook Canal, Ten Mile Brook Canal, and Buxton Proprietors of Canals, Locks, and Slips.

Hancock Brook Canal

The Proprietors of Hancock Brook Canal were incorporated by the Massachusetts Legislature in February 1811 for the purpose of floating wood products down the brook from Barker Pond to the Saco River. The original investors were Philip Eastman, James Osgood, Robert Bradley, Robert Page, James W. Ripley, William Evans, John Evans, Abiel Farnum, Thomas Spring, Seth Spring, Joseph Howard, John McMillen, and John Spring.

The proprietors were to complete the canal in five years, but on February 23, 1818, were granted a further three years, and, on January 24, 1820, another five, which included expansion to the town of Denmark. When the canal opened, the tolls were to be: for each mill log, eight cents; for each thousand clapboards and shingles, at the rate of five cents for one thousand; for each thousand feet of boards, plank, and slit work, at the rate of six cents for each thousand feet; for masts, spars, ranging, and other timber, at the rate of six cents for each ton.

The tolls were expensive, considering a toll was paid for each dam, and the brook was "canalled by building twenty-two dams and slips from Hiram Bridge to Barker Pond,"[140] but there was no other feasible way to bring products to market. The proprietors had difficulties collecting fees and ensuring a smooth flow of logs due to incompetent or inattentive mill owners. The configuration of rates for logs was changed from eight cents per log to thirty-two cents per thousand board feet, to be surveyed at four logs per one thousand feet to mitigate the damage caused by large logs. In 1822 proprietors[141] won the power to compel delinquent owners to "do their duty" or "to pay their just proportion of expenses incurred by others."[142]

In 1825, the proprietors enlisted the aid of the sheriff in collecting from Simeon Chadbourne and Henry Flye $335.20 for debt or damage and $15.08 for costs of the lawsuit. Appraisers of the property to be seized were Thomas B. Watson, Ephraim Kimball, and John Bucknell. If the debt was not paid in full, Chadbourne and Flye were to be jailed.[143]

The canal was in operation in 1838, but was not mentioned in Well's 1867 survey of water power. It noted that "Over hundred millions of pine lumber have been driven out of this canal into the Saco river."[144] Nine of twenty-five "powers," existing or potential, noted in that survey were on Hancock Brook. In order from Hiram bridge, they were "Allen's mill; Clark & Co.; a dam formerly a shingle machine; Rankin's sawmill; two wooden dams used for log-driving; Barker Dam; a stone dam 50 feet long at the foot of the Great Hancock Pond."[145]

Ten Mile Brook Canal

The governor approved the Ten Mile Brook Canal on February 27, 1813, under the name Ten Mile Brook Canal Corporation. The named proprietors were William Lane, Isaac Bradbury, Thomas Howard, and Joseph Howard Jr. The canal was to run from Clemons Pond in Hiram to the Saco River in Brownfield. It was given the right to charge tolls when it

---

140 Walter Wells, *The Water-Power of Maine* (Augusta, ME: Sprague, Owen & Nash, 1868), 158.

141 James Steele, Elias Berry, John Perley, Samuel Osgood, Cyrus Ingalls, Charles L. Wadsworth.

142 An Act to Regulate the toll and passage of logs, Private and Special Laws, 1822, chap. 147.

143 Oxford County Registry of Deeds, July 20, 1825, Book 10, 550–552.

144 Walter Wells, *The Water-Power of Maine* (Augusta, Maine: Sprague, Owen & Nash, 1869), 308.

145 Wells, 158.

opened. The rates were to be: "for each board log, mast or spar, passing a slip or lock, one cent each; for each thousand of boards, planks and slit work, three cents; for each thousand of clap-boards and shingles, one cent each; and in all cases one cent shall be paid for the use of the canal, for each of the said articles."

The Canal Corporation missed the deadline of five years to build and did not petition for an extension of time.

Not until 1824 did Frederick Howard and Jackson Wood petition to incorporate for the purpose of transporting logs, masts, and other timber products. On February 16, 1824, the Committee on Turnpikes, Bridges, and Canals, to whom the petition was referred, commanded the petitioners to publish their petition three times successively in the *Eastern Argus*, a newspaper printed in Portland, the last publication to be thirty days, at least, before the first Wednesday of the first session of the next legislature, "that all persons interested, may then appear and shew cause, (if any they have) why the Prayer of said Petition should not be granted."[146]

Trouble ensued. James Osgood, a landowner along Ten Mile Brook, remonstrated on January 31, 1824. He claimed the petitioners incurred trifling expense in erecting two wooden dams across the brook, and, by this act, the private individuals had betrayed the public trust and trespassed upon his rights as owner, having expressly forbid it. He accused the petitioner of being impoverished and owners of large tracts of land of hiding under the names of Frederick Howard and Jackson Wood. Furthermore, the trivial expense expended did not warrant tolls, the petitioners did not own pine timber on the brook, and the late appearance of the newspaper notice did not give interested persons, who lived fifty miles away, sufficient notice. He stated bluntly, "Your remonstrant would further urge that the whole transaction has upon the face of it, the appearance of finesse and trick—that the notice, the shortness of which is unparalleled in all the legislative proceedings of which your remonstrant is acquainted, was delayed on publication till the 27th

January & the petition to be acted upon the 1st of February, & this notice to reach individuals interested, who live <u>fifty</u> Miles distant, is a fact, which will not escape the observation of your honorable body." He asked the legislature to give the petitioners leave to withdraw or postpone action until the next session so that all parties may have timely notice to prepare to represent the facts in a proper light and manner.[147]

It didn't take long for Simeon Pease, Mark Pease, and John Pease to air their opinions. Their letter was read and referred to the Committee on Turnpikes, Bridges, and Canals on February 6, 1824. The Peases stated that the petitioners owned little or no real estate on the brook and that a canal would enable them to enrich themselves at the expense of others, "the brook being at present one of the best the country affords for the transportation of logs to Saco River." Furthermore, granting a monopoly would greatly injure owners of large tracts of timber land on the brook.[148]

Despite remonstrations, the legislature passed the Act of 22 February 1826, incorporating the Ten Mile Brook Canal.[149] Not coincidentally, the proprietors were Simeon Pease, Theophilus Smith, and John Pike II.

This time, rates took into consideration distance. For timber sufficient to make one thousand board feet passing the full extent of the stream, twenty-five cents; passing as far as Lane's dam, eight cents; to Wadsworth's mill dam, four cents; at the lower dam, eight cents. It was further enacted "that no individuals be deprived or injured in the exercise of any rights or privileges, they might or could have enjoyed, in regard to the stream aforesaid, previous to the passing of this Act."

In the run-up to the petition of 1826, large tracts of land passed back and forth among James Osgood, Seth Spring, Joseph Howard, and Simeon Pease, and smaller parcels went to Theophilus Smith and John Pike. It is not known how long the canal was in operation, nor if the corporation was profitable. Most likely, John Pike and Simeon Pease felt

---

146   Maine State Archives, Hiram Box 14.

147   Ibid.

148   Ibid.

149   Private Acts of the State of Maine passed by the Sixth Legislature at its Session, held in January 1826, chap. 407.

pinched in 1841. The sheriff, having had no one show up to pay taxes of $2.33, sold two hundred acres of John Pike's on the Ten Mile at auction to Simeon Pease for $4.58 on September 2, 1841. Likewise, on the same day, eighty acres of Simeon Pease's land on the Ten Mile, including the house, were struck off to Samuel P. Small for $4.63. But 1841 wasn't the end. Wells reported in the survey of 1868 "at outlet of Ten Mile pond 100,000 boards and staves yearly, valuable power, only partially improved."[150]

---

150 Walter Wells, *Provisional Report upon the Water-Power of Maine* (Augusta, ME: Stevens & Sayward), 66.

SCHOOLS

Peleg Wadsworth's mission

Prior to building a schoolhouse, residents taught classes in their homes. The house of Gen. Peleg Wadsworth, not yet occupied,[151] is the first-known location in Hiram in which classes were held. In 1805, after the town voted not to raise money for schools, the general sent his son Peleg Wadsworth Jr. from Portland to Hiram to teach school there. Peleg Jr. boarded with his older brother Charles Lee Wadsworth. Peleg Jr. was fourteen, the youngest teacher on record. Young teachers were common because eighth-grade equivalence qualified one for teaching. School terms were short and frequently lasted only a few weeks, especially in winter. Often farmers, innkeepers, and the like taught a few weeks or months in their off seasons.

By 1806, Hiram had a schoolhouse, as noted in the warrant to James Eastman, collector of taxes, on November 29, 1806, requesting him to assemble eligible voters in "the" schoolhouse, singular, for a meeting.

After 1810, Hiram's population grew quickly, as did the number of students. The number of scholars (as students were called) more than doubled between 1810 and 1812, increasing the number of school districts from two to six, and thus the schoolhouses. Some areas, such as "Stanley's" District 6 in South Hiram, started with as few as six scholars. Meanwhile, District 5 grew from thirty-three to sixty in one year and was split into three districts in 1814.

Geography class at Mt. Cutler School c. 1916.

---

151 The family moved to Hiram in 1807.

Watson District School, c. 1890, King Street. Miss Lillian Wilson, teacher (back row, right). It no longer exists.

In 1812, Hiram allocated $100 for 175 scholars in six districts. There must have been several schoolhouses because the warrant for the annual Town Meeting of 1814 called men to meet "at the Schoolhouse near Simeon Bucknell,"[152] indicating there were several school buildings. Simeon Bucknell's house was in District 1 in the area around the west bank of the Saco River known as "the Bridge."

The year 1816 was an important one for schools in Hiram. An indictment for deficiency of schools likely prompted improvements. At the January 4 Town Meeting, voters considered hiring a public schoolmaster for the winter term. A committee of three was initiated to superintend the business of the schools, to recommend location of buildings, and to allocate students to districts. Peleg Wadsworth, Alpheus Spring, and John Pierce were elected to the new committee.

The town then doubled the school budget from $100 to $200. In an unusual vote, voters agreed to appropriate money received from Haverhill, Massachusetts, for support of pauper William West, to the school budget, and to hire a teacher for six months. Peleg Wadsworth, a champion of education, was elected agent to defend the town against the charge of deficiency of schools.

The student population more than tripled, from seventy-nine to 292, between 1810 and 1820, and the annual school budget also tripled to $300. The number of districts increased to nine. Growth continued, with the town, by 1824, adding two more districts filled with 356 scholars.

By 1829, the districts increased to thirteen. Further growth added one more district in 1836 and triggered redefinition of districts. In 1838, fifteen districts were identified, but only thirteen school agents named, implying two were null. The highest number of districts in Hiram was eighteen,[153] though not all were active at the time.

---

152 Simeon Bucknell lived on Pequawket Trail on the west side of the Saco River near Thomas Spring's tavern, today Old Homestead Farm.

153 The 1823 school ledger showed eighteen districts plus the name of Nicholas Peterson, owner of 104 Ten Mile Brook Road.

School Agents

Each school district had a school agent elected at annual Town Meetings. Agents carried out the business of schools. Duties included hiring teachers, assisting selectmen in allocating students to districts (voted at Town Meetings), convincing parents to send their children to school, occasionally disciplining students if a teacher could not "govern" them, seeing that firewood was supplied, helping to raise money for repairs or a new school, and collecting school taxes. Agents were paid, and could also teach, as did William Cotton, John Warren, and Charles L. Wadsworth.

The budget was voted at the Annual Town Meeting. Taxes were levied on families whose children attended school and were proportionate to the number of scholars in each district.

School attendance was encouraged, but not mandatory. It is unknown what proportion of Hiram children attended school. Early school records are spotty and not included in the Hiram town clerk's records. Only one list of attendees exists, that of 1811–1812 for the combined Districts 5 and 6 in the neighborhood of Durgintown.[154]

In 1828, Gen. Peleg Wadsworth offered an alternative to tax-funded schools. At age eighty, a year before he died, the general rode through town on horseback to tell of a free school he was offering for "good little boys" and, we trust, for good little girls.

Power of Town Voters

Townsmen controlled school districts and exercised it at Town Meetings. Male voters decided which students attended school in which districts, when to add a new district, whether to repair or rebuild a schoolhouse, and which agents would serve in school districts. An article at the March 1819 Town Meeting was to give the ability of children of any one district to attend school in the others. It was voted down. At the Town Meeting of April 3, 1826, districts tried to take more power by asking for approval to choose their own school agents. The town voted against it. Indeed, the town continued to be involved in the minutiae of school business well beyond 1830, the period studied, voting details at every Town Meeting.

For example the Town Meeting of April 1, 1826, was adjourned and extended to April 15, 1826.

> The town met agreeable to adjournment and proceeded to business as follows viz
> 1st Chose Ephraim Kimball Moderator
> 2nd voted that John Wadsworth, Obediah Gerrish, Daniel Allen, Nicholas Peterson, William Huntress, Nathaniel Parker & Dean (Deacn?) Irish compose a School District by themselves
> 3rd voted to annex the tenth School District to District No. 2
> 4th voted to Set Solomon Hartford off from School District No. 5 and annex him to District no. 6
> 5th voted to annex Aaron Rand and Henry W. Barnes to School District no. 3[155]

Under this system, votes were frequently rescinded and reconsidered, and it sometimes took years for issues to be presented and addressed. In an extreme case, the need to make up deficiencies in the school budgets of 1809 and 1810, was voted at the April 1, 1822, Town Meeting. Making up deficiencies of 1809 was voted down, but the town decided to make good the deficiency of 1810 by paying it out of money raised for 1815.[156] The amounts of the deficiencies are unknown.

Schoolmasters (Teachers)

John Burbank may have been the earliest teacher in 1778—his father taught in Kennebunk before moving to Hiram. Not until 1804 is there a record that named a teacher. John Goodenow was paid $42 for teaching twelve weeks (a much higher rate than given in 1821). Other known teachers before 1830 were Miss Mary A. Merrill (District 1 at "the Bridge") and Miss Mary

---

154   Maine State Archives, Hiram Box 8.

155   Hiram Town Clerk Record, 15 April 1826, 221.

156   Hiram Town Clerk Record, April 1, 1822, 141.

Benton of West Baldwin (District 5 in Durgintown) in 1821, Alpheus Spring (District 1 for three months) in 1822, and Asa Osgood Jr. (District 2 on the east side of the Saco River).

Most teachers were men prior to the 1820s in what were called the common schools (public schools). Male teachers often used their positions as stepping stones to higher occupations. For example, Peleg Wadsworth taught school after graduating from Harvard College, and afterward opened a store, a common pursuit among the upper class in New England.

Women could teach, privately, out of their homes. Academic subjects such as geography, history, arithmetic, Latin, reading (articulation) and English grammar, recitation, orthography (spelling), penmanship, and science were common subjects.

In the larger cities, women also taught in dame schools, so called because they emphasized preparing girls for entry into society. These schools instructed girls of the wealthier classes and taught manners, comportment, playing musical instruments, and fancy sewing skills. It may have been a reason for the Barkers to move from Hiram to Portland. Twins Flavilla Ann and Mary Jane Barker attended Miss Fellow's school in Portland and probably learned to stitch their samplers there in 1818, at age nine. Very young boys also attended dame schools, as did Henry Wadsworth Longfellow at age three to four.

Writing and reading were taught separately. This is an important distinction, as people who could read but not write should not automatically be considered illiterate. This may have been the case with Elizabeth Ayer, wife of the preacher John Ayer. When John sold their property, she signed the deed renouncing her dower with an "X" and the notation "Her Mark." Also signing petitions, deeds, and letters with an "X" were Rebecca Baston, Moody Brown, Royal Brown, James Flye, Samuel Jelerson, George Whales, and others.

Teacher Pay

In the 1820s, due to the scarcity of male teachers and the realization that women could be paid one-third as much, teaching in public schools became one of the few acceptable occupations open to young women. Records for 1821 and 1822 show there were more female than male teachers in Hiram.

Pay varied by district in Hiram. It is unknown if or how experience was valued. Duration of school terms also varied, and could be as little as three weeks. Often, there was no winter term. Teacher rates of pay appear in Appendix 18.

Teacher Rules

In the mid-to-late nineteenth century, an influential education reformer, Horace Mann, urged higher and more uniform standards.

Teachers did more than teach school. They were expected to be models of behavior in the community, read the Bible (scriptures) in class, attend church services, and be of good moral character. Some rules for teachers of the nineteenth and early twentieth century have been published and widely quoted, but have not been verified as associated with particular towns or schools and may not be accurate. These rules, among others, purported that female teachers must not be married, must carry a bucket of water and a scuttle of coal to school each morning, must board in the town in which they teach, and must not dance or play games of chance. Male teachers may be allowed one night a week to court a lady, or two nights if they attend church.

What is true of school rules was that teachers were responsible for janitorial services of the schoolhouse[157]—cleaning floors and lamps and keeping the wood stove going when needed, but teacher contracts that are documented were less specific in terms of duties. They called for good governance in the classroom and care in preservation of school property.

Schoolhouses

Schoolhouses of the early period were one room. The architecture and furnishings were simple and primitive, dictated by the circumstances of individual towns. Prior to Henry Barnard's treatise

---

157 Contract from Story County, Iowa, 1874, Ames Historical Society, Ames, Iowa.

Tear Cap School, 48 Tear Cap Road, 2014.

Durgintown School, 339 Durgintown Road, c. 1891. Teacher Chester Chapman (right), Supervisor Dr. Charles Wilson (far right).

This school, formerly on Sebago Road at Four Corners, East Hiram, was moved in 1895 to 80 Main Street to become Rufus Small's store, seen here with bunting during Hiram's Centennial celebrations in 1914.

Durgintown School, 2014. The cupola was added during WWII to spot enemy planes.

The former school, formerly Rufus Small's store, is today a private residence, 2014.

Tripptown School, Oak Hill, Tripptown Road, date unknown.

South Hiram School, a two-room schoolhouse built in 1916.

South Hiram School, currently the Hiram Town Office, 16 Nasons Way (formerly 25 Allard Circle), 2010.

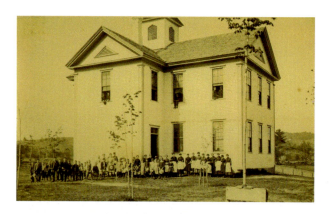

Mt. Cutler School, the only three-room school, 20 Historical Ridge, Hiram, built in 1883, now Great Ossipee Museum, home of Hiram Historical Society. Tallest girl in front is Jennie Bosworth. Walter Young has both feet out the window, c. 1885.

Great Ossipee Museum (former Mt. Cutler School), 2016.

in 1838,[158] school architecture received little thought. Barnard believed these generally poorly designed buildings hindered rather than promoted learning. His book, *School Architecture,* laid out detailed plans for school construction, covering everything from siting buildings, size, grounds, lighting, heating and ventilation, desks, and seating, to teaching apparatus such as maps, charts and globes, play areas, and, of course, blackboards, textbooks, clocks, and the teacher's bell. Barnard included arrangements designed "to promote habits of order, and neatness" such as cloak hooks, scrapers and mats for the feet, and sinks and

Ridlon School, 117 Brownfield Road, South Hiram, 2012. It was established as "Stanley's," School District 6, and may have built as early as 1819.

---

158   Henry Barnard, 1811–1900, was the first U.S. Commissioner of Education. He began writing on the improvement of schoolhouses in 1838. His reports were published in journals, and his book *School Architecture* went through many editions.

Map showing schools (locations indicated by gray ovals) in Hiram in 1858.

towels for hand washing. Last but not least, schools should provide separate "places of retirement" for children of either sex for the "offices of nature."[159]

The exact build dates of Hiram's schoolhouses are unknown. Most likely, the remaining one-room schoolhouses were built later in the nineteenth

159 This meant separate outdoor toilets. Sally Zimmerman, *Historic New England*, Winter 2015, 7.

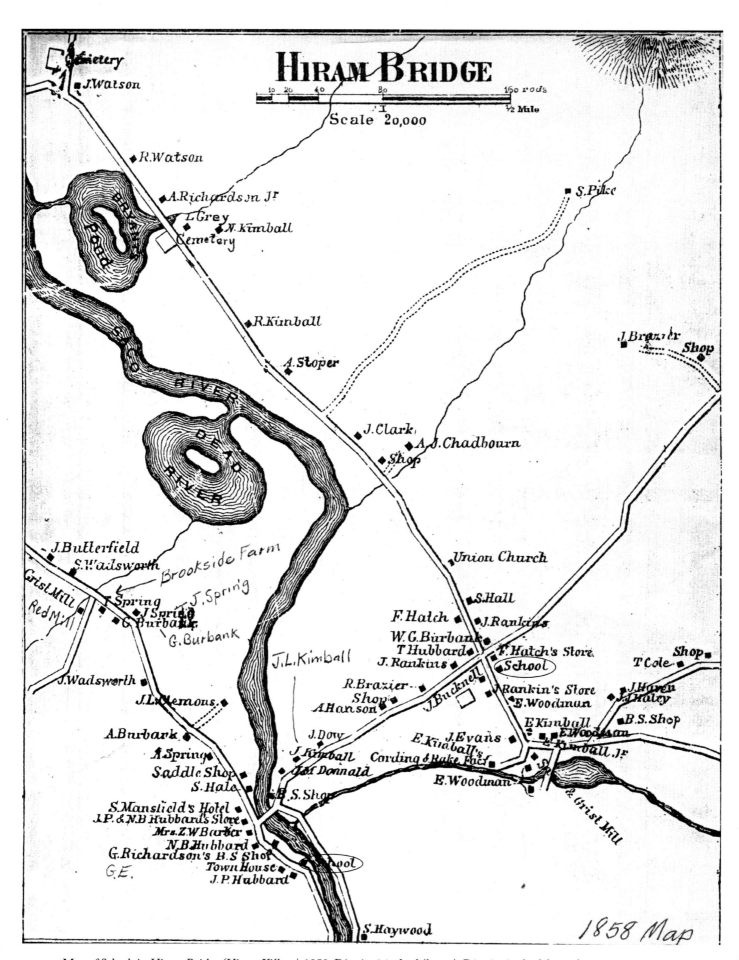

HIRAM BRIDGE

Scale 20,000

1858 Map

Map of Schools in Hiram Bridge (Hiram Village) 1858. District 14 school (lower), District 2 school (upper).

century. Four currently survive: Tear Cap, Ridlon, Durgintown, and the District 2 building that was adjacent to Four Corners Store and moved in 1895 to 80 Main Street, opposite Hiram Village Cemetery. All are privately owned. The Ridlon School may have been built by William Stanley as early as 1819, and would be the earliest remaining schoolhouse.

These schoolhouses are small and simple with one door for both sexes. Mt. Cutler School is the exception. The present building, built in 1883 to replace a similar one that burned a year earlier, is a three-room schoolhouse with many improvements, such as separate doors for each sex, large windows and high ceilings, running water, and separate indoor toilets in the basement. The South Hiram School, a two-room schoolhouse, which had one door for both sexes, was built in 1916.

Other schools, which no longer exist, for which there are images, were Tripptown, Watson, and Hiram Hill.

Two Extraordinary Teachers

Hiram's history includes three extraordinary teachers from later years: Priscilla Adams (1850–1924), Madison K. Mabry (1824–1915), and Jesse Rowe (1876–1969). Included are excerpts for Miss Adams and Mr. Mabry because they were the grandchildren of early settlers.

Priscilla Adams, granddaughter of Joseph Adams, taught at several schools, one of which was Hiram Hill School, located near the junction of Hiram Hill Road and Richardson Road.

From the *Oxford County Record*, Kezar Falls, Maine, January 2, 1886: "Miss Priscilla Adams is teaching in the Tearcap district. In the matter of firm and quiet discipline, clear and plain explanation of every point and particular, systematic and methodical arrangement, and untiring devotion to duty, we have never seen her excelled in a schoolroom (Submitted by Llewellyn A. Wadsworth, Hiram)."

From the *Oxford County Record*, Kezar Falls, Maine, March 5, 1887: "On Friday, Feb. 25, after the storm and blizzard that has become historic from Maine to Chicago, Miss Priscilla Adams walked from her school on Hiram Hill to the house of her father, N.W. Adams, in South Hiram, some six miles. On Monday she came back on foot and on time, through drifts eight feet deep, that had been impassable for oxen for three days. The present is her forty-third term. Tell us no more of Bonaparte crossing the Alps. If anybody wants somebody to take children anywhere, and make them ladies, gentlemen, and scholars, let them send for the greyeyed school-ma'm. We cross examine our memory of forty years in vain to recollect her superior. (Submitted by Llewellyn A. Wadsworth)."

Madison K. Mabry was a grandson of early settler Josiah Mayberry (also spelled Maybury). Llewellyn A. Wadsworth, town historian, wrote of him, "Our memory spans a period of seventy years and we endorse the opinion of persons still older that no other person has ever done as much in Hiram as he did for the cause of education, especially for the Common Schools."[160]

Hiram Hill School, located near the junction of Hiram Hill Road and Richardson Road, c. 1891. Back Row: John Sargent (holding book), Winfield Hutchins, Fulton Babb, Millard Ridlon, Bertha Hutchins, Cora Witham. Center row: Frank Witham, Maurice Robbins, Charles Clemons, Alice Clemons, Annie Goodwin, Edna Sargent, Francena Sargent, Ruth Sargent, Priscilla Adams (teacher). Front row: Florence Ridlon, Florence Sargent, Albert Babb, Clifford Clemons, Walter Hutchins, Harry Sargent, "Dee" Witham, Lee Hutchins, Harry Goodwin, Walter Sargent.

---

160   Llewellyn A. Wadsworth, *Centennial, Hiram, Maine, 1814-1914* (Cornish, ME: Webb Smith Printing Co., 1914)

Madison K. Mabry's eighty-fifth birthday tribute, published in an unknown, undated newspaper, c. 1909

North Turner, Me., Oct. 19—Madison K. Mabry, who celebrated his 85th birthday, the 17th, at his home at North Turner bridge, was born on a farm in Hiram, Oct. 17, 1824, of parents noteworthy for their moral, intellectual and physical excellence.

He was educated in the schools of Hiram and Westbrook Seminary and began teaching when 17 years of age, teaching for 40 years in Oxford, York and Cumberland counties; also for five years as principal in Limerick and Parsonsfield Academies. He was Justice of Peace in Hiram for seven years and served often as supervisor of schools. For three years he was supervisor of York county. In fact Mr. Mabry led the vanguard for

This portrait of Lt. Madison K. Mabry with commemorative sword hangs in Soldiers Memorial Library in Hiram. It was painted by Arthur Spear.

temperance, freedom, morality and education in Hiram for 30 years.

He enlisted 17 June 1862, was active in enlisting others, was commissioned as lieutenant in the 17th Maine but was discharged for disability the same year. He was an organizer in I.O. G. T.,[161] for some years. His life has been a very active one and any real reform is sure of his sympathy and support.

In 1876, Mr. Mabry experienced religion and joined the Methodist church. Receiving a local preacher's license, he served in Mercer, Fairfield, Livermore, Turner, Rumford, Andover and North Yarmouth, with good results, for 11 years. His home has been at North Turner Bridge with no regular pastorate.

He married first Dorcas True, by whom he had seven children, who are settled in Maine, Massachusetts and Wisconsin. In 1886 he married Ella T. Safford of Turner.

At 85 years of age he is still physically strong, mentally unimpaired, hopeful and cheerful, taking a lively interest in everything and is well informed on many lines relating to the welfare of the country and humanity.

Excerpt from the Diary of Florence Small

Oct. 27, 1903—The 17th of this month Madison Mabry was 78 and he had a reunion of all the pupils that went to school to him here in Hiram. I went and was glad that I did go. I helped set the tables and wait on the folks and washed the dishes—nearly a hundred at dinner. The tables were fine. I carried a pumpkin pie and three baskets of grapes. After dinner Madison made a speech. Next Llewellyn Wadsworth read a poem that he composed. Next Samuel Gould[162] had a

---

161   International Organization of Good Templars, a fraternal order for temperance or abstinence of alcohol and drugs.

162   Samuel Wadsworth Gould (1852–1935), son of Elias and Ruth Clemons Gould, former Hiram student, was an unsuccessful candidate for Maine Governor in 1902, was elected representative from Maine 1911–13, and practiced law in Skowhegan.

few words to say. He was a disappointment. Then Leland Kimball "thought it was too bad to spoil a good teacher to make a poor minister." Sophia Stuart spoke well, followed by Willis Mabry, Irving Mabry, Bertha Mabry Abbott, and Cora Mabry. Then Mrs. Madison Mabry and Fannie Young Clifford read four letters.

The old "flyer" below was reproduced from the original donated to the H. H. S. by Abbott Spear of Warren, ME. Mr. Spear is a descendant of Madison K. Mabury.

HIGH SCHOOL.

A High School will be opened, in

HIRAM,

TUESDAY, AUG. 27, 1872,

AND CONTINUE TEN WEEKS.

M. K. Mabury, Principal.
Miss Abbie Mabury, Assistant.

TUITION.

Primary,	$2.50.	Languages,	$5.50.
Common English,	3.50.	Music,	10.00.
Higher English,	4.50.	Penmanship,	Free.

Instruction in Penciling, Wax Flowers, &c., will be furnished if desired.

The large experience of the Teachers, warrant success.

Board will be furnished in good families, at reasonable rates. Room for those who wish to board themselves are plenty.

Further information given on application to Principal.

HIRAM, July 10th, 1872.

Poster advertising M.K. Mabry's high school.
Miss Abbie Mabry was his daughter.

CHURCHES AND TITHINGMEN
hand in hand

Before the first church was built in Hiram, services were conducted in people's homes by itinerant preachers or, in the case of John Ayer, who conducted the town's first religious services, in his own house. After the first schoolhouse was built, prior to 1806, services were conducted there. The first organized religious group was the Methodist Society, formed in 1810, the first year funds for the ministry were requested at Town Meeting. The vote was not recorded. The Baptist Society was founded in Hiram a year later by act of the Massachusetts Legislature. There were seventeen sponsors: Loammi Baston, Royal Baston, Winthrop Baston, Aaron Cross, John Fitz, James Fitz Jr., James Gilmore, Samuel Hooper [probably Samuel Sloper], Ephraim Kimball, Edward Lewis, Josiah Maybury (Mabry), Asa Osgood, Aaron Richardson, Edward Richardson, John Watson, John Watson Jr., and Thomas B. Watson, with their families and estates.

Though the Bastons were sponsors of the Baptist Society, membership was not assured, as Jane Baston discovered when she was excluded in 1824, while her sisters were admitted. She confessed her faults to the church in 1826 and was received into fellowship.

The first church building in Hiram was built for the Baptist Society c. 1834 and it shared its meeting house with the Methodists. Susan Spring funded the building of the Universalist Church in 1871. The Congregational Church formed in 1826, with charter members Peleg and Elizabeth Wadsworth, and

dedicated a building in 1872. The Methodists realized their own church building in 1885.

The First Universalist Society was organized May 9, 1834, at a meeting held at the Town House. Officers elected were Alpheus Spring, moderator; Dr. Levi A. Hannaford, clerk; Benjamin Barker, treasurer and collector. The Standing Committee was composed of Daniel Small, Sewell Fly, Benjamin Barker, Joseph Butterfield, and Simeon Bucknell. Appended to the constitution of that date were names of charter members of the Society: John Goodenow, Rebecca Goodenow, Thomas Spring, Sally Spring, Mehitable Kimball, Caroline W. Hannaford, Martha Hamblen, Hannah Bucknell, Elisa W. Spring, Elizabeth E. Fly, Sarah H. Kimball, Mary G. Collins, L. A. Hannaford, Simeon Bucknell Jr., Benjamin Barker, Daniel Small, Isaac Hamblen, Thomas Mabry, Joseph Butterfield, Sewell Fly, Alpheus Spring Jr., John Kimball, Marshall Spring, I. W. Haven, Andrew R. Bucknell, John Bucknell, William Warren, and John Eldridge.

Until the meeting house was given by Susan Spring in 1871, special and annual meetings of the Universalist Society were held at the Town House and various other locations, including the selectmen's office above Barker & Hamblin's store, the counting room of Barker & Butterfield, the space over Spring's store, the village schoolhouse, the inn of John P. Hubbard, Hanson's Hall, and the home of Elisha Woodman.

Free Will Baptist Meeting House, King Street, built c. 1834. The meeting house was razed in the 1920s.

Looking north up King Street from Four Corners, Free Will Baptist Meeting House in center, before 1895.

Universalist Church, Pequawket Trail in Hiram village, was built in 1871 in Gothic Revival style, with funds from Susan Spring and on land of Marshall Spring.

Hiram Universalist Church and the Marshall Spring house, 1597 Pequawket Trail, 2013.

The "new" Methodist Church, 8 Hancock Avenue, was built in 1885. It became the Congregational Church and later the Hiram Community Church. It was deeded to the Friends of Soldiers Memorial Library in 2015 and converted into an arts center.

Hiram Community Church before conversion into the Arts Center at 8 Hancock Avenue, 2014. The Arts Center and Soldiers Memorial Library combined to form the Hiram Cultural Center in 2020.

Hiram Community Center, run by the Hiram Community Club, 14 Historical Ridge, 2016.

The Congregational Church was built in 1872. In 1955 it was taken over by the VFW, and it reverted to the Hiram Community Club in 2014. The steeple was razed in the 1960s.

The Union Church in South Hiram, built in the early 1800s at Stanley Pond, was the scene of many baptisms. It was called the Union Church because it was free to every denomination who preached the gospel. One winter Sunday, when there was about two inches of snow on the ground, a large company gathered there, cut a channel in the ice, and immersed three candidates for baptism. They sang "On Jordan's Stormy Banks," appropriate for the occasion.

The church had the distinction of being the only church in Maine in which a meeting was appointed and date set for the same before the sills were laid. At a Baptist quarterly meeting in Easton, New Hampshire, the question arose, where should the next meeting be held? One brother extended an invitation to come to South Hiram for the yearly meeting, to be held about six weeks later. Someone asked about the accommodation, there being no church building at that place. The brother replied, "If you will make the appointment, we will furnish the building." The date was set for mid-October.

The brother went home and the people then began in earnest to get ready for the yearly meeting. They gave lumber, time, and the use of teams, and when the middle of October arrived, they had a church, framed, shingled, clapboarded, and plastered; temporary seats and a pulpit were put in and people

Union Church at Stanley Pond, South Hiram, 1907.

from miles around came to the first meeting, filling it to overflowing.[163]

The church became deserted, except for the occasional funeral, and is longer standing.

Though the town had power to police moral behavior through elected tithingmen, the church had its own authority over moral values. The Free Will Baptist Church denied membership to supplicants deemed to have violated its code, as it did, temporarily, to Jane Baston, who recanted and was admitted into the fold. In 1874, the Universalist Church officials banned member Madison K. Mabry because of hearsay. Madison pressed three charges against the pastor of the Society, Rev. I. J. Mead, on April 19, 1874, as follows:

First. A hasty accusation of falsehood under circumstances that rendered me unable to vindicate myself.

Second. Accusing me of unfatherly and unchristian conduct toward my son, tending to estrange him.

Third. Manifesting a determination to shield a bad woman and encouraging her in wicked practices.[164]

The pastor was exonerated, and Dorcas M. Mabry, Hannah E. Mabry, Thomas Mabry, and John P. Hubbard voluntarily removed their names from the Society.

Tithingmen

Tithingmen (also spelled tythingmen) in Colonial America throughout the nineteenth century were not the collectors of ten percent of income to benefit the church, as they were in early England; rather, they were responsible for maintaining order in church and in the community on the Sabbath. They were the moral police. Tithingmen were sober and sedate men of dignity and stature suitable to the importance of the position, and were held in high regard. Selectmen

---

163 Information taken from an old undated newspaper clipping.

164 Hubert W. Clemons, Clerk, First Universalist Society, Hiram, Maine, *Madison K. Mabry and the First Universalist Society of Hiram, Maine,* typescript summary of events in 1874, July 30, 1989.

were warned to use due care in their selection and to choose them annually. Tithingmen were voted into office at annual Town Meetings.

The regulations respecting behavior on the Lord's day appear excessively restrictive today, and included financial penalties for disobeying. Rude or indecent behavior in a house of public worship carried a fine of not more than forty shillings or less than twenty shillings. Due observance called for no traveler, drover, waggoner, teamster, or any of their servants to travel (except from necessity or charity) on penalty not more than $6.66 or less than $4. The same sum applied to being caught keeping a shop open or doing any business or work (works of necessity and charity excepted). These regulations were in effect "from midnight preceding to sunsetting."[165]

Extending past sunset, from midnight preceding to midnight following, no person could execute any civil process.

Even more restrictive were the regulations on entertainment, which was prohibited from Saturday night to Monday night. This meant no attending any concert of music, dancing, or any public diversion, show, or entertainment, including sport, game, play, or recreation on the evening preceding or succeeding the Lord's day. An innkeeper serving alcohol (except to travelers, strangers, or lodgers in such public houses) was fined $3.33 for each person and, after the first conviction, a fine of $6.66 for each offense. After three times convicted, his license was revoked and every person drinking or spending their time, either idly or at play, was fined between $2 and $4 for each offense.

Though preachers railed against the use of alcohol, settlers liked to imbibe, and Hiram's innkeepers, victuallers, and retailers were ready to oblige. During the period 1821-1832 up to four licenses to sell "strong liquor" were granted annually.

Tithingmen were obliged by law to inform of all offenses against the due observation of the Lord's day, including idleness, disorderly behavior, profanity, and the like. Tithingmen had the right to enter any of the rooms of an inn or public house of entertainment on the Lord's day and the evening preceding and succeeding, examine all persons whom they suspected of unnecessary travel or other violations,

Licenses to victuallers, innholders, and retailers of strong liquors in Hiram

Licenses were granted for one year to:

September 11, 1821. Benjamin Barker, shop. Thomas Spring Esq., innholder in his dwelling House.

September ?, 1822. Thomas Spring, innholder in his dwelling house.

December 2, 1822. Levi Morrell, innholder in his dwelling house. Benjamin McDonald, shop.

September 9, 1823. Thomas Spring Esquire, innholder in his dwelling. Benjamin Barker, shop.

November 6, 1823 Benjamin McDonald, shop. Levi Morrell, innholder in his dwelling house.

September 14, 1824. Thomas Spring Esq. and Levi Morrell.

September 10, 1827. Thomas Spring Esq., innholder in his now dwelling house. Benjamin Barker, dwelling house or shop.

January 19, 1828 John Kimball, dwelling house or shop. Levi Morrell, innholder in his dwelling house.

September 9, 1828. Benjamin Barker, dwelling house or shop.

January 19, 1828. Thomas Spring Esq., innholder in his dwelling house.

September 15, 1829. Thomas Spring and Benjamin Osgood, innholders in their dwelling houses. Benja Barker Esq., shop. Asa Dyer, shop.

October 23, 1830. Thomas Spring Esq., innholder in his dwelling house.

September 13, 1831. Thomas Spring, Levi Morrell, innholders. Isaac Hamblin, Mark Treadwell, retailers.

March 27, 1832 A.A. Pike, retailer.

---

165 Freeman, *The Town Officer*, 1808, 187–190.

and make a complaint before a justice of the peace of the county. If the offender lived elsewhere, the grand jury considered the case.

Attendance at church was mandatory. Absence from the public worship of God for three months was cause for a fine of ten shillings. The choice of church and place of worship was left to the worshiper as long as it was Protestant.[166]

There were compensations as well as incentives for tithingmen. One half of fines collected were applied to the town and one half to the informer.

It is not known how strictly these laws were enforced in Hiram. Receipts for such fines were not found.

Tithingmen

1811	Peleg Wadsworth, Asa Osgood
1815	James Fly, Asa Osgood
1816	James Fly, Thomas B. Watson
1817	James Fly, Jeremiah Trafton
1818	James Fly, Jeremiah Trafton
1820	John Watson, Loammi Baston
1821	William Stanley, John Hodgson, Thomas B. Watson, Benjamin Bucknell
1827	John Watson, Simeon Chadbourne
1828	Thomas Goodwin, Thomas B. Watson

---

166   Article III of the Constitution of the Commonwealth of Massachusetts, 1780.

PAUPERS

myth of self-sufficiency

A myth held of the pioneers was that they were always self sufficient. Another was that once a pauper, always a pauper. Neither was fact. What was true was that neighbor helped neighbor.

Early settlers felt a responsibility for those in need, and this carried over into law. Settlements and towns were obligated to support the poor and indigent who were lawfully settled therein, upon request of the individual or other person. People who received public support were called paupers. Money for support of the poor was voted at Town Meetings and raised by taxation; it was a significant part of the annual budget. Amounts sometimes equaled that voted for support of schools, $100 to $200, but were always less than voted in support of highways.

Also obligated for support, in proportion to their ability to pay, were kindred—parents, grandparents, children, and grandchildren. A husband was always liable to support his wife and his children, but not illegitimate offspring. The ability to pay was recognized as a sensitive and difficult subject. It was not the intent of the law to unfairly burden the kindred family or to force sacrifices and dangers that would hazard the sustenance of said family. Thus, careful judgment was called for.

Most of the early settlers made a go of it. Exceptions were Stephen Burbank, John Mariner [Marriner], Jeremiah McLucas, John McLucas, Robert McLucas, William West, and, occasionally, David Durgin Jr. and Eleazer Strout. Some, like Lemuel Howard and Richard Trippe, needed aid only in old age. Other settlers were surviving on their own, but their children or grandchildren were not. Moody Brown had to rescue his daughter, Louisa, who married Isaac Merrifield and became a pauper in Wells, Maine. John Whales received support for his grandson.

Poor people were under the care of Overseers of the Poor. In Hiram, this function fell to the selectmen who were also assessors. Overseers had the power to set the level of support, within the approved budget, and to indenture those who could work. At public Town Meetings, townsmen could bid to have minors and adults work for them and the town would pay. Naturally, the lowest bid won.

By statute, any two overseers could commit paupers to confinement in municipal workhouses so that they could be gainfully employed and be less of a burden on the taxpayers. Any two overseers could also commit to workhouses "all persons able of body to work and not having estate or means otherwise to maintain themselves who refuse or neglect to do so; live a dissolute, vagrant life, and exercise no ordinary calling or lawful business, sufficient to gain an honest livelihood."[167] If one did not have a legal settlement, overseers could strike preemptively to put people to work before they became in need of financial support.[168] Some people resented this power, but controls were in place.

There were rules about selling an indigent's property, posting public notices, statutes of limitations on recovering expenses from towns and paupers who later gained income or property, paupers in jail, and who could be reimbursed for support provided. There were penalties for bringing a pauper into a town and for leaving a pauper behind.

Paupers were more common than is generally believed of our forebears, who, in our minds, were self-reliant.

At the first Town Meeting after Hiram was incorporated as a town, after choosing a moderator, the first order of business was "to see what the Town will do with regard to the disposal of family of David Durgin jr who are become paupers in Cornish."[169] The town voted in the affirmative but there is no record of what action was taken.

Most likely the action was to put up able-bodied members to vendu (auction), as Hiram had no

---

167   Hugh G. E. MacMahon, *Progress, Stability and the Struggle for Equality* (Portland, ME: Drummond Woodsum & MacMahon, 2009) 48.

168   Freeman, *The Town Officer*, 1808, 230.

169   Clerk's Record, Town of Hiram, November 7, 1814.

workhouse until late in the nineteenth century—1879. Not everyone was happy to be sent there, and one person declared he would not go.

Town Farm

On March 3, 1879 the citizens of Hiram "voted to buy a town farm not to exceed $2,500.00" and the farm of Charles B. Davis on Hampshire Street was dutifully purchased for $2,500 on April 21, 1879. The town operated it for forty-one years, closing it in 1921. In 1923, Fred W. Hill bought it for $3,475. When Conrad and Jane Hartford came to the farm in 1959, the house was derelict, and they sold the property at the end of the century to an out-of-state buyer, who dismantled and removed it.

Caring for indigents was not a trivial pursuit. Dozens of people were involved with either procuring provisions or delivering them or services such as chopping and "holling" (hauling) wood, usually in four-foot lengths, fetching doctors, giving rides to

meetings or lending horses or cows. Homeless paupers had to be boarded with other Hiram residents, and there was much moving around because these stays were not usually long term. The McLucas family lived in seven households in five years between 1819 and 1824—the homes of Joseph Howard, Ephraim Kimball, Winthrop Baston, William Gray, Eleazer Strout, Joseph Gray, and Solomon Hartford.

When an indigent died, there were funeral and grave digging expenses. The overseers reimbursed people for such services if they were approved before expenditure.

Support could be one time or it could go on for years. Only "reasonable" expenses were allowed, but occasionally tobacco and alcohol were supplied. In 1821, Simeon Chadbourn was reimbursed 83 cents for "2 qts wine for Grace Merrifield." Wine, gin, rum, and brandy were sent to various paupers (there were no references to beer), but in April 1820 a reimbursement for "absinth" was controversial. John McLucas regularly received rum, but Stephen Burbank was

The town purchased the Town Farm on Hampshire Street in 1879 and closed it in 1921. Photo copied by permission of Conrad Hartford.

given "2 qts. ginn" once, around the time his wife died, and he was "crazy."[170]

Sometimes the overseers reduced the amount requested for reimbursement or denied it altogether, as they did when James Burbank, a relative of Stephen Burbank, requested money for support, the reason being it had not been approved in advance. John Pierce Jr. received a more drastic cut in 1837 when he claimed he had lost $238.04 in support of the poor and was allowed $16.75 because the committee was not convinced his statement was entirely correct.

Eligibility

Any person of twenty-one years of age residing in a place for five continuous years and not receiving any supplies or support as a pauper could gain a "settlement" of the town.

A married woman had the settlement of her husband, but it was lost if she divorced or the husband died. Legitimate children had the settlement of the father and illegitimate children had the settlement of the mother. Minors could have a settlement of their own. One such way was to serve an apprenticeship to any lawful trade for four years in a town and set up in trade within one year of the end of the term. Minors were people under the age of twenty-one. Males usually were cared for until age twenty-one, but it was hoped that girls could be married off at eighteen.

The rules defining who was eligible for a settlement were complicated, especially if paupers "fell into distress," perhaps by becoming ill in a place where they were not legally settled. It became important to establish legal settlement because paupers had to be removed back to their legal residence. Much of the business of the overseers was spent communicating with other towns about indigents and who was responsible to pay to support them and relocate them and what were reasonable expenses.

Although taking place later in the century, the following letter is typical of the contests between towns.

List of Reimbursements for Pauper Support, 1813[171]

1813 April 5 town of Haverhill to Dist Hiram William West sundry supplies, Peleg Wadsworth 31.29, T Spring 26.92, J Eastman 3.80, E Kimball 2.82, J Chadbourn 4.00, J Watson 2.98, April 4, 1814 Dr J Benton 7.25, Dr Richardson 8.60, Lemuel Howard 3.91 (milk 2.42, milk 1.17, 1 lb butter .25, 1 peck potatoes=3.91, J Clemons 2.17, Daniel Lane 6.00, P Wadsworth 14.33, June 1814 T Spring 11.44, J Watson .25, Overseers 15.00

List of Reimbursements for Pauper Support, 1823[172]

Joseph Gray 25.00 [boarded McLucas]
John Warren 11.00
Simeon Chadbourne 10.00
Benj Barker 2.68
James Fly 10.00
Cotton Lincoln 18.34
Doct Benj Thompson 3.00
William Lane—
William Pierce—
Inhabitants of Brownfield—
April 23 1823 accounts allowed
George Sutton 1.48 wood, beans & potatoes
Joseph D. Boynton 77.87 7 ½ cord wood, 1½ bushel wheat 5.62 per ½, 2.25
Benj Barker 13.10
Simeon Chadbourn 2.25
James C. Burbank—we think he ought not have anything as he was not engaged by the overseers
Benj Swett 41 lb pork 5.12 ½
Benj Thompson doctor bill 6.05
Benj McDonald 20 days at 3 = 10.00
Patience Gray .67
Alpheus Spring 1.50
John Watson Jr. 10.83 = 64.71

---

170   Stephen Burbank's first wife, Mary, died April 17, 1823, aged forty-one years.

171   Maine State Archives, Hiram Box 14.

172   Maine State Archives, Hiram Box 14.

To the Overseers of the town of Brownfield

Gentlemen

Your letter of the 12th inst. stating that Royal McLucas & family had fallen into distress and been furnished relief by your town at the charge of the town of Hiram, was duly received. Upon inquiry we are satisfied this town is not the place of the lawful settlement of the paupers. We cannot therefore cause his removal, nor contribute to his support.

Dated at Hiram Aug. A.D. 1858

John P. Hubbard—Overseer of the Poor.[173]

John Mariner

The battle between Hiram and Cape Elizabeth over the case of John and Betsy Mariner and child was more heated. John Mariner was in Hiram when the 1800 census was taken. He and his wife were twenty-six years of age or under, living with their son, who was ten years old or less. In 1801, John signed Timothy Cutler's petition to incorporate Hiram as a town, and he also signed Charles Lee Wadsworth's counter petition. No more is heard of them until 1821, when they are declared paupers in Cape Elizabeth. It was a stretch for Cape Elizabeth in 1821 to claim Hiram residency as far back as 1801, and eventually that town agreed.[174]

The following correspondence illustrates some challenging aspects of legal settlements.

1821 April 17. Betsey Marriner wife of John Marriner and her child have become chargeable to this town as paupers by an act of incorporation passed Feb 1800. Mr. Marriner & Betsey his wife moved into your town the year before it incorporated[175] and lived on land belonged to Gen Wadsworth until the year 1801. Of course they gained inhabitancy thereby. We conceive it necessary to give this information that you may order their removal or otherwise provide for

them as you may judge expedient. We have charged the expense which has ahead arisen to your town & shall continue to do so as long as we are obliged to provide for them. James Dyer, Woodberry Jordan—

Overseers Cape Elizabeth

1821 May 12. Gentlemen, We have received your letter dated April 17, 1821 informing us that Betsey Marriner & child have become chargeable to the town of Cape Elizabeth & that you have charged their expense to the town of Hiram & shall continue so to do. We do not consider them inhabitants of the town of Hiram and refuse to pay any expense that may arise from their support.

If John Marriner had gained an inhabitancy in the town of Hiram in the year one thousand eight hundred, as you state, & if he had not lost it before, he has lost it by the new laws of this state, passed at the last session of the legislature.

Gentlemen, we are with much respect, Yours, etc.

Peleg Wadsworth Jr., Simeon Chadbourn, John Watson Jr.—Overseers of the Poor.

1821 June 14. Gentlemen, We have received your letter dated May 12. You say if John Marriner had gained an inhabitancy in the town of Hiram in the year one thousand eight hundred and had not lost it before, he has lost it by the new laws of this State, passed at the last session of the legislature…please note…persons residing in a town twelve months previous to passing of said Acts who have not directly or indirectly received any supplies from a town as a pauper have a legal settlement therein, but this is not the case with Mrs. Marriner, part of that time she had lived in Westbrook & part in

---

173   Maine State Archives, Hiram Box 14.

174   Maine State Archives, Hiram Box 14.

175   Refers to the incorporation of the act, not the town.

Cape Elizabeth as a pauper of course she has not gained an inhabitancy of any town by the late law passed, etc.

As we conceive the said Betsey has not gained any legal settlement in any town since she left the town of Hiram therefore we present to you the amount of the Bill which has already arisen to $6.35 Cts & for the further expense of 26 cents per week. We wish you to pay to the Bill as soon as Convenient and without any further trouble.

Gentlemen, We are yours with much respect. James Dyer, John Armstrong, Woodberry Jordan, Overseers of the Poor, town of Cape Elizabeth

1821 July 6, Hiram. Gentlemen, We have received your letter dated June 14. We cannot yet, find any Act of Incorporation which makes John Marriner an inhabitant of the town of Hiram. We should like to see such an Act, and be convinced that John Marriner is an inhabitant of this town before we pay any expense for Mrs. Marriner. We should be glad if you would send us a copy of the Act you allude to, or direct us where to find it.

Someone from this town will probably see you, before long, about the matter; and when you convince us that John Marriner is an inhabitant of this town, we shall be willing to take charge of his wife, without further expense.

Gentlemen, we are with much respect, Yours, etc. Peleg Wadsworth, Jr., Simeon Chadbourn, John Watson, Junior— Overseers of the Poor of the town of Hiram

1821 Nov. Peleg Wadsworth account. Settling the question of maintenance of John Marriner with the Overseers of Cape Elizabeth in our favor $1.00.

Accounts of services and supplies to paupers appear in the Appendix. Some of the stories follow below.

Stephen Burbank

Stephen Burbank seemed to be well off. He and his brother John Burbank owned 269 acres. In 1808, he was elected collector of taxes, a position of responsibility for which he received three cents for every dollar collected. In 1809 he owned real property. He was charged tax on one poll, one dwelling house, one barn, four acres tillable land, eight acres mowing land, ninety acres unimproved land, one cow, two cattle three years old, two cattle one year old, one horse, one colt one year old, and three swine. But only a year and a half later, on November 29, 1810, the Overseers of the Poor in Portland, Maine, wrote to the overseers of Hiram.

Gentlemen, Stephen Burbank, an inhabitant of your town has now become chargeable in this town as a pauper. We conceive it necessary to give you this information so that you may order his removal, or otherwise provide for him as you may judge expedient. We have charged the expense of his support, which has already arisen to your Town, and shall continue to do so, so long as we are obliged to furnish him with supplies.

We are, Gentlemen, with much respect, your most obedient humble servants,

Per order, Oliver Bray, Secretary, board of Overseers of the Poor.

Stephen Burbank continued to be an expense to Hiram off and on until he died in 1850.

Solomon Hartford

The Solomon Hartford family was temporarily in distress. At the September 1816 Town Meeting, $60 for the support of their children and other town paupers was voted. It was also voted to set up the children at vendu (auction) to the lowest bidder as follows:

"Mr. Humphrey A. Chadbourn bidd off John Hartford at 1/0 per week. John Pierce Jr bidd off James Hartford at 2/5 per week. William H. Hartford bidd off by Moody Brown at 1/ per week. The Selectmen are to furnish suitable clothing for each of them until otherwise provided for."

On April 7, 1817, the town voted "to dispose of the Hartford children at vendue to the person who will take them the cheaper. Jacob Lord took John Hartford at four shillings per week. He is to find him victuals & clothes. David Newcomb took James Hartford at 4/ per week & ??? victuals & clothes. Jeremiah Trafton took William Hartford at 5/ per week provides him victuals & clothes and that the Overseers dispose of the family of Stephen Burbank discresionally."

Yet in 1821 there was an agreement of Solomon Hartford to support John McLucas and two children.

McLucas Family Support
Jeremiah 1821
John 1819–1824, 1853
Robert & Mrs. 1823

Isaac Merrifield

In this tragic story the facts remain elusive. Isaac was born in Porter in 1798 of Samuel Merrifield and an unknown mother. He married Louisa Brown, born in Hiram five years earlier than he, daughter of Moody Brown and Susannah Smith of Hiram, who settled on Cutler's Lower Grant. Moody was a private in the Revolutionary War on the Massachusetts line, for which he received a pension.[176] In 1820, he was living in Hiram with a household of five.

There are several puzzling aspects of the details about Isaac Merrifield and Louisa Brown. Isaac purchased fifty-two acres from Peleg Wadsworth in 1806 (when he was eight years old? Was there another Isaac?) In April 1815 he mortgaged it for the sum of $258 to be paid back with interest in four annual notes.[177]

According to Hiram Historical Society notes, Isaac Merrifield of Hiram married Louisa Brown on May 12, 1816, in Hiram, with a marriage certificate signed by Peleg Wadsworth. But marriage at this late date would be unusual if her children were born as family genealogy states—Oliver, August 5, 1811, and Elvira, November 13, 1815. There is agreement that Louisa was born in 1793, but when did she

marry, and how old was she when she married Isaac Merrifield? And is Oliver the right child? There is no other record of Oliver, but there is a record of Isaac Merrifield Jr.

Presumably, with fifty-two acres of land and a father who was doing well, Isaac would be solvent or at least supported, but by October 1820 he had become a pauper. In November, Moody Brown fetched Louisa from Wells, and Hiram was discussing what to do with Isaac Merrifield Jr. Two months later, Isaac Jr. fell ill and died. Father Isaac died soon after. Descendants put the death date at May 19, 1820, but this date is five months before he became a pauper, and eleven months after Winthrop Baston claimed he boarded Isaac and the child. In May 1822, Abijah Lewis was reimbursed $2 for making Isaac's coffin, but because requests for reimbursement could be submitted up to two years from the date of incurring the expense, it is not a clear indicator of the date of death.

Louisa remarried in 1825, to David Lowell. Louisa's new family did not escape poverty, receiving support again in 1832, when Richard Heath was reimbursed $31.44 "for support of A. Lewis and D. Lowell's family." When she received support again in March 1843, for the coffin of her child,[178] Louisa was listed under her name, indicating that she was a widow. Although she lived to be ninety-five, she did not remarry. Their children were David Lowell II, born 1827; Willoughby, born 1831 (drowned in Hiram in 1888); Susan B., who married Ebenezer Lowell; Lizzie S. (Louisa?), who died at age nineteen; Lida (Lydia?); and Jane, who married James Day Jr. of Brownfield.

Eleazer Strout Family
On March 9, 1819, Alpheus Spring submitted a bill for $3.50 for removing Eleazer Strout's family from Standish.

April 1819: Simeon Chadbourn's account was for goods delivered to Eleazer Strout, $1.81.

---

176 Annual allowance was $96, and he received a total of $1424.53 before his death in 1851 in Cornish.

177 The lot was "on the southerly side of the brook running from the Gold place so called to the Dyer place so called at the same place where the westerly line of Levi Lords lot strikes said brook," which we believe was in Durgintown and would place it near his father's property.

178 John Bucknell made the coffin, presumably for Louisa's daughter Lizzie S. MHS Coll. 146, Vol. 2: 32.

Support of Eleazer Strout was temporary. In a few years he was helping support others, and when the 1850 U.S. census listed him as a pauper, he was seventy-seven years old.

William West

William West's story is interesting in that he sold his house and property on the east side of the Saco at the Bridge to Simeon Chadbourn, who opened a store (later Lemuel Cotton's) directly opposite on the west side of the Saco. Much later, West sued to retrieve property he claimed the town had taken illegally.

William West was in Hiram by 1808. He was on the List of Rateables of 1809 with one poll, a dwelling house, two acres of tillable land, one cow, four horses, and two swine. This is not much land or livestock, but no one in Hiram in 1809, including Peleg Wadsworth or son Charles Lee Wadsworth, had as many horses.

William West was a legal voter in 1810 and 1811. To be so, one needed to be a white male over the age of twenty-one, a resident of Hiram for one year, and have annual income of $10 or estate valued at $200.

His name appears in the List of Rateables of 1810, but the data is blank. In 1811, he was elected to the position of surveyor of boards. Even though he received cash for selling his house to Simeon Chadbourn in 1811, he was heading toward insolvency. In March of 1812, the town tried to help by paying William West $1.48 for some unspecified service regarding David Durgin Jr. and Levi Lord. But the next month, April, Peleg Wadsworth began supplying the West family and seeing to it that they were boarded with Hiram families. Somehow, William West got to Haverhill, Massachusetts, which charged Hiram for supplies in April 1813. The town's policy of applying such funds to pauper accounts changed, because at the Town Meeting of January 1816, it was voted to allocate money received from Haverhill in support of the William West family to the support of Hiram schools. There is more on this story in the chapter on Schools.

These are some of the stories of paupers. More correspondence and receipts for services rendered are in Appendix 19.

The Founders

TIMOTHY CUTLER

October 14, 1735–April 7, 1817

Married February 24, 1759

Mary Norton, dates unknown

Timothy Cutler was a founding father of Hiram, supposedly a Freemason,[179] who helped name the town of Hiram for Hiram, King of Tyre, by flipping a coin with Gen. Peleg Wadsworth and the general's son Charles Lee.[180] (Read more about the town's naming in the bio of Charles Lee Wadsworth, later in this section.) Cutler was associated with Hiram in November 1787, when the Massachusetts Legislature awarded him a grant of land, more than two years before Peleg Wadsworth purchased his land.[181] Mt. Cutler is named for him. He became the first U.S. postmaster in Hiram, appointed in October 1800. He led a petition to Massachusetts to incorporate Hiram as a town in 1801, but Gen. Peleg Wadsworth, then in the Massachusetts Legislature, opposed it and it was denied.

Cutler was fifty-two when he became acquainted with Hiram through his land grant. He was born in Boston, the son of Robert and Anna Cutler, and he married Mary Norton there. He died in South Berwick, aged eighty-two. There is no record that he served in the military or held any town office in Hiram. When he bought land with his wife, Mary, in Falmouth (now Portland) in 1765, his occupation was listed as "Baker." Later his occupation was "Trader," but after the "Britains" burned his bakery on India Street in 1775, he moved to Scarborough and bought land there in 1783, where he again became a baker. By the time the Massachusetts Legislature approved his grant of land in Hiram and Porter in November 1787, his occupation elevated to "Gentleman."

The land deals that led to the award of Cutler's Grants are fascinating. Cutler was granted land in Hiram to compensate for land he owned in Cumberland that Massachusetts granted to others. Cutler explained that he had made improvements with the intention to move there, but was not living on the land by January 1, 1784, as required by law, so was not able to claim it.

For his five hundred acres in Cumberland, he was rewarded with six thousand acres in Hiram and Porter, some thirty-eight miles from Scarborough and less developed. The Upper Grant in Porter was thirty-eight hundred acres. The Lower Grant in Hiram was twenty-two hundred.

Though free to sell the granted land in hundred-acre lots, the deed required his assurance to grant title to those who petitioned claiming settlement before January 1, 1784. In Hiram there were seventeen such settlers claiming twenty-one hundred acres; most of them had settled on Cutler's Lower Grant. Furthermore, the prior owner of the Cumberland property shared it with his brother, a fact not known to Cutler. In negotiations, Cutler gave him thirteen hundred acres in his Upper and Lower grants.

Read more in the chapter on Land Grants.

Cutler lived at what is now 1608 Pequawket Trail. "His house was where George W. Osgood has since lived."[182] On the 1880 map of Hiram, G. Osgood is shown as owner of a house, shed, and two barns across the street from the Universalist Church.

Cutler's residency in Hiram was irregular. As a Hiram resident, he bought thirty acres of the Prescott Grant on the east side of the Saco in 1800, but more frequently he was recorded in Scarborough. In 1791, Cutler bought from John Ayer fourteen acres of "the Danforth lot at the Bridge" on the west bank of the Saco River. The Danforth lot of one hundred acres had been purchased by John Ayer in 1782. It was included in Cutler's grant, but because Ayer proved

---

179 The Masonic Grand Lodge has no member card for him, but it also has no card for Peleg Wadsworth, who was proved to be a member in the book *10,000 Famous Freemasons*.

180 According to Ridlon, *Saco Valley Settlements and Families*, the coin was tossed by Peleg and Timothy. Others say Peleg and Charles.

181 Peleg Wadsworth purchased his land on March 10, 1790.

182 Ridlon, *Saco Valley Settlements and Families*, 148.

he had settled on and improved his farm before the cut-off date (and also had deeds to his properties), Cutler deeded back this property on March 10, 1791. At the time, Cutler lived in Scarborough. In June 1792, when he sold another hundreds-acre lot, he resided in Flintstown (Baldwin), and from October to December 1792 he was in Brownfield. Therefore, it is likely that Cutler built the simple Cape-style house between 1793 and May 13, 1794, when he listed himself in a property deed as residing in Hiram.[183]

Why didn't Cutler choose to build on one of his land grant plots? Land along the Saco River was more desirable—close to the Bridge village, river transportation, and roads—but it was not available because it was reserved as "settlers' plots," plots that reverted to those who could prove they had settled before January 1, 1784.

By 1806, Cutler was in South Berwick, paying the lesser tax as nonresident in Hiram. Although associated with Hiram for nearly thirty years, he lived in Hiram perhaps twelve years.

Twelve years in Hiram was not long compared with Peleg Wadsworth's time in town—he was associated with Hiram for thirty-nine years and lived there for twenty-two years, until his death. Peleg's son Charles Lee Wadsworth lived in Hiram fifty-four years. In 1811, Cutler sold the Hiram house and property to Asa Burbank and his wife, Mary, and he was not living in Hiram in 1814, when it was officially incorporated as a town. Therefore, it is likely that Cutler, with one or both Wadsworths, flipped the coin to name Hiram for Hiram, King of Tyre, earlier, perhaps in 1806, when Hiram petitioned for the second time to become a town. The area was first known as "Great Ossipee," was called "Hiram town" in the 1790 census and "Hyram and Cutler's Grant"[184] in 1800, long before they flipped the coin to name Hiram for the King of Tyre.

Read more about Timothy Cutler in the Incorporation and Land Grants chapters.

Timothy Cutler house, 1608 Pequawket Trail, 2019.

Yankee style barn and outbuildings of the Timothy Cutler house amid ancient butternut trees, 2009.

The front north parlor of the Timothy Cutler house, under restoration, 2014.

---

183 York County Registry of Deeds, Alfred, Book 2, 556, from copy in Oxford County Registry of Deeds, Fryeburg, now in Paris.

184 Cutler was spelled Luttler in the original 1800 census document.

GEN. PELEG WADSWORTH

May 6, 1748–November 12, 1829

Married c. 1772

Elizabeth Bartlett

August 9, 1753–July 20, 1825

At forty-two, Brigadier General Peleg Wadsworth began thinking about retirement and making a permanent home in Hiram. The wealthiest, most prestigious, and most active man in community affairs during his thirty-nine-year association with Hiram, Peleg dedicated himself to his adopted community. Well educated, entrepreneurial, a thoroughly decent and fair man, he devoted himself to his family, his soldiers, his farm, and his town.

Born and raised in Duxbury, Massachusetts, Peleg attended Harvard College. Graduating in 1772, he became a school teacher, along with his former classmate Alexander Scammel. He ran a store in Plymouth, Mass., where he met and married Elizabeth Bartlett. A brilliant military career followed, after which he shone in politics: local, state and federal. His military exploits in the Revolutionary War are well documented and include his capture and escape from British soldiers at Bagaduce (Castine). He was a friend of George Washington and served with Paul Revere.

Though not a tall man, his military bearing commanded attention and respect. In 1848, Zilpha recalled her father vividly:

"Imagine to yourself a man of middle size, well proportioned with a military air, and who carried himself so truly that many thought him tall. His dress,

Silhouettes of Elizabeth Bartlett Wadsworth and General Peleg Wadsworth, the only known likenesses created during their lives.[185]

---

185   For a portrait drawn after his death see James Thacher, *Military Journal* (Hartford: Silas Andrus and Son, 1854), 256.

a bright scarlet coat, buff small clothes and vest, full ruffled bosom, ruffles over the hands, white stockings, shoes with silver buckles, white cravat bow in front; hair well powdered and tied behind in a club so called."[186]

He must have brought an air of culture and refinement to the settlement of Great Ossipee, where most residents were preoccupied with the hard sweaty work of cutting the forest to make tillable lands. He was a skilled surveyor, a talent in great demand in a nascent settlement, especially in laying out roads, which he did as selectman. Peleg joined the Congregational Church long before moving to Hiram. A devout man, he conducted the family in morning and evening prayers. The Wadsworths probably attended church services held in private homes, as there was no church building until 1826.

In line with his moral sentiments, he became a Master Mason of St. John's Lodge No. 1 in Boston, shortly after the close of the Revolutionary War. Freemasonry is a fraternity based on the belief that each man has a responsibility to help make the world a better place. Masons value and promote ethics, personal growth, tolerance, education, diversity, philanthropy, family, and community. His membership in this fraternal organization proved fateful in naming the town of Hiram.

Military Man

Peleg and Elizabeth lived in Kingston, Massachusetts, at the onset of the Revolution. He joined the militia and recruited a company of minutemen, which chose him captain. In response to the alarm of April 19, 1775, his company marched to Lexington and Concord the next day.

In 1776, Wadsworth served as aide to Gen. Artemas Ward and as an engineer under Gen. John Thomas, assisting in planning the defenses of Roxbury, Massachusetts. He fought in the Battle of Long Island in 1776 and was made brigadier general

of militia in 1777 and adjutant general of Massachusetts in 1778.

In 1779, he served as second in command to Lt. Col. Paul Revere, leading a force sent to attack the British at Bagaduce, Maine. The so-called Penobscot Expedition resulted in the destruction of most of the American vessels involved. Wadsworth organized and led the only successful part of the expedition, the retreat. Revere and Commodore Dudley Saltonstall, the commander of the fleet, faced court-martial charges for their roles in the debacle.

In March 1780, Peleg took command of all troops raised for the defense of the Province of Maine. He liked to keep his family close and took them with him to what he thought would be a safe post in Thomaston, Maine. However, on a bitterly cold night in February 1781, British troops advanced on the house, wounded Wadsworth in the arm, and captured him. Soldiers helped him dress, but did not allow Elizabeth to dress his wounds. He wrote anxious letters to his pregnant wife from prison in Fort George at Bagaduce:

"I am extremely afflicted with the idea of your situation. The windows dashed, the doors broken, the house torn to pieces and blood and slaughter around you."[187]

Peleg and fellow prisoner Maj. Benjamin Burton escaped by cutting a hole in the ceiling and crawling out along the joists. Within four months he had made his way back to his family in Plymouth, where he remained until the war's end.

Peleg treated his men with loyalty and kindness. After the war, he employed Daniel Hickey, who was his bodyguard when he was captured, and instructed his son Charles Lee Wadsworth to look after him. Hickey worked at the Hiram farm driving back and forth to Portland doing errands for Peleg, carrying produce and pigs from the farm to sell and returning with coffee, tea, sugar, molasses, cotton, brandy, rum, fish, ginger, and onion seed. Before Elizabeth moved to Hiram in 1807 he occasionally brought an orange for the children or pies and gingerbread she had baked.[188] He lived in a

---

186 Joyce Butler, "The Wadsworths: A Portland Family," in *Longfellow's Portland and Portland's Longfellow*(Portland, ME: Maine Historical Society, 1987), 4.

187 Peleg Wadsworth, *A Story about a Little Good Boy* (Portland, ME:: Privately printed at the Press of Lefavor-Tower Co., 1903), viii.

188 Various family letters, Maine Historical Society, Coll. 16.

cabin in an area along the Saco River, at the approximate location of Hiawatha Campground, known for many years as "Hickey's Field." Daniel married Sophia Cole of Hiram in 1793 and ended as a pauper, supported first by the town of Hiram in 1809,[189] and then, beginning in 1811, by the town of Baldwin,[190] where he is buried.

Portland

Peleg purchased 1.5 acres of land on the outskirts of Falmouth (Portland) in April 1784. In 1785, he built an impressive brick home on Back Street (now Congress Street). No brickyards existed in Portland, so Wadsworth imported them from Philadelphia to complete the first brick home in Portland. The Wadsworths had the largest drawing room in town and completed the décor with the city's first spinet. The house is now the Wadsworth-Longfellow House, owned by the Maine Historical Society.

Peleg engaged in surveying and opened a store, an honorable enterprise among New England gentry. The location, on a commercial route to Falmouth Neck, was good for business, and was next to his house, making it easier for his wife, Elizabeth, to operate it, as he was often away.

Political Man

The general led a very active political life. Intimately involved in the movement for Maine statehood, he became chairman of the first convention to address the issue—in 1785 in Portland, well before the movement during the War of 1812 that popularized the separation that was legalized in 1820. In 1792, he was chosen a presidential elector and a member of the Massachusetts Senate. He went on to represent the Third Eastern District of Maine and was reelected as a Federalist to the six succeeding Congresses. He served fourteen years from 1793 until 1807, when he declined to run again, retired, and moved to Hiram. There, beginning at age 59, he devoted the remainder of his life to farming, business, family, and local concerns.

Family Man

Peleg and Elizabeth lived in Kingston, Massachusetts, until 1775, when he joined the militia. Ever the family man, he, Elizabeth—"my dear Betsy"—and their first child, Alexander Scammel, born May 9, 1774, lived on base. Tragically, Alexander took

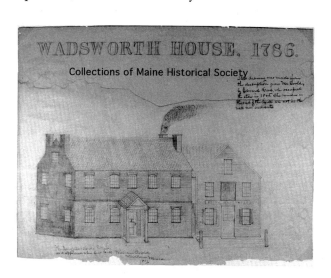

Peleg Wadsworth house and shop in Portland.
Later, a third story was added to the house.
Collections of Maine Historical Society.

Peleg Wadfworth,

Defires to acquaint his friends, acquaintance and the people in general—That he has juft open'd a Store at Falmouth, juft above the Hay-market,

With an Affortment of

G O O D S,

Suitable for the Seafon,

WHICH he will fell on as good terms, as at any ftore in town, for cafh, lumber, or PUBLIC SECURITIES of every kind.

He has a quantity of Lifbon SALT.

Advertisement for Peleg Wadsworth's store.
Falmouth Gazette, *Saturday, January 22, 1785.*

---

189 Massachusetts General Court Resolves, Pauper Accounts, March 4, 1809, March 10, 1810.

190 Massachusetts General Court Resolves, Pauper Accounts, February 27, 1811, June 1812, June 1813, January 1814, January 1815, January 1816, June 1816, November 1816, June 1817, June 1818, June 1819.

sick and died there on August 28, 1775. Ten more children followed, all of whom survived to adulthood. The oldest, Charles Lee Wadsworth, born January 26, 1776, became a captain of the militia and a prominent founder of Hiram. Daughter Elizabeth, born September 21, 1779, died of consumption in Portland shortly before she was to marry Stephen Longfellow, who subsequently married daughter Zilpha, born January 6, 1778. Zilpha became the mother of the world-famous poet Henry Wadsworth Longfellow. Son John, born September 1, 1781, attended Fryeburg Academy and graduated from Harvard College in 1800, and was admitted to the Bar of Cumberland County, Maine, in 1808. An accomplished linguist and scholar, he was described as charming and "remarkably comely and graceful."[191] Returning to Hiram after his father died in 1829, he operated a silk industry at Wadsworth Hall from about 1832 to 1849. Daughter Lucia, born June 12, 1783, never married and ran the house with the Longfellows in Portland. Son Henry, born June 11, 1785, became a lieutenant in the U.S. Navy at age nineteen. He died at Tripoli on September 4, 1804, while assisting in running a torpedo ship into the enemy's fleet. Son George, born January 6, 1788, said to one of the best penmen in the U.S., died in Philadelphia in 1816. The son named Alexander Scammel who lived, born May 7 1790, served forty years in the navy, and was said to be one of the finest-looking officers. He served in the War of 1812 and became a commodore. Samuel Bartlett, born September 1, 1791, owned a store in Eastport, Maine, and served as a state legislator. The youngest, Peleg Jr., born October 10, 1793, became a general in the militia and inherited and ran the homestead upon the death of his father. Like his namesake, he was civic minded, serving as selectman, clerk, surveyor of highways, treasurer, and fence viewer.

While Peleg pursued his political career and business enterprises in Hiram, Elizabeth ran the Portland household, seeing their children were well educated and cultured as they entered adulthood. In a letter-journal written in 1797, Zilpha provided a vivid vignette of the Wadsworth family, which had gathered on a Sunday evening in the front parlor.

> There sits Mama in her lolling chair by the fire. [Eliza] is playing on the piano "Ye Tribes of Adam Join." John and Lucia are singing at the back of her chair. George, Alexander, and Sam are singing in different parts of the room. Little Peleg is stepping about the floor surveying one and another. Charles is sitting at the table with me. He was writing. His pen dropt from his fingers, and he listens to the music. Harry is reading beside me, you know he is always self collected.... I have been singing as I wrote.... Ten children! What a circle! I should like to know what are Mama's thoughts as she looks around on us.[192]

By 1797, when Zilpha wrote in her journal, Charles was married with a family and living in Hiram. Zilpha and Elizabeth (called Eliza) were cultured and refined young women whose favorite pastimes were reading, writing letters, playing the spinet, and drawing. John would go on to Harvard College. Lucia and Harry attended school in Portland. The four youngest boys made up the rest of Elizabeth's charges.

Two years later, in December 1799, the death of America's first and most revered president produced great national mourning. Eliza wrote to her father, asking for a copy of the death march composed for Washington's funeral or a scrap of Washington's handwriting, adding, "Papa had he hair? A lock of that...I should value more highly still." Peleg shared Eliza's request with Martha Washington, who sent him a lock of her husband's hair. In an undated note, Eliza wrote, "I wish it may be preserved in our own family while it can be safe. Some years hence...if Maine is

---

191 Joseph Palmer, *Necrology of Alumni of Harvard College 1851-2 to 1861-2* (Boston: Printed by B. Wilson and Son, 1864), 295.

192 Elizabeth Wadsworth to Nancy Doane, February 2, 1799, Wadsworth-Longfellow Papers, Craigie House, Longfellow National Historic Site, Cambridge, MA. Cited in Butler, *Longfellow's Portland*, 12.

GENERAL WADSWORTH AND SON.   P. 258.

Portrait of General Wadsworth and unnamed son.[193]
Painted after his death, it is not a true likeness.

a separate state…I had rather it would be preserved among its treasures."194 This loyalty to Maine and thoughts of its future were typical of the family. Today, the Maine Historical Society holds Eliza's treasure.

Though often away on business, the general wrote letters to his family almost daily. The letters usually contained advice to the children to behave well, study hard, and respect other people.

Letter to George, Philadelphia, May 13, 1798:

I hope my dear George that you will be very good to help Henry[195] make the garden & do all the work; & remember that in order to please God & your parents & everybody it must be done with good nature and pleasantness. Whatever is cross is wicked. I know you do not mean to be wicked—then you & all the little Boys must always be very good natured in all you do… your affectionate Papa, P Wadsworth.[196]

Not only did he write letters, he composed stories with moral themes for the children. Two such stories are preserved at the Maine Historical Society. "The Story of a Blind Girl" relates an encounter with a blind girl begging in the streets of Philadelphia in which he admonishes sons George, Alex, and Samuel to find ways to secure employment for her and others like her, for he fears for her future. "A Little Good Boy and How He Grew Up to Have Good Little Boys of His Own" is autobiographical and instructional, and reveals a sentimental and sensitive side of his character. He tells how deeply the illness and death of his first child, Alexander Scammel, saddened and affected him. The story also introduces a theme of respecting nature, a consciousness ahead of his time. He tells of a boyhood pastime of stealing the eggs of birds from nests, which he regrets, and urges his children not to do it:

…how crewel it is for little Boys to get away the poor little Birds Eggs when they have taken so much pains to build their Nests & taken so much pleasure in laying their Eggs in them to hatch their little young Birds! Did you never see how sorry the poor little Birds are when they flutter round a Boy when they think He is going to get their Eggs or their young one? They seem to cry & take on so much as your Mama would do if the Indians were going to catch her little Boys & carry them away.[197]

The general had a special relationship with his grandchildren as well, specifically a strong, mutual bond with his grandson Henry Wadsworth Longfellow. Henry, named for his uncle who perished in a war, looked forward to his visits to Wadsworth Hall to sit on his grandpa's knee and hear stories of his exploits, particularly his capture and escape.

---

193   James Thacher, *Military Journal* (Hartford: Silas Andrus and Son, 1854 edition), 256.

194   Maine Historical Society, Coll. 16, Box 2/1.

195   Henry was George's younger brother.

196   Maine Historical Society, Coll. 16, Box 2/4.

197   Maine Historical Society, Coll. 16, Box 1/10.

Wadsworth Hall

Well before he resigned from the Legislature in 1807, the general had planned his retirement. After returning to Maine, he settled in Portland and engaged in land speculation. His 1790 purchase of seventy-eight hundred acres in Hiram was part of that plan. Shortly after, he started farming and building his mansion and mills in Hiram.

As with many of his other pursuits, Peleg immersed himself in the project. In a letter to son Charles Lee on October 13, 1799, he described the results of testing clay for making the best bricks for the chimneys:

> ...three samples of clay have all turned to Brick. Watson's is rather the best, the Dragon Meadow & Ingall's Capeway are much alike altho they will do tolerably. To that you may dismiss the Gondola if you have not already done so.[198]

Theophilus Smith of Cornish, mason, constructed the chimneys. Master carpenter Stephen Jewett of Cornish built the house. Wadsworth's sawmill on his property at Great Falls Brook provided the lumber. Author Pat Higgins describes the mansion:

> One of the largest houses in the area, it has a seven bay facade and an unusual floor plan. The house is constructed with an unusual full cellar; a team of oxen could pull a load of produce completely into the cellar for easy unloading and then continue out the opposite side. The front door allows admission directly into a room so large and high ceilinged that it was used by the local militia for drill during inclement weather and at other times as a school. The customary stairway hall usually associated with the front door is found at the side of the house. The house, the third oldest house in Hiram, still stands today although it was extensively

Wadsworth Hall, the largest home in Hiram, took three years to build and was under way by 1798; 82 Douglas Road, 2014. Wadsworth Hall was later found to be the fifth oldest house in Hiram. Houses older are: 6 Hiram Hill Road (part between 1774 and 1781); 287 King Street (1785); 1608 Pequawket Trail (c.1794) and 1912 Pequawket Trail (1796).

198 Maine Historical Society, Coll. 16, Box 2/4.

Aerial view of Wadsworth Hall, c. 1930.

The older barn (right) was built in English style with the door under the eaves. When updated, the door was relocated but the "lights" remained under the eaves. The "new" barn (left) was built in Yankee style with the door under the gable, c. 1830. Photo 2009.

The original cooper shop (left) and the sap house (right) where maple sap was boiled into syrup and sugar, 2009.

The front hall of Wadsworth Hall depicted on a postcard, c. 1930.

remodeled in 1875. Windows were changed, a piazza was added and a roof top outlook was removed. Originally yellow, the exterior paint was changed to white.[199]

Community Leader

Before he moved to Hiram in 1807, Wadsworth served as one of three members of the Committee on Accounts in 1806 and 1807. He may have been re-elected, but there is a gap in the records for the Committee for the years between 1808 and 1811. By 1808, he served as treasurer and one of three selectmen.

General Peleg Wadsworth's desk, Wadsworth Hall, 1927.

Jury boxes measured six and three-eighths inches by five and one-eighth inches by five inches and contained names of eligible men of good character to serve as jurors. The box was locked and carried to meetings by the town clerk.

199   Pat Higgins, "Peleg Wadsworth," Mainestory.com, 2014, www.mainestory.info/the-hidden-history-of-midco/peleg-wadsworth.html.

From 1809 to 1828, a year before his death, he served as justice of the peace. As a petit juror on the Circuit Court of the County of Oxford[200] he was instructed to "fix"[201] the Jury boxes to meet new standards every five years, in 1808, 1813, and 1818.

Likely a man of great strength and agility, in 1811 at age sixty-three, he was elected one of the hog reeves, a strenuous office.[202] According to *New England Families*, he served as selectman for six years and treasurer for twelve.[203] Judging by the number of financial receipts, he was one of the most active selectmen in their other roles as assessors and overseers of the poor.

Town officers and committee members received payment for services in express amounts and were reimbursement for authorized expenses. A typical request for reimbursed for services comes from the year 1813, when Peleg served as selectman:

April 10 warrant for meeting to choose County Treasurer .25

½ day giving limits to Surveyors of Highways .34

April 24th ½ day on the demand of Portland viz John McLucas[204] .34

April 26th ½ day fixing Jury boxes .34

May 17th Warrant for meeting to regulate Jury box .25

May 24 ½ day fixing Jury box, 26th ½ day on valuation .67

May 31 ½ day on highway tax bill .34

June 2 ½ day attending on John McLucas' matters & distributing bill .34

June 3 ½ day attending to Suit of Paris on the West cause[205] .34

July 2 ½ day appraising McLucas' ??? .34

August 24 postage of letter to Overseers .08

1 day to Brownfield and Fryeburg on Town business, School taxes .67

Horse expenses on Ditto .75

Sept 27 laying out Road from Nathaniel Williams, James Fly Jr. & J. Eastman 1.00

Oct 4 1 day appointing & fixing the place of School House of Dist. 4 .67

Nov. 19 examining County Road for amendment .25

Dec. 16 Warrant for Meeting on the subject of separation[206] .25

1814 Feby 21 ¾ day making list of voters & warrant for annual meeting .50 = 7.72

~~Feby 28 warrant for Class meeting no. 1~~[207] ~~.25~~ (crossed out)

March 7th service as treasurer 1813 5.00 [total] 12.72[208]

After incorporation in 1814, the townspeople elected him moderator for the first three official Town Meetings[209] and dozens of times afterwards—a strong indication of his esteem. A position of importance, the moderator controlled the flow of the meeting. On March 6, 1815, the town elected him both selectman and treasurer, and on June 3, 1815, chose him to defend the town against an indictment for bad roads in Hiram.[210] He was chosen again in 1816 and 1817 and 1818.

---

200 A petit jury is a trial jury, unlike a grand jury.

201 Make a list of eligible names to be drawn from the box.

202 Hogs were more difficult to catch than stray cattle.

203 William Richard Cutter, editor, *New England Families Genealogical and Memorial: A Record of Achievements of Her People in the Making of Commonwealths and the Founding of a Nation* (New York: Lewis Historical Publishing, 1913), 735.

204 John McLucas was a pauper chargeable to Hiram.

205 Refers to William West, a pauper.

206 Refers to the separation of Maine from Massachusetts.

207 Probably a meeting of School District No. 1.

208 Maine State Archives, Hiram Box 6.

209 November 7, 1814; January 16, 1815; April 3, 1815.

210 Indicted by the Circuit Court of Common Pleas at Paris.

Educator

Peleg set a high priority on children's education. His letters to his children continuously urge them to study hard. He uses his own past as an example in "A Little Good Boy and How He Came To Have Little Good Boys of His Own." He relates how he rose early in the morning to walk miles to school, saying his prayers and studying his lessons while he walked. "Papa" assigned less farm work in exchange for his studies, a big benefit in Peleg's view. After graduating from Harvard, he taught school.

As selectman, Peleg helped set school taxes, decide when to build new schools, and rearrange school districts according to shifts in population. During his time in Hiram, he saw growth to thirteen school districts.

He and son Charles L. taught in School District 3. In January 1813, this district had thirteen children, eight for Charles L., five for Peleg. Peleg's children at that time ranged in age from twenty to twenty-eight, and were not likely to be in school in Hiram. Were these students (called scholars) children of servants or workers on his farm? It is possible they were children of paupers living at his farm, such as Betsy Mariner before she left in 1801.[211]

His youngest son, Peleg Jr., became the youngest teacher in Hiram. He stayed with his uncle Charles Lee and taught limited terms at Wadsworth Hall before the family moved to Hiram.[212] Peleg also established a free school in the Town House in his eightieth year and rode horseback through the village to invite children to attend."[213]

Farmer

Only three seasons after Peleg purchased the land, Portland's *Eastern Herald* newspaper published a story on September 10, 1792 about his success. "The General thinks the farm raised more than 1000 bushels of corn on burnt land at a place called Great Ossipee."[214]

It was possible. Farmers commonly prepared land for farming by felling the trees for lumber, burning the land, and planting gardens in the spaces between the stumps. Later, oxen teams pulled up stumps and piled them into fences—hence the old saying, "Ugly as a stump fence."[215]

Peleg gave his oldest son Charles Lee Wadsworth five hundred acres in Hiram and instructed him to start farming. In 1795, Charles built a house farther up the mountain from Peleg's farm. That same year, Charles married Ruth Clemons and the couple welcomed their first child, Betsey,

Peleg focused intensely on his Hiram property—building his mansion took three years—and, ever the entrepreneur, he developed the land for both farming and logging. Copious letters between father and son show Peleg giving advice and Charles keeping him informed. In one letter, Peleg stated his opposition to incorporating his land as a town, but included advice on buying sows, logging, hay, and procuring corn, as well as some praise for Charles's decisions.[216]

Accustomed to commanding troops and attention in Congress, Peleg lamented he could not be in Hiram more and had to depend on others for news of progress at the farm. In a plaintive letter to son Charles L. from Washington, January 13, 1801, he wrote:

> Dear Charles,
> Altho I have now & then some news of you by way of Portland, I have not had the pleasure of one line from your hand since I left Hiram.
> I know you must be very busy but that ought not to prevent you writing sometimes,

---

211 Maine State Archives, Hiram Box 14, Overseers of the Poor.

212 Llewellyn A. Wadsworth, Centennial, *Hiram, Maine, 1814-1914*, 14. Peleg Jr. was fourteen in 1805 when he taught at Wadsworth Hall.

213 Cutter, ed., *New England Families Genealogical and Memorial*, 735.

214 *Americana*, Vol. 14, 1920, 379, quote from *Eastern Argus*.

215 Raymond C. Cotton, *Hog Reaves, Field Drivers, and Tything Men* (Hiram, ME: Hiram Historical Society, 1983), 6.

216 Maine Historical Society, Coll. 16, Box 1/3.

as I am anxious to hear & to know how you go on—whether well or ill.[217]

Slow mail delivery only increased his impatience. On May 1, 1801, he wrote: "I did not receive yours of 19th till 27th. The mail is worse than none."[218]

Logging became a successful business for Peleg and Charles L. They discussed when, where, and how to cut and who was best to cut and transport or "drive" logs on the Saco and Ossipee rivers and Canal Brook, which ran through his property. Always entrepreneurial, by 1809 Peleg had built a blacksmith shop, a sugar house, a carding mill, sawmill, and three barns on his property.[219] Later he owned a saw and gristmill in Brownfield on Ten Mile Brook. In 1813, he researched building a salt works in Saco, which was not built, but is an example of his broad interests and energy.

He had the cash and position to expand his holdings. He regularly bid on properties up for auction due to unpaid taxes. One such sale netted Peleg 1,159 acres of James Osgood's land in 1815. Also in 1815, Peleg foreclosed on the mortgage to Joseph Howard and bought William Woodsome's property. These were not necessarily permanent sales, because owners could contest and buy back properties within two years.[220]

Of his many endeavors, the farm occupied most of Peleg's time. Two years after moving to Hiram, a "List of Rateable Polls & Estates for 1st May 1809" showed Peleg owning one dwelling house, two outbuildings, three barns, one potash,[221] one sawmill, eight acres tillable land, twenty acres mowing land, three acres meadow land, twenty acres pasture land, five thousand acres unimproved land, two oxen, six cows, no head stock three years old, one two years old, two one year old, three horses, no colts, and two swine.[222]

The same list credited Charles L. with one dwelling house, one outhouse, one barn, no potashes, one-quarter sawmill, seven acres tillable land, twenty acres mowing land, two acres meadow land, forty acres pasture land, thirteen hundred acres unimproved, and two oxen, five cows, no head stock three years old, two two years old, three one year old, two horses, one colt three years old, three swine.

At this time, Peleg and Charles owned the largest farms in Hiram, by far. The next biggest acreages of unimproved lands were owned by Joseph Durgin with 380 and John Pierce with 312. Thomas Spring had three barns but only one horse. Only William West owned more horses than Peleg. West, however, fell into poverty and as selectman, assessor, and overseer of the poor, Peleg saw to it that the town provided for the West family.

Peleg depended on horses to travel back and forth to Portland, where his wife managed the household and store before moving to Hiram. His value of the animals became clear when Daniel Coolbroth took advantage of his generous nature. Peleg loaned a horse and saddle to Coolbroth, who sold them instead of returning them. Peleg proved his wrath over the incident in a letter:

The horse you left in Vermont has returned & is worth only his skin. My black horse has got lame so that I am completely unhorsed. These accidents will prevent Ma's coming to Ordination I believe tho I could hire a Horse if she would go.

Love to the family.

P. Wadsworth

So Coolbroth[223] in Buxton where He was known universally to be a Villain. So this is not the first prank of the kind he has

---

217 Ibid.

218 Ibid.

219 1809 List of Rateables. Maine State Archives, Hiram Box 14.

220 Oxford County Registry of Deeds, Fryeburg, Book 6, 198–201.

221 Evolved from "pot ash," wood ashes seeped in water to make soap. Not a mill.

222 Maine State Archives, Hiram Box 9.

223 Daniel Coolbroth, born in 1750, served in the Revolutionary War as a private on the Massachusetts line, for which he received a pension beginning October 25, 1826. He resided in Buxton in 1810 (U.S. census) and Denmark in 1820. There is no record he resided in Hiram, nor is there a record of the result of the prosecution.

played. The purchaser must therefor know that the horse was not his property & therefore attempts to secrete him.

Hiram 4 June 1809
Dear Sir:

On Thursday before last (the day you left us) at noon I leant Daniel Coolbroth (the same ragged laboring man whom you saw here) my Hilton Horse, your saddle Bridle & Saddle bags to go to his family at Buxton & to return here again the next day. Since which he instead of returning according to promise has sold my horse etc. at Buxton & tis said has gone to Portland. The above intelligence I have just received by Mr. Phillip Page just from Buxton, also that a Mr. Palmer near bog Mills Buxton on Moderation Falls knows where the horse is secreted & ty'd in the woods for fear of a pursuit, that Doct. How of Standish has bought the saddle bags.

Charles has been in quest of the horse, man, etc. ever since last Thursday but has not returned. He may be in Portland possibly without knowing the above—to whom you will communicate this.

My request is that Mr. Longfellow[224] would institute the severest suit against Coolbroth that the case will admit of. if you find him there or elsewhere & deal with him with the utmost severity of the law, tho the Villain is not worth a cent, I will pay the cost of punishing to the utmost extent. Coolbroth if in form (& I hear he was threatened to be confined in the workhouse) will probably be drunk about the streets or at the Grog Shops with the proceeds of the horse etc.[225]

Another laborer, Edmund Eastman, took greater advantage when he stole not only a horse and saddle but money and clothing of Peleg Jr.

Farmers of that period had to be versatile and prepared for many seemingly unrelated occupations.

STOP THIEF !!!

STOLEN from the Barn of the subscriber, on the night of the 20th inst. a Chesnut Coloured MARE, five years old, with a white stripe or spot in her face, slim and round built, strikes her fore feet rather across each other and sometimes over-reaches a little and is a smart trotter, carries her head high, and nose out; her main and tale rather light, and has not been trimmed lately. Also a saddle and bridle, blue Surtout, calf-skin Boots, napt hat, port bags, spurs, red morocco Pocket Book with silver clasps, with sundry Notes, receipts,&c. in favour of Peleg Wadsworth, jr. with three or four dollars, and one silver dollar, a pair of leather Gloves marked P. Wadsworth, jr., Mittens, two penknives, &c. &c.

A youth about 18 years old, a hired labourer by the name of EDMOND EASTMAN, absconded from the House at the same time, and is supposed to be the Thief; he has black hair and black eyes, wore off a snuff-coloured short jacket, and a pair of gray mixed cloth trowsers: but the surtout will be rather long for him Whoever shall stop said Thief, Horse, &c. shall be well rewarded by
PELEG WADSWORTH.
Hiram, Feb. 21st. 1825.

Advertisement published in the Portland Advertiser *newspaper February 21, 1825. Collection of American Antiquarian Society.*

Peleg studied the science of agriculture, and in 1812 the newly formed Oxford Agricultural Society elected him a member.

The Wadsworths also produced shoes and boots. Daniel Small, a cooper on Sebago Road, kept a diary between 1821 and 1863. He mentioned going to Peleg's to buy boots for himself and his children. Among the items listed in the 1830 inventory of Peleg's estate was "soaleather" valued at 58 cents.

Peleg always needed labor for his extensive farm. He hired neighbors—Clemons, Cotton, Durgin, Huntress—and indentured servants. The contract between Peleg and fourteen-year-old orphan Sambo Foddee[226] of Portland was signed February 12, 1808, to expire when Sambo turned twenty-one. In return for labor on the Hiram farm, Peleg was to teach Sambo to read and write, supply room and board, and

---

224 Stephen Longfellow, his son-in-law, was a lawyer in Portland.

225 Maine Historical Society, Coll. 16/2 Vol. 2, CLIX, 44.

226 May also be interpreted as Lobdell, Loddee, or Toddee.

at the conclusion, two suits of clothes, one suitable for the Lord's day, and one for working.[227]

There is no further record of Sambo. Descendants of Peleg surmise he ran away—a fourteen-year-old city boy may not have relished the hard life of a rural farm. If so, he could have melted back into the black community in Portland, from which he came. In doing so he would have forfeited free room and board, his freedom after seven years, and a suit of clothing, assuming he was wearing one suit he was given.

Money Lender

With cash difficult to come by, Peleg often wrote to Charles L. asking if he had enough money and offering to bring some. Unlike most Hiram residents, Peleg had cash to spare, due to his logging enterprises, mills, and land deals.

If a settler needed money and didn't have a trade to earn income or goods or produce to sell, he had few options—he could mortgage his real property or he could borrow from the general.

Peleg made a startling number of loans, some of them lasting years, with interest. At his death, the 1830 inventory of his estate listed forty promissory notes worth $3,379.77, almost as much as the value of his real estate, $3,775. Some notes dated as far back as June 1822, some for hundreds of dollars. Some loans were dated just days before his death. Most of the borrowers were Hiram men.[228]

Illness and Death

The general fell ill with what seemed like a cold on October 17, 1829. After six days, Drs. Hannaford and Benton were called and round-the-clock watches and medications began. He died on November 12, 1829, at age 81. His daughters meticulously documented his illness. The diary reveals much about life in Hiram and medical practice at the time.

My father & I left Portland last Thursday at ¼ past 12. Stopped at Gorham a few minutes, stopped at Whitneys in Standish & got tea & we got to Fitches about 7 o'clock. Stopped there about an hour till time for the moon to rise. Got home about ½ past 9 apparently without much fatigue or cold.

Friday morning Pa appeared Smart. Rode down Side meadow & over hill. Toward night not very Smart. Saturday hoarse & had got a cold. I slept with him Saturday night. Sunday not so hoarse. Went to Meeting in PM.

Monday not so well. Rather bewildered. I sat up with him. Tuesday Dr. Hannaford[229] came in PM. Took Pills & I believe went out of doors in PM. I & Lucy sat up with him. Wednesday Dr. Benton[230] came. Miss Page sat up with him & Lucy[231] last night. Thursday quite sick, high fever—wandering. Dr. Benton & Dr. Hannaford here in AM. Thought his case very alarming. Dr. H towards night. Mr. B. Barker[232] here toward night & stayed all night. CLW's wife[233] & I sat up with him & Mr. B last night. Rested pretty well & slept considerably.

23rd Friday. a little more comfortable. Pain in lungs subsides. Drs. B & H here in morning gave more physic & dripped blisters & sat up some 30 or 40 minutes in AM.

---

227   Maine Historical Society, Coll. S-7829, Misc.

228   Appraisers were Benjamin Barker, Ephraim Kimball, and John Bucknell on May 19, 1830.

229   Levi A. Hannaford, physician in Hiram, was born in Parsonsfield March 29, 1803. He married Caroline Collins of Windham on March 4, 1829, and she gave birth to daughter Nancy McIntire December 20, 1829, five weeks after Peleg Wadsworth died. He served as Hiram town clerk and selectman, moved to Illinois in 1835 or 1837.

230   Joseph Benton, physician in Baldwin, was twenty-six when he attended the general. His grandson Albion Benton settled in the New Settlement, Hiram.

231   Probably the general's niece Lucia.

232   On December 27, 1824, Benjamin Barker married Zilpha Wadsworth, daughter of the general's brother Dura and Lydia Wadsworth.

233   Ruth Clemons, wife of the General's son Charles Lee Wadsworth.

24th Saturday. Lucy sat up last night & I tonight. Pa not so well today as yesterday, wandering part day, sleepy, just gone at 10:30 quite rational for about 10 minutes. Hickup sometimes.

25th Monday. Mr. Barker & I sat up with Pa & Miss Page ½ night. CLW here part night. Wandering most day. Hickups one hour at a time last night & today.

26th. Cousin Peleg,[234] Jane Ingalls[235] sat up part night. Pa rested pretty well thru most of the night & appears Smarter this AM & except the Hickups is quite rational this AM.

27th Lucy & her father sat up last night. Pa rested for ??? there was Mr. Cotton[236] part of the night & partly smart in the AM. Kept his bed most AM & Hickups most day. Some sharp pains at night & soarness over his body.

28th Miss Page & I sat up last night. Pa did not rest very well. Had Hickups most night. Calomel & other Physic operated in morn & PM. Feeble in AM a little Smarter in PM. Hickups most of day but not so bad toward night. The Drs. were doubtful in morning of Pa's recovery by tonight. Dr. B ???

29th Lucia & I sat up last night. Pa slept most night but not very easy. Kept his bed most day. Hickups most all night & most day.

30th CLW's wife & I sat up last night. Slept pretty well but not very Smart in AM. Slept pretty well in PM & a little better at night than in morning. Hickups most times night & day.

31st Saturday. Lucy sat up last night. Pa did not rest very well last night & not so well in AM.

Nov. 1 Sunday. I sat up with Pa last night. Rested pretty well most night. Kept his bed most day, not very Smart. The Hickups has abated considerably.

Nov. 2 Miss Page sat up with Pa last night & rested pretty well. Kept his bed most day. Hickups not so frequent.

Nov. 3 Tuesday. I sat up last night. Pa rested well part the night & part today has ???…

[Nov. 11] Theodosia Wadsworth[237] & I sat up with him the last night. He seemed to sleep considerable the first part of the night & expired without a struggle a quarter before seven in the morning Thursday the twelfth day of Nov. 1829.[238]

Peleg's symptoms point to pneumonia, specifically bacterial pneumonia,[239] which presents as high fever, coughing, shortness of breath, rapid breathing, sharp chest pains that are worse with breathing, abdominal pain, lack of appetite, severe fatigue, sweating, chills, mental confusion, and hiccups due to irritation of the nerves in the lower lobe of the lung.

Typically, doctors and patients of the period expected medical treatment to produce a reaction to the medicine to indicate the medicine was doing "something." For example, if one vomited or perspired or stopped hiccupping shortly after taking the medicine, the treatment was seen as having an effect, whether positive or negative.

Summary of Medical Treatment of General Peleg Wadsworth, October 23 to November 11, 1829

Day 1 medical treatment consisted of Dover Powder, Ammoniac & Liquorice and Pills (of unknown content). On **Day 2** a blister on his left arm was noted and Calomel, Red Pepper, Molasses water, Wine, and Columbo were added. The **next day** Rheubarb & Salts of Wormwood were included. **Day 5** saw Arrow root tea in the mix, followed by Balsam Peru on **Day 6.** Treatment was the same until Bark was added. **Next** to be tried was Ether, then Senna, and Snakeroot & Saffron. On **Sunday** 8 November Brandy and Port and a cordial every six hours was prescribed. The

---

234 Probably Peleg C. Wadsworth, son of Charles Lee, married Bethia Spring in 1821.

235 Daughter of Lt. Benjamin Ingalls, first settler in Hiram, married Charles Lee Wadsworth in 1846.

236 Probably William Cotton.

237 Theodosia Wadsworth, the daughter of Israel Burbank, was married to Peleg Wadsworth II.

238 Maine Historical Society, Coll. 16, Box 1/10.

239 Suggestion of medical historian Dr. Richard Kahn.

Wadsworth Hall Burying Ground, 2009. Brigadier General Peleg Wadsworth's grave at Wadsworth Hall in Hiram is marked by a simple slate stone to the right of the family obelisk.

On Peleg Wadsworth's gravestone is written "Sacred to the memory of Gen. Peleg Wadsworth, born at Duxbury, Mass., May 6, 1748, died Nov. 12, 1829, at 81. He was a patriot, philanthropist, and a Christian." Photo 2014.

last notation was on **November 12, 1829,** at 6:45 a.m. "Died easy."[240] The complete diary is in Appendix 20.

The General's obituary writer was effusive in summing up his life.[241]

DIED.

At Hiram, 12th ult. Gen. PELEG WADSWORTH, aged 81 years. He was born at Duxbury in Massachusetts, and was educated at Harvard University. The war of the Revolution commencing soon after he graduated, he took an active and zealous part in that contest, and distinguished himself as an officer. After the peace he removed to Portland. He represented the town several years in the General Court of Massachusettts, and filled many other important offices in the town. When Cumberland District was formed he was chosen Representative in Congress, and continued in that station for many years, the duties of which he performed with great fidelity. In 1807 he removed to his farm in Hiram, where he resided till his death.

---

240 Maine Historical Society, Coll. 16, Box 1/10.

241 *Portland Advertiser and Gazetter of Maine (*Portland, ME), December 1, 1829, 2. In *America's Historical Newspapers* database, Readex, a Division of Newsbank (Naples, FL).

No person ever possessed a more kind and benevolent disposition—and he delighted in promoting the happiness of those around him. The cause of Religion, and the education of the rising generation engaged much of his attention, and constituted much of his happiness. Relying on the mercies of the Redeemer, his death was as calm and peaceful, as his life was active, useful and benevolent. 'Blessed are the dead that die in the Lord.'

Will and Inventory of Peleg Wadsworth's Estate

Though ill, Peleg Wadsworth signed his will on November 11, 1829, the day before he died.[242]

He bequeathed the house in Portland that the Longfellows occupied to Zilpha Wadsworth Longfellow and her unmarried sister Lucia, "with all the privileges & appurtenances thereunto belonging in common & undivided, with the rent that is unpaid." To son Alexander Scammel he left a house lot in Portland he had purchased from William Vaughan. Another house lot in Portland, bought of William Gorham, was left to the sons of his son Samuel B. Wadsworth. Samuel, who operated a store in Eastport, Maine, was not included.

To Peleg Jr., he left "the home farm with all the stock, household furniture & everything appertaining thereto including builds etc." and some additional land, except the part of the Bucknell lot sold to the Town of Hiram for the Town House.

To son Charles Lee, Peleg left a tract of land adjacent to that of Charles L. Frank Wadsworth, son of Charles Lee, received Lot No. 3 of the fourth range, excepting the pine timber. Peleg divided the mill property and pine timber among his five sons (Charles Lee, John, Alexander Scammel, and Samuel Bartlett, but gave Samuel Bartlett's share to Samuel's children and Peleg Jr.). Alexander Scammel and the children of Samuel Bartlett received half of the remainder of his land in Hiram and Brownfield that was part of the Wadsworth Grant.

Inventory of the Portland Property

An inventory of the Portland property signed April 22, 1830, valued the Longfellow house at $5,000, Alexander's lot at $50, and the children of Samuel Wadsworth's lot on Washington Street at $100, for a total of $5150.[243]

Inventory of the Hiram Estate

A committee to appraise the inventory of the Hiram estate was appointed on May 19, 1830, and completed May 22. On the committee were Benjamin Barker, Ephraim Kimball, and John Bucknell, all of Hiram. The inventory consisted of three parts: Real Estate; Personal Estate and Notes, Cash on Hand; and Additions to the above demands.[244]

Real Property

Peleg's real property consisted of acreage on the Wadsworth Grant, Cutler's Grant, and the borders of Middle Pond, and saw and gristmills in Brownfield. The combined properties were worth $3,775.

Personal Estate

1 horse & chaise	$100
31536 feet of boards 2 $3 per M	94.60
2600 R.O. Hhhd Stves 2 $4 per M	10.40
17 ¾ yds of mill cloth @ 3/	8.87
3 ½ Hs soaleather @ 1/	.58
300 of white & hard pine logs in the Ten Mile Brook	150.00
A small lot of oak planks	1.00
Total	$365.45

The full will and inventory appears in Appendix 22.

The General's One-Horse Chaise

People who bought some of his possessions revered them. Two examples are Peleg's one-horse chaise and his sleigh. Collector Charles Soden, proprietor of The Hayloft, an antiques treasure house in Naples, Maine, purchased the two-wheeled pleasure carriage,

---

242 Maine Historical Society, Coll. 16, Box 2/4.

243 Maine Historical Society, Coll. 16, Box 2/4.

244 Ibid.

Peleg Wadsworth's one-horse chaise in the Peterborough, New Hampshire, bicentennial parade in 1939 was driven by Drs. Morse and Cutler. Courtesy of Goyette Museum.

and it became one of his prized possessions. When his widow closed the museum and auctioned the contents in 1936, Maj. A. Erland Goyette, president of the First National Bank of Peterborough, New Hampshire, after coveting it for many years, realized his dream and purchased the shay for his transportation museum for $80. He located Wadsworth descendants and Portland's *Sunday Telegram* published interviews of their recollections.[245] According to the paper, Mrs. John B. Pike [Cora Hubbard] and Mrs. James Maclaren [Minnie Hubbard], granddaughters of Peleg Wadsworth Jr., Mr. and Mrs. Clarence Douglas [Margaret Pike] and three children lived at Wadsworth Hall at the time. Margaret Pike Douglas was the daughter of Cora Hubbard Pike. The children born later [Kathleen, Mary, John, Susan] were the sixth generation that lived at the Hall. The seventh generation is Margaret, James, Nathan, and Amy.

From the *Sunday Telegram:*

Mrs. Pike cannot recall seeing the old one-horse chaise but does remember hearing her grandmother [Lusannah Wadsworth Hubbard] tell about a visit she made with her father-in-law, the senior general, to Duxbury, Mass. going in the old chaise.

Mrs. Davis [Frances (Wadsworth) Rounds] is the oldest living person raised on the old farm, she being of the fourth generation. Upon being asked if she remembered the old chaise she replied, "Oh yes, I always rode to church in it on Sundays. My mother died when I was very young and my grandparents, Gen.[Peleg Jr.] and Mrs. [Lusannah] Wadsworth Jr. brought me up. I used to ride on a cushion between them.[246]

---

245   Special Dispatch to the *Sunday Telegram*, Portland, ME, August 23, 1936.
246   Ibid.

The Goyette Museum closed in September 1977, and contents were auctioned, buyers unknown.

Fifty-Nine years after he died, the general was remembered in daily observations. A comment about the general's sleigh:

> Hiram, Feb. 11, 1888 (E)—Dr. Charles E. Wilson has recently been riding in a sleigh of the half moon style that Gen. Peleg Wadsworth, of Revolutionary fame, brought from Duxbury, Mass., in 1784. It remained in his possession till his death in 1829. His youngest son preserved it till his death in 1875. It is still in a good state of preservation, having been made equally sound and substantial in every part... Llewellyn.[247]

This half moon sleigh is similar to one Peleg Wadsworth owned. Courtesy of 19th Century Willowbrook Museum, Newfield, Maine (now called 19th Century Curran Village at Newfield).

The general was particular on how his sleigh should look. He wrote to son George from Philadelphia on December 15, 1798, directing that the "sley should have green Baize curtains on all sides," repeating and adding on December 20 that George, age ten, should enjoy riding in it and be careful to avoid being stepped on by the horse.[248]

---

247   Llewellyn Wadsworth, *Oxford County Advertiser* (Norway & Paris, Maine), February 11, 1888.
248   Letters to George, Maine Historical Society, Coll. 2378.

CAPT. CHARLES LEE WADSWORTH

January 26, 1776–September 29, 1848

First marriage October 9, 1795

Ruth Clemons, May 27, 1772–January 1, 1839

Second marriage November 19, 1846

Jane Ingalls, June 2, 1781–March 28, 1847

Though a prominent Hiram citizen by his own merits, Capt. Charles Lee Wadsworth is overshadowed in history by his father, Brigadier General Peleg Wadsworth. Charles came to Hiram from Portland in 1795, nineteen years old and newly married in Fryeburg to Ruth Clemons. Peleg gave Charles five hundred acres adjacent to his own farm, making father and son the largest landowners and farmers in Hiram. Both built large estates and were taxed heavily.

Capt. Charles Lee Wadsworth House

Imposing is the view from the site of Capt. Samuel Wadsworth's home, on the Mountain Road, about a mile to the west of Wadsworth Hall. What a delightful situation! From this vantage point the Saddleback Mountains of Baldwin stand out in all their grandeur. A tumbledown outbuilding, caved-in cellars, covered wells, and the remains of a burying ground are all that are left of the old homestead, once the prize of the countryside. The spacious mansion was built in 1795 by Gen. Peleg Wadsworth

The Capt. Charles L. Wadsworth house, built in 1795, sited above Wadsworth Hall on Mountain Road, no longer exists.

for his son, Capt. Charles Lee Wadsworth, subsequently becoming the property of the latter's son and grandson, Capt. Samuel Wadsworth and Arthur Wadsworth. Arthur established himself later in South Hiram.[249]

In 1806, before Peleg retired to Hiram, Charles's highway tax was $52.09—making him the most heavily taxed man in Hiram; the next highest was innkeeper Thomas Spring at $16.58. Considering those working on the roads received pennies per day in tax deductions, these were steep amounts.

Road Building

Road building and maintenance were high priorities. In 1800, men from all thirty-four families in Hiram were kept busy laying out and maintaining roads on their farms, work that reduced their taxes.

Charles Lee Wadsworth served as surveyor of highways in several years between 1807[250] and 1828. Surveyors of highways were elected to recruit workers in their respective districts, keep accurate records of hours worked, and collect the highway taxes.

Finding enough men to work on the roads must have been time consuming, even with the incentive of trading work for taxes. When Charles Lee was a surveyor of highways in 1807, there were only three names beside his on his list: neighbors Peleg Wadsworth, Ely Clemmonds (Eli Pope Clemons), and John Rounds. The distance covered was well over two miles, most of it on mountain terrain. This was time consuming and hard labor for four men.

The highway tax was composed of poll tax, real estate tax, and personal property tax. In 1807, the highway taxes of Peleg and Charles Lee Wadsworth

---

249 William Teg, *Hiram* (Cornish, ME: Carbrook Press, 1941), 61.

250 He may have served as surveyor in prior years, but records are incomplete.

View of Capt. Charles L. Wadsworth house. It fell into disrepair under ownership of son Capt. Samuel Wadsworth and grandson Arthur Wadsworth.

consisted of all the elements, Peleg paying $49.68 and Charles Lee paying $16.36. Clemons and Rounds paid only the poll tax of $2.16. The poll tax was a "head" tax levied on all and needed to be paid in order to vote. Paying only a poll tax indicates Eli Clemons and John Rounds did not own property, but had residency in Hiram.[251] It is unknown how long John Rounds stayed in Hiram and worked on roads. He does not appear on further tax lists. Eli Clemons, however, remained in Hiram, acquired property, and hence paid a higher tax.

Charles' highway tax list of 1809 jumped to ten residents and four nonresidents. The number of surveyors rose, also. There was a steady increase from six in 1807 to eleven in 1820, seventeen in 1825, and twenty-five in 1830, which reflected the rapid population growth of the period.

Community service

Like his father, Charles Lee was entrepreneurial, active in the community, and gaining logging and building experience. It is said he built the first bridge over the Saco River in 1805 with joiner[252] John Ayer. An honest man who could judge the quality and ensure standards of cut boards, Charles served as surveyor of lumber in 1807. In 1812 he served on the Committee for Bridge Repairs.

Charles served as clerk of Hiram in 1805 and perhaps longer. The clerk kept the official records and recorded the actions of Town Meetings. As a member of the Committee on Accounts in 1812, 1813, and 1816, he helped approve reimbursements to individuals for services. He also served with the local militia, which elected him captain, making him responsible for training his men at musters. Mustering, or training,

---

251   Highway tax 1807, Maine State Archives, Hiram Box 14.

252   A joiner is one who fitted posts and beams together.

took place in Fryeburg, Brownfield, and Denmark, and, in inclement weather, inside Wadsworth Hall. Securing ammunition (good powder and blank cartridges) was difficult and frequently involved travel to Cornish, Portland, and elsewhere. Charles Lee served eight years before requesting a discharge in 1830 for reasons of "hard times and ill health." He left service with the militia having achieved the rank of lieutenant colonel.

Though well off, Charles, like many others, considered resettling westward. In 1819, his brother John wrote him in an attempt to entice him to upstate New York "south of the large lakes," Geneva or Canandaiga, rather than Ohio or Illinois.[253] Charles didn't leave, but other settlers tried their luck out west. John Clemons Jr. took his family to New York in 1804 and to Ohio in 1817. As the trend continued, town historian Llewellyn A. Wadsworth bemoaned the loss of population in his journals written in the 1870s.

Like his father, Charles valued education. He sent eight children to school in 1813 and in 1819 served as school agent and class master for the twelve students in his district (No. 3).

Perhaps Charles's most well-known act was in helping to name Hiram. According to legend, Freemasons Peleg Wadsworth, Charles Lee Wadsworth, and Timothy Cutler[254] flipped a coin to decide if Hiram was to be named for Hiram Abiff, a central character in an allegory passed down in Masonic lodges, or Hiram, King of Tyre, a biblical king who also plays a part in the Masonic allegory. It was decided in favor of Hiram, King of Tyre.

Of "Captain Charlie" many quaint stories are told. He was an owner of extensive timberland and rode a mule on his excursions among the lumbermen. One night this animal carried him safely over the Saco on a bridge stringer; an event the rider did not know of until the following day when the workmen making repairs discovered the print of the shoe-caulks in the stringer.[255]

The fact that he did not remember may indicate he was slightly inebriated. Then, too, nights were dark—the first lamps on the covered bridge were lit in 1889,[256] long after Charles Lee rode his mule on it.

Charles Lee fathered eleven children in Hiram. First-born was Betsey (December 26, 1795). She married Henry W. Barnes of Hiram in a ceremony performed by the general. Next was Peleg Clemons Wadsworth (April 26, 1797), who married first Bethiah Spring and second Mary Richardson. He fathered nine children with each wife. John (December 2, 1798) married Mary Benton, West Baldwin, daughter of Dr. Joseph Benton, who attended the general during his fatal illness. Col. Charles (January 20, 1800) married Sarah Lewis. Col. Charles and Sarah's youngest, Llewellyn A. Wadsworth, a poet, essayist, and civil servant, was Hiram town historian, whose journals and records are much valued today. Jane (May 29, 1801) became the second wife of pioneer Benjamin Ingalls. Lucia (December 13, 1802) married Edmund Butterfield, and as a widow worked with her uncle, John Wadsworth, at Wadsworth Hall reeling silk. She received state bonuses in 1848 and 1849. This was an interesting find because it was supposed the silk industry collapsed after a severe winter in 1844. Child number seven was Henry (born November 3, 1804) who married first Mary Ann Wentworth and second her sister Catherine S. Wentworth. Alexander (May 6, 1806) became a noted landscape architect in Boston. Frank (June 29, 1808) married Mary Ingalls. Eli (February 7, 1811) married Mary Chaney. The youngest, Capt. Samuel (May 19, 1815), married Jane Clemons. When Charles died in 1848, age seventy-two, he left a large family of whom four sons settled in Hiram. Alexander was a son that left.

---

253   Letter of December 28, 1819, Maine Historical Society Coll. 16/6.

254   There is no record that Timothy Cutler was a member of the Masons, but many in Hiram were. There is no record of who tossed the coin or how many times it was flipped. It would be reasonable for only the two grant holders, Peleg and Timothy, to have flipped the coin.

255   Ridlon, *Saco Valley Settlements and Families*, 149.

256   Lamps were lit by Marshall Spring, who was paid seven cents per night.

Alexander Wadsworth (1806–1898)

Born in Hiram, Maine, Wadsworth studied civil engineering at the Gardiner Lyceum. In 1825, he obtained a job in Boston as a landscape surveyor where he established a reputation through his work on Washington Square in Lowell and Mount Auburn Cemetery in Cambridge, both in 1831. During the fall of that year, Wadsworth was hired by the Garden and Cemetery Committee as its civil engineer. Shortly thereafter he began work on a topographic survey plan for Mount Auburn Cemetery, collaborating with Henry A.S. Dearborn. Wadsworth and Dearborn's Picturesque plan would be the first of its kind in the United States and a model for other rural garden cemeteries. Wadsworth continued to work on plans for Picturesque cemeteries, parks, and suburbs including the cemetery at Harmony Grove, Salem; Auburn Park, Newton; Pemberton Square, Boston; and the suburbs of Roxbury and Malden Highlands.[257]

Llewellyn A. Wadsworth (1838-1922) was a distinguished son of Col. Charles Wadsworth and Sarah L. Lewis and grandson of Charles L. Wadsworth. Llewellyn was a poet and essayist, and, as town historian during Hiram's centennial celebrations in 1914, he wrote a brief history of Hiram that was published in the Centennial program. He was a founder of Soldiers Memorial Library, built in 1915, a trial justice, a representative in the Maine State Legislature, a town selectman, and a superintendent of schools. He and his wife, Annette Clemons Wadsworth, owned Mt. View Farm, a guest house on Wadsworth Road, off Hiram Hill Road,[258] which burned in 1916. Subsequently they moved to the adjacent John Spring farm. His son Eli lived there with his son Paul and wife, Ada Cram Wadsworth, until it, too, burned, in 1947.

Town Offices Held by the Wadsworth Family

Agent to Defend Town vs. Bad Roads
1815	Peleg Wadsworth

Clerk
1805	Charles Wadsworth
1827	Peleg Wadsworth Jr.

Committee on Accounts
1806	Peleg Wadsworth
1807	Peleg Wadsworth
1812	Charles L. Wadsworth
1813	Charles L. Wadsworth
1816	Charles L. Wadsworth
1817	Charles L. Wadsworth
1820	Peleg Wadsworth Esq.
1824	Charles L. Wadsworth
1827	Charles L. Wadsworth (voted to excuse C. L. Wadsworth, chose Alpheus Spring)

Committees on bridge building and repairs
1812	Saco River: Charles L. Wadsworth
1822	Saco River repair: Charles L. Wadsworth agent
1823	Ossipee River build: Charles L. Wadsworth, Peleg Wadsworth Esq.
1824	Ossipee River repair: Charles L. Wadsworth
1826	All bridges: Peleg Wadsworth Jr. agent to view

Committee on a Plan for a Town House
1816	Peleg Wadsworth

Fence Viewers
1816	Charles L. Wadsworth
1828	Peleg Wadsworth Jr.

---

257 "Alexander Wadsworth," *Cultural Landscape Foundation*, 2001–2015, http://tclf.org/pioneer/alexander-wadsworth.

258 Earlier called Howard Lane.

Hog Reeves

1811	Peleg Wadsworth
1822	Seth Wadsworth,
	Peleg C. Wadsworth

Justices of the Peace (incomplete list)

1809	Peleg Wadsworth
1810	Peleg Wadsworth
1813 or 1814	Peleg Wadsworth
1815	Peleg Wadsworth
1821	Peleg Wadsworth
1822	Peleg Wadsworth
1824	Peleg Wadsworth
1825	Peleg Wadsworth
1827	Peleg Wadsworth
1828	Peleg Wadsworth

School Agents

1819	Charles L. Wadsworth District #3
1820	Charles L. Wadsworth #3
1821	Charles L. Wadsworth #3
1822	Charles L. Wadsworth #3
1823	Peleg Wadsworth Jr. #3,
	Peleg Wadsworth #8
1824	Peleg Wadsworth Jr. #3,
	Peleg C. Wadsworth #8
1825	Peleg Wadsworth J.,
	Peleg C. Wadsworth,
	Charles Wadsworth
1826	Peleg Wadsworth Jr.,
	Peleg C. Wadsworth,
	Charles Wadsworth
1827	Peleg Wadsworth Jr.,
	John Wadsworth,
	Charles Wadsworth
1828	Peleg Wadsworth Jr.
1829	Peleg Wadsworth Jr. #3,
	John Wadsworth #10
1830	Peleg Wadsworth,
	Peleg C. Wadsworth

School Committees

1816	A committee of 3 was chosen instead of an additional school agent. Chose Peleg Wadsworth, Alpheus Spring, John Pierce
1817	Selectmen: Peleg Wadsworth Esq.

1818	Selectmen: Peleg Wadsworth Esq.
1823	Peleg Wadsworth Jr.
1824	Peleg Wadsworth Jr.
1825	Peleg Wadsworth Jr.
1826	Peleg Wadsworth Jr.
1827	Peleg Wadsworth Jr.
1828	Peleg Wadsworth Jr.
1829	Peleg Wadsworth Jr.
1830	Peleg Wadsworth

School Teachers

1805	Peleg Wadsworth Jr.
1819	Charles L. Wadsworth District #3

Sealer of Leather

1827	Peleg Wadsworth 3rd
1828	Peleg Wadsworth 3rd

Selectmen

1805	Charles Wadsworth
1808	Peleg Wadsworth
1809	Peleg Wadsworth
1812	Peleg Wadsworth
1813	Peleg Wadsworth
1814	Peleg Wadsworth
1815	Peleg Wadsworth
1817	Peleg Wadsworth Esq.
1818	Peleg Wadsworth Esq.
1821	Peleg Wadsworth Jr.

Surveyors of Wood & Bark

1827?	Samuel D. Wadsworth

Surveyors of Highways

1807	Charles L. Wadsworth
1808	Charles L. Wadsworth
1809	Charles L. Wadsworth
1813	Charles L. Wadsworth
1814	no record
1815	Charles L. Wadsworth
1816	Charles L. Wadsworth
1817	Charles L. Wadsworth
1818	Charles L. Wadsworth
1819	Charles L. Wadsworth
1820	Peleg Wadsworth Jr.
1821	Dura Wadsworth
1822	Peleg Wadsworth Jun.

1823	Peleg Wadsworth Jr.
1824	Peleg Wadsworth Jr.
1825	Peleg Wadsworth Jr., John Wadsworth
1826	Peleg Wadsworth Jr., John Wadsworth
1827	Peleg Wadsworth Jr., John Wadsworth (voted to excuse)
1828	Peleg Wadsworth Jr., Charles Wadsworth
1829	Peleg Wadsworth Jr., John Wadsworth, Peleg C. Wadsworth
1830	Charles Wadsworth, John Wadsworth (voted to excuse), Peleg C. Wadsworth

Tithingmen

1811	Peleg Wadsworth
1825	Dura Wadsworth
1826	Dura Wadsworth

Treasurers

1808	Peleg Wadsworth
1812	Peleg Wadsworth
1813	Peleg Wadsworth
1814	Peleg Wadsworth
1815	Peleg Wadsworth
1816	Peleg Wadsworth
1817	Peleg Wadsworth
1818	Peleg Wadsworth
1821–1830	Peleg Wadsworth Jr.

JOSEPH ADAMS
September 21, 1774–1858

First marriage April 12, 1802
Mercy Elwell of Gorham
April 16, 1780–?
Second marriage September 21, 1821
Dorothy L. Warren
February 18, 1784–August 10, 1844

Hiram historian Dr. William Teg wrote, "Joseph Adams, a native of Buxton, moved into Hiram in 1822, settling on the Waters Grant."[259] If Teg had consulted Hiram Plantation records or Oxford County deed records he would have learned that Joseph Adams settled in Hiram well before 1822.

Joseph paid a highway tax in 1806, and was on the list of eligible voters in 1809, 1810, and 1811. The 1809 List of Rateables, an inventory of property to be taxed, showed him to be prosperous, with property of two hundred acres, double that of the typical lot. He was listed with one poll (the compulsory "head" tax), one dwelling house, two barns, two tillable acres, twenty acres mowing land, ten acres pasturage land, 168 acres unimproved land, three oxen, four cows, two cattle two years old, two cattle one year old, one horse, and two swine. He had strong ties to Gorham and married his first wife there. In 1821 he married Dorothy Warren, daughter of Col. Nathaniel Warren, popular Revolutionary War soldier, who, according to Teg, settled on the Waters Grant in 1813.[260]

Oddly, the next early record of Joseph dates to 1830, when he was included in the U.S. census. In 1838 he was a school agent for District 7. Where was he in between these dates? He is not on the list for the bridge tax in 1815 and he does not appear on voting lists after 1811. According to the 1820 census, there were fourteen Joseph Adamses in Maine. Was he the Joseph Adams in Gorham, the hometown of his wife and where his oldest son, Nathaniel W. Adams, was born in 1822?

In the 1850 census Joseph is seventy-eight years

Nathaniel W. Adams may have built this blacksmith shop before it was named Apple Acres, 363 Durgintown Road. Photo 2019.

old and living in Hiram with his son Nathaniel W. Adams (age twenty-seven), Eliza Adams (twenty-five), Rebeckah Adams (forty), Mercy Adams (twenty-three) and Prisilla [sic] Adams (one month). Joseph died in Hiram in 1858.

Joseph's oldest son, Nathaniel W. Adams, became an important man in Hiram. After marrying Eliza K. Chadbourne, he went on to own the largest apple orchard in Hiram[261] (on Durgintown Road where Apple Acres is today). Nathaniel was an enterprising man in a thriving time. In addition to the orchard, he and Joseph D. Lord owned a mill between the old Porter road and Ossipee River, which was still operating the year before he died in 1908.[262]

Nathaniel and Eliza had three children: "Stephen Adams, who settled on the Durgin Grant; Orison Adams, who settled on the Waters Grant; and Priscilla

---

259   William Teg, *History of Hiram, Maine, Sesquicentennial Edition* (Cornish, ME: Carrbrook Press, 1964), 55.

260   Ibid, 55.

261   Ibid., 55.

262   Mitchell, Davis and Daggett, *The Town Register: Brownfield, Denmark, Hiram and Porter* (Brunswick, ME: H. E. Mitchell Co., 1907), 94.

Workers boxing apples at Pendexter's, Hiram, 1941. Photo by George French. Courtesy of Maine State Archives.

*Apple Acres orchard, 1944, owned by H. Granville, at present owned by the William Johnson family.
Photo by George W. French of Kezar Falls (1882–1970), photographer of the Maine Development
Commission, 1936–1955. The house and barn burned in 1981. Courtesy of Maine State Archives.*

The name Apple Acres is identified by the sign on the truck in this photo of the crew in 1944. From the back of the photo: Harry Granville, Marie Granville, Alma McInnis, Louella McInnis, Beverly Granville, Steve Lajoie, Arlene Gilmore, Harvey Pendexter, Bertha Cousins? Photo by George French. Courtesy of Maine State Archives.

Adams, a highly gifted school teacher, who remained with her parents."[263] Read more about her in the chapter on Schools.

Obituary of Nathaniel Warren Adams

From the *Oxford Democrat*, Paris, Maine, 12 May 1908:

Friday afternoon, April 24, the long and useful life of Nathaniel Warren Adams came to a peaceful end. He had been ill for 6 days with pneumonia. His age was 85 years, 6 months and 17 days. He was the last survivor of 13 children. He leaves an aged and devoted wife. Miss Priscilla Adams, his only daughter, graduated from Gorham Normal School and for many years was one of the most successful teachers in Hiram. Even a dull pupil could be stimulated by her energy and enthusiasm and people in our own and other towns will remember with gratitude her patience and devotion, as well as her admirable ability as a teacher, but for about 12 years she has been suffering with an incurable mental disease.[264] Mr. Adams resided with his two sons, Orison W. and Stephen J. Adams, on the old home place settled by their grandfather, Joseph Adams. Internment was at Cornish Cemetery. Llewellyn A. Wadsworth, Hiram

---

263 William Teg, *History of Hiram: Sesquicentennial Edition* (Cornish, ME: Carbrook Press, 1964), 55.

264 Priscilla Adams was born in 1850 and died in 1924, suffering mental disease for 28 years.

JOHN AYER

March 27, 1727–1812

Married November 18, 1767

Elizabeth Pike, October 2, 1748–?

John Ayer was the son of Lt. Ebenezer and Susannah Kimball Ayer, born in the part of Methuen, Massachusetts, that is now Salem. The family relocated to Pepperellborough, Maine (now Saco). His father fought with Lovewell at Pequawket (Fryeburg), the disastrous Indian fight in 1725. John married Elizabeth Pike of Salisbury, Massachusetts, who bore him twelve children: Sarah, Timothy, Elizabeth, Humphrey, John Pike, Jacob, Mary (died young), Anne, Nancy, Susan, Hannah, and Lydia.

John purchased property in Standish in 1770, and in 1777 he and Elizabeth were members of the Congregational Church there. The house they lived in is no longer standing—it is dust on the Randall Apple Orchard in Standish, at the corner of Route 25 and Randall Road—but part of the house they bought in Hiram still stands.

In April 1782, Ayer purchased one hundred acres from John Curtis, one of the surveyors of Hiram in 1774. The property included a house and barn, a fact that became important later.

Ayer held the first Christian religious services in Hiram in this house. "John Ayer was evidently of strong religious convictions, for he is spoken of by historians of the period as an exhorter and itinerant preacher."[265] In early property deeds he listed his occupation as "joiner,"—a timber framer who cuts the mortise and tenon that joins a post and beam without the use of nails, screws, or other metal fasteners. Above his house, about 1785, he built the first mill in Hiram, a gristmill on Thirteen Mile Brook, so named because it was thirteen miles from Fryeburg (now called Red Mill Brook after a later mill built below Ayer's). With Captain Charles L. Wadsworth, he built the first bridge over the Saco River in Hiram in 1805. Prior to this, travelers crossed the Saco River on Ingalls Ferry.

Ayer sold the property to his second son, Humphrey, in 1797 and moved to Cornish, as did

Brookside Farm, 6 Hiram Hill Road, 2012. Part of the house is the oldest known structure in Hiram. The part built between 1774 and 1781 is the side door with side lights and two windows in what was a single-story Cape facing south (left of the two-story Cape facing Pequawket Trail). The second-story shed was added prior to 1894 and has not changed much.

Humphrey. Two years later, Humphrey sold the farm to his brother-in-law Thomas Barker, husband of the Ayer's eldest child, Sarah (Sally) Ayer.

Brookside Farm has seen many owners. Among them in the nineteenth century was Dura Wadsworth, brother of Peleg Wadsworth, and in the twentieth, Joseph Rankins Jr., Frank and Estelle Merrifield, who bought it after their house was burned in the 1947 wildfires, and Doris Lombard, a dealer who sold antiques in the barn.

The property has an interesting history of ownership. The first owner was John Curtis. A letter written by Lt. Benjamin Ingalls on August 5, 1774, describing his surveying expedition to Great Ossipee, as Hiram was first known, indicated they laid out lots for Ingalls himself, Ebenezer Herrick, Daniel Foster, Abiel Messer, and John Curtis. The earliest deeds

---

265 George Thomas Little, *Genealogical and Family History of the State of Maine* (New York: Lewis Historical Publishing Company, 1909), 1053.

Brookside Farm, 1894, when it was owned by Caleb Clemons. Pictured are Anna Clemons, Ella Clemons, and Mame Clemons with children Lillian and Sumner Durgin. Ella Clemons Butterfield owned it in 1930 in a property trade with Anna Lowell.

found are dated 1782. In April of that year, John Ayer of Pearsontown (now Standish) purchased one hundred acres with a house and barn from John Curtis for 150 pounds. Earlier, in February, he had purchased from Eliphalet and Martha Danforth one hundred acres with a dwelling house and barn, south of the Curtis lot, for 102 pounds. Later in July he bought one hundred acres of land from John Lane, north of the Curtis lot, for 60 pounds. The lots were adjacent along the Saco River, part of a group called "Settlers' Lots." Ayer settled on the Curtis lot. Llewellyn Wadsworth, town historian, noted that "John Curtis had a similar lot, extending from the place where Samuel L. Clemons now lives, by Red Mill brook to a point opposite of Hancock brook."[266] Hiram Historical Society members confirmed that Clemons had lived across the street from Brookside Farm, placing it on the Curtis lot described as

bordering the lot of John Lane, closer to Brownfield to the north. No, Samuel L. Clemons was not Mark Twain (he worked on the railroad that passed near his house), but he was related distantly.

Although John Ayer held deeds to properties dated February and April 1782, in November 1787, the Massachusetts Court awarded a grant to Timothy Cutler that included Ayer's. Because Ayer could prove he had settled before the cut-off date of January 1, 1784, he petitioned for title to four hundred acres[267] and was deeded title to two hundred on March 10, 1791. Ayer paid a small fee of 3 pounds 2 shillings, but lost one hundred acres, if the registered deeds are correct, or two hundred acres if the notation on the petition of men who settled before January 1, 1784, is correct.

Cutler still desired the property and two months after Ayer received title, Ayer sold fourteen

---

266   Llewellyn A. Wadsworth, *Centennial, Hiram, Maine, 1814-1914* (Cornish, ME: Webb-Smith Printing Co., 1914).

267   Deeds for three hundred acres, not four as petitioned, were recorded in York County Registry of Deeds, Alfred, copied for Oxford County Registry of Deeds, Fryeburg, now in Paris.

acres of the Danforth lot at the Bridge to Timothy Cutler, where Cutler built his house (now 1608 Pequawket Trail).

Ayer continued to sell pieces of his property. On February 21, 1793, he sold to John Burbank of Brownfield and Stephen Burbank of Flintstown (Baldwin) forty acres "of the Danford [Danforth] lot that John Burbank, Junr improved" for 40 pounds. Research by Joan and Roger Brown proved this was the property of J. L. Clemons, indicated on the 1858 map of Hiram, and Eli Clemons on the 1880 map.

As if the situation wasn't complicated enough, the deed giving Ayer title to two hundred acres also included Joseph Bean, who was allowed one hundred acres for the fee of 1 pound 11 shillings. Who was Joseph Bean? Where was his property? Why was he included on the deed? Other deeds settled the question of location, but not the reason. A deed of October 25, 1815, conveying from Bean to Daniel Gibson,[268] states that the property is "the same as laid out agreeable to the General Court on July 24, 1789 duly executed to Timothy Cutler, containing 75 acres more or less, and is the farm I [Bean] live on" in Brownfield in Cutler's Upper Grant that Cutler called "Happy Valley." What was earlier "Happy Valley" is presently in the center of Brownfield.[269]

Brookside Farm, 2009.

---

268 The Gibson Farm was on the Little Saco River near the Fryeburg line.

269 Larry Glatz, letter to the author, September 24, 2009.

BARKER FAMILY

Thomas Barker
1766–July 25, 1819

Married June 22, 1789

Sarah Pike Ayer, 1768–January 27, 1825

Founders left Hiram for many reasons—cheaper land elsewhere, pioneer adventure farther west, better mercantile prospects on Maine's seacoast, or to be cared for by their children in old age, to mention a few. In his move to Portland after nearly thirty years of accumulating wealth and prestige in Hiram, Thomas Barker was able to ensure educational opportunities not available in Hiram for eleven of his twelve children still at home, especially for his young daughters.

Thomas Barker in Hiram

Thomas Barker, from Cornish, was already farming in Hiram in 1789, the year he married Sarah Ayer and purchased two one hundred–acre lots in Cutler's Lower Grant on Hiram Hill.[270] He continued to buy, sell, and mortgage land in Cornish, Baldwin, and Hiram between 1792 and 1815, some with his brother Noah Barker and some with his brother-in-law Humphrey Ayer. He identified himself as yeoman or trader, but in 1799, when he purchased the property of John and Elizabeth Ayer, his wife's parents, his occupation was innkeeper.[271] By 1806 he was the third largest landowner in Hiram.[272] In that year he took out a mortgage for $2,100, a great deal of money, and he paid it back a year later. Perhaps it funded the dam he built on the pond in 1807, for which he is remembered.

The split stone dam was on the outlet of one of several ponds named Hancock Pond (so called because they were all fed by Hancock Brook), and it became known as Barker Pond.[273] The purpose of the dam was to raise the water level to float logs down the brook to his mill and to the Saco River.

Llewellyn A. Wadsworth credits Thomas with building a mill "nearby," and Josiah Mayberry with tending the gristmill.[274] At the time, the mill was in Baldwin.

Thomas was active in town affairs before he built his mill and dam. He was elected collector of taxes/constable in 1804, a member of the Committee on Accounts in 1806, and selectman in 1804 and 1805.

But the mill and dam must have taken up his time. Siting the mill on Hancock Brook was prescient—harnessing the brook was profitable because fees could be charged. The Proprietors of Hancock Brook Canal thought so, too, and incorporated February 26, 1811, to do so. The group completed twenty-two dams and slips in 1825, for which it charged tolls, one of which was eight cents for each mill log floated down the brook to the Saco River.[275] Thomas was not an investor and did not profit from it as he had moved to Portland and had died by then. The dam, however, was still operating when the 1867 survey of water power in Maine was conducted, in which it was noted that nine of the twenty-five actual and potential water-power sources in Hiram were on Hancock Brook.[276]

The prospect of Hancock Brook Canal siphoning Thomas Barker's dam and mill business may have contributed to his decision to leave Hiram. Thomas, a man of wealth in Hiram, also may have desired opportunities only a city could bring for his

---

270   One one–hundred–acre lot adjoined Daniel Baston's (lot 10), and the other one hundred–acre lot adjoined "the same where said Thomas has his corn planted." Oxford County Registry of Deeds, Fryeburg, Book 51, 277A.

271   Ibid., Book 1, 15. It may have been the first inn in Hiram. Where was it?

272   His property tax portion of the highway tax was $9.80, compared with that of Charles L. Wadsworth ($50.52) and Thomas Spring ($13.44).

273   The earliest name of Hancock Pond was "Gotts Ponds." Llewellyn A. Wadsworth, Journal, November 17, 1870.

274   Llewellyn A. Wadsworth, Journal, November 17, 1870. Was this the sawmill later owned by the Rankins of Wards Hill Road, Baldwin, who were annexed to Hiram in 1822 by petition to the legislature?

275   Approved by the governor of Massachusetts, February 23, 1818.

276   Walter Wells, *The Water-Power of Maine* (Augusta, ME: Sprague, Owen & Nash, 1868), 158.

Barker Lake Dam, 1931 postcard. In 1867, the head and fall of the original was over eight feet. The present dam is less high.

Barker Pond dam, 2014.

large family. The twelve surviving Barker children were born in Hiram and Cornish between 1790 and 1811. Sometime in 1815, when the youngest was nearly four, the family moved to Portland. Possibly this occurred in February 1815, when Thomas sold his homestead farm[277] to Daniel Fox. By April

---

277   Brookside Farm, 6 Hiram Hill Road.

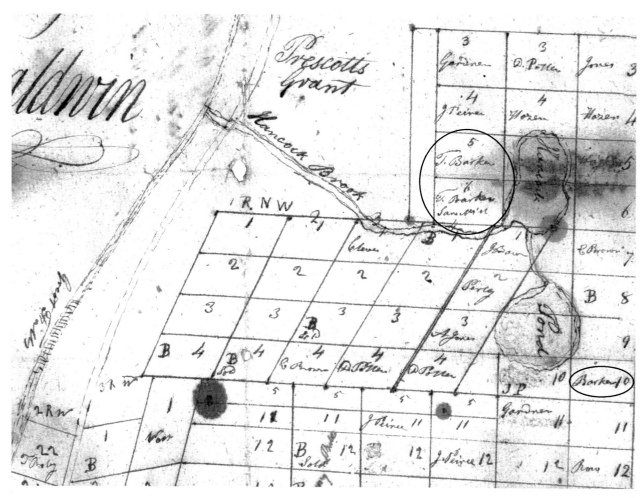

The Baldwin Lot Plan of 1806 shows T. Barker owning three lots—Range 5 Lot 1, Range 6 Lot 1 with a sawmill on Hancock Brook, and Lot 10. Also shown is Northwest Range 1 Lot 1, Range 2 Lot 1, and Range 3 Lot 1 owned by Rankin family members when they petitioned in 1820 to be annexed to Hiram.

1815, when the bridge tax list was made, it was the eldest son, Thomas A. Barker, who was taxed, not his father.[278] Thomas did not pay his taxes on his three hundred-acre lots and sawmill for 1811–12 and forfeited them in October 1815, by which time the family had moved. The notice of sale[279] was under the auspices of Stephen Longfellow, husband of friend Zilpha Wadsworth of Hiram, daughter of General Peleg Wadsworth, and his neighbor in Portland, so he must have known, or perhaps he didn't care, since he appears to have opened an inn in Portland, as did his namesake son, Thomas A. Barker, in November 1815. T. A. Barker quickly established a larger tavern. But it didn't last.

New and Cheap Boarding-House.

THOMAS A BARKER,

HAS taken the house opposite the Court-House, together with the convenient Stable adjoining, where he has opened a HOUSE OF ENTERTAINMENT for the accommodation of those country people who visit this town for a market. He assures the public that his conveniences, both for man and beast, are such as cannot fail to give satisfaction—as the terms will be more reasonable than can be obtained in town.

. Three or four Boarders may be accommodated as above.

Portland, Nov. 22.

Newspaper Eastern Argus *(Portland, Maine), November 29, 1815.*

---

278   Listed as Thomas Barker Jr.
279   Cumberland County Registry of Deeds, February 15, 1816, Book 73, 271.

Newspaper Portland Gazette *(Portland, Maine),*
January 9, 1816.

Sampler sewed by Flavilla Ann Barker, aged
nine, born at Hiram, daughter of Thomas and
Sarah Ayer Barker. Photo courtesy of Androscoggin
County Historical Society, Auburn, Maine.

Thomas Barker Family in Portland

The Barker family was well established in Portland by 1818, when twin daughters Mary Jane and Flavilla Ann Barker stitched samplers that survive. The Barkers had known the Wadsworths in Hiram, and they settled near Stephen and Zilpha Wadsworth Longfellow in Portland. It was the twins' privilege to walk "hand in hand" to the same school as their playmate and near neighbor, Henry Wadsworth Longfellow. Henry's first teacher, at age three or four, was "Ma'am Fellows,"[280] who ran a private "finishing" school for the wealthy, also known as a "Dame School," and it is likely the school where Mary Jane and her twin learned the fine art of fancy sewing and stitched their samplers at age nine.[281] Each made a silk and linen cross-stitched sampler, as expected of young ladies of society. Mary Jane's is identified and described in *American Samplers* by Bolton and Coe.[282] In 2000 her sampler was auctioned by Butterfield, a large auction house in San Francisco.[283]

Butterfield Auction Catalog description of the sampler of Mary Jane Barker, aged nine

Silk and Linen Genealogy Sampler; Mary Jane Barker

First Quarter 19th Century

Executed in blue, beige, ecru, brown and black silk threads on a linen ground centering a genealogical chart of the names and births of Thomas and Sarah Barker's children below inscribed with a verse and inscribed: Mary Jane Barker, Age 9, all within a trailing foliate and floral border.

Provenance was stated, dimensions given as twenty-one inches by sixteen inches, and the estimate of sale price was $2,000–$3,000.

---

280 Likely Abigail Fellows, second wife of Nathaniel Fellows.

281 Information from Leslie Rounds, executive director of Dyer Library/Saco Museum, Saco, Maine, an expert on samplers.

282 Ethel Stanwood Bolton & Eva Johnston Coe, *American Samplers* (Boston: Society of the Colonial Dames of America, 1921), 124–5. The description includes a note that Mary Jane walked to school, hand in hand, with playmate and near neighbor Henry W. Longfellow.

283 *Catalog* (San Francisco: Butterfield Auction Galleries, 2000).

Mary Jane's twin, Flavilla, also stitched a sampler with the names, places, and dates of birth of all of Thomas and Sarah's children. It is at the Androscoggin County Historical Society, Court House, Auburn, Maine. The samplers are nearly identical, but differ slightly. Flavilla recorded Peleg Barker's birth date as May 19, 1804, instead of 1807. Mary Jane recorded the birth place of Sarah in 1792 as Limerick rather than Hiram.[284]

Verse on the Samplers

Jesus permit thy gracious name to stand
As the first efforts of the infants hand
And while her fingers over this canvas move
Engage her tender heart to seek thy love

When the twins were ten years old, their father Thomas died in Portland on July 25, 1819, age fifty-three, a year after his daughters' samplers were stitched. He left a widow with eleven children at home, and the family struggled. Oldest son Thomas Ayer Barker had joined the family in Portland in 1817, but by 1820 was back in Hiram with a bride, Sarah (Sally) Fitch, daughter of innkeeper Richard Fitch of Baldwin.

Within months of his father's death, Thomas A. lease-deeded the Hiram farm to his mother for the remainder of her natural life "in consideration of the Love & good will I bear Her."[285] It is not likely she ever lived there, for in 1820 she was managing the inn in Portland, with thirty-one in her household, including ten under sixteen, fourteen over twenty-five, four "foreigners," and one in manufacturing.[286] The Portland City Directory for 1823 confirmed an inn on Main Street (now Congress Street) near Brown Street, probably in their home, but the eldest

Fitch Inn, Pequawket Trail, West Baldwin, built 1785, where Sarah Fitch lived before her marriage to Thomas A. Barker of Hiram. It no longer exists.

---

284 This may not be a girlish mistake. In two property deed transactions in 1792 and 1793, Thomas was identified as a trader from Limerick, but he was also in Hiram and Cornish during that period. Oxford Country Registry of Deeds, Fryeburg, Book 1, 202–208, 210.

285 Oxford County Registry of Deeds, Fryeburg, March 31, 1820, Book 8, 287.

286 U.S. Federal Census 1820, Portland.

daughter Susan M., only twenty-three, was the inn holder.[287] Sarah Barker, the mother, died two years later in January 1825, age fifty-six.

Mary Jane's sister Asenath had married Levi Morrell of Windham on May 6, 1819, a few months before Thomas died, but Susan M., Sarah, Pamela, Sophia, Elizabeth Pike, Mary Jane, Flavilla Ann, and Caroline needed to be wed.

A procession of marriages ensued. Sophia was first, age twenty-three, marrying Stanley Nay of Portland on May 27, 1823. Sister Elizabeth Pike Barker was next, marrying William A. Rogers of Portland, September 29, 1824, at age twenty. A portrait of Elizabeth is owned privately, one of two portraits auctioned along with Mary Jane's sampler.

Two months after Elizabeth was espoused, Sarah, age thirty-two, married Benjamin Chandler on December 30, 1824. Mary Jane followed in 1825, just a few months after her mother died and she was orphaned. She was sixteen.[288] The eldest sister, Susan M., age thirty-six, married Ephraim Cross on April 29, 1826, and died a year later on April 29, 1827.

Six months later, Mary Jane's twin, Flavilla, at age seventeen, married James Mason Williams of Taunton, Massachusetts, on November 21, 1826, and died there in 1882. Caroline, the youngest daughter, was the last to marry, at age twenty-two, on May 18, 1833, to Joshua Pike.

Son Noah married Tabitha Page and lived and died in Burlington, Maine, a suburb of Bangor. He must have had a close relationship with his older brother, as all the children of Thomas A. and Elizabeth Clement were born at Noah's house between 1822 and 1837, regardless of where Thomas A. and Elizabeth were living.[289]

Innkeeping was in the family blood. Thomas

Elizabeth Pike Barker Rogers, sister of Mary Jane and Flavilla Ann, about 1840, painting unsigned.

A. Barker, a widower in 1820, left Hiram shortly after his second marriage in 1821 to Elizabeth R. Clement, daughter of Jacob H. Clement, a prominent innkeeper in Gorham, and kept a public house there with his father-in-law.[290] Younger brother Peleg later leased the tavern. Reuben Lowell of Hiram also ran taverns with Jacob H. Clement in Gorham.[291]

The Barker inn in Portland remained in family hands after Susan Barker's death. It appears that daughter Sophia's husband, Stanley Nay, who ran a grocery store on Haymarket (now Middle Street), took it over until his brother-in-law Peleg Barker returned sometime around 1834.[292]

287 Portland City Directory and Registry, 1823.

288 The typical age of a bride was 18.

289 Burlington, Maine, records: Ellen, September 21, 1822; Peleg, April 13, 1824; Augustus, January 25, 1826; Jacob C., June 16, 1828; Caroline, May 3, 1830; Eveline, July 12, 1835; Flavillah A., May 2, 1837.

290 Hugh D. McLellan, *History of Gorham, Maine* (Somersworth: New England History Press, facsimile of the 1903 edition, 1980), 318.

291 "Jacob H. Clement and Reuben Lowell kept large taverns at West Gorham, designed with their immense stables especially to accommodate the teaming travel to Portland, which came down through the White Mountain Notch." Ibid, 273, 318.

292 Portland City Directory of 1827 lists Stanley Nay as inn holder on Main (Congress Street). Portland City Directory of 1834 lists him as clerk at Peleg Barker's, and Peleg Barker as inn holder, Main.

A portrait of Mary Jane Barker Eastman and her family was painted in Maine before they left for the Michigan wilderness in 1835. It was photographed in 1915 by the Michigan Historical Commission.[293] *It bears a striking resemblance to a family portrait attributed to George Washington Appleton, itinerant Maine artist, c. 1830, published in* Maine Antiques Digest, *January 1995, page 41E.*

A Barker Pioneer Daughter in the West

Mary Jane's life after marriage stood in stark contrast to that of her city sisters and her urban society education. When still a teenager, she moved with her husband, Timothy Eastman, a physician apprenticed in Portland, to Canaan, Maine, a small rural village between Skowhegan and Pittsfield in Somerset County, where Mary Jane gave birth to five children between 1826 and 1832. In the spring of 1835, Dr. Eastman fulfilled a boyhood dream and headed west, as did many. Mary Jane followed in August. It was an arduous trip with five young children, journeying across New England, up the Erie Canal, by sailing ship to Detroit, then by stage coach, and, finally, birch bark canoe, to their new log cabin home in the Michigan wilderness. Their house in Grand Haven burned six years later, in 1841, and they relocated to his land upriver, where some "rough improvements" had been made. Eastman organized a new settlement he named Polkton after President Polk. In a show of esteem for the doctor, residents named a nearby pioneer settlement Eastmanville. Dr. Eastman's professional services were in demand and required long journeys throughout the forest on horse and afoot,[294] leaving Mary Jane to cope alone for long stretches.

For ten years Mary Jane bore no more children, either through absence of her husband or miscarriage, but gave birth to four more, the eighth eponymously named Octavia. Mary Jane died, probably exhausted, in 1853, age forty-four. Six years later Timothy married her sister Sophia, who was a widow and nine years older than Mary Jane.

A Barker Scoundrel Son

Thomas Ayer Barker
October 23, 1794–October 25, 1842
First marriage December 5, 1819
Sarah Fitch of Baldwin, dates unknown
Second marriage November 25, 1821
Elizabeth Clement of Gorham,
December 26, 1800–November 14, 1871

Being remotely located, Mary Jane escaped the havoc her older brother Thomas A. rained upon his sisters in Portland and Hiram.

He started married life well, with his bride, Sarah Fitch, daughter of prosperous innkeeper Richard Fitch of West Baldwin.

---

293 Ibid., following 420.

294 Mary Eastman Bridges, "Timothy Eastman, M.D.," *Michigan Historical Collections*, 39 (1915), 420.

After Sarah died, he married Elizabeth Clement, daughter of Jacob H. Clement, an innkeeper in Gorham. But Thomas A. began a downward spiral, causing much angst in the family, beginning in July 1822, when he was forced to sell sixteen acres of the homestead farm in Hiram by the Baldwin line on the "Portland road" (old Pequawket Trail road)[295] to pay off a tax debt of $32.40 plus fees.[296]

Sister Susan M. purchased one-half. Brother-in-law Levi Morrell, innkeeper, leased it for ten years and continued to invest in adjacent land and to participate in Hiram town affairs. As an innkeeper, Levi was granted a license to sell spirits from his house in 1822. Contributing to the town, he was elected to the school committee in 1823 and 1824, and constable and collector of taxes in 1825 earning 5.75 percent on each tax collected and 25 cents for each notification of a Town Meeting or vote.[297] He was more physically challenged as field driver in 1827. He and Asenath sold the property in April 1827 to her uncle, Noah Barker, who lived with them, and they moved to Westbrook. After a year Noah sold the Barker homestead back to Levi Morrell.

That same year, 1827, Thomas A. bought 230 acres of land in Gorham. With a mortgage to pay, he sold land in Hiram to his brother-in-law Levi Morrell, his uncle Noah Barker, and John Kimball, but it wasn't enough. In 1829, perhaps when he was innkeeper in Gorham, he was convicted of larceny and fled to Standish, selling seventy acres of the Gorham land to four investors, who included his sisters' husbands William A. Rogers and Stanley Nay, and his wife's brother Simeon C. Clements.[298] With no money, he turned up in Biddeford, whose officials wrote to Hiram officials in 1831 requesting payment for support of pauper Thomas A. Barker. The Hiram Overseers of the Poor, one of whom was

his cousin Benjamin Barker, voted it down at Town Meeting, September 20, 1831.

Town Clerk's Record of Town Meeting
September 20, 1831

5th Voted that T.A. Barker be set up at auction to be struck off to the lowest bidder with the reservation that the Overseers have the care of said Barker unless he be bid off for the sum of one less than one dollar eighty seven & a half cent

7th Voted that the Overseers have five days to review proposals for keeping Thos A. Barker and that they let the person have him who makes the most favorable proposals all things considered [illegible] that this person taking him have five days to prepare in.[299]

The Hiram men who supported him this time were John Pierce Jr. ($25), Richard Heath ($6), and Mark Treadwell ($2.50).

In 1832, William A. Rogers, Thomas's brother-in-law, bought ninety acres of Thomas A.'s mortgaged Gorham property at a sheriff's sale for $18. At a sheriff's sale in Hiram, nineteen acres was sold for $47.50. "Three disinterested and impartial and discreet men"[300]—John Warren, Alpheus Spring, and Levi A. Hannaford (who became Hiram's first physician)—appraised it. In another family transaction in 1832, Noah Barker deeded some of his land, which had been mortgaged for $50, to niece Sarah Barker Chandler of Portland (now a widow?). Also in 1832, Levi Morrell finally sold the Thomas A. Barker homestead. Later owners were John P. Hubbard and abutter John McDonald. In 1858 it was occupied by Samuel Haywood. It no longer exists.

Brother Peleg moved back to Portland, sold for $50 "one half of Pew No. 132 situated in the lower

---

295 Part of 300 acres of the Prescott Grant his father had purchased in 1809. Oxford County Registry of Deeds.

296 Likely a tax debt. Peleg Wadsworth, Peleg Wadsworth Jr. and Marshall Spring appraised the land at $128, twice the amount requisite to satisfy the Execution, with the creditors holding the land jointly with Susan M. Barker who owned half. Oxford County Registry of Deeds, Fryeburg, 28 June 1822, Book 9 page 326.

297 He posted 8 notices in 1825, earning $3.00.

298 Cumberland County Registry of Deeds, Portland, 13 March 1829, Book 117, 122.

299 Hiram Special Town Meeting, September 20, 1831.

300 Fryeburg Registry of Deeds, Book 14, 362.

floor in the Stone Church belonging to the first Parish,"[301] and ran his family's inn. Thomas A. was at the same address in 1834, as was brother-in-law Levi Morrell.[302] Thomas Ayer Barker died October 25, 1842, in Portland and is buried in Evergreen Cemetery alongside his wife and son Peleg. Thomas A. was the fifth wealthiest resident of Hiram in 1818. Before he died at age forty-eight, he was dependent on the kindness of family and friends.

No more information about Thomas A.'s long-suffering younger brother Peleg Barker or Peleg's wife, Sarah, not even a death date, could be located.

Others in the Barker Family

Noah Barker Jr. was Thomas Barker's brother. He was born at Stratham, New Hampshire, son of Noah and Susannah Merrill Barker, who moved to Cornish, Maine. He married Sarah Clark and lived in Cornish.

Children

Benjamin Barker, 1798–January 10, 1848, married December 27, 1824, Zilpha Wadsworth of Hiram, May 23, 1800–March 29, 1896.

Mary W. Barker, 1802–1877, married Andrew R. Bucknell of Hiram, September 15, 1792–August 20, 1873.

Benjamin Barker came to Hiram from Cornish as a clerk in the store that Capt. Simeon Chadbourne opened in 1816. Afterwards he traded as proprietor. This was the store that Benjamin sold to John P. Hubbard in 1845 and Noah Hubbard expanded in 1846. It became Lemuel Cotton and Son General Store, 1238 River Road.

Benjamin Barker, with his business acumen, formed a partnership in 1826 with Isaac Hamblin. Barker & Hamblin was a successful retail enterprise in Hiram, selling such items as herring and nails, caps and capes for the militia, and, for the ladies, lace, calico, ribbons, buttons, and slippers, many imported

Benjamin Barker's house (left), opposite his store (later Cotton's general store), lower right. The house, on the corner of River Road and Mountain View Avenue, was owned by Seth Clemons during Hiram's centennial in 1914 when this photo was taken. Seth Clemons's grain store is on the upper right, adjacent to the railroad.

---

301 First Parish Church, 425 Congress Street, Portland. Cumberland County Registry of Deeds, Portland, April 29, 1835, Book 140, 566.

302 Portland City Directory and Register, 1834.

A letter addressed to Messrs. Barker and Hamblin, Hiram, dated 1832.

from England by George L. Drinkwater of Portland. They were also licensed to sell liquor in their store. Messrs. Barker and Hamblin sold their shop in 1836 to Benjamin Morrison of Hiram.

Benjamin held many town offices. He was measurer of wood and bark in 1817 at age nineteen. He first appeared on a list of voters in 1822. He was town clerk and selectman (listed as Lt. Benjamin Barker), and surveyor of highways. He was selectman and overseer of the poor and had the disagreeable duty of judging his nephew Thomas A. Barker when he came before Town Meeting as a pauper in 1831.

He was said to be well posted in public affairs and one of the most clear-headed men in the county. In 1824 he married Zilpha Wadsworth, daughter of Dura (brother of Gen. Peleg Wadsworth) and Lydia Bradford Wadsworth. He was one of the last people to see Gen. Peleg Wadsworth alive, when he attended to the general on his death bed, staying all night to keep watch and administer medications.

Benjamin fell off Hancock Brook Bridge by the Saco River January 10, 1848, and either died from the fall or froze to death.[303] He was fifty years old. Zilpha Barker outlasted him by fifty years. They are buried in the Hiram Village Cemetery.

Children

Zilpha W. Barker, born August 5, 1827, married Samuel E. Spring of Brownfield.

Benjamin Barker, born in 1829, died in 1850.

Erastus H. Barker, born in 1832, died in 1875.

Clark H. Barker, born 1837, married Hattie Robie in Portland.

Virginia Barker, born in 1841, married James Jordan and lived in Portland, died May 22, 1916. Virginia Barker Jordan is important because her gift

---

303   Daniel Small, *Papers*, Maine Historical Society, Coll. 1449.

Soldiers Memorial Library, 85 Main Street, built with funds from Virginia Barker Jordan in 1915. It is across the street from Hiram Village Cemetery and adjacent to the former Methodist Church, built in 1885, now the Arts Center at 8 Hancock Avenue.

of $3,000 made it possible for the Soldiers Memorial Library in Hiram to be built in 1915.

Barker Pond remained undeveloped until the Bridgton and Saco River Railroad gave it exposure and access beginning in 1883. Cottages built around that time are prized today and handed down from generation to generation for summer recreation.

DANIEL BASTON (BOSTON)
c. 1746–after 1822

Marriage date unknown
Catherine Harmon of Sanford, dates unknown

The Bastons were a force in Hiram for a century, from 1783 to 1883. Today there are none.

In 1884 town historian Llewellyn A. Wadsworth told part of their story. Excerpted from the *Oxford County Record*, Kezar Falls, Maine, June 28, 1884:

> A hundred years ago, in June 1784, Daniel Baston came from Denmark to Hiram, crossing Saco river on a raft, capsizing, and losing his kettles and crockery on the route; he settled on the farm owned by us.[304]

It was significant that Llewellyn pointed out the loss of kettles and crockery. Like many early settlers, Baston owned few possessions and the loss was a hardship unimaginable today. Without kettles and crockery Daniel's family couldn't cook or store food. There were no stores in Hiram, and perhaps no blacksmiths or potters at the time. To travel to other towns seeking replacements—Fryeburg, Brownfield, Baldwin, Porter, or Cornish—meant walking miles and carrying a heavy load or finding a horse and possibly fording the river as there were no bridges across the Saco until 1805.

> He was, we believe, a native of Kennebunk, or vicinity. He had settled in Denmark in 1775, near Baston Hills [Boston Hills], that still bear his name; being the first settler of Denmark, as we are informed. He was one of the Assessors of Hiram in 1803. The remnants of two huge pine stumps still cling to the soil near our buildings, on what must have been the first clearing—the only relics of the forest primeval.
>
> Of his children, Winthrop settled on the farm now occupied by us, and known as the Craige place. Royal settled below on the farm long known as the Thomas Goodwin farm. Loami [Loammi] Baston, son also of Daniel, settled with his father on the farm where we now reside. He died about 1821.[305] Daniel Baston lugged on his shoulders in a basket the clay used in building his chimney, a distance of half a mile, up a very steep hill—bringing it from the banks of Saco river. The old house gave place to another, which was burned in 1815.
>
> The late Hiram Baston, proprietor of the Mt. Cutler house, told us that he well remembered that he was taken and put over the fence among the currant bushes for safe keeping, he being *four* years old. Hiram was a son of Loami. Benjamin and Joseph, two sons of Daniel, settled on Hiram hill, on the road from Lemuel Cotton farm to the Gen. Wadsworth farm. Daniel Baston at length removed to Vermont, where he died.

Who Were They?

Daniel Baston was the progenitor of the Hiram Bastons. He was the son of Gershom Baston of Wells, Maine, occupation "joiner."[306] Daniel served in the Revolution in the summer of 1775,[307] after which he settled in Denmark with his wife, Catherine, in a small log cabin. He and Catherine had five sons, Winthrop, Loammi, Royal, Benjamin, and Joseph, and perhaps some daughters. He was one of the first settlers of Denmark; the Boston Hills are named for him. He removed to Hiram Hill, across the Saco River, in June 1783 or 1784, in search of more fertile land, and thus is a founder of both towns.

The date he arrived is important. When he

---

304 The farm was about one-half mile up Hiram Hill Road.

305 Loammi died December 19, 1820, a suicide.

306 A joiner attached posts to beams.

307 He served in Captain Joshua Bragdon's company, Colonel Scammon's regiment.

settled in Hiram it was on "unappropriated" land, subsequently given to Timothy Cutler in 1787 by the Massachusetts Legislature. The legislature passed a law that allowed men who had settled on and improved land and were living on it by January 1, 1784, to petition for ownership of one hundred acres. In 1788, he signed the petition, along with sixteen others, claiming one hundred acres of land, and Timothy Cutler wrote him a deed. But if Wadsworth was correct that Baston settled in June 1784, six months after the deadline, Baston did not qualify to sign the petition claiming land. However, in the face of powerful forces in remote Boston, and given significant land injustices, residents of the struggling pioneer community could be forgiven for not betraying a productive neighbor. If an undated untitled newspaper account is true, then Baston settled in June 1783, and there is no other story.

Indeed, the Bastons served Hiram well.

Daniel Baston was one of the earliest known selectmen in Hiram. The year was 1803; there is no earlier record of the governance of Hiram. He served along with John Pierce and John Burbank.

Town Offices Held

Collectors of Taxes

1807	Winthrop Baston received $9.75 for services as collector in 1807
1808	Winthrop Baston

Constables

1807	Jacob Lord Jr., elected on March 24, resigned and was replaced with Winthrop Baston

Field Drivers

1815	Loammi Baston
1818	Royal Baston

The house of John Thomas Boston (c. 1812–1905), Denmark Road, also known as South Road, on the Hiram line, shown with Clerment (1862–1924) and Mamie Jewell Hartford (1871–1969) and seven of their eleven children. The house collapsed in 1920. Courtesy of Conrad Hartford.

Hog Reeves

1811	Loammi Baston
1815	Winthrop Baston

Selectmen & Assessors of Hiram

1803	Daniel Baston
1804	Daniel Baston
1805	Daniel Baston
1806	Daniel Baston

Surveyors of Highways

1807	Benjamin Baston
1811	Benjamin Baston

Tithingmen

1819	Royal Baston
1820	Loammi Baston

Daniel was more aware of the market value of his property than were other Hiram settlers. He had a penchant for recording family transactions in registered deeds. He sold land to his sons Winthrop, Loammi, and Royal, and bought it back several times. One of the more unusual is the deed selling the use of his field for two years to son Loammi for $100. The deed dated June 23, 1816, specifies that it will take effect nine months and eleven days later, on April 2, 1817, possibly the beginning of the new farming season.[308]

Another deed helped to fill a gap in Daniel's voting and tax records between 1809 and 1812, when he was listed as a nonresident on John Spring's tax bill. Daniel paid $400 for one-half of Royal's homestead, valid for the rest of his natural life. The deed was dated August 3, 1811, and stated that Daniel lived in Standish. Standish tax records[309] revealed he paid taxes there in 1808, 1809, and 1810 and received two abatements. He returned to Hiram and began voting again in 1813. Why he left and returned is a mystery.

It is believed Daniel went to Vermont late in life with his grandson Jason, son of Loammi, and died there. What possessed him? If he did so, it was after he broke the life deed on half of Royal's homestead in

1822. Another question is why he left. Was it adventure in his old age? Was it was his desire to leave Hiram after the death of his son Loammi and settlement of Loammi's estate on July 10, 1822?

Loammi Baston
?–December 19, 1820
Married c. 1806
Rebecca Powers of Sanford,
August 26, 1789–May 10, 1871.

After marriage, Loammi and Rebecca followed a traditional path. On January 12, 1807, for $1,800 he bought one hundred acres of the farm his father lived on, lot 11 of Cutler's Grant on Hiram Hill. But in October of that year, he sold one-half to his brother Royal. Loammi acquired twenty acres on lot 12, adjacent, from Cutler's lawyer on June 17, 1814, and built a house. Unfortunately, the deed, which was not recorded, burned in his house fire in October 1815. Cutler agreed to deed it again, and charged $60.[310]

Tragedy was common among the early settlers—illnesses for which there were no cures, accidents on roads, at farms, and in logging, as well as fire from fireplaces, the principal source of heat, or from candles and lanterns, the only sources of lighting. But what befell Rebecca Baston when her kind and affectionate husband took his life on December 19, 1820, must have been particularly hurtful. Not only was suicide shameful, but Loammi died intestate and in debt to his father, Daniel. Daniel did not forgive the debt, even though it meant his daughter-in-law's share of the property would be sold, and she and his grandchildren, who lived surrounded by their Baston relatives, would be evicted.

It was Rebecca's great fear of being thrust onto the public dole that prompted her to seek relief for herself and six children ranging in age from a thirteen-year-old daughter to a baby, and begging the court to allow her some personal property. In defense of Daniel, it was difficult for him to support himself in his old age. He was seventy-four, probably no longer able to farm properly, at a time when

---

308 Oxford County Registry of Deeds, Fryeburg, June 23, 1817, Book 6, 526.

309 Standish Town Office, Tax Records, 1808–1810.

310 Oxford County Registry of Deeds, Fryeburg, March 16, 1816, Book 10, 49.

cash was short and "social security" was the immediate family and/or taxpayers of the town who voted for support of the poor at Town Meetings.

Luckily for Rebecca, James Evans, a Hiram lawyer, intervened. He wrote the letter for her because she couldn't write.[311] He bought her property, sold at vendue to David Cole of Cornish, and arranged for her to buy a smaller property that he owned in East Hiram on the other side of the Saco River, farther from the Bastons.

It took three-plus years to wrap up the estate.

December 19, 1820—Loammi Baston died.

January 25, 1821—Rebecca wrote to probate judge.

April 24, 1821—Probate Court awarded Rebecca Baston $300 out of Loammi's personal estate and that she may choose articles to that amount.

April 30, 1821—John Watson and Mary A. Watson witnessed that furniture in the amount of $300 was received by Rebecca Baston and signed "X her mark."

April 19, 1822—Benjamin Bucknell bought twenty acres of Loammi's land at auction to pay Loammi's debts of $31.20.

July 10, 1822—David Cole of Cornish paid $354.33 at auction to buy thirteen acres of the homestead for debts, excepting the present year's crops, 7.25 acres woodlot, and 19.25 acres allowed for the widow's right of dower.

April 7, 1824—James Evans paid David Cole $675 for the same land.

April 15, 1824—Rebecca Baston paid James Evans $250 for ten acres and 151 rods, after deducting land for a road.[312]

Rebecca Baston's Plea to Probate Court

Hiram January 25th 1821

To the Honble [sic] —

Benjamin Chandler Esq Judge of Probate for the County of Oxford __

Sir I am under the necessity of Representing the unfortunate & distressing Situation of myself & family from that Ever memorable day, the 19th of December

Last! My Kind, and affectionate Husband, being Subject to fits of Insanity, Put an End to his Life, Leaving me disconsolate, with Six Small Children: The Eldest a daughter about 13 years old: & one at the Breast—4 weeks old, also an aged father, of the Deceased being 74 years of age and what adds Poignancy to my present Grief is my Pecuniary Circumstances, being in Such an Unsettled State. My father Baston gave the deceased a Deed of Sixty acres of Land Lying in Hyram & took Securities to the full Value or more which he now holds in his hands for his maintenance & Support, and Refuses to make any Settlement, and will agree to nothing for Our mutual benefit. But is determined to bring in his Claim as Creditor; in a proper Time which will Cover all the Real Estate; furthermore, we Suppose the debts of the Deceased amount to 100 dollars, which will Take The Personal Estate principally at present. Leaving myself & family in distress, & Indigence; which will doubtly Oblige me to cast myself upon the public for support.__

These & such Like, Humiliating Inflictions, Together with my Loss, & manner of my Bereavements, Render my Situation Truly Deplorable. ___

Under These Circumstances I pray your Honour to look upon my afflictions & if you Can Legally & Justly Give me the Personal Estate; or any part Thereof; you may deem proper I Shall always feel myself; under the strongest Obligations of Gratitude for any favour.

Rebecca Baston

More information is available about some of Loammi's children than for their farmer father, yet this information is also incomplete. All were born in Hiram—Lucy (Lizzie) S. (October 1808), Phebe O. (December 1809), Hiram (November 1811), Jason (October 1813), Rebecca P. (May 1817), and Mary E. (November 1820).

---

311   Rebecca signed with an X, her mark, Oxford County deed, July 10, 1822, Book 10, 316-318.

312   Oxford County Registry of Deeds, April 15, 1824, Book 11, 259.

Mt. Cutler House, built 1846, razed 1968.

Lucy S. never married. Her gravestone in Hiram Village Cemetery is marked "Miss Lizzie S. departed May 10, 1871, ae. 81 yrs. 9 mos." Phebe O. married Uriah Wadsworth, son of Dura Wadsworth, brother of General Peleg Wadsworth. Jason in 1836 married Eliza E. Kimball, daughter of Hiram settlers Ephraim and Rachel Ackerman Kimball. Jason, the grandson believed to have gone to Vermont with Daniel Baston, died in Hiram in 1847. Mary E. married Reverend John C. Perry, and became the mother of the Honorable Albion Perry, mayor of Somerville, Massachusetts. Hiram became proprietor of Mt. Cutler House. When Hiram's son, a doctor, died, he was so distraught, he committed suicide by cutting his throat. He was seventy-two.

The Other Sons of Daniel Baston

Winthrop Baston was born in Brownfield c. 1775–80. He married Huldah, daughter of John Robbins, and settled at Hiram between land owned by his father and the farm of Joshua R. Ridlon on Hiram Hill. In the War of 1812 he served in Colonel McCobb's regiment. Children, all born at Hiram, were Andrew S. (June 1806), Mary (July 1808), Calvin (October 1810), Luther (November 1812), Hannah (1814), and Daniel (February 1817).

Several times Winthrop bid for the work of paupers and boarded them. Stephen Burbank, Isaac and Louisa Merrifield, and John McLucas were among them. Was it out of the kindness of his heart or the necessity of operating a farm? Winthrop was not wealthy, but in 1818[313] he owned more than his father, Daniel, and brother Royal, but less than Loammi.

The following is an example of Winthrop's support.

In 1820, Winthrop took in the pauper family of Isaac Merrifield and wife Louisa Brown, a former neighbor, their son Isaac and daughter Grace, for which he was paid for room and board at the rate of $2 per week. Details appear in Services to Paupers in Appendix 19.

The agreement was unusual in that it was recorded.[314] The reason it was written is unknown.

---

313   1818 inventory compiled in May, Maine Historical Society, Coll. 146, Box 1.

314   Maine State Archives, Hiram Box 14.

Hiram Novm 13th 1820

This agreement made this day between the Overseers of the Poor of the Town of Hiram and Winthrop Baston of said Hiram witnesth [sic] that the said Winthrop promises and agrees to supply Isaac Merrifield and his first child with good food harmonious lodging at his own dwelling house from this time to the first Monday of April next at the rate of two dollars per week for all the time he shall so supply them and the said Overseers on their part agree to furnish said Winthrop with an order from the selectmen on the receiving of said Winthrop for whatever their supplies shall amount to at the above rate. Said order to be made payable in one year from this date. [signed] Alpheus Spring, Ephraim Kimball, John Warren—Overseers of the Poor of Hiram, & Winthrop Baston

NB The wife and youngest child of Mr. Merrifield are to have the privilege of making their home at Mr. Baston's

Royal married Sally Leathers of Hiram on March 1, 1809. There is no further information about her. Their children were Susan (May 8, 1810), Enoch M. (August 15, 1817), Royal Jr. (February 19, 1819), and Sally (October 27, 1820).

Benjamin, born c. 1771–1780, married Martha Clark. They had eight children: William was born in 1796; Harriet (dates unknown); Deborah (c. May 23, 1811); Mary Ann (c. February 11, 1812); Louisa (dates unknown); Royal (dates unknown); Jane (dates unknown); Gardner (dates unknown).

The Bastons were members of the Free Will Baptist Church in East Hiram. Benjamin's daughters Mary Ann and Deborah were accepted as members on August 19, 1824, but Jane was a problem and was not admitted. Two years later, Jane received a letter of admonition dated January 25, 1826. Jane repented and came forward on Monday, June 5, 1826, confessed her faults to the church, and was received into fellowship.[315] Her faults were not reported, but apparently, her sins were not grave enough to deter Abner M. Black of Lowell, Massachusetts, from marrying her, and together they raised six children in Lowell.[316]

Joseph paid taxes in 1806 and was not heard from again in Hiram.

Other Baston Mysteries

Catherine Boston married John Burbank in 1795. Lois Boston, his second wife, married him in 1800. According to the marriage intentions they filed in Fryeburg, they were from Hiram. There is no further information, so their stories remain hidden. It is possible they were unrecorded daughters of Daniel and Catherine Baston.

---

315   Free Will Baptist Church records.
316   1860 U.S. census.

BUCKNELL FAMILY

Simeon Bucknell
1754–1836
Married March 21, 1782
Hannah Burbank
January 2, 1757–April 11, 1813

Simeon Bucknell and his sons and nephew were early settlers in Hiram and active in town affairs. He was living in Fryeburg when he and Hannah Burbank were married by the Reverend Mr. William Fessenden. They had seven children: Sarah (1783), John (1785), Mehitable (1787), Benjamin (1790), Andrew R. (1792), Simeon Jr. (1795), and Mary (1798).

Shortly after their first child, Sarah, was born in Fryeburg, the family settled in Hiram on land on the west side of the Saco River that was awarded to Timothy Cutler in 1787. Simeon and his nephew John Jr. both signed the petition of 1788 claiming one hundred acres each that they had settled on before January 1, 1784, as required by law. Cutler deeded to John Bucknell Jr. not one hundred acres claimed, but seventy-five acres, "in Consideration of Good

The house, Capt John Lane's second, was purchased by Simeon Bucknell and was known as the Andrew R. Bucknell house (Andrew was Simeon's son). It was built after 1779, when the Clemons family visited the Capt. John Lane family. The view in this photo is from Pequawket Trail, which had been relocated because of Saco River erosion in the freshet of 1869.

Services done me." This lot, where John Jr. was living, was on the south side line of lot number one. There were six "settler's lots" along the Saco River in a plot plan that has not been found.

There is no deed from Cutler to Simeon Bucknell, but Simeon settled north of John Jr. along the Saco, near Thomas Spring, in the house Capt. John Lane built. Lane's daughter Anne was born there in 1792. Unaware of Anne, the newspaper *Oxford County Advertiser*, December 9, 1910, noted that only two persons had been born in the house: Mary (1798), daughter of Simeon Sr. and Hannah Bucknell, and much later, on November 20, 1889, Thomas C. Clemons, son of Samuel L. and Mary Allen Bucknell Clemons. At any rate, the house was built too close to the changing Saco River and was demolished c. 1940 before it fell into it.

Simeon had the distinction of living near the District 1 school and will forever be remembered for it. The first Town Meeting of 1814 (and later meetings) called men to meet "at the Schoolhouse near Simeon Bucknell." The schoolhouse is long gone, as is the house.

The Bucknells were respected and enterprising, but not wealthy—not many in Hiram were. In 1790, Simeon had enough cash to purchase from John Lane and Henry Brown a gristmill and twenty acres on Ten Mile Brook in Brownfield, on the condition that he would keep it in good order for sixty years. He sold it the next year to William Lane, and this mill was later bought by Peleg Wadsworth, who, presumably, kept the bargain. John Bucknell was taxed in 1809 for a gristmill and three-quarters share of a sawmill in Hiram, but the location is unknown.

Simeon was on the Committee for Bridge Repair in 1812. When property was assessed for the bridge tax of 1815, Simeon's was valued at $270, which placed him fifteenth of eighty-five, below that of John Pierce, Aaron Richardson, Thomas Spring, Samuel Merrifield, and John Warren, and well above the Durgins, Abraham Gray, Levi Lord, Morgan Lewis, and Samuel Sloper.

Simeon was a captain in the militia, as was his son Andrew R., who was a constable in the town

The Andrew R. Bucknell house, built by Capt. John Lane, was demolished c. 1940 before it fell into the Saco River. The back of the house, viewed here from the river bank, was the front before the Pequawket Trail was relocated.

for twenty-five years.[317] Andrew R. was less successful as a tax collector, which in some years was a joint position. He was subject to a sheriff's warrant for being "A Deficient Tax Collector" in 1819. He owed the sum of $33.33 to the town, for which his property would have been sold or his body sent to jail had Sheriff Cyrus Hamlin of the Commonwealth of Massachusetts been able to find any property, or his body, after which the sheriff returned "in no part satisfied."[318] Andrew must have redeemed himself, for after nine years, in 1827, he was elected again, bidding $12.50 for the job.[319]

Son Benjamin fought in the War of 1812 and was a magistrate, served as town clerk in 1814 and 1817 to 1819, and selectman 1823 to 1826. John took over as clerk in 1820, 1821, 1823 to 1826, and again in 1837 and was selectman in 1829.

John Bucknell Jr.
April 20, 1796–January 4, 1880
Married August 6, 1818
Hannah Gray, January 26, 1799–October 3, 1871

John Bucknell Jr., a nephew of Simeon Sr., was constable in 1812 and 1813. The Bucknells were also fence viewers, hog reeves, and surveyors of highways. Simeon Bucknell Jr. held the uniquely named position of money clerk in 1828. In one of the earliest records found, John Bucknell was mentioned as class master in 1804.

Town Offices Held

Clerk
1814	Benjamin Bucknell
1815	Benjamin Bucknell
1817–1819	Benjamin Bucknell, Esq.
1820–1821	John Bucknell
1822–1823	Benjamin Barker
1824–1826	John Bucknell
1837	John Bucknell

Collector of Taxes
1814	John Bucknell
1818	Andrew R. Bucknell (at 5 percent)
1827	Andrew R. Bucknell (bid at $12.50)
1828	Andrew R. Bucknell (bid at $30.50)

Committee on Accounts
1812	Benjamin Bucknell
1817	Benjamin Bucknell
1819	Andrew R. Bucknell
1821	Benjamin Bucknell

Committees on Bridge Building and Repairs
1812	Simeon Bucknell
1818	Ossipee River bridge repairs: Simeon Bucknell
1821	Saco River repair: John Bucknell

Constable
1812	John Bucknell Jr.
1813	John Bucknell Jr.
1818	Andrew R. Bucknell
1827	Andrew R. Bucknell

---

317 Ridlon, *Saco Valley Settlements and Families*, 147.

318 Hiram Town Clerk records, Nov. 19, 1819.

319 In 1818 the rate was 5 percent.

Cullers of Hogs and Steeres

1826–1829	John Bucknell Jr.

Fence Viewers

1816	Simeon Bucknell
1827	John Bucknell
1828	John Bucknell Jr.

Field Drivers

1818	Benjamin Bucknell
1819	Andrew R. Bucknell
1823	Simeon Bucknell Jr.
1824	Andrew R. Bucknell
1827	Simeon Bucknell Jr.
1828	Andrew R. Bucknell

Hog Reeves

1812	Benjamin Bucknell

Justices of the Peace

1816	Benjamin Bucknell
1822	Benjamin Bucknell
1823	Benjamin Bucknell
1828	Benjamin Bucknell

Money Clerk [unique title this year only]

1828	Simeon Bucknell Jr.

School Agents

1820	John Bucknell School District #1
1821	John Bucknell #1
1823	John Bucknell #1
1825	John Bucknell
1826	John Bucknell
1830	Simeon Bucknell Jr.

School Committees

1821	Benjamin Bucknell Esquire
1822	Benjamin Bucknell
1824	Benja Bucknell
1825	Benj Bucknell

School Teachers

1804	John Bucknell

Selectmen

1823	Benj. Bucknell
1824	Benj. Bucknell
1825	Benj. Bucknell
1826	Benj. Bucknell
1829	John Bucknell

Surveyors of Highways

1825	Andrew R. Bucknell
1827	Simeon Bucknell Jr.
1829	Simeon Bucknell Jr.

Surveyors of Lumber

1829	John Bucknell Jr.

Tithingmen

1821	Benjamin Bucknell

BURBANK FAMILY

Benjamin Burbank
c. 1725–?

Married November 6, 1750
Jane Sewell, dates unknown

Benjamin Burbank was almost sixty when he moved in 1782 to Brownfield from Arundel, Maine (Kennebunkport), where he taught in 1770. He or his son John may have been the first teacher in Hiram. His children, all born in Arundel, were Mehitable, Israel (c. 1750–1755), John (born c. 1760), Benjamin (c. 1757–1760), and Stephen (born before 1770). The oldest, Mehitable, married Abel Merrill of Arundel, and may have remained there. The four boys accompanied Benjamin in the move to the part of Brownfield that became Hiram in 1807.[320]

Benjamin and Benjamin Jr. signed the petition of 1788 claiming land as settlers before January 1, 1784. Two Benjamin Burbanks were listed in the U.S. census of 1790, one in Hiram and one in Brownfield.

On June 15, 1791, Benjamin and Israel Burbank assisted in appraising the estate of John Clemons of Hiram. Three days later, June 18, 1791, the same day Cutler transferred one hundred acres to him, he sold the property where he lived in Hiram and moved to Brownfield. His wife, Mary, signed the deed, releasing her right of dower, indicating the seller was Benjamin Jr.

The buyer, Thomas Spring of Grafton, New Hampshire, opened a tavern there in 1796 servicing the stage line from Bartlett, New Hampshire, to Portland. It was a good location, since it was twelve miles from Fryeburg and horses needed to be refreshed every twelve miles according to postal rules. This property is now known as Old Homestead Farm (1912 Pequawket Trail). Paul and Ada Wadsworth bought the property from the last

Spring heir in 1948 after their house on Hiram Hill was burned in the wildfires of 1947.

It is odd that no Benjamin Burbanks were listed in the 1800 census,[321] yet Benjamin of Brownfield Addition signed Cutler's petition of 1801 to incorporate Hiram.

The death date of Benjamin Burbank is unknown, but after 1790 only one Benjamin appears in records. After 1801, the Burbanks who appear are Israel, John, and Stephen.

Benjamin Burbank Jr., born 1766, according to his Revolutionary War military enlistment record, was drafted for service in Cambridge, Massachusetts, July 4, 1778. As he was only twelve years of age, and the age requirement for a soldier was fifteen, most likely he served as a musician or errand boy.

Benjamin Burbank Jr. of Brownfield married Mary Richardson of Hiram on December 20, 1786. He was then twenty years old.

The dates of death of the two Benjamin Burbanks are not known. In 1800, Benjamin Burbank lived in Brownfield. He signed Timothy Cutler's petition for incorporation in 1801 as a resident of Brownfield's Addition,[322] as did John Burbank, Israel Burbank, and Israel Burbank Jr., but not Benjamin Jr. The lack of the title "Jr." may indicate that the father died before 1800.

Where the son Benjamin went after he signed the petition to recover his land in 1788 is unknown, but the application in Michigan for a pension for Revolutionary War service in 1836 stated he had resided in Maine during the war, stationed at Winter Hill, Cambridge (now in Somerville). He wrote "Have been absent from said District, the county of my nativity for 40 years." The application was suspended for lack of proof of service from Massachusetts Rolls.[323]

---

320   George Burbank Sedgley, *Genealogy of the Burbank Family* (Farmington, ME: Printed by Knowlton and McLeary Co., 1928), 48.

321   A Benjamin Burbank of the right age is listed in the 1800 census of Grafton, New Hampshire.

322   Brown's Addition became part of Hiram in 1807.

323   Sedgley, *Genealogy of the Burbank Family*, 48–49.

Israel Burbank
c. 1750 to 55–September 9, 1836

Married December 16, 1776

Ruth Merrill of Arundel (Kennebunkport)

c. 1753–April 4, 1843

Israel Burbank, brother of Benjamin Burbank Jr., both sons of Benjamin and Jane, also served at Cambridge in the Revolution. In 1790 he lived in Brownfield. In a deed dated June 20, 1791, he received from Henry Young Brown "the Southwardly half of a Tract of land in Brownfield where he now lives being in the whole Tract Two hundred and Twenty Seven acres.... The Northwardly half of said Tract belongeth to John and Stephen Burbank." In 1800 he lived in Brownfield and his age was given as forty-five and over. He had seven or more children, but the names of only four are known—Israel Jr. (1785), Asa (1786), Theodosia (1792), and Dorothy (c. 1795).

Did Israel move from Brownfield to Hiram where he served in several town offices? No. The town border was redefined in 1807, annexing his property to Hiram. The anomaly is that he was elected to office in Hiram while a legal resident of Brownfield. He was collector of taxes in 1805, and in 1806 was a selectman. The fact that both Israel and John were elected to office in Hiram while living in Brownfield[324] is puzzling because only legal inhabitants of the town were eligible to hold office. There is a possible explanation. Inhabitants of a town, at an annual Town Meeting, could vote to make a person a legal inhabitant if it was declared on the agenda in advance, but there is no record this happened.[325] Another explanation may be that residents presumed that Brown's Addition would be added to Hiram and prematurely considered it so. Regardless, the Burbanks were elected and purported themselves well in office as responsible citizens. Israel voted in all of the elections for which records were found and was the second U.S. postmaster in Hiram, in 1803.

Israel Burbank was a man of modest means. On the List of Rateables (inventory for tax purposes) for 1809 he was charged for two polls, meaning living

1812 highway tax list showing Israel and Israel Burbank Jr., Daniel Cram, Josiah Pierce, and Alpheus Spring with valuations of zero. The reason is unknown.

with him was another white male over twenty-one with the potential to vote, meaning he had sufficient property or income.

Israel had a dwelling house, a barn, three tillable acres, four acres of mowing land, four acres of pasturage, sixty-four acres of unimproved land, two cows, one head of cattle, one horse, and five swine, and his tax bill was on the low side. When he was a selectman in 1806 he paid highway taxes of $2.95, compared to Daniel Baston's $6.20, but higher than Enoch Baston, Joseph Durgin, James Fly, Jacob and Levi Lord, and John McLucas at $1.30.

Curiously, in 1812 neither Israel nor his son Israel Jr. were charged any tax on real or personal property, nor was Daniel Cram, Josiah Pierce, or Alpheus Spring. The real and personal property of the four were valued at zero, but they were all charged the poll tax of $2.10.[326] Why was this year exceptional? What could have accounted for it? None were paupers, none had property seized, none were soldiers, none were ill. Israel was advancing in age

---

324   John was elected selectman in 1803, 1804, 1805; Israel was elected in 1806.

325   Freeman, *The Town Officer*, 1808.

326   Maine State Archives, Hiram Box 14.

and in the last seventeen years of his life (he died in 1836) was ill, but not in 1812. Israel Jr. served in the War of 1812 but not until 1814, so the zeroes in the tax list are puzzling. Possibly it was an unfinished document. All but Israel Burbank Jr. were back on the list for 1813, paying the poll tax, which had increased from $2.10 to $3. Daniel Cram still had no real or personal property, but Josiah Pierce, who was twenty-three years old at the time, had property worth $81 and Israel, whose age was between fifty-nine and sixty-three, had property valued at $174.50.

In her pension application, Israel's widow, Ruth Merrill Burbank, wrote:

> Israel Burbank died Sept. 9, 1836, after an illness of several years. Had a "shock of palsy" two or three years before death and was unable to speak. He had lived with Peleg Wadsworth, 2d[327] (born about 1791) and family for 17 years. Served 4 months in Capt. John Elder's company, 1776. Also, 4 months, Capt. Joshua Nason, Col. Stover's Reg. when Burgoyne was taken.[328]

Lt. Asa Burbank
1786–October 26, 1858
Married July 1814
Sarah Bucknell
January 24, 1783–October 30, 1865

Asa voted for the first time in 1809, probably the second "poll," a male over twenty-one years of age, living with his father, Israel. He served in the War of 1812 as lieutenant in Capt. Alpheus Spring of Hiram's company under James Steele's battalion of artillery from September 13 to September 24, 1814, raised at Hiram, service in Portland. He signed up again, serving from the next day, September 25, to November 7, 1814, as lieutenant in Capt. W. Wheeler's company, Lt. Col. W. Ryerson's regiment raised at Rumford, Maine, service at Portland, along with other Hiram men: Josiah Mayberry (Mabry), corporal; Thomas B. Watson, sergeant; Privates Stephen

Burbank, Noah Lewis, Moses Lowell, Asa Osgood Jr., Nathaniel Tripp.

Asa voted in 1813 and every year after that for which there is a record. He was elected constable for four years, from 1813 to 1816, when the office was merged with that of collector of taxes. How he managed to conduct business as constable in the nearly two months of 1814 from September to November when he was serving his country as lieutenant in the war is not known. Perhaps there was not much crime or need for the public warrants for meetings or services of a constable at the time, or perhaps he

Israel/Asa Burbank house, built c. 1803, 20 Shotgun Gulch, 2014. The original door under the center chimney was converted into a window.

had a substitute. In 1815, when he returned from war service, he was elected selectman, and his property was valued at twice that of his father's.

The children of Lt. Asa and Sarah Bucknell Burbank were George W., 1815; Hannah, 1816; Lydia Jane, 1819; Benjamin, 1821; Mary B., 1823.

Benjamin Burbank, January 18, 1821–April 28, 1898, married November 4, 1858, **to** Georgia Eastman, October 5, 1838–1916.

The Benjamin Burbank house, built c. 1849, is depicted on the 1858 map. Of several Benjamin

---

327   Israel Burbank's daughter, Theodesia, married Peleg Wadsworth II, son of Dura Wadsworth, brother of Gen. Peleg Wadsworth.

328   Sedgley, *Genealogy of the Burbank Family*, 94.

The Israel/Asa Burbank house in 1940, seen from the back of the house.

Israel/Asa Burbank house, 1995, seen from the back. Courtesy of the Town of Hiram.

Painting of the Benjamin Burbank house, Lewis Kelley Road, off Pequawket Trail, burned in 1947. Artist signature is faint. Collection of Hiram Historical Society.

Burbanks, the house was most likely built by Benjamin Burbank (1821–1898), son of Asa and Sarah Bucknell Burbank. Subsequent occupants were Henry N. Burbank and wife Louise Clemons, and Irving and Ella Cram. At the time it burned in the wildfires of 1947, it was the summer home of Lewis Kelley of Massachusetts.

John Burbank
c. 1760 to 1765–?
First marriage April 16, 1795
Catherine Boston, dates unknown
Second marriage February 24, 1800
Lois Baston, 1778–February 21, 1848

John Burbank, the brother of Benjamin Jr. and Israel, was born in Arundel, Maine (Kennebunkport), and, like many others who came to Hiram, was a soldier in the Revolution. He was a schoolmaster in Hiram in 1778, perhaps the first. The land he settled on with his wife Catherine Boston of Hiram was deeded by Henry Young Brown, founder of Brownfield, and conveyed to John and Stephen Burbank of Brownfield, "Husbandmen," on December 30, 1790. It consisted of 229 acres of land on the east side of the Saco River "exclusive of an allowance for Bryants pond in said tract in Brownfield."[329] In the U.S. census of 1800, his age was given as under forty-five and he was living in Brownfield with a wife and four children—two sons and two daughters all under sixteen years of age, implying they were children of John and his first wife, Catherine.

They soon moved across the river. On February 21, 1793, John Ayer sold to John Burbank of Brownfield and Stephen Burbank of Flintstown (Baldwin) forty acres "of the Danford [Danforth] lot that John Burbank, Junr improved" in Hiram on the west bank of the Saco, for 40 pounds. Research done by Joan and Roger Brown disclosed that Hiram's first physician, Dr. Hannaford, owned this property in 1833, and Eli Clemons owned it in 1880. The Eli Clemons house on the river burned in 1919.

The property on the Saco River in the village is across Pequawket Trail from where the Israel/Asa Burbank house sits on a rise overlooking the west bank of the Saco.

---

329   Brownfield ceded this property to Hiram in 1806.

Property improved by John Burbank Jr., later owned and improved by Eli Clemons, on the west side of the Saco River just above the bridge. In his diary, Daniel Small records helping Dr. Hannaford raise his house in 1833.[330] The "new" house burned in June 1919.

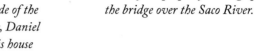

View of the property looking upstream from the bridge over the Saco River.

Stephen Burbank
dates unknown

Marriage date unknown

Mary (Polly) surname unknown, dates unknown

Stephen Burbank is a puzzle. Vital statistics are scarce. It is presumed he was the brother of John when Henry Young Brown deeded 229 acres to John and Stephen Burbank, husbandmen, of Brownfield on December 30, 1790. Three years later, when John Ayer deeded forty acres of the "Danford [Danforth] lot" to John and Stephen, Stephen was living in Baldwin. He does not appear in the Brownfield, Hiram, Baldwin, Cornish, or Fryeburg censuses of 1790 or 1800. He had a wife, but she was identified only once, in 1809, when Polly cosigned the deed selling John and Stephen's 229 acres, waiving her dower. The name of only one child is known, Samuel, born in 1803.

Back in Hiram in 1808, Stephen was elected collector of taxes, a position of responsibility for which he received 3 cents for every dollar collected. In 1809 he seemed to be doing well. He was charged tax on one poll, one dwelling house, one barn, four acres tillable land, eight acres mowing land, ninety acres unimproved land, one cow, two cattle three years old, two cattle one year old, one horse, one colt one year old, and three swine. He probably received some of the $780 paid for the 229 acres sold in 1809. But the next year, on November 29, 1810, the Overseers of the Poor in Portland notified Hiram that Stephen Burbank was a pauper in their town.

Subsequently much effort and many people involved themselves in caring for the family of Stephen Burbank, who moved around and had to be carried back to Hiram several times between 1810 and 1850 when he died. Perhaps the reason he enlisted in the War of 1812 was to earn money for his family. The saga of Stephen Burbank, pauper, whom Hiram recognized as a legal resident—except in 1823 when Cumberland recognized responsibility—is told in correspondence, bills, and receipts of expenses in the chapter Paupers of this book. Yet Stephen may have had money to buy twenty acres of his former property in partnership with the father of the owner in 1836.[331]

Why did Stephen fail when he and his brothers John and Israel owned about the same number of buildings, acreage, and livestock? Alcohol may have played a part. When he was a pauper he received "2 qt ginn 50 cents" after he went crazy around the time his wife died, which was charged to the town on April 8, 1823, by Benjamin Barker (a store keeper in Hiram).

---

330   Collections of Maine Historical Society.

331   Stephen Burbank and Moses Richardson purchased twenty acres adjacent to Thomas B. Watson's property in 1836, paying $150. Oxford County Registry of Deeds, Book 18, 59.

Another puzzle is Henry S. Burbank. There are four records of him. One was his request for reimbursement of $20 on April 8, 1823, for taking care of Stephen Burbank "while crazy" for twenty days and ten nights, for which the overseers deducted $10. Another was his marriage to Mercy Wentworth on April 6, 1824, in Hiram. In militia records his name appears in 1829. Presumably, initials H.S.B. on the back of the draft of the Constitution of the Hiram Light Infantry indicate he was involved in writing it. Lastly, his gravestone in the Wentworth Cemetery reads "Henry S. Burbank, Died Aug. 31, 1855, ae. 59 yrs. 7 mos. his wife Mercy, d. Jan. 27, 1873 ae. 72 yrs. 2 mos." He may have been "Harry," the son of John and Catherine Baston Burbank.

According to the Burbank genealogy, the Hiram Burbanks descended from one family. There is no mention of Henry S. or any other Henry of the same age.[332] Not until much later do we see another Henry Burbank. Henry N. Burbank, 1863–1948, lived in the house Benjamin Swett and his wife, Dolly Burbank, purchased from Simeon Bucknell in 1818 at 1232 River Road.

Town Offices Held

Collectors of Taxes

1805	Israel Burbank
1805	Israel Burbank
1806	Israel Burbank
1808	Stephen Burbank
1813	Asa Burbank
1815	Asa Burbank
1816	Asa Burbank (Voted to merge office with Constable)

Committees on Bridge Building and Repairs

1815   Saco River: Marshall Spring, Asa Burbank—to distribute subscription papers and obtain donations ; John Pierce, Asa Burbank, Isaac Gray—to view and ascertain the best place to erect said Bridge; John Pierce, Asa

John Burbank Finds Livestock on His Property

Regardless of how much livestock a farmer owned, he was always aware of his herd as it was valuable. Fencing was necessary to keep the animals from straying onto others' property and possibly causing damage, or a pound keeper's fee.

> To John Pierce Clerke of the Plantation of Hiram December 10, 1806
> This to ~~certify~~ give you notice that on the tenth day of December I found a Stear in my Barn yard three years old last Spring with a white Strip in his face and all four legs white his body Sparked black and white with long Sharp Horns the owner whereof to me is unknown. John Burbank.

Farmers depended upon livestock and would know by appearance the "Stear" was "three years old last Spring," but John Burbank did not know who the owner was. The steer was obviously marked and the owner should have registered the markings with the clerk. The clerk would publish the notice and report it to the pound keeper, who would collect it, and if no owner responded, had the right to dispose of it, which usually meant selling it.

Burbank, Marshall Spring—super intend the erecting of said Bridge (work to be paid at $1.25 per day up to July 15, 75 cents after).

---

332 Sedgley, *Genealogy of the Burbank Family*, 97.

1816   Hancock Brook: Chose John Pierce, John Watson, Asa Burbank a Committee to Superintend building the Bridge

Constables

1812	John Burbank
1813	Asa Burbank
1814	Asa Burbank
1815	Asa Burbank
1816	Asa Burbank (Voted to merge with office of Collector)

Fence Viewers

1830   William C. Burbank

Field Drivers

1816	Asa Burbank
1820	Asa Burbank

School Teachers

1778	John Burbank
1804	John Burbank

Selectmen

1803	John Burbank
1804	John Burbank
1805	John Burbank
1806	Israel Burbank
1815	Asa Burbank

Surveyors of Boards

1820	Asa Burbank
1822	Asa Burbank
1824	Asa Burbank

Surveyors of Boards and Clapboards

1823   Asa Burbank

Surveyors of Boards, Clapboards, and Shingles

1817	Asa Burbank
1821	Asa Burbank

Surveyors of Boards and Logs

1818   Asa Burbank

Simeon Bucknell, married to Hannah Burbank, sold this house in 1818 to Benjamin Swett, who had married Dolly Burbank. The house was later owned by Roland and Cora Clemons, stepfather and mother of Hubert W. Clemons.

Surveyors of Boards, Plank Timber, Slitworks, Clapboards & Shingles

    1816   Asa Burbank, Marshall Spring

Surveyors of Clapboards

    1819   Asa Burbank, Marshall Spring

Surveyors of Clapboards Shingles

    1820   Marshall Spring, Asa Burbank
    1821   James Evans, Marshall Spring, John Warren

Surveyors of Lumber

    1815   Asa Burbank
    1827   Asa Burbank
    1828   Asa Burbank

Surveyors of Highways

    1813   Israel Burbank
    1827   Henry S. Burbank

The Burbank/Clemons house at 1232 River Road in 2019 more closely resembles the house built in 1817. The barn was moved by Henry N. Burbank to attach to the shed, in the mode of "big house, little house, back house, barn."

CHADBOURNE FAMILY

Joseph Chadbourne
c. 1763–December 24, 1844?

First marriage May 23, 1793
Elizabeth Ayer, c. 1774–April 1812
Second marriage April 8, 1813
Dorcas Gray, died March 16, 1860

The Chadbournes were an interesting family from a long line of civic-minded souls with a religious bent. Before arriving in Hiram, Deacon Joseph Chadbourne held services in private homes in Cornish before a church was established in 1792. Elder John Chadbourne was an exhorter[333] doing the same. But it was Joseph who came to Hiram first, continuing to be a pew holder in Cornish as there was no organized church in Hiram.

Joseph was the son of Joshua and Susanna Spinney Chadbourne of Cornish. He married Elizabeth Ayer, daughter of the Hiram exhorter John Ayer. Although they were living in Cornish, their children Humphrey A., Benjamin, and Nancy were born in Hiram, likely in the house of Elizabeth's parents (now 6 Hiram Hill Road) before the parents sold it and moved to Cornish. Daughter Martha was born in Cornish c. 1802 after her parents, Joseph and Elizabeth, moved to Hiram.

The earliest record of Joseph in Hiram was his signature on the 1801 petition of Timothy Cutler to incorporate Hiram as a town, and he was established enough to be elected selectman of the newly established plantation in 1807. In 1811, sons Humphrey, sixteen, and Ben, fourteen, were in school in District 5, covering the area around Hiram Falls. Joseph's wife Elizabeth Ayer died in 1812, and he married Dorcas Gray of Hiram.

Joseph was active in town affairs, elected as a surveyor of highways in 1813, 1816, and 1821, and a fence viewer in 1815. Also that year, he served on the Committee on Bridge Repairs that led to the 1815 bridge tax for building a new bridge. His property was valued at $253 and his tax was $5.11. In 1820 and 1821, he was culler of hoops and staves, an impartial judge of the quality of wood for coopers, a trade several Chadbournes plied.

The children of Joseph and Elizabeth lived in Hiram for a while but left. Son Humphrey Ayer Chadbourne, born in Hiram April 2, 1795, served in Wheeler's Massachusetts Militia in the War of 1812. He voted in 1819, and was a school agent for three years—1821, 1822, and 1823. He moved his family to Fryeburg in the 1830s and died there February 23, 1872. Their son Humphrey A. died in the Civil War.

Son Benjamin Chadbourne, born February 14, 1798, married Nancy R. Richardson on October 31, 1827. She was the daughter of Artemas and Mary Thompson Richardson of Hiram. Benjamin was a natural mechanic and a cooper, a trade he left to farm. The Chadbournes were famous for their large frames and immense strength. Another Benjamin Chadbourne was driving a load uphill from Standish when the wagon stalled. He offloaded a barrel of pork onto his shoulders and trudged uphill behind the wagon.

Joseph's son Benjamin was also active, as tax collector in 1824, culler of hoops and staves in 1827, constable in 1828, a surveyor of highways in 1828, and, with his great strength, culler of hogs 1828. In 1849 and 1850, he was a selectman, but he moved from Hiram in 1852, age fifty-four. In Bridgton, on Chadbourne's Hill Road, he was "prominent in public affairs, a lieutenant in the militia, justice of the peace, selectman and constable, identified with the early temperance reform movement and a consistent member of the Methodist Episcopal Church."[334] He died December 18, 1875, in Bridgton.

John Wilson Chadbourne
August 6, 1786–March 19, 1866

Married May 29, 1811
Lydia Boynton, dates unknown

Also from Cornish, the son of William and Eleanor

---

333 Exhorters: religious "men of loud speech and pronounced demonstration, who could rub their hands and emphasize with stamp of foot." *Ridlon, Saco Valley Settlements and Families*, 230.

334 G. T. Ridlon, Sr., "William Chadbourne…," *Portland Sunday Telegram*, January 15, 1911, Hiram Historical Society.

Wilson Chadbourne, John W. joined Joseph in Hiram in 1809, age twenty-three, and continued to grow his farm, but not his family. In 1811, Patsy and Nancy were listed as scholars of John Chadbourne, but they are a better match to be Joseph's. By 1813, Joseph had five children in school and John had one.

By 1815 when the tax on the new bridge was calculated, John W. lagged Joseph in wealth, but had more than his neighbors. His property, valued at $177, was worth a little more than Abijah Lewis's and similar to Loammi Baston's, compared with neighbors William Storer ($136), Samuel Durgin ($91), and Levi Lord ($43), but Joseph's property was worth $253.

John W. held an office in almost every year from 1813 to 1825—surveyor of highways 1813, 1816–17; hog reeve 1815, 1816; field driver 1817; fence viewer 1818; culler of hoops and staves 1819–21; pound keeper 1825. John W. left Hiram sometime between 1830 and 1840. In 1850, he lived in Cornish with his son and daughter-in-law and their children, and was without his spouse. He is buried in Cornish.

His brother Samuel Chadbourne lived for many years in Hiram. Born February 1795, he is first on record for voting in 1819. He was still living in Hiram in 1860, but he was not elected to any office. He married Sophronia W. Odiorne.

Rev. John Chadbourne
May 10, 1788–March 24, 1860
Married January 25, 1798
Seviah Littlefield
November 11, 1778–June 20, 1860

Born in Sanford to Deacon Ebenezer and Anna Harmon Chadbourne, Rev. John was ordained in Shapleigh Baptist Church in 1818 and was pastor of the Second Baptist Church, Sanford, 1832–1834. He also preached in Eaton, New Hampshire, Hollis, and Hiram. He was known as Elder John Chadbourn, Second, to distinguish him from his uncle, who preached in Cornish. He married Seviah Littlefield January 25, 1798.

Some of their children married locally and remained.

Tax Rate Determinations of Joseph and John W. Chadbourne, 1809 and 1811

Valuation of real property (rateables) combined with the head (poll) tax determined the amount of tax owed. It illustrates the rate at which land was cultivated and farms grew. The Chadbournes' rateables, typical of many in Hiram, show how long it took some settlers to make improvements.

In 1809, Joseph had one hundred acres, of which he had tilled five and hayed five. He had a house and barn, two oxen, four cows, and two swine. In 1809, when John W. first came to Hiram, he owned one hundred acres, none of which was cultivated, but he also owned two oxen. Two years later, the year he married Lydia Boynton, John W. had built a house, increased his tilled acreage to two, and had two oxen, but still no barn. Both had added village land—Joseph three acres and John W. two. Joseph had another eligible voter under his roof (two polls), which usually meant a strong young man to help, had added one year-old cattle, and increased his swine to three—not big farms by any means, but showing steady growth.

George married Louisa Watson; Phebe married Royal Watson; William married Betsy R. Rankin; Mehitable married Freeman Hatch of Cornish,[335] an early owner of the store at Four Corners.

Simeon Chadbourne
January 29, 1783–February 6, 1872
Did not marry

Simeon was the most liked of the Chadbournes. Son of Humphrey and Elizabeth Libby Chadbourn of

---

335 William Morrell Emery, *Chadbourne-Chadbourn Genealogy* (Fall River, MA, 1904), 29.

Berwick, Maine, he never married and did not have children of his own, but he loved children and they loved him, calling him "Uncle Sim."

Simeon Chadbourne was living in Cornish when, on December 17, 1811, he bought the house of William West at the east end of the Hiram bridge over the Saco. William soon became a pauper, and Simeon boarded his wife, Mary West, for nine weeks in 1812, for which he received payment of $5.22.

It was thought that the store Simeon Chadbourne opened in 1816 was the first one in Hiram. However, the property deed places one and one-half acres sold by Asa Burbank to Simeon on June 20, 1816, adjacent to Whitten Pike's store. The Pike property had been sold by Asa Burbank three months earlier, on March 20, 1816.[336]

Simeon was just as active, if not more so, than his relatives, particularly from 1816 to 1827, and he was more willing to engage in politics. In 1816, a meeting in Simeon Chadbourne's house was held to discuss separation from Massachusetts. A vote taken showed forty-three in favor, fourteen against. Those opposed became fewer in number as the years passed. A

cooper, he was culler of hoops and staves in 1816 and 1821. He held the simultaneous positions of collector of taxes and constable from 1819 to 1821, was on the important Committee on Accounts in 1817 and 1818, and served as selectman in 1818, and from 1821 to 1823. Interestingly, although several of the Chadbournes were clergymen and respected men in town, Simeon was the only one to serve as tithing-man, an office he held in 1827.

Simeon Chadbourne Fountain

Years later, Simeon was fondly remembered with an impressive fountain in his memory. From an unknown undated newspaper article in the collections of Hiram Historical Society:

Mrs. Zilpha W. Spring, of Portland was in town Friday, on business connected with the public drinking fountain that she is erecting in her native village. Capt. Simeon Chadbourn, to whose memory the public fountain at Hiram was erected, was born in

Fountain honoring Simeon Chadbourne at the west end of Hiram Bridge, 1905. Mt. Cutler House, left, between Cotton's Store and Timothy Cutler house left of Pequawket Trail. Right of the road is Marshall Spring house (1593 Pequawket Trail) and Walter Bowie house (demolished 1990). Ella Butterfield Album, Hiram Historical Society.

336   Oxford County Registry of Deeds, Fryeburg, June 20, 1816, Book 7, 364, and March 20, 1816, Book 7, 113.

Gorham, Me., 29 January 1783 and died in Hiram 6 February 1872. He left no relatives in Hiram, excepting a large number of nephews and nieces, he having been "Uncle Sim" to all the inhabitants of Hiram. He came to Hiram about 1815.[337] He traded a while about 1817, on the site of Hon. N.B. Hubbard's house. Rev. John Pike had a store some six feet from his, and as he was Deputy Sheriff, and frequently absent, he sometimes employed Mr. Chadbourn to tend his store also. Mr. Chadbourn was a great reader, and was well informed on most subjects of general interest. He remembered the famous raising at Gorham in 1795, and was present when a portion of a church fell and killed Dr. Bowman, an event immortalized by Tom Shaw, the poet laureate of Gorham, in stanzas as follows, etc.

> 'Town of Gorham,
> Foolish people
> Killed Dr. Bowman,
> Raising a steeple.'

At a Special Town Meeting of November 4, 1884, it was voted to accept the Chadbourn Fountain and any changes and alterations that may be made by Mrs. Spring, also to thank her for the gift of the fountain, and to thank Charles E. Hubbard for his work on the fountain.

This fountain was about eight feet tall and made of cast iron. It was located at the westerly side of the last covered bridge and was supplied by gravity flow of water from a fountain on the side of Mt. Cutler in the area which is now the Merrill Botanical Park. Near the top was a cup for the benefit of birds. A little lower down a stream jetted forth for the benefits of thirsty horses that came along. Some of the overflow of this found its way into a cup near the base for the benefit of passing dogs. Sometime around 1920 one of

Notes on Simeon Chadbourn's life by Town Historian Llewellyn A. Wadsworth

Mar. 19, 1872—Capt. Simeon Chadbourn died in Hiram, Feb. 6, 1872, at the residence of Capt. A.R. Bucknell, where he has lived some 8 years. He was born in Berwick, Me., Jan. 27, 1783, to Humphrey and Mary Libby[338] Chadbourn, and was, therefore, 89 years and 8 days old. He was never married. He removed to Cornish in 1806, where he remained as a cooper till April 1814; thence to Gorham. He came to Hiram May, 1814. He recently informed me that at that time there was but one house in the vicinity of Hiram Bridge, in which Israel Burbank, Jr., kept the Post Office. It stood very near the site of the Mt. Cutler House. He commenced the first store in Hiram about 1816, near the present residence of Hon. Noah. B. Hubbard. Rev. John Pike commenced a store about 6 feet from Mr. Chadbourne's, which he finished first. Mr. Pike was for a time Deputy Sheriff and during his absence, Mr. Chadbourn frequently attended both stores, making or receiving payments. He has held the office of Constable, Selectman, Collector, etc., and was also Captain in the Militia. In politics he was a Republican and in religious faith a Calvinist Baptist. He was engaged in mercantile affairs some years with the late Benjamin Barker, Esq., of Hiram, whose daughters, now residing in Portland, have contributed to furnish the comforts of life in his declining years.

L. A. Wadsworth, *Oxford Democrat*, March 19, 1872

---

337 He bought from William West in 1811 a house at the east end of the Hiram bridge across the Saco.

338 This is incorrect. His wife was Betsey Libby.

the teams from A. & P. B. Young's sawmill ran away with a load of lumber which crashed into the fountain and tore it from its base. For several years it lay beside the River Road and them, mysteriously, it disappeared. Fortunately, someone salvaged the bronze plates which adorned it. Two of the plates are at present on display in the museum of the Hiram Historical Society.[339]

Town Offices Held

Collectors of Taxes

1819	Simeon Chadbourn
1820	Simeon Chadbourn (was paid Five Cents on a Dollar)
1821	Simeon Chadbourn (was paid 5.5 percent)
1823	Benjamin Chadbourn (was paid 5.5 percent)
1824	Benjamin Chadbourn

Committee on Accounts

1817	Simeon Chadbourn
1818	Simeon Chadbourn
1827	Simeon Chadbourn
1828	Simeon Chadbourn

Committees on Bridge Building and Repairs

1815	Joseph Chadbourne, agent, to build bridge across Hancock Brook
1818	Thomas Spring, Joseph Chadbourn, Simeon Bucknell; John Warren agent, Ossipee River bridge repairs
1830 Sept. 13	Ossipee River: Voted to choose Ben Chadbourne an Agent to consult with Cornish respecting the repairs of the upper bridge

Constables

1819	Simeon Chadbourn
1820	Simeon Chadbourn
1821	Simeon Chadbourn
1823	Benjamin Chadbourn
1824	Benjamin Chadbourn
1826	Benjamin Chadbourn
1828	Benjamin Chadbourn?

Cullers of Hogs and Steeres

1828	Benjamin Chadbourn

Cullers of Hoops & Staves

1816	Simon Chadbourne
1820	Joseph Chadbourn
1821	Joseph Chadbourn, Simeon Chadbourne
1822	Simeon Chadbourn, Benjamin Chadbourn
1823	Benjamin Chadbourn
1824	Benjamin Chadbourn

Fence Viewers

1815	Joseph Chadbourn
1818	John W. Chadbourn

Field Drivers

1816	Joseph Chadbourn
1817	John W. Chadbourn
1822	Simeon Chadbourn
1827	Simeon Chadbourn

Hog Reeves

1815	John Chadbourne
1816	John W. Chadbourne

Pound Keepers

1825	Joseph Chadbourn

School Agents

1821	Humphrey A. Chadbourne District #6
1822	Humphrey A. Chadbourn #6
1823	Humphrey A. Chadbourn #6
1824	Benja Chadbourn #6
1825	Benj Chadbourn
1826	Benj Chadbourn
1827	Benj Chadbourn
1828	Benj Chadbourn
1829	Samuel Chadbourne #6
1830	Ben Chadbourne

Selectmen

1807	Joseph Chadbourne

---

339   Raymond C. Cotton, *Hog Reaves, Field Drivers, and Tything Men*, Hiram, ME: Hiram Historical Society, 1983), 19.

1818	Simeon Chadbourn
1821	Simeon Chadbourn
1822	Simeon Chadbourne
1823	Simeon Chadbourne

Surveyors of Highways

1813	Joseph Chadbourn, Joseph W. Chadbourn
1816	Joseph Chadbourn
1817	John W. Chadbourn
1821	Joseph Chadbourn
1822	Simeon Chadbourn
1823	Simeon Chadbourn
1824	Simeon Chadbourn, Benja Chadbourn
1826	Ben Chadbourn
1828	Benj. Chadbourne Jr.

Surveyors of Lumber

1825	Simeon Chadbourn, Benj Chadbourn
1828	Simeon Chadbourne [first use of "e" at end]
1830	Benja Chadbourne

Surveyors of Split Lumber

1830	Simeon Chadbourne

Tithingmen

1827	Simeon Chadbourne

JOHN CLEMONS
Before 1743–after 29 June, 1790

Married October 27, 1757

Abigail Southwick, c. 1728–January 8, 1832

The Clemons surname was also spelled Clammons, Clammonds, Clamons, Clemens, Clement, Clemmonds, Clemonds, and Clermont.

One of the earliest settlers in Hiram was John Clemons, who arrived with his family from Brownfield via Fryeburg via Danvers, Massachusetts, in 1780. Traveling south on foot from Brownfield in 1779,[340] they were looking for a place to settle when they came upon the home of the Capt. John Lane family on the Pequawket Trail.[341]

John's son Eli Pope Clemons was four years old, but remembered when they first came to Hiram. Town historian Llewellyn A. Wadsworth wrote in his journal in 1870:

> The date of their coming in 1779 is proved by the fact that Eli P. Clemons who was born in Danvers, Mass., 8 Sept. 1775, remembers that they passed the night at Capt. John Lane's, Eli being then four years old…also that they had some bean porridge poured into the hollow or sag of a leather bottomed chair and the children ate it with spoons.

William Teg tells the story with more flourish:

> The story of their first coming to Hiram in 1779 has often been told, but loses none of its savor in the retelling. So here it is: John Clemons, his wife and six children—originally natives of Danvers, Massachusetts, started from Fryeburg, coming on foot along the Pequawket Trail, arrived at the home of Capt. John Lane on the Saco. Although their coming was unexpected, they were hospitably received and entertained, as was the custom among the early pioneers. But, as it may be supposed, any elaborate reception was out of the question. As for food, well, it seems to have been restricted to only one dish, bean porridge. This was served to the children from a depression in the leather bottom of an old arm chair![342]

Mrs. Lane was not expecting company, let alone six more children, and did not have enough bowls, so came up with the creative solution of serving the porridge in the seat of the chair, a solution that was not to be forgotten and was related down through the generations. Other versions imply that there were not enough spoons either, saying the children ate the porridge with spoons and clam shells.

> The next problem that confronted John Clemens was to discover a place in the wilderness suitable for a farm. Such a find presented itself to him one day while out hunting along the shores of two beautiful ponds. In October 1780, the Clemens family domiciled itself between the two ponds—now bearing its name. And here, through industry and frugality, became comfortably situated.[343]

The Clemons family settled on land included in Gen. Peleg Wadsworth's Grant, sometimes referred to as a patent. In a deed dated June 29, 1790,[344] Wadsworth described the property, for which John

---

340   William Teg, *Hiram*, 1941, 26.

341   The Clemons were living at Island Bridge in Brownfield per Ridlon, *Saco Valley Settlements and Families*, 582.

342   William Teg, *Hiram*, 1941, 26.

343   Ibid.

344   York County Registry of Deeds, Book 57, 76, written June 29, 1790, recorded September 24, 1794. Deed Book 55, 216, from Peleg Wadsworth to Abigail Clemons for 1 pound 10 shillings "adjoining Ten Mile Pond" west of Bill Merrill Mountain for one hundred acres surveyed in 1789 was written September 11, 1794.

Photo of Clemons Pond from above the Clemons homestead. Photo by Andrew Zelman, 2019.

Clamons [Clemons] paid 63 pounds, as being "two hundred acres of new Land situated in Hiram and laying on the northerly Decent of Bill Merrill's Hill, so called, being the two hundred acre Lotts formerly laid out to Lemuel Haywood [Howard] by Joseph Frye Surveyor...." Lemuel Howard married John's daughter Hannah.

John built a log cabin and lived there for the rest of his life, happy to be near good hunting and fishing in a beautiful spot in "the Notch." For seven years the only neighbors were Tom Hegon, Native American hunter and trapper, and his wife, who lived in their wigwam on a ridge near Clemons Pond (formerly called Ten Mile Pond). Tom Hegon was an Abenaki Pequawket and one of fourteen warriors who became soldiers on the side of the patriots during the Revolution.[345] These two families were friendly and the Hegons and Clemonses share the same resting place near the "Indian Mound."[346]

It is not known how old John was when he married Abigail Southwick on October 27, 1757.

Most likely he was born before 1743, as he was a colonial soldier in 1755. There is much speculation as to who Abigail Southwick was, and there are several possibilities, chiefly that Abigail was born in Danvers, Massachusetts, c. 1728, as her obituary noted that she died in Hiram on January 8, 1832, at age 104. If so, she would have been twenty-nine years old when she married and forty-nine when her sixth child, Eunice, was born on October 10, 1777. She bore two more girls, Tamar and Delilah.

The first white woman to call at the house was Mrs. Keazar [Kezar] of Parsonsfield, who accompanied her husband on snowshoes when on his way to Fryeburg.[347] Another story related by G. T. Ridlon illustrates the isolation and hardship of that time. When John and his eldest son were at Fryeburg to get corn ground, a snowstorm came up, and so deep were the drifts that father and son were detained for several days. Meanwhile, on the last day, Mrs. Clemons had only a cupful of beans made into porridge to feed her five children.[348]

345 Hubert Clemons, *The Clemons Family of Hiram, Maine*, 1981, 7a.

346 Ibid., 3. The site is unconfirmed.

347 Ridlon, *Saco Valley Settlements and Families*, 581.

348 Ibid.

View of Clemons Pond from the house, spring 2014.

An interesting side note is that the family was summoned to the dinner table by a primitive "trumpet," a conch shell brought with them from Danvers.

Though it is not known when John was born, the year John died is known—1790—and it was probably after June 29, when Peleg Wadsworth and John Clemons wrote the deed granting John two hundred acres. On June 15, 1791, Philip Corey, Benjamin Burbank Jr., and Israel Burbank, appraisers, took an inventory of the estate of John Clements [Clemons], late of Hiram in the county of York,[349] yeoman, deceased. In August the Court of Probate in Waterboro granted Abigail administration of the estate. She gave bond of 40 pounds with two sureties, namely son Jonathan Clemons and Simon Frye, Esq., for the faithful discharge of her trust.

Shortly after John's death, the two young girls, Tamar and Delilah, died suddenly. The widow then walked miles through the woods to her nearest neighbor, Daniel Baston, for help in burying her daughters.[350]

Why didn't the girls' brothers help bury them? Where were the older sons in 1790 when their sisters died?

The oldest child, John Clemons Jr., was born on June 4, 1763, in Danvers, Massachusetts. He served in the Revolutionary War. He was enlisted January 1780 by Sergeant McCoy from the 15th Regiment to serve to the end of war. The descriptive list of enlisted men dated West Point, January 10, 1781, Light Infantry Company, Col. Rufus Putnam's 5th Regiment, identifies him as "aged 16 years, stature 5 feet 7 inches, complexion dark hair and eyes dark; resident of Salem."[351] He married Mary McLellan on February 6, 1789, in Gorham, Maine. In 1790, they resided in Hiram in a cabin behind John's and up the mountain on what became Capt. Artemas

---

349   Hiram was assigned to the new county, Oxford, in 1805.

350   Ibid., 581.

351   Danvers was then part of Salem.

Richardson's, between what later was Capt. Samuel Wadsworth's and the mill brook. According to Gideon T. Ridlon, it was here that Gen. Peleg Wadsworth passed his first night in Hiram. In the morning, he and John Clemons ascended Bill Merrill Mountain and made an optical survey of the grant of land of seventy-eight hundred acres assigned to Wadsworth, from which he sold two hundred acres to Clemons.

In 1804, John Jr. moved his family west to Hamilton, Madison County, New York. At the urging of their son Alexander in 1817, they moved farther west to Sandusky, Ohio, then to Marblehead, Ottawa County, Ohio, in 1835. Their son William settled farther west, and he served in the Mexican war. Later he and his wife and two children were killed by Native Americans.

The second son, Jonathan, born May 7, 1770, married Hannah Lane, daughter of Capt. John Lane, who had provided the initial hospitality to the Clemonses. Jonathan settled on a farm situated about one mile east of the family homestead and had eight children born between c. 1803 and 1829: Samuel C.; Caleb C.; John L.; Mary; Ruth; Lavina; Daniel; Marshall. For 45 pounds he bought one hundred acres from Gen. Peleg Wadsworth in a deed dated June 8, 1795. The northwesterly end line was the property of Lemuel Howard, who had recently bought from Wadsworth and was later to marry John's daughter, Hannah.

It was Jonathan to whom the widow Abigail conveyed her property in 1825. However, son Eli Pope Clemons recovered judgment against Abigail for $800 debt or damages and $18.55 costs of suit, and the bulk of the homestead was conveyed to Eli in 1826.[352] She conveyed the remaining property to Jonathan.[353]

Thus, Abigail lost her property. How could this happen? As a property owner, the widow had to pay taxes, but a woman had very little means to support herself and her children before they married, usually by 18 years of age.

About this time the present farmhouse was expanded, presumably by Eli, who had received title.

Eli Pope Clemons, born five years after Jonathan, married Ruth Hanscum [Hanscomb] on March 6, 1804, and settled near his parents. They had eleven children between 1805 and 1830, nine of whom reached adulthood: William, Sudrick, Bartlett, Lorinda, Aldrick M., Jane I., Peleg W., Ruth, and Lafayette. Ruth, who died in 1917, was the last Clemons to own the homestead.

The farm at what is now 133 Notch Road has one of the finer prospects in Hiram, with gently sloping fields to frame the view of Clemons Pond and the hills behind. The Cape-style house with its recessed porch, an addition built c. 1826, is attractive and well kept. The barn is a fine example of a Yankee barn with extensions. It, too, has a recessed open area.

Of John and Abigail's other children, Hannah Clemons married her neighbor, Lemuel Howard, the uncle of Judge Joseph Howard of Brownfield, in 1779, and in 1785 settled behind the Clemons homestead on Hiram Hill, on the farm subsequently owned by William Cotton, who married their daughter.[354] Lemuel signed Timothy Cutler's petition for incorporation of Hiram as a town in 1801 and voted regularly. In April 1812, he was reimbursed $2 for four weeks board of Mrs. West, a pauper, and

Clemons homestead, 2014. The recessed entry likely dates from c. 1826.

352   Registry of Deeds, Fryeburg, ME, Book 11, 359.

353   Jonathan died on June 15, 1855, and his epitaph reads, "The land I cleared is now my grave."

354   Ridlon, *Saco Valley Settlements and Families*, 581.

Clemons homestead. Mt. Cutler forms the background. The older part of the house is to the right. Photo mid-nineteenth century.

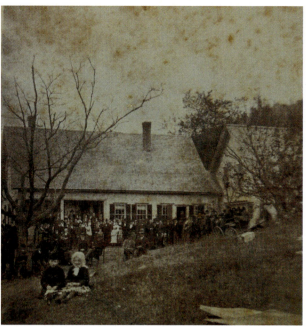

Clemons family reunion, 1880.

two years later $3.91 for milk, butter, and a peck of potatoes for her. Their son John served in the War of 1812 and was a hog reeve in Hiram in 1817.

Daughter Ruth married Capt. Charles Lee Wadsworth in 1795. Daughter Eunice married Elder James Fly, who came to Hiram from Gorham, Maine, in 1794. Elder James was the son of James Fly, a Revolutionary soldier who also served at Ticonderoga in 1758 during the French and Indian War. Elder James and Eunice settled on Hiram Hill above the John Clemons farm. Elder Fly, ordained on September 5, 1822, organized the Free Will Baptist Church in Hiram in 1825.

When Abigail Clemons died on January 8, 1832, at age 104 she left 164 descendants. In 1880, more than ten percent of the population living in Hiram was descended from John Clemons or connected with the family by marriage, more family links than to any other early settler. In 2014, there was only one Clemons from Hiram still living in Hiram, Hubert Wentworth Clemons, born January 27, 1929, town historian and one of the founders of the Hiram Historical Society.[355]

Yankee style barn with extensions, 2014.

---

355 Hubert W. Clemons passed away on April 17, 2019, at ninety years old.

WILLIAM COTTON
October 5, 1776–December 7, 1859

Married May 25, 1800
Hannah Howard, June 16, 1771–May 28, 1871

William Cotton was the progenitor of the extensive Cotton family in Hiram. Born in Gorham to John Cotton, the fanatical enthusiastic Baptist known as "the mad preacher," William lived in Cornish and in about 1799 settled northeast of Bill Merrill Mountain, above John Clemons's farm.

His wife, Hannah, was the daughter of Lemuel and Hannah Clemons Howard. Together they had six children. They were Lydia, 1800; Lemuel, 1801; John H., 1804; Living, 1805; Ruth W. 1806; and William Jr., 1809. William and Hannah Howard Cotton are buried in the William Cotton I family cemetery on Richardson Road.

William served in the War of 1812 under Capt. Alpheus Spring, another Hiram resident. They held muster in Captain Thomas Spring's field and marched to defend Portland against the British. William held neighborhood town offices of fence viewer, school agent of District No. 4, and surveyor of highways. Sons Lemuel and Living were also elected surveyors of highways. A neighbor of the Wadsworths and a trusted employee, William sat one night with Peleg Wadsworth toward the end of Peleg's fatal illness in 1829.

Son William Jr. married Levina Clemons and raised eight children on Hiram Hill on his farm on the old Schoolhouse Road, now called Maple Hill Run Road. William Jr. and Levina are buried there in the William Cotton II family cemetery.

L. A. Wadsworth thought William Jr.'s place worthy of comment in his 1876 diary when he rode to buy skunk oil for Marshall Spring, who was ill with pneumonia:[356]

> Jan 30. I rode to Mr. Moulton's[357] with Mr. M. thence to Albert Lowell's, borrowed a bottle, and went to Joshua Sargent's and bought of the boys a bottle ½ pint of Skunk's Grease for twenty five cents for Marshall Spring. I rode with Darius R. Lewis & Lincoln Cotton. I came via Wm. Cotton's & Lafayette Clemons (whose wife was ill with Lung Fever).[358]

The Cottons, like most of Hiram's settlers, were farmers. The first notable industry established by the Cotton family was in the 1870s, when Living's son Lemuel II (1840–1916) started making ax handles at his home on Hiram Hill.[359] Lemuel and his son Charles and grandson Raymond ran the factory until World War II, shipping handles treated with their trademark "Ebonoak" all over New

Almon Storer (left) and Cyrus Goodwin (right) at the old ax handle factory behind Lemuel Cotton's house on Pequawket Trail before it burned in 1919. It was rebuilt in 1920.

---

356   Skunk oil was used for respiratory problems.

357   Reuben Moulton's farm, 818 Notch Road.

358   Llewellyn A. Wadsworth, *Journal*, Manuscript, Hiram Historical Society, January 30, 1876.

359   Raymond C. Cotton, *Split, Rive and Whittle: The Story of Lemuel Cotton's Axe Handle Factory* (Hiram, ME: Hiram Historical Society, 1989), 5.

Leon Lombard, salesman, poses with the largest white oak "bolt" ever received at the axe handle factory. It grew in Porter and took a pair of strong horses to transport to the factory, 1927.

Lemuel Cotton II delivered a birthday present bicycle for grandson Raymond Cotton, c. 1912.

England and northern New York. The patterns and machinery were sold to the King Axe & Tool Co., Oakland, Maine.

Ever industrious, Lemuel started another enterprise. In 1884, he purchased from John P. Hubbard one-half acre, with buildings, adjacent to Mt. Cutler House in the village, and he moved there. The next year he partnered with Hubbard at the store. After the partnership with Hubbard was dissolved, it became the legendary general store handed down to son Charles and grandson Raymond. The store was owned and operated by the Cottons for 102 years until sold to Edmund P. Chernesky in 1987.

Raymond Cotton (1904–1998), third-generation Cotton store owner, was exceptional all his life. Customers who flocked to the store listened to tales while seated on cracker barrel stools and bought tripe and cheese while hearing the crackle of Ray's ham radio. During the 1947 fires that radio proved invaluable in communicating with the outside world. While running the store, Raymond was town clerk for fifty years, storyteller, author, filmmaker, lover of children, educator, a founder of Hiram Historical Society, and

curious about everything—a warm, friendly, civic-minded, fair, and decent man. The seventh generation still lives in Hiram.

Cotton's store stands on part of Timothy Cutler's grant, awarded in November 1787. The land[360] was purchased by Israel Burbank and John Burbank. The mortgage to Cutler was $562. Israel's son, Asa Burbank, took possession in 1811 after Cutler relocated to Berwick.

It has been said that Simeon Chadbourne built the first store in Hiram, but Whitten's store was finished before Chadbourne's. Trader John Pike of Hiram purchased the land from Asa Burbank on March 28, 1816, and partnered with Simon J. Whitten of Parsonsfield. When trader Simeon Chadbourne of Hiram purchased 1.5 acres from Asa Burbank to build his store in June 1816,[361] it was at

---

360   150 acres plus the Danforth lot adjacent to John Burbank's land and across the road from Cutler's house.

361   Oxford County Registry of Deeds, Fryeburg, now in Paris, March 28, 1816, Book 7, 113; Asa Burbank to John Pike; June 20, 1816, Asa Burbank to Simeon Chadbourne, Book 7, 364. Chadbourne may have traded from his house on the east bank of the Saco.

Lemuel Cotton & Son Store c. 1895. It was considerably expanded and altered from the store built by Simon J. Whitten or Simeon Chadbourn c. 1816.

the corner of Whitten's store. Pike sold the store to Whitten on December 6 1817.

Benjamin Barker, who had clerked at Chadbourne's store and filled in at Whitten's store, was familiar with both, and he bought both in 1823, Whitten's in August and Chadbourne's in October.

When Benjamin Barker and Peleg Wadsworth sold the store to John P. Hubbard in 1845 for $800, the property contained the store, shed, chaise house, blacksmith shop, dwelling house, and the right of way on the County Road to Cornish, a total of one acre, more or less. This right of way established that Whitten's store was the location of the present Cotton's store. Barker reserved the right of way at the north end and the privilege of occupying the garden in common with Hubbard as long as Hubbard improved the land around the "ditch."[362]

Earlier owners of the store were Benjamin Barker (1823), John P. Hubbard (1845), Wilson, Tennant, Hogan & Gray (1870), Charles E. and John W. Hubbard (1871), John Pierce and A. P. Sanborn (1872), T. B. Seavey & Co. (1879), Noah B. Hubbard (1880) and James M. Young and J. W. Hubbard (1880), John W. Hubbard (1881).

Cotton's store was considerably expanded by John P. Hubbard in the mid-nineteenth century. The building is now owned by David Foley, a Cotton descendant, who is renovating it.

Lemuel Cotton & Son Store as it appeared in 1914 with centennial bunting.

Town Offices Held

Fence Viewers

1825	William Cotton

School Agents

1819	William Cotton
1821	William Cotton

School Teachers

1819	William Cotton
1820	William Cotton

---

362 Oxford County Registry of Deeds, Fryeburg, now in Paris, January 18, 1845, Book 23, 256.

Cotton's store became the Hiram Village Store. Photo 2017.

Surveyors of Highways

1819	William Cotton
1820	William Cotton
1821	William Cotton
1822	William Cotton
1824	William Cotton
1825	William Cotton
1828	Lemuel Cotton
1829	Lemuel Cotton
1830	Living Cotton

JOSEPH CRAM
May 15, 1762–January 28, 1815
Marriage date unknown
Abigail Pugsley
November 4, 1770–April 13, 1841

Joseph Cram left a legacy that exists today, but it was not always in Hiram. He and Daniel were in Hiram from 1812 to 1814, Daniel staying through 1815,[363] paying taxes and voting, but without much wealth. In 1812, Joseph had no real estate and his personal property was valued at only $10, hence his tax was a combination of the poll tax of $2.10 and twenty cents in personal property. Daniel had no property in 1812, but by 1815 was taxed in the upper third of taxes paid.

In the War of 1812, Daniel was a corporal in Capt. Alpheus Spring's company of Major James Steele's battalion of artillery, with service in Portland in 1814. Joseph's son John was a private in the same company, age eighteen.

Joseph died in 1815, and the Crams moved to Baldwin and were not heard from again in Hiram until Joseph's grandson, Joseph Cram Jr., of Cornish, bought property on Tear Cap in 1866, after which the Crams became a prolific Hiram family, led by Joseph and Adeline Chick Cram. But because they did not hold office in their early brief years, and because of their late arrival in later years, the family is not considered founders of Hiram.

The Cram family:

Joseph Cram and Abigail Pugsley, Baldwin

Son Daniel Cram (1789–1861) and Eliza Spencer (1803–1888), Baldwin

Son John Cram (1796–1868) and Lydia Thorn (1796–1864), Baldwin

Grandson Joseph Cram (1820–1901) and Adeline Chick (1824–1897), Hiram

Great-grandson Daniel Bela Cram (1852–1925) and Bertha Jane Allen (1862–1933), Hiram

The Cram homestead, Tear Cap, Hiram, was built or enlarged by Joseph Cram or his son Daniel Bela Cram. It burned in 1911. Note laundry drying on the lawn.

---

363 Weldon J. Cram was also taxed in 1815. No further information about him is known.

DAVID DURGIN
August 20, 1749–1820

Married 1771

Abigail Haines, November 29, 1746 or 1749–?

The families of David Durgin and his eldest son, Samuel, were among the first settlers on the Waters Grant in what is now South Hiram. They were the only two Durgin families in 1800, but by 1820 there were six in what became known as Durgintown, the neighborhood that spanned the Waters Grant and part of the Wadsworth Grant. According to descendants, three brothers emigrated from Ireland and one settled in Hiram after living in Scarborough and serving in the Revolutionary War. Brothers David, John, and Silas served in Capt. John Rice's company.[364]

The earliest record of David and Abigail Haines Durgin in Hiram is in 1800. They were in their fifties with four children in their household. The sons were Joshua (twenty-five years old), David Jr. (seventeen), and John (nine). David Jr. had married Sally Lord on March 15, 1800, and may have been living at home when the census was taken in August. The daughter counted in the census is likely Elizabeth, birth date unknown and probably at home until she married Samuel Tibbetts Jr., of Buxton, in 1816.

According to Hiram Historical Society records, eight children were born before 1800, but four were not listed in the census. Who were the four not counted? Samuel M. had his own household in 1800. Eighteen-year-old Abigail married Levi Lord in 1800 and was probably not living at home. This leaves two sons unaccounted for: Timothy H. (sixteen) and Joseph (fourteen), old enough to be hired out, living and working on other farms, as was common.

David and Abigail's oldest son, Samuel M., married Phebe Day in 1793. In the 1800 census, Samuel's household consisted of him and Phebe and three children under ten. Later arrivals were Abigail, Margaret, Dorothy, Naomi, and Caleb, born between 1804 and 1813. Of these, only Naomi married a spouse from Hiram, Abner McDonald, on November 2, 1829.

Cutler's petition of 1801 to incorporate as a town caused some initial difference of opinion in Durgin households. David Jr. and Samuel were in favor of incorporation, but were swayed by Charles Lee Wadsworth and joined father David and brother Joseph signing against incorporation.

These Durgins—Samuel, Joseph, David, and David Jr.—were all named on the list of voters for 1809. To be on the list for this year, one had to be a resident of Hiram for one year and be a white male of twenty-one years with an annual income of $10 or an estate worth $200.

Curiously, David and John don't appear on the tax lists of 1809. Called rateables, or inventories, they detail the number of polls, dwelling houses, outbuildings, barns, acres of land, and livestock on which taxes were based, but all appear in 1810 and 1811. Joseph had triple the land and double the livestock of the others.

Although the Durgins were counted in the 1800 U.S. census of "Hyram," the first recorded real estate deed is October 26, 1809, when David Durgin Jr., yeoman, of Hiram, sold to Bennet Pike, of Cornish, twenty acres of the land and buildings where he lived.[365] The next earliest deed is December 3, 1810 in which David Durgin conveys to David Jr. one hundred acres of land extending from the Ossipee River to his land.[366] In 1813, David Durgin sold fifty acres to Ephraim Tibbetts and referenced it as the lot Peleg Wadsworth sold to him.[367] Descendants consider the Durgin homestead was most likely built by 1809 when David was taxed on one house and one barn. A late recording of deeds is not surprising, as

---

364   Massachusetts soldiers and sailors in the Revolutionary War.

365   Oxford County Registry of Deeds, Fryeburg, Book 5, 134.

366   Oxford County Registry of Deeds, Fryeburg, Book 6, 76.

367   Oxford County Registry of Deeds, Fryeburg, Book 6, 318.

Durgin homestead at 339 Durgintown Road, 2017, shown between the Durgintown School (left) and Yankee barn (right). The front portico and sun porch were added.

The Durgin/Ordway Cemetery lies below the homestead and school and adjacent to Apple Acres. Eighteen Durgins/Ordways are buried there.

the Durgins worked in the forest for Peleg Wadsworth to earn a fifty-acre deed from him.[368] The Durgins sent their children to school in District 5-6.

Durgin children in school in 1811, listed under the fathers' names:[369]

Samuel Durgin
   Betsey and Daniel
   Joseph
   Abigail
   Peggy
   Dolly
David Durgin
   John
Joseph Durgin
   Rebecka
   Mary
   Silas
David Durgin Jr.
   Sophia
   Timothy
   Lovey

With all the Durgins nearby, family support would seem to be assured, but David Jr. ran into financial difficulties in 1814, as did Samuel in 1824. In the Town Meeting of November 7, 1814, the first held after incorporation as a town, the first order of business, after choosing Peleg Wadsworth as moderator, was "to see what the Town will do with regard to the disposal of the family of David Durgin jr who are become paupers in Cornish."[370] The typical "disposal" of paupers was to auction the able-bodied to board and work for the lowest bidder, but no action was recorded in this case. David Jr. must have reacquired some of his wealth and returned to Hiram, because he is listed in the 1820 census of Hiram. All but Joseph, who died in 1820, are on the 1822 list of voters. Joseph must have had some skill because in the same first Town Meeting, November 7, 1814, he and another Durgintown resident, Jacob Lord, were elected "to nail that part of Cornish Bridge belonging to Hiram and make any other necessary repairs, and to put up a fence to prevent passengers from falling into the gully made by the Freshet and

---

368 According to Susan Douglas Moulton, Peleg Wadsworth descendant, in conversation with Sally Williams, February 28, 2021.

369 Maine State Archives, Hiram Box 8.

370 Hiram Town Clerk Record, November 7, 1814, 5.

immediately & that their Labours thereon shall be accounted for in their future Highway Taxes."

In February 1824, John Wadsworth, son of Peleg, won a judgment against Samuel, and the sheriff threatened Samuel with jail in lieu of paying his debt or having the equivalent amount of his goods sold. The debt was $14.55, which burgeoned to $42.03 with the added costs of the suit.

David Jr. and Sally Durgin's children were Sophia, Daniel, Love, Daniel III, Hannah, Sarah, William, and Abigail, born between 1801 and 1820. Two daughters, Sarah and Judith, died in infancy.

Joseph Durgin, born in 1786, married Ruth Farnham of Hiram. Their children were Rebecca, Mary, Silas, Jane, Patience, and Betsey, born between 1803 and 1819.

John Durgin owned a sawmill on the Ossipee River at Warren Bridge, built in 1824 by Capt. Theophilus Smith of Cornish. Smith was the mason employed by Peleg Wadsworth for Wadsworth Hall.

Col. John Warren purchased the mill in 1834. Shortly thereafter it was consumed by fire.

Durgins held offices of field driver and hog reeve in their neighborhoods, but otherwise were not active in town affairs.

Town Offices Held

Field Drivers
1811	David Durgin
1815	Joseph Durgin

Hog Reeves
1817	John Durgin
1818	Joseph Durgin
1822	Daniel Durgin

Surveyors of Highways
1829	Joseph Durgin

JAMES EASTMAN
c. 1750/51–November 13, 1833
Married January 12, 1787
Sarah Whitehorn, c. 1760/61–March 10, 1852?
and

THOMAS TRIPP
October 31, 1776–December 31, 1854
Married April 11, 1801
Polly Hamilton, c. 1779–c. March 9, 1850

James Eastman, a soldier of the French and Indian Wars and the Revolution, settled on the top of Hiram Hill. His grave, off what is now called Richardson Road, is marked by a plaque and a veteran's flag.

James was a collector of taxes for the years 1805, 1806, and 1807, for which he was paid 3 cents on the dollar he collected. He and his wife were remembered for dressing the crop of flax for farmers in the region, even late in life. Eastman lived into his eighties,

presumably with the support of Richard Tripp and others plus a Revolutionary War pension.[371] The pension of half-pay, which commenced on March 4, 1833, at a rate of $40 per annum, benefited him nine months and his widow until her death in Denmark, where she was living with daughter Lucy and her husband Rand Chadbourne Sr.

Tripptown is the neighborhood settled first by Thomas and Polly Hamilton Trippe of Sanford, Maine. Several of their children would have been born in Sanford—Richard, 1801; Isaiah, 1803; Eliza, 1804; Hiram, no information available; Thomas Trippe Jr., 1808; Sarah A., 1810; Roxana, 1812; Nancy, 1814.

Richard married Elizabeth (Betsey) Eastman on April 15, 1821. The next year Richard and his father, Thomas, bought property from Betsey's father, James Eastman, and with this property Richard first appeared on a voter list in 1822.

The Tripps were intricately interwoven with the Eastmans by marriage, ensuring family support, as were many of Hiram's families. Deed transactions among James Eastman, Richard, and Richard's father Thomas Tripp[372] in 1822 and 1823 were several and complicated. Richard and Thomas bought fifty-five acres on the Waters Grant for $350 from James Eastman, Richard's father-in-law, on March 25, 1822.[373] A month later, on April 25, 1822, Thomas paid Richard $350, provided that Richard pay James Eastman "the Sum of $800 or Shall Well and Truly Maintain James and his wife agreeable to a certain Bond given to James by Thomas and Richard Tripp."

James Eastman burial site, located at the end of Richardson Road, 2019.

---

371 He served one year, 1775–76, as private under Captain Clough's regiment, commanded by Colonel Poor, on the New Hampshire line.

372 The "e" at the end of their name was dropped.

373 Property James Eastman had purchased from Peleg Wadsworth on October 23, 1801.

Four days later, on April 29, 1822, Richard paid Thomas $175 for an undivided half of their property, the lot on which Thomas lived. The property was adjacent to that of John Clemons. On May 13, 1823, Thomas Tripp paid Peleg Wadsworth $275 for fifty-five acres of the lot called the Day Lot, the same lot on which Thomas lived. On September 13, 1823, Richard and Thomas sold to the selectmen of Hiram the same property for $500. Either the Tripps failed to provide support for the Eastmans or the Eastmans needed more support than the Tripps could give, for a month later Solomon Hartford sold his adjoining property to the selectmen for $500 in return for support of the Eastmans and "a certain sum to Lucy Eastman," a daughter who was thirteen at the time. Town support returned to Richard Tripp in 1831 and 1835, authorized by a new set of selectmen.[374]

Town Offices Held

Field Drivers
| 1824 | Richard Tripp |

Hog Reeves
| 1822 | Richard Trippe |

School Agents
| 1828 | Richard Trippe |
| 1829 | Richard Tripp District #11 |

---

374 Lucy Eastman married Solomon H. Gilpatrick of Hiram in 1847 at age forty-seven.

JAMES FLYE

September 27, 1741–?

Married November 21, 1761

Jerusha Freeman, c. 1741–?

James Fly and wife Jerusha Freeman Fly migrated northwest from Gorham to Baldwin, then to Hiram, in 1794, settling on the River Road along the Saco River below the Great Falls.

In 1815, their son, Elder James Fly, became a tithingman, a position of high esteem, and was a founder of the Freewill Baptist Church in 1825. He married Eunice Clemons, daughter of early Hiram pioneers John and Abigail Clemons. Another son, John Fly, settled at the end of Fly's Lane, off the Pequawket Trail, below the Great Falls. The cellar of his house, according to Dr. William Teg, Hiram historian, is located in a long-overgrown pasture on the western slope of Jameson's Mountain.[375] Llewellyn A. Wadsworth of Hiram depicted John Fly as "tall, erect and healthy; a good house carpenter; a collector of taxes in 1803; a good wheelwright, making a pair of cartwheels as the age of 86."[376]

John took a different route from his clergy relatives. He was elected collector of taxes in 1803 and 1804, and to the combined positions of collector and constable in 1809 and 1810. Collectors of taxes were given an amount of money to collect and were paid a small percentage for every tax collected. Early tax collectors were sometimes unable or unwilling to collect the required amount in the time allotted, and were subjected to actions by the sheriff, which included selling goods and property, if sufficient, to pay uncollected amounts plus fees. The alternative was having their "body" put in jail. John Fly was declared remiss in his duties as tax collector for 1809 (as was Andrew R. Bucknell ten years later in 1819). John Fly's deficiency was failure to collect $100.58, a large sum, or pay the same to the treasurer by the first day of May 1810, resulting in the sheriff's warrant in 1812 for $112.58, including fees.

Remembering Winfield Flye

From Bernice Stevens Dupree:[377]

"Rarely, one saw dear old Winfield Flye stivvering carefully down the road toward home after going up to get the mail on a winter evening. Usually he could be seen in his humble home, at the foot of Mt. Cutler School hill, reading, always reading…a familiar, spectacled, bald little man, hungry for more knowledge."

From Roger W. Flint:[378]

"Winfield Flye lived in an old house by the Mt. Cutler School. Like all the Flyes, he was considered eccentric. What he did and how he lived I do not recall.

"In those days as now there were food fads, and Winfield was quite concerned about his diet. At the time there was some theory that milk was improved by agitation, particularly by turning it back and forth from one container to another. I can see him now, sitting on his shed steps with a can of milk in his hands, pouring it into another held between his knees. He would be wearing his black suit and an old hat. Back and forth he would alternate the cans. So far as anyone could determine, he ended with just milk. It may have benefitted him, for he lived to a ripe old age. Old Winfield, a mystery to us ten-year-olds. June 1965."

In a society where cash was in short supply, it was often difficult to collect taxes. A person's highway tax

---

375 Jameson's Mountain is a small rise southeast of Peaked Mountain and Barnes Brook. Part of the old Pequawket Trail was along now called River Road.

376 Hubert W. Clemons, "The Fly/Flye Family," *Downeast Ancestry*, October 1980, 4:3, 13.

377 Bernice Stevens Dupree, *Hiram Historical Society Newsletter*, June 1, 1986, 4.

378 *Hiram Historical Society Newsletter*, Special Issue, November 10, 1978, 1.

This former East Hiram Post Office at 62 Main Street was once the home of Winfield Flye. Photo 2020.

men were deficient in paying taxes in 1808. They were Royal Baston, John Browne, William Cotton, John Eames, James Gilmore, Samuel Henderson, Samuel Merrifield, and Abijah Lewis. Simeon Bucknell paid his tax and was crossed off the list.

Collector John Fly survived the sheriff's assault of 1812, but was afterward elected only to neighborhood offices, such as fence viewer, hog reeve, and surveyor of highways.

The Flys were not wealthy, but were more comfortable than some. Like most settlers they were subsistence farmers who engaged in another trade, like being a cooper, blacksmith, cobbler, or, in the case of James Fly, a clergyman, for a little cash. John was relatively well off. In 1809 his grown son provided extra labor, was eligible to vote, and living on his farm consisting of taxable property of one house, one barn, six tillable acres, six haying acres, three meadow acres, 185 acres of unimproved land, two oxen, two cows, one horse and two swine. Son James Fly Jr. had less than half as much, a situation that continued through 1818.

could be reduced by laboring on roads, but general taxes and money for schools, for those who had children attending, could not be worked off.[379] Eight

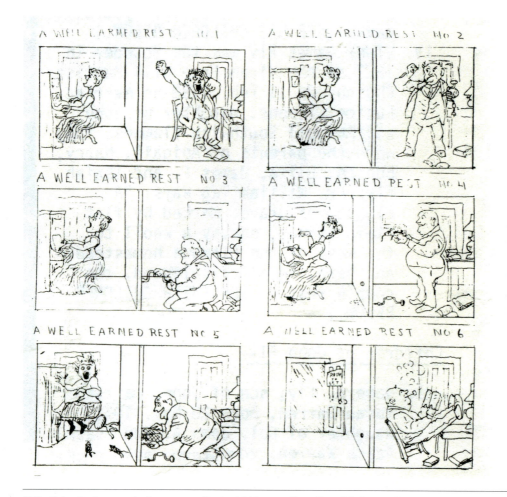

Cartoon of Winfield W. Flye. The following comment was written by him on the back of No. 1: "This set of pen pictures were made Wed. Eve. Nov. 29th, 1893—Night before Thanksgiving.

---

379   John had two scholars to pay for in 1811, sons Sewell and John, and three in 1813.

Town Offices Held

Clerk

1838	Col. Sewell Fly
1840	Col. Sewell Fly

Collectors of Taxes

1803, 1804	John Fly

Constable/Collector of Taxes

1809	John Fly
1810	John Fly

Cullers of Hoops & Staves

1829	John A. Fly

Fence Viewers

1815	John Fly
1828	John Fly

Hog Reeves

1815	John Fly
1816	James Fly

Surveyors of Highways

1807	John Fly
1811	John Fly
1819	James Fly
1820	James Fly
1821	John Flye
1822	John Fly, James Fly
1823	John Fly
1827	John Fly
1828	John Fly
1829	John Fly

Tithingmen

1815	James Fly
1816	James Fly
1817	James Fly
1818	James Fly
1830	John Fly

Sketched Nov. 28, 1896, by Winfield W. Flye, Hiram, Me.

Pencil drawing of a dog pointing by Winfield Flye, 1896.

Pencil drawing of the head of a buck by Winfield Flye.

Pencil drawing of a bunch of grapes by Winfield Flye.

Isaiah Fly, born in 1809, son of Elder James and Eunice Clemons Fly, married Jane S. Burbank. Their son, Winfield Flye, was an artist noted for fine drawings and humorous cartoons. Members of the families of Isaiah Fly and Isaiah Flye Jr. are buried in the Hiram Village Cemetery. Note the spelling change in the family name. Both spellings are found in the cemetery.

OBEDIAH GERRISH
August 24, 1796–October 21, 1861
Married February 20, 1821
Deborah Littlefield
December 2, 1796–June 20, 1866

Obediah Gerrish, of Kittery, was living in Parsons-field when he bought land from Capt. Charles Lee Wadsworth in 1820[380] and built his homestead on what is now called Gerrish Road, off South Hiram Road. Eight months later he married Deborah Littlefield of York, and when their first son was born, in 1823, Obediah named him Peleg Wadsworth Gerrish. Gen. Peleg Wadsworth was pleased and rewarded him with a sheep.

Several of their children found spouses in York, but Peleg W. Gerrish became a successful farmer in Hiram and was elected a selectman in 1877. He was also a stage-coach driver who supplied much information to the historian Gideon T. Ridlon, author of the book *Saco Valley Families and Settlements*, published in 1895, an important source of information for this book.

Obediah was elected to a few town offices: school agent in 1828, presumably of the Ridlon School in South Hiram; surveyor of highways in 1823, 1827, and 1830. In 1830 he was excused from the office of surveyor of highways and was promptly reelected.

Obediah is buried in the Gerrish family cemetery on the property, as is his father, Capt. Timothy Gerrish, a retired sea captain who came to live with his son Obediah and family.

Obediah Gerrish homestead, 55 Gerrish Road, spring 2015.

Town Offices Held

School Agents

1828	Obediah Gerish [Gerrish]
1830	Obediah Gerrish

Surveyors of Highways

1823	Odebiah Gerrish
1827	Obediah Gerrish
1830	Obediah Gerrish

---

380   Obediah Gerrish is not listed in the U.S. census of 1820, but he voted in 1822.

JAMES GILMOR
c. 1765–c. 1814

Marriage date unknown
Martha ? c. 1767–August 22, 1816

James Gilmor (also spelled Gillmore, Gilmore, Gilman) came from Durham, New Hampshire, and settled with his wife, Martha, on the old Tear Cap Road to Denmark, now called Fletcher Road, sometime before 1800, when he was listed as James Gilman in the U.S. census of 1800, for Prescott's Grant, York County, which was separate from the U.S. census of 1800 for "Hyram and Luttler's [sic Cutler's][381] Grant."

The Gilmors appeared to live a typical farm life with their seven children, James having sufficient property to allow him to vote.[382] In 1809, he was taxed on one house, one barn, two oxen, two cows and a yearling, and four swine. Of his one hundred acres he had cleared only one for cultivation and eight for hay. Neighbor Samuel Sloper on King Street had double Gilmor's tillable acres, but had fewer livestock and no barn. Longer established neighbors, the Watsons, had tilled two acres each, owned oxen, cows, swine, and horses, but shared a barn.[383]

Early receipts shed light on James Gilmor's life in the Hiram community. In April 1810, he was paid for two and a half hours of labor repairing the Great Bridge over the Saco River, job pay not specified. He, along with King Street neighbors the Watsons and Samuel Sloper, and Ephraim Kimball on the other side of Bull Ring Road (also known as Christian Hill), was a founder of the Baptist Society, enacted into law in 1811.

The War of 1812 shattered the Gilmor family.

As he departed for war on December 23, 1812, James sold to Stephen Pease of Cornish, for $125, his hundred acres, excepting twenty acres he had deeded to Eleazer Strout and ten acres sold to Ephraim Kimball. Stephen Pease was known to give mortgages, so perhaps James did this to secure cash for his family when he was gone. He did not return. Martha Gilmor purchased the same property for the same amount of money on September 1, 1814, and James's estate was probated on November 19, 1814. [384]

James had enlisted in New York in the First Artillery Regiment, Capt. James T. B. Romayne's company, as a private. Why New York? There were Gilmors living in Manlius, New York, near where James is thought to have died. Although there is no record of his death,[385] he is named on the plaque honoring

The marked graves of Daniel, Mary, and Martha Gilmor, and possibly James, under an unmarked stone in Old Settlers Cemetery on King Street, 2017.

---

381 Misspellings of Hiram and Cutler's Grant.

382 Voting lists 1809, 1810, 1811. We found no list for 1812. He is not on the list of 1813. Maine State Archives, Hiram Box 14.

383 John Watson, John Watson Jr., and Thomas B. Watson were listed as each owning 0.33 Barns. *List of Rateables 1809*, Maine State Archives, Hiram Box 14.

384 James died intestate and his property was ceded to Martha, probated in Fryeburg by Judge Judah Dana.

385 *Index to War of 1812 pension files*, transcribed by Virgil D. White (Waynesboro, TN: National Historical Pub. Co., 1989).

veterans of the war in the Soldiers Memorial Library in Hiram, and it is family legend that he was killed in a battle at Sackets Harbor. After 1813, his name appears on no official record in Hiram, neither real estate deeds nor lists of voters, taxes owed, fathers of school children, town officers, paupers, or the like. At the time, he would have been approximately forty-seven years of age.

More tragedy struck a few years later, in 1816—a perilous time in Maine, the "Year without a summer" was particularly hard for the Gilmors. On July 26, 1816, the oldest child, Mary, born December 28, 1796, died at age nineteen. One month later, her mother, Martha, died, age forty-nine. Six children ages five to seventeen were orphaned.

Wealthy neighbor Ephraim Kimball became the guardian of the orphans. The eldest son, Daniel S. Gilmor, died December 9, 1819, age twenty, and is buried next to his mother in Old Settlers Cemetery. It is believed that James is buried nearby under an unmarked stone. Of the surviving children, James (born July 12, 1801), Samuel V. (born December 19, 1803), David (born May 25, 1805), John Watson (born February 28, 1809[386]), and Martha (born August 7, 1811), the fate of three sons is known, thanks to descendants.

Son James Gilmor died in Durham, New Hampshire, in 1832 at age thirty-one and left property to his wife Tirzah. To his beloved brothers, David and John W., he left a promissory note for $92.70 against James Brazier and Ephraim Kimball of Hiram dated July 12, 1820. David bought land in Denmark in 1830, and died in Durham, New Hampshire, in April 1833, age twenty-eight. He left the Denmark property to his brother John W. Gilmor, a blacksmith by trade. He left his "joiners tools" to Nathaniel Hale in Denmark, provided he reached the age of fourteen. John W. was living in Denmark when he married Rebecca Paine of Standish on March 6, 1833, and they lived in Denmark with the first three of their six children until moving to Corinna, Maine, in 1841, and then to Stetson, Maine. John W. died in 1853 and received the first Masonic funeral held in Stetson.

James Brazier bought James and Martha's property from Simeon Chadbourne and Ephraim

Kimball in three transactions in 1826 and 1827. Brazier and his family lived there until 1897, when his daughter, Marie Brazier Wilder, wife of James D. Wilder, began to sell off parcels.

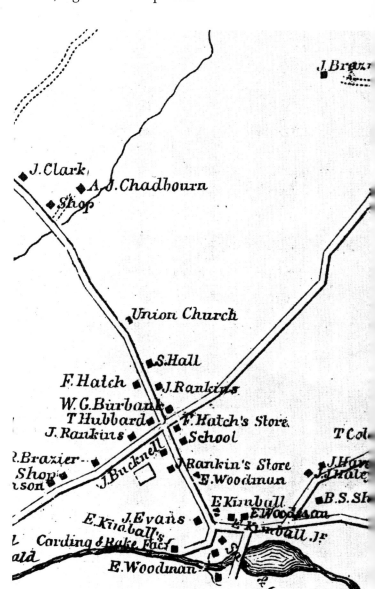

An 1858 map of Hiram Bridge showing the four corners of what is now Main Street, King Street, Bullring Road, and Sebago Road. J. Brazier's house and shop, formerly James and Martha Gilmor's, is on the upper right, off Bull Ring Road. Note there are no houses between W. G. Burbank's and J. Brazier's.

---

386   He was born in March 1809, according to family records.

1816: The Year Without a Summer

Mount Tambora in Indonesia erupted on April 10, 1815, and spewed volcanic ash into the atmosphere for six days. An estimated ten thousand people died immediately, and more died later from the effects of the catastrophe. Sulfur in the ash was converted to sulfuric acid, which blocked incoming light from the sun for several years, causing extraordinary cold around the globe. New England and Canada were especially hard hit during the agricultural growing cycle, from March to September. There was frost in every month. It snowed in June and July. Newly shorn sheep froze to death. Birds froze and fell from trees. Staple crops of hay, Indian corn, and wheat failed, causing prices to rise. Oats became so expensive, rising from 12 cents to 92 cents per bushel in 1816, farmers could not feed their horses. Without good nutrition, diseases such as cholera spread. Subsistence farmers, already on the edge in northern New England, left in droves for greener pastures in New York and Ohio. On a single day a wagon train of 120 men, women, and children passed through Haverhill, Massachusetts, headed for Indiana. Some returned to Maine in the summer of 1817, finding no better place to live.

STEPHEN GILPATRICK
June 16, 1791–July 21, 1882
Married November 25, 1813
Charity Brown, April 27, 1793–March 5, 1875

Lt. Stephen Gilpatrick arrived before 1817 from Cornish with his wife, Charity Brown, also of Cornish. When he purchased fifty acres from David Trafton of Cornish in 1817 for $250, he was already in Hiram and his occupation was "Gentleman." In 1815, David Trafton had paid $600 to Peleg Wadsworth for one hundred acres at Bartlett's Pond,[387] later known as Trafton Pond, and, still in Cornish a year later, David, a trader, sold the other half to Edmund Trafton of Cornish, combmaker, for $250. Edmund didn't settle in Hiram, either, and sold his half back to Peleg Wadsworth in 1823 for $300.

Another Trafton, Jeremiah Trafton, however, served in the War of 1812, lived in Hiram for thirty years, married Sarah Lewis, and was elected tithingman in 1817 and 1818, school agent in 1825, culler of hoops and staves in 1826, and surveyor of highways in 1827.

A year after Stephen Gilpatrick bought his fifty acres he hadn't done much with it. In the 1818 inventory he had a house but no barn, he had not improved his fifty acres, and had only one cow. His tax was $38 on real property and $10 on personal property; the total put him near the bottom, at eighty-third out of 113 residents. Unfortunately his house burned in the 1940s and no photo has been found.

Stephen sold his half to Simeon Pease of Cornish in 1820, but he remained in Hiram, perhaps on the same property,[388] and was counted in the 1820 census along with his parents, John (age seventy-six) and Eunice Tarbox Gilpatrick, of Saco, and John Jr., Stephen's older brother, who was then forty-six years old.

Stephen participated in town affairs. At Town Meeting in May 1818, when the topic was repair of the Ossipee Bridge, $100 for repair was voted, John Warren was chosen agent and Stephen was elected surveyor. Stephen was elected a surveyor of highways

in most of the years from 1819 to 1829 and a school agent for District 4, formerly William Cotton's, in 1824 and 1830.

The Gilpatricks stayed in Hiram and became a prolific and important family. Stephen and Charity bore ten children. Son Stephen B. married Thankful Rand of Hiram. Son Sewell married Olive Lewis of Hiram. Son Clement B. married Martha J. Gould of Hiram. Son Benjamin F. married Elizabeth Owen and lived on what is now called Ben Gilpatrick Road, off Route 160 near Trafton Pond.

Stephen's older brother John Jr. and Betsey Hamilton produced five children. Son Ammi married Esther Gray of Hiram. Son Solomon H. married Lucy Eastman of Hiram. And so on through the generations.

"The Greatest Marvel of the Age"
Charles F. Gilpatrick, the healthy son of Ammi and Esther Gray Gilpatrick, developed ankylosis at age 12 or 14, a rare progressive disease of ossification, which prevented him from moving. To earn a living he exhibited himself from Maine to California as the "ossified man."

Obituary of Charles F. Gilpatrick
Portland Press Herald newspaper, February 9, 1914.

South Hiram, Maine—At the home of his sister, Mrs. Alpheus Gilpatrick, Charles F. Gilpatrick, known all over New England and many other states as the "the ossified man," passed out of life Feb. 7 [1914]. His was the only known case of complete ossification in the world, and the like may never be recorded in history again. He was a strong, healthy boy with no apparent disease until 12 or 14 years of age, when this hardening process began, which no medical skill could reach, and which made rapid work until the summer

---

387 Who was Bartlett?

388 Simeon Pease was known to give mortgages.

of 1898 when it had completely gone over him and since that time he has been unable to move or help himself in the least, but has lived and breathed in a living tomb of stone. It seems wonderful that in all that time his mind has never become impaired. He was a great reader and had the most wonderful memory. He was always pleased to see his friends and always very cheerful. He said to many he was the happiest man in the world, that although the Almighty had seen fit to encase his body in a case of stone he had never felt a pain in all these years and felt perfectly satisfied with his lot.[389]

Charles Gilpatrick, the ossified man. Photo courtesy of Shirley Welch, Brownfield, Maine. Published in Hiram Historical Society Newsletter, *Vol. 7, No. 2, Jan.–Feb. 1988, 5.*

Town Offices Held

Fence Viewers

1830	Stephen Gilpatrick

Surveyors of Highways

1819	Stephen Gilpatrick
1820	Stephen Gilpatrick
1822	Stephen Gilpatrick
1823	Stephen GIlpatrick
1824	Stephen Gilpatrick
1826	Stephen GiIpatrick
1829	Stephen Gilpatrick

Charles F. Gilpatrick was exhibited on a pillow on a pedestal.

389 Hubert W. Clemons, "South Hiram's Ossified Man," *BitterSweet: The magazine of Maine's Hills & Lakes Region*, Christmas 1980, Vol. 4:1, 9.

BARTHOLOMEW GOULD

1774–August 11, 1855

Married 1798

Mary Goodwin, 1776–November 5, 1852

Gould Mountain is a legacy of the Gould family, but for whom was it named? Was it Moses, who legend says came with Aaron? Was it Aaron who was in Hiram for the 1790 U.S. census, but was gone by 1800? No further information about him is known. After 1790, no surname Gould/Goold is recorded in a U.S. census of Hiram until Daniel and George Gould in 1840. Their father, Bartholomew Gould, was born in Wells and lived in Parsonsfield and Porter, but could have come to live with one of his children in Hiram. He is buried in the Stanley Cemetery in South Hiram.

The nine children of Bartholomew and Mary Goodwin were not born in Hiram, but several came to live in Hiram and became prominent families, although later than founders of the town. The children were Abigail, Hannah, George, Susan, Daniel, Mary, Elias, Lydia, and Major.

The Gould and Stanley families were intertwined. George Gould, born c. 1805, married Olive Stanley, daughter of William and Susannah Stanley, in 1826. The following year he was elected one of twenty-three surveyors of highways in Hiram, but he moved out of town and Isaac Stanley replaced him. In 1830 he was living in Porter. By 1837, he was back in Hiram, where he lived until he died in 1869. His son, Civil War Lt. George F. Gould, married his cousin Ruth Ann Bickford, inherited the homestead, and passed it on to his widow when he died in 1891.

George Gould's sister, Susan Gould (born c. 1807), married Isaac Stanley in 1824. Brother Daniel (born c. 1810) married Deborah Stanley in

Aerial view of Hannaford's Riverside Greenhouse, photographed by George Burnell in the 1960s. The barn was separated from the house in 1948.

George Gould (1805–1869), son of Bartholomew Gould, may have built this homestead in 1826 when he married Olive Stanley.

The Gould/Hannaford house in its present location, 2014. When the greenhouse business was sold c. 1976, the house was moved about a hundred yards up the hill to 77 South Hiram Road.

1833 and they lived at "Gould Place" on the eastern slope of Gould Mountain. Mary Gould (born 1812) married John Lord in 1838.

Elias Gould (born 1815) married first Julia (Sally) French. Their son, Samuel Wadsworth Gould (1852–1935), settled in Skowhegan, where he operated the Oxford Hotel, was a successful lawyer, postmaster of Skowhegan from 1896–1900, and a representative of Maine in the U.S. House of Representatives, 1911–1913. Elias Gould's second wife was Ruth Hanscum Clemons. He and Ruth lived at Gould Farm on Gould Farm Road, off Pequawket Trail, near the Brownfield line. Ruth received the Boston Post Cane in 1914 as the oldest woman in Hiram. The farm burned in 1947.

A story told over and over about Bartholomew Gould is that he stuck his oxgoad—a rod for driving oxen—into the ground beside the road and it sprouted and grew into a beautiful shade tree known locally as the "Ox-Goad Willow."[390] It stood on the property of Frank Stearns (1877–1946) at 72 South Hiram Road in South Hiram (Kezar Falls Village) until it succumbed of old age.

---

390 Teg, *History of Hiram*, Sesquicentennial Edition, 58.

GRAY FAMILY

William Gray Jr.
1786–May 7, 1862
Married June 4, 1809
Margaret McLucas
March 22, 1790–September 6, 1879

William Gray Jr., the son of William and Lucy Day Gray of Sanford, was the first of the Grays to arrive in Hiram, but he never accumulated much wealth and died a pauper. After fighting in the Revolutionary War, his father migrated to Cornish. The earliest record of William Gray Jr. in Hiram is 1809, the year he was taxed for two tilled acres and one cattle—but no house, barn, or other livestock. He also paid a poll tax in Hiram in 1810 and 1811. In the 1815 bridge tax he was charged only 58 cents for one poll (head tax) and had no real or personal property—the bottom of the barrel, so to speak.

On April 21, 1813, at age twenty-seven, William Gray Jr. enlisted in Sanford in the 33rd U.S. Infantry, but he was rejected on June 15, 1813. The only description given was his height—five foot seven and a half.

Isaac Gray
1775–December 30, 1850
First marriage July 7, 1796
Betsey Sullivan Hart, died pre-1815
Second marriage 1815
Mary Jordan, 1783–July 5, 1852

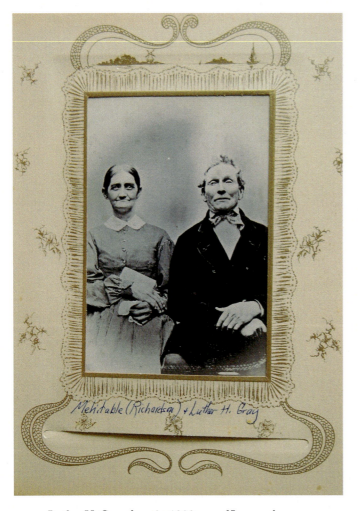

Luther H. Gray, born in 1800, son of Isaac and Betsey Sullivan Hart Gray, and his second wife, Mehitable Richardson, ten years his junior. Luther H. died in Hiram December 27, 1879.

Isaac Gray's great-grandchildren Alice, Minnie, and Luther S., children of Isaac W. Gray. Luther S., born in 1897, fought in World War I.

Isaac, son of Daniel and Patience Hamilton Gray, was more successful and civic minded than William, voting regularly beginning 1813, serving on the important Committee of Accounts in 1813, the Bridge Committee of 1815 for a new bridge over the Saco River, and as surveyor of boards and surveyor of highways after that. But he slipped up. He was elected agent for repair of the bridge over the Saco River in April 1821, but was dismissed in September. The reason was not printed. Marshall Spring, John Bucknell, and Ephraim Kimball were chosen for a new committee. Shortly after, Isaac bought one hundred acres in Baldwin. In Naples in 1840, he sold his property of 120 acres in Hiram and Baldwin, and he died in Naples in 1850.

Children of Isaac and Betsey, born between 1797 and 1800, were Lydia, Patience, Hannah, and Luther H. Children of Isaac and Mary, born between 1816 and 1826, were Albert, Isabella, Ansel, Arthur, and William, who was born in 1826 in Naples and died in 1870 in California. Son Luther H. inherited his father's skill with wood, listing himself as a "joiner" in a deed signed in 1849.[391]

Joseph Gray
1789–June 20, 1864
Married 1810
Susan Brown, December 11, 1789
or 1790–1860, age 71

Joseph joined his older brother Isaac in Hiram before 1815, and, like Isaac, amassed some wealth. He paid about half the 1815 bridge tax as Isaac. His occupation was blacksmith.

The children of Joseph and Susan were born between 1812 and 1835: John B., Elizabeth, Artemus, Mary Ellen, Lucy Ann, Thankful, Christopher, George H.

Abraham Gray
April 9, 1787–April 20, 1865
Married June 9, 1811
Abigail Pugsley, April 4, 1793–January 11, 1867

Abraham Gray was also assessed for the 1815 bridge tax and was still in Hiram in 1830, but moved to Lovell and died there.

The known relationship was between Isaac and Joseph—brothers, sons of Daniel and Patience Hamilton Gray, long-time residents of Cornish. The relationship of William, Isaac, and Abraham is unknown. The repetition of given names may be a clue, but is not definitive.

William was the only confirmed Gray resident of Hiram in 1810.[392] All the above Grays were in Hiram in 1820.

Town Offices Held

Committee to View Site of New Bridge Over the Saco

January 16, 1815 John Pierce, Asa Burbank, Isaac Gray

March 27, 1815 Charles L. Wadsworth, John Watson, Isaac Gray

April 1, 1816 Voted to allow Isaac Gray $4.00 on his account

Superintendant on Saco River Bridge Repair

April 1821 —Elected Isaac Gray

September 1821 —Voted to dismiss Isaac Gray [no reason given]

Surveyors of Boards & Logs

1818 Isaac Gray

Surveyors of Boards & Shingles

1819 Isaac Gray

Surveyors of Boards

1820 Isaac Gray

1826 Abraham Gray

1929 Abraham Gray

Surveyors of Highways

1821 Isaac Gray

---

391 Oxford County Registry of Deeds, Fryeburg, now Paris, July 26, 1849, Book 32, 60.

392 Maine Historical Society, Coll. 146. Box 1/2, 1810 inventory.

JOHN HARTFORD

1759-c. 1811

Marriage date unknown
Hannah Fly, November 4, 1762–?

John Hartford was the progenitor of the prolific Hartford families of Hiram, Denmark, and Brownfield. A Revolutionary War soldier, by 1800 he had settled with his wife, Hannah Fly Hartford, on the River Road, on or near the property later known as the Joseph Warren place. He and Hannah had eleven children, but by 1811 Hannah was widowed with six children in school in School District 5. There were five student "scholars" in 1813.

Hannah was not well off. In 1811 she was taxed on one house, one barn, one acre of "village land," ninety-eight acres unimproved land, and two cows. There was one poll in her household, possibly son Simeon, who had enough property two years later to vote in 1813.

Some of the children remained significant to Hiram. Benjamin married Adeline Ingalls of Hiram, daughter of Lt. Benjamin Ingalls, who organized the first survey expedition to the west bank of the Saco River in 1774. Solomon married Sarah Eastman, daughter of Revolutionary War veteran James and Sarah Whitehorn Eastman. James married Betsy Hill and sired

ONCE UPON A TIME...

Rolling The Snow

Out on the Hartford brothers' farm near Hiram, in the days before snowplows they broke winter roads with this snow roller pulled by oxen. (This photo was submitted by Philip Douglass of Convene, Maine)

The Hartford brothers gathered to pack snow for winter sleighing.
Undated, untitled newspaper clipping. Hiram Historical Society.

Sylvanus, who was the father of Clement, grandfather of Grover, and great-grandfather of Conrad, who died in Hiram in 2014.

Samuel B. was the son of Sylvanus B. Hartford (born May 16, 1820, in Coventry, New Hampshire), and Eliza Ann Black of Hiram (born March 22, 1823). Sylvanus was the grandson of John Hartford. From the Samuel B. Hartford Farm on Tear Cap near the Denmark line, the Hartford brothers rolled snow with a team of four oxen.

Many Hartfords followed John and Hannah: Solomon and Sarah had eight children; Sylvanus and Eliza Ann Black conceived seven survivors; Clement and Mamie A. Jewell had sixteen, of whom thirteen survived to adulthood; Grover and Mildred F. Douglas raised four. In addition there was Augustus, William B., several Hermans, Humphrey, Alonzo, and others. The manuscript *Hiram Cemetery Inscriptions, 1989* lists 102 Hartfords and wives buried in Hiram.[393]

Solomon Hartford, son of the first Hartford, John, did not start well. When taxed for the new bridge in 1815, he had no property, and in 1816 and 1817 was a pauper whose sons John, James, and William H. were auctioned by the town to the lowest bidder for labor and board. But Solomon demonstrated resilience. By 1819, he had accumulated sufficient property to vote, and in 1824 and 1826 was chosen agent of School District 5. He also served as surveyor of highways in 1825 and 1826.

Town Offices Held

School Agents
1824	Solomon Hartford	District #5
1825	Solomon Hartford	
1826	Solomon Hartford	

The Samuel B. Hartford Farm on Tear Cap near the Denmark line no longer exists.
Photo courtesy of Brownfield Historical Society.

---

393 Typed manuscript: *Cemetery Inscriptions, Hiram, Maine*, 1989 Recheck of Hiram, Maine Cemeteries presented through Molly Ockett Chapter, D.A.R., Genealogical Chairman Mrs. Ola-Mae Wheaton.

HOWARD FAMILY

Lemuel Howard
April 6, 1752–March 20, 1842

Married June 4, 1779

Hannah Clemons, c. 1759–?

In many ways, the Howards were typical Hiram settlers—not because Lemuel was a very early settler to town, but because he and the second and third generations had their ups and downs. They struggled to stay afloat, bought and sold and mortgaged property, defaulted and recovered with family help, contributed to the community when they could, and used their skills in new ventures. Because there are contradictions in the stated secondary histories of the family and ambiguities because of the many Howards named Joseph, including the name of Lemuel's more famous nephew, the story has been difficult to tell.

The Hiram Howards did not achieve the high status heaped upon the Brownfield Howards through Lemuel's nephew, Judge Joseph Howard. Judge Howard graduated from Fryeburg Academy and Bowdoin College. He was named United States district attorney for Maine by President Martin Van Buren. He served as associate justice of the Supreme Judicial Court until 1855 and was elected mayor of Portland in 1860.

In contrast, Lemuel was destined to be a yeoman. He may have been a private in the Revolution in Capt. Joel Green's company, seeing service in White Plains in 1778–1779.[394] Lemuel Howard lived and farmed near the Hiram/Brownfield/Porter line around Clemons Pond and the Notch Road. Howard properties were near each other, though in different towns—Hiram, Brownfield, and Porter.

The children raised by Lemuel and Hannah Howard were John, born c. 1790; Hannah, 1782; and Mary, 1801.

Son John and his first wife, Ruth Hartford, were the parents of Joseph Howard (born c. 1811). John served in the War of 1812. John's second wife was Catherine Benton, daughter of Dr. Joseph and Kate Britton Benton of West Baldwin. Dr. Benton treated Peleg Wadsworth during Peleg's fatal illness. Hannah Howard married William Cotton of Hiram in 1800. Mary Howard married Jonathan Lowell of Hiram in 1821.

Joseph Howard Jr.
Dates unknown

Marriage date and spouse unknown

Joseph Howard was a housewright of Hiram when he purchased one hundred acres from Peleg Wadsworth for $500 in 1811.[395] Even though Joseph Jr. earned money by selling half to Isaac Lane for $250 on the next day, Peleg Wadsworth foreclosed in 1813. Joseph Jr. must have earned it back, because in the 1818 inventory he was taxed on a poll, a house, a barn, ninety-eight acres, and some animals. The next year he was elected a selectman and to the School Committee.

In 1825, he sold his Hiram homestead on Ten Mile Brook to Theophilus Smith, an investor in the Ten Mile Brook Canal. This time Howard described his occupation as "mechanic."[396]

Lemuel, a farmer, did not participate in Hiram affairs, but his son John, along with Joseph Howard Jr., did.

Town Offices Held

Collectors & Constables
1820	Joseph Howard

Field Drivers
1817	John Howard
1818	John Howard

Hog Reeves
1817	John Howard
1819	John Howard

School Committee
1819	Joseph Howard

---

394 Two Lemuel Howards served.

395 Oxford County Registry of Deeds, Fryeburg, February 11, 1811, Book 5, 288.

396 Oxford County Registry of Deeds, Fryeburg, May 5, 1825, Book 10, 495.

Selectmen

| 1819 | Joseph Howard |
| 1820 | Joseph Howard |

Surveyors of Highways

1815	John Howard
1816	John Howard
1817	John Howard
1818	John Howard, Joseph Howard Jr.
1819	John Howard, Joseph Howard
1821	John Howard
1822	John Howard
1824	John Howard
1825	John Howard
1826	John Howard
1829	Joseph Howard
1830	Joseph Howard

ROBERT HUNTRESS
December 6, 1771–April 20, 1850
Married October 29, 1795
Hannah Wadleigh, June 6, 1775–June 20, 1857

"The Huntress family was noted for industry, economy and strength."[397]

Robert Huntress came to Hiram in 1807 at age thirty-six. He was born at Berwick, as were seven of his nine children:[398] Temple, William, Elizabeth (Betsey), John, Darling, and Frances (Fanny). Samuel was the first born in Hiram, on July 8, 1808, and was followed by Hannah in 1810. A son, Robert, died young.

Robert and Hannah's farm was on the northeast side of the Ossipee River near Warren Bridge, in what became known as the Huntress neighborhood. There were Huntresses in South Hiram into the 1940s.

Like the Lords, the Huntresses were active in their Durgintown neighborhood; they intermarried with the Lords. Robert, especially, was thought of as an upstanding citizen and was elected tithingman in 1822. When he was elected again in 1827, and he declined, the town's men voted not to excuse him.

Harrison Huntress (1840–1912), grandson of Robert, son of John (1803–1855), built a house in the neighborhood that is recognizable today.

The Harrison Huntress house, 49 Durgintown Road, 2020.

---

397   Ridlon, *Saco Valley Settlements and Families*, 742.
398   Ibid., 741.

Robert Huntress

Town Offices Held

Field Drivers
1824   Robert Huntress

Surveyors of Highways
1821   Temple Huntress
1822   Temple Huntress
1823   Temple Huntress
1824   Temple Huntress

1826   William Huntress
1827   John Huntress
1828   John Huntress
1829   John Huntress
1830   Temple Huntress

Tithingmen
1822   Robert Huntress
1827   Robert Huntress [voted not to excuse him]

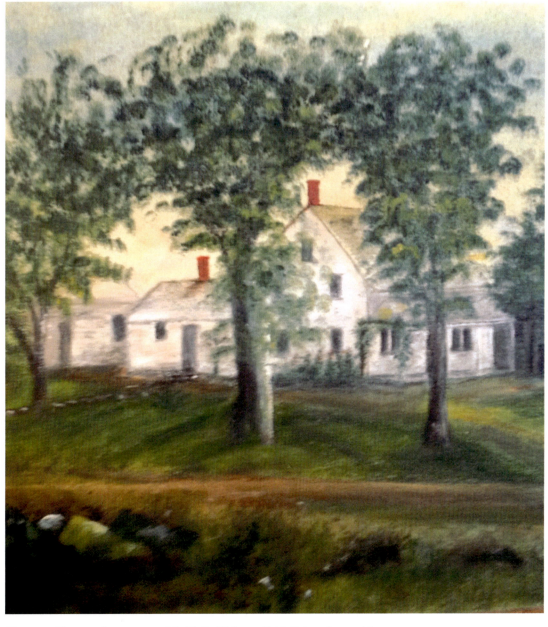

Harrison Huntress house, painted by E. D. Holmes, 1914. Privately owned.

EPHRAIM KIMBALL
June 17, 1751–1832

Married September 23, 1773

Hannah Emerson, February 13, 1754–?

When Ephraim and Hannah Emerson Kimball moved from Farmington, New Hampshire, to Hiram in 1809, Ephraim was fifty-eight years old with ten children ranging in age from eight to thirty-four. Four—Elizabeth, Jesse, Deacon Ephraim, and John—joined their parents, at different times. Sarah, Mary, Samuel, Solomon, Nehemiah, and Eleanor Cooper stayed in New Hampshire. Daughter Abigail had died the year before at age seventeen. In 2003, there were 164 descendants of Ephraim and Hannah Emerson Kimball.[399]

The spouses of the children and grandchildren who came and remained in Hiram include many of its notable families: Alexander, Baston, Bucknell, Burbank, Chapman, Chipman, Clark, Clemons, Cram, Eastman, Evans, Howard, Hubbard, Kimball, Mabry, McDonald, Meader, Moulton, Rankin, Richardson, Sanborn, Seavey, Spring, Stanley, Stuart, True, Watson, Wentworth, and others.

Ephraim had bought, with Benjamin Furber, also of Farmington, New Hampshire, 348 acres in Prescott's Grant in July 1809. The next month they partitioned the land and the Kimballs settled on 225 acres beginning at Hiram Bridge on the east side of Saco River along Hancock Brook and adjoining lands of James Gilmor, John Bucknell, and Samuel Sloper, on what is now called Main Street, Fletcher Road, and King Street.[400]

Elizabeth Kimball married Jonathan Wentworth in 1791 in New Hampshire. Their children Ephraim (married Mary Walker), Moses E. (married first Mary Canney, second, her sister Debora), Noah, and Mercy (married Henry S. Burbank) were all born in New Hampshire and buried in the Wentworth Cemetery in Hiram. Hannah (married first Asa Osgood, second John Bucknell) is buried in the Spring Cemetery). All the following children and spouses are buried in Hiram Village Cemetery: Eliza (married William G. Burbank, merchant), Lydia W. (married Joseph Rankin, builder of Rankin's Mill), Abigail H. (married Thomas B. Seavey—their first child was born in Hiram in 1815), and Mary Jane (married Jonas Alexander).

Jesse Kimball, son of Ephraim and Hannah, was married to Abigail Varney, and already had four of their twelve children when his parents moved to Hiram. Jesse followed on March 20, 1817, according to Teg,[401] and he was chosen a surveyor of highways in 1819 and surveyor of lumber in 1825. He was active afterwards, but he is not listed in Hiram between those dates in the 1820 census or the 1822 voting list.

Children of Jesse and Abigail Kimball
Nathan Kimball married Isabella Watson, daughter of Thomas B. and Mary Hill Watson. They lived adjacent to her father at what is now197 King Street.

The house, known as the Nathan Kimball house, enlarged and renovated, 197 King Street, 2009.

---

399 James Leonard Ackerman, *Rachel Ackerman (1787–1858) and the Kimballs of Strafford County, New Hampshire and Oxford County, Maine,* May 2003.

400 This land extended from Hancock Brook to King Street.

401 William Teg, *History of Hiram, Maine* (Cornish, ME: Carbrook Press, 1964), 31.

Hannah married Thomas Mabry, son of Josiah H. and Rebecca Mabry.

Louisa married Arthur Livermore True, both born and lived in New Hampshire.

Abigail married Amos C. Hanson, both buried in Hiram Village Cemetery. Their granddaughter was Evie Hanson of Hiram, a well-known commercial artist.

Hope married Enoch Rankin, son of Joseph and Jane Perry Rankin.

Ephraim died at age ten.

Reuben married Bethia Cram. They are buried in the Wentworth Cemetery on Hampshire Street.

James married Nancy A. Caverly.

Cyrus died at age twenty-seven.

Elizabeth W. married Isaac Chapman.

Emerson died at age two.

Sophie died at age sixteen.

Deacon Ephraim Kimball, son of Ephraim and Hannah, was born in 1786 and married Rachel Foss Ackerman in 1808 before moving to Hiram and settling on Tear Cap near the Mabry place. In Hiram he was elected to almost every office—selectman, Committee on Accounts, committees to lay out roads and repair bridges, constable and collector of taxes, fence viewer, field driver, school agent for District 2, surveyor of highways, surveyor of boards and lumber, and captain of the militia. An upstanding citizen, he was appointed guardian of James and Martha Gilmor's children after James was killed in the War of 1812 and Martha died in 1816. In the War of 1812 he served as sergeant in Capt. Alpheus Spring's company, service in Portland September 13–September 24, 1814. A man of esteem and discretion, he was asked to appraise property in executive actions and was a founder of the Baptist Society in 1811. He ran for state senator in 1821 and lost, but was elected state representative in 1827.

Later he operated a wool-carding and cloth-dressing mill on Hancock Brook in association with Henry McGrath.[402] In 1832, the mill was a thriving cabinet factory, employing ten to twelve men and producing annually from eight thousand to ten thousand chairs, four hundred to six hundred bedsteads, and other products.[403] On the 1858 map of Hiram Bridge, it is identified as "E. Kimball's Carding & Rake Factory."

The Flint and Burnell Mill on Hancock Brook was photographed by Iza Hubbard c. 1915. It was believed to be the mill owned by Ephraim Kimball in 1858, and earlier, the cabinet factory of Spring & Haskell, at which eight to ten thousand chairs were made annually in 1832.

Children of Ephraim and Rachel Ackerman Kimball

Esrom [Ezrom], born in 1808 in Farmington, New Hampshire, and died in Albany, Maine in 1895

    James Madison, born 1810 in Hiram

    Abigail, born in 1812 in Hiram

    Eliza

    Ellen

    Ephraim, died in infancy

    Ephraim, born in 1819 in Hiram

    Ezrom

    Albion King Parris, born in Albany, died in Waterford, Maine

    Peter Ackerman, born in 1826 in Hiram, died in 1848

John Kimball, son of Ephraim and Hannah, was born 1796 in New Hampshire. On February 15, 1815, he married Mehitable Bucknell, daughter of Simeon

---

402 Mitchell, Davis and Daggett, *Town Register: Brownfield, Denmark, Hiram and Porter, 1907* (Brunswick, ME: The H. E. Mitchell Co., 1907), 93.

403 William D. Williamson, *History of the State of Maine, Vol. 2* (Hallowell, ME: Glazier, Masters & Co., 1832), 609.

Bucknell and Hannah Burbank Bucknell, of Hiram. John, a surveyor of lumber, was the lowest bidder to build the bridge over the Saco in 1829 at $750, and was on the committee to investigate repairing the bridge over the Ossipee. He opened a shop in his house in East Hiram on Bridge Street (Main Street) in 1826[404] and was licensed to sell liquor there in 1828. He also served as school agent and had enough money to be one of the bondsmen for the constable charged with collecting taxes.

Children of John and Mehitable Kimball: Sarah H., married Andrew J. Otis; John L. Kimball, born 1821; Emeline B., born 1824. All were buried in Hiram Village Cemetery.

Town Offices Held

Clerk
1839   Nathan Kimball

Collectors of Taxes
1822   Ephraim Kimball (was allowed 4.75 percent of collections)

Committee on Accounts
1816   Ephraim Kimball
1818   Ephraim Kimball

Committees on Bridge Building and Repairs
1821   Saco River repair: Isaac Gray agent (work to be paid at 75 cents per day). Sept 1821 voted to dismiss Gray as agent. Chose Marshall Spring, John Bucknell & Ephraim Kimball a committee to Superin tend the repair of the bridge
1823 Sept.   Ossipee River build: Charles L. Wadsworth, Peleg Wadsworth Esq., Alpheus Spring Esq., John Warren Esq., Capt Ephraim Kimball

1827   Saco River repair: Voted that Benjamin Barker be an agent to superintend the repair of the bridge across Saco river under the direction of the Selectmen. Voted not to excuse Mr. Barker as agent for the bridge, & Ephraim Kimball (being one of the Selectmen), to direct him

Constables
1822   Ephraim Kimball

Fence Viewers
1819   Ephraim Kimball
1820   Ephraim Kimball
1821   Ephraim Kimball
1822   Ephraim Kimball
1824   Ephraim Kimball

Field Drivers
1816   Ephraim Kimball
1818   John Kimball

Money Clerk (unique title this year only)
1828   Jesse Kimball

School Agents
1819   Ephraim Kimball District #2
1820   Ephraim Kimball #2
1821   Ephraim Kimball #2
1822   Ephraim Kimball #2
1824   Ephraim Kimball #2
1825   John Kimball
1828   John Kimball

School Committees
1829   Nathan Kimball
1830   Nathan Kimball

---

404   Daniel Small, *Papers*, January 2, 1826, Maine Historical Society, Coll. 1449, 38.

Selectmen

1812	Ephraim Kimball
1819	Ephraim Kimball
1820	Ephraim Kimball
1825	Ephraim Kimball
1826	Ephraim Kimball
1827	Ephraim Kimball
1828	Ephraim Kimball
1831	Ephraim Kimball

Surveyors of Boards

1826	Jesse Kimball

Surveyors of Boards, Clapboards and Shingles

1821	Ephraim Kimball

Surveyors of Lumber

1825	Jesse Kimball
1827	Ephraim Kimball (voted to excuse, chose Jesse Kimball)
1828	Jesse Kimball
1829	Jesse Kimball
1830	Jesse Kimball

Surveyors of Highways

1817	Ephraim Kimball
1818	Ephraim Kimball
1819	Ephraim Kimball
1821	Jesse Kimball
1822	Ephraim Kimball
1824	Ephraim Kimball
1825	Ephraim Kimball, John Kimball
1829	Ephraim Kimball

LANE FAMILY

Three Lane brothers from Buxton, John, Daniel, and Jabez, all captains in a solidly military family, were involved in early Hiram.

Capt. John Lane
July 4, 1734–July 14, 1822

First marriage, Elizabeth Hancock
Second marriage, Hannah Boynton Hazeltine
Third marriage, Hannah Bean

Son of a military man, John was trained early for a soldier's life. At age twenty, then a cordwainer of Biddeford, he was commissioned second lieutenant in the French and Indian Wars under his father at Fort Halifax on the Kennebec. When his father died in 1756, the command became his. In the Revolutionary War, at age forty-one, he commanded a company of 120 men in 1775 that he and his subordinate officers raised. He was assigned to "treat" with the members of the Penobscot tribe, who were about to form an alliance with the British in Canada. He was successful in convincing Penobscot Chief Orono and others to travel to Cambridge, Massachusetts, and ratify a treaty, after which he was placed in command at Cape Ann Harbor and repulsed the British.

"He was strong minded, possessed of true military genius and its important accompaniment, invincible courage. It was his glory to defend his country against every form of oppression."[405]

After the war, in 1777, he migrated from Buxton, Maine, to Hiram and built a house on the west bank of the Saco River on the Pequawket Trail in the area between what is now Hiram Hill Road and the Notch Road. In this house, his daughter Anne Lane was born in 1792. It was here that John Clemons and his family took refuge on the evening of their first excursion exploring Hiram as a place to settle in 1779. In brief, the Lanes did not have enough bowls for all, so served the children porridge from the seat of a chair.

This hospitality took place in Lane's first house. The cellar hole of this original house, which was built one hundred feet southeast and closer to the river than the second house, was swept away in the freshet of 1869, causing the town to spend $1,000 to relocate the road farther from the river, which was on the other side of the house. The second house, built farther from the river, later known as the Bucknell house, lasted longer, but was razed in the early 1940s as it teetered over the bank one hundred feet above the river. The house was said to be built in 1792[406] and was called the oldest house in Hiram. It was not the oldest house in Hiram, if it was built in 1792 as claimed. Both the Curtis/Ayer house, erected before 1782, and the John Watson house, 1785, were built earlier.

By 1810, Lane was living in Buxton, and died there. Capt. John Lane's obituary noted:

> As a relative and friend he was exemplary and faithful. He submitted to the relentless power of death with Christian calmness, fortitude, and resignation which characterized his life in its various relations. The evening before his death he summoned his

"Old Bucknell House" Built in 1792, Hiram Me. 73.

Capt. John Lane's second house, later known as the Andrew R. Bucknell house, in a view from the relocated Pequawket Trail.

405 Ridlon, *Saco Valley Settlements and Families*, 111.
406 Ibid., 147.

children around his bed and admonished them to live in peace through the journey of life, and cautioned them against excessive sorrow at his departure.

He was eighty-eight years old.

The bedroom must have been crowded—he had nineteen children by three wives.[407] Some of his children lived in Hiram, but records are few. One son was William Lane, who was born in Buxton May 19, 1769, married Alice Haines on November 7, 1793, lived in Hiram as a farmer, and died in Brownfield on August 23, 1862. His brother, John, had purchased a mill from Henry Young Brown in 1789. This was sold to Simeon Bucknell. In 1791, before William's marriage, he bought back from Simeon Bucknell the corn mill with a small log house on Ten Mile Brook. Seven years later, in 1798, he bought from Eliza Brown, Henry Brown's widow, sixty-five acres in Brownfield on the west side of the Saco bordering "Rattle snake pond" to the mouth of the "Eleven mile brook."[408] This is the earliest known reference to the name Rattle Snake Pond. Previously it was known as Lane's Lake; at present it is Pequawket Pond. In 1813, William became one of the charter proprietors of Ten Mile Brook Canal.

William and Alice's son, William Henry Lane, July 9, 1804–January 25, 1882, married Lavinia Wakefield on November 12, 1832, and settled in Hiram. Their children married into the Hiram families of Chadbourne, Buck, Pierce, and Durgin.

Captain John's son Daniel Lane, March 28, 1771–December 21, 1858, married Keziah Hanscomb on November 30, 1797, and signed Charles Lee Wadsworth's counter petition to block incorporation of Hiram as a town. He had sufficient property to vote from 1809 to 1819, but not much more. In 1809 he had one house, no barn, two tillable acres, two acres of mowing land, forty-six unimproved acres, and one cow. In 1813, he worked off his taxes as a surveyor of highways, the only office he appears to have held, and he earned $12 by boarding pauper

William West's children. He was able to add some land and was taxed on ninety-seven acres in the 1815 bridge tax. His tax of $1.87 was one of the lowest in town.

Captain John's daughter, Alice Lane, married Hiram farmer Aaron Williams on February 21, 1831, and died in Hiram on March 11, 1870.

Captain Jabez Lane
September 21, 1743–April 30, 1830

Of the brothers, Jabez had the most tenuous connection with Hiram. Like them, he served in the army in the Revolution. He received a pension and a warrant for three hundred acres of land granted December 14, 1790, in Buxton. On July 25, 1782, before he settled in Buxton, he bought from his brother John land on the west side of the Saco. John had bought the land from John Curtis, one of the original party that surveyed the west bank of the Saco in 1774. It included one-half of the intervale and "Curtis's pond," adjoining that of John Ayer. No more is heard of Jabez in Hiram.

Capt. Daniel Lane
May 11, 1740–September 11, 1811
Married October 21, 1762
Mary (Molly) Woodman, dates unknown

Capt. Daniel Lane, a brother of Captain John, imbued with the military by his father, also served in his father's company, at age sixteen, under his brother. During the siege of Quebec under Gen. James Wolfe, he was engaged in erecting the fortifications at Halifax, Nova Scotia, and subsequently enlisting soldiers and arresting deserters in Maine and Massachusetts. After enlisting in the Revolution, he was taken prisoner near Fort Edward, New York, stripped of his clothing and his watch, and carried to the headquarters of Gen. Burgoyne. The general released him upon parole, with a note dated August 9, 1777, allowing Daniel to pass through lines

---

407 Wife 1 Elizabeth Hancock, Wife 2 Hannah Boynton Hazeltine, Wife 3 Hannah Bean. Maine Genealogical Society, *Maine Families in 1790* (Camden, Maine: Picton Press, 1990), 156.

408 Oxford County Registry of Deeds, Fryeburg, October 18, 1798, Book 1, 214.

on his way home, an act for which his family was very grateful.[409]

After his discharge in 1780, Daniel returned to Buxton and lived there for some time with his wife Mary "Molly" Woodman Lane and seven children, then moved to Hollis across the river. But after his house burned, he relocated to Hiram, where his brother John had settled. Daniel built a house about two miles west of John's on the hill, on the farm later known as the Daniel L. Clemons farm.[410]

Isaac, son of Capt. Daniel and Molly Lane, was the third generation of Lanes to enter the military. Too young at thirteen to be a soldier, he enlisted in the spring of 1777 as a fifer in his father's company and served until discharged at West Point. He reenlisted in 1781 and served until 1783, when he was honorably discharged by Major General Knox, commander of forces on the Hudson River. Isaac and his brother Daniel raised the 33rd Regiment of Infantry for the War of 1812, and he served as colonel. Afterwards he was a prominent citizen of Buxton, a merchant and mill owner. He speculated in property in Hiram, paying the unpaid direct tax of 1815[411] and selling for $10 one hundred acres of the widow Hannah Hartford to Solomon Hartford. He sold thirty-five acres of Israel Burbank's at Hiram Bridge to Simeon Chadbourne, who built his store on it in 1816. John Lane Hancock, 1757–1835, the son of Col. Isaac and Joanna Lane Hancock, was the first person to traverse Hancock Brook with an eye to "canal" the channel for driving logs.[412]

This house, known as the Archie Wyman Lane house, was consumed in the 1947 fire. Archie Lane was born in 1907[413] and died on January 18, 1987. His parents were Jessie E. and Alice M. Lane. His spouse was Hazel Wentworth of Denmark.

By 1820 there were no descendants in Hiram bearing the surname Lane. But a later house known as the Lane House on Pequawket Trail in Brownfield near the Hiram line at Pequawket Pond (formerly called Lane Lake and Rattlesnake Pond) was burned in the 1947 wildfires.

Town Offices Held

Surveyors of Highways
1813   Daniel Lane

---

409 *Lane Genealogies*, Vol. 1 (Exeter, NH: The Newsletter Press, 1891), 232.

410 Llewellyn A. Wadsworth, *Centennial, Hiram, Maine, 1814-1914*, 11. See the 1858 Hiram map above Clemons Pond.

411 This tax was separate from the 1815 bridge tax.

412 Llewellyn A. Wadsworth Journal, November 17, 1870.

413 December 22, 1909. per Ancestry.com.

LEWIS FAMILY

Abijah Lewis
1756–December 17, 1830

Married February 24, 1785
Betsey Eldridge, c. 1756–October 11, 1841

Abijah Lewis, a Revolutionary War soldier from Buxton, Maine, claimed one hundred acres he had settled on Hiram Hill before January 1, 1784, on land that became Cutler's Grant. Yet Abijah Lewis was not one of the eighteen families listed in the U.S. census of Hiram in 1790. Abijah Lewis appeared in the census of Buxton with a household of five, including two young boys. Though it could have been Abijah's father, Abijah, and mother, Rebecca Lewis, the household matches that of son Abijah.

The earliest Abijah listed in the Hiram census was 1800, by which time the household had eleven members. The Buxton Abijah's household had seven.

Abijah and Betsey's children, all born before August 1800, when the census was taken, were Edward, Noah, Rebecca, Alice, Sally, Abijah III, and Alpheus. All remained in Hiram and settled near their parents on Hiram Hill.

The oldest, Edward, was born in 1784. If the date is correct, it was before Abijah married Betsey. Who, then, was Edward's mother? Was she a first wife of Abijah, unidentified? Was she Betsey Eldridge who bore Edward out of wedlock? If so, Betsey and Abijah did not have another child for six years until Noah was born on July 17, 1790.

Noah sparked a controversy when the town proposed to lay out a two-rod-wide road through his field, taking one-ninth of an acre. He claimed damages at the Town Meeting of April 21, 1821. He asked the town for $25 or to abate his taxes yearly until they reached that amount. In exchanges common in Town Meetings, first it was voted not to allow Noah Lewis $25 for damages for a road passing through his land. Then it was voted not to allow Noah $15. It was then voted to allow Noah $10

and to abate his taxes, commencing in the following year, 1822. Voters reconsidered and decided not to allow Noah Lewis $10 out of the next year's tax. But Noah persisted.

At the next Town Meeting, September 4, 1821, the warrant was to see if the town would alter the time of the payment to Noah. The meeting was extended to the next day. Apparently the selectmen agreed with Noah—the warrant for the meeting was to see if the town would allow $25 in damages "as assessed by the Selectmen."[414] The warrant was not taken up—the meeting was devoted to a discussion about building a new pound and where it would be located. There is no record of whether Noah Lewis received the $25.

There is also no record of what his taxes were in 1821 or 1822. His town tax in 1818 was $93. Thus, fifty-eight people paid more than Noah and sixty-five paid less.[415]

Alpheus, the youngest son of Abijah and Betsey, fared less well. He became a pauper. In 1827, Josiah Mayberry bid $70 for him for a year, and in 1831 Richard Heath bid $47.50 for him and his family.[416]

Marshall Lewis
?–May 14, 1814

Married, date unknown
Elizabeth (Betsey) Cross
August 17, 1780–March 1867

Marshall Lewis served in two wars. He was the son of John Lewis, an English immigrant, and veteran of the French and Indian Wars. Two of John's sons fought in the War of 1812 and neither survived. Joseph died trying to make it home. Marshall was killed in the Battle of Oswego of a musket wound to his shoulder.

Marshall's widow was left with six children between the ages of eight and fifteen. Their children were Sarah Howard, Alexander, Daniel, Olive,

---

414   Hiram Town Clerk's Records, September 1821, 127.

415   Maine Historical Society, Coll. 146, Box 1.

416   Alpheus Lewis and Mary Ward of Hiram filed intention of marriage September 12, 1820. Richard Heath may have been the brother of Abner Heath, who married Rebecca Lewis, sister of Alpheus.

Hannah, and Abigail Wilson, all of whom stayed in Hiram. Three years after Marshall's death, Betsey married Joseph Durgin and bore five more: Phebe, Almira, Marshall, Samuel, and John, none of whom remained in Hiram. Betsy Durgin received a pension of $4 per month for Private Marshall Lewis until September 4, 1862.

Before his war service, Marshall barely got by. In 1809, his sole possession was one cow. By the 1810 inventory, he had built a house and cultivated four bushels of corn and one-half acre of English hay out of fifty acres, but was never eligible to vote in Hiram.

Morgan Lewis
1776–September 11, 1838
Marital data unknown

Morgan Lewis was the son of Maj. Morgan Lewis, who had settled in Alfred, Maine, in 1772. The earliest record of him in Hiram is the 1806 highway tax. In 1812, he paid a tax of 50 cents, the lowest charged, on real property valued at $13 and personal property of $12.

He amassed sufficient property to vote in 1814, and paid his 1815 bridge tax of $1.02. By 1818, he is listed as nonresident owner of fifty acres of unimproved property. In the U.S. censuses of 1800, 1810, 1820, and 1830 he is a resident of Alfred, which may explain his absences.

Town Offices Held

Field Drivers
1822	Abijah Lewis Jr.
1823	Alpheus Lewis
1828	Noah Lewis

Hog Reeves
1816	Noah Lewis
1817	Noah Lewis
1819	It was voted to let hogs run at large but not horses, thus no need for a hog reeve
1820	Abijah Lewis

Surveyors of Highways
1812	Edward Lewis
1821	Edward Lewis
1822	Edward Lewis
1823	Edward Lewis
1824	Edward Lewis
1825	Edward Lewis
1830	Noah Lewis

LORD FAMILY

Jacob Lord
February 3, 1777–June 10, 1850
Marriage date unknown
Emma Day, c. 1779–?

Jacob and Emma Day Lord were in Hiram by 1800, the only Lord household in the U.S. census of 1800. By 1806, Jacob's brother Levi Lord had joined the Durgintown neighborhood, and by 1820, Thomas Bradbury Lord had relocated from Limerick, making four Lord households in Hiram, including Jacob Lord Jr., who had just turned twenty-one and was eligible to vote.

Jacob, son of Jacob and Mary Huntress Lord[417] of South Berwick, Maine, and Emma had seven children: Jacob Jr., born in 1799; Dorothy "Dolly," born in 1800; Hosea, 1804; Emma, 1807; Mary, 1811; Rhoda, 1816; Isaiah died young. In 1811 and 1813, four were sent to school.

Jacob signed Cutler's petition of 1801 to incorporate Hiram as a town, but changed his mind and signed Charles L. Wadsworth's counter petition against incorporation. Jacob was elected constable in 1896, but when reelected in 1807 he resigned and was replaced with Winthrop Baston. Afterwards he held only neighborhood positions.

In addition to being a farmer, Jacob had some skill as a carpenter. In 1814, he and David Durgin were elected "to nail that part of Cornish Bridge belonging to Hiram and make any other necessary repairs, and to put up a fence to prevent passengers from falling into the gully made by the Freshet" and to be paid by having future highway taxes be reduced by that amount.[418] Jacob was also hired to repair the bridge in 1820 and to be paid 75 cents per day.

By 1818, Jacob had a house and barn, and of one hundred acres had two in cultivation, six in mowing, and three in pasture for his two oxen, three cows, five cattle, and two pigs. His real property was worth $175 and his personal property $117, which totaled $292, well above the median.

Levi Lord
1786–July 20, 1861
Married 1800
Abigail Durgin, 1782–November 25, 1858

Levi, born nine years later than brother Jacob, did not amass as much wealth as Jacob, accumulating less than half, and by 1830 had left Hiram for Porter. Children: Henry died young; Henry, born in 1806; John, 1808; Levi, 1816; Jacob, no information; David, no information; Albert, 1823.

Thomas Bradbury Lord
June 7, 1796–January 27, 1882
Married October 17, 1824
Clarissa Watson
September 28, 1805–October 9, 1884

Thomas B.'s parents were firmly grounded in Limerick. His mother, Sarah Bradbury of Buxton, came to Limerick to marry his father, Thomas. He was the grandson of Hannah Dennett of Saco, and Ammi Ruhamah Lord, a founder of Limerick, who drew up plans for the Baptist Church there. But Thomas B. had been living in Hiram for several years when he married Clarissa Watson, daughter of John Watson Jr. Seven of their eight children survived to adulthood: William G., born 1827; Clara O., born 1830; Mary, 1832; Irania, 1834; Hannah, 1836; Sarah, 1839; John T., 1841.

Town Offices Held

Constables

1806	Jacob Lord Jr.
1807	Jacob Lord Jr., resigned and was replaced with Winthrop Baston

Fence Viewers

1823	Jacob Lord

---

417 Mary was the daughter of Darling and Lorie Huntress of South Berwick, Maine.

418 Hiram Clerk Records, November 7, 1814.

Field Drivers

    1823   Jacob Lord

Hog Reeves

    1823   Jacob Lord Jr.

Money Clerk [unique title this year only]

    1828   Thomas Lord

School Agents

    1830   Thomas Lord

Surveyors of Highways

    1807   Jacob Lord Jr.
    1818   Jacob Lord
    1819   Jacob Lord
    1821   Levi Lord
    1823   Levi Lord
    1824   Joseph Lord
    1826   Joseph Lord

Surveyors of Lumber

    1827   Levi Lord

JONATHAN KNOWLTON LOWELL
1756–1852

Married December 11, 1794
Rachel Morton, 1758–?

It was fortuitous for Hiram when Jonathan Knowlton Lowell in 1802 traded, with Seth Spring of Bridgton, two hundred acres of land in Foster's Gore in Denmark for 110 acres of better farm land on Cutler's Lower Grant in Hiram. Thus began a long succession of Lowells in Hiram and Gorham, where Jonathan K.'s wife, Rachel Morton, resided before marrying him.

Like his father, Moses Lowell, Jonathan K. fought in the Revolution. Jonathan was at the battle of Bunker Hill.

Children

Abigail, born 1786, married Capt. Greenleaf Cram of Standish.

Moses, born 1787, married Rachel Newcomb of Gorham, and brought her and her brother David Newcomb to Hiram.

Reuben, born 1790, married first Rhoda Lord of Hiram, second Charlotte Jewell of Cornish.

Thomas, born c. 1791, married Eliza Paine of Standish.

Miriam, born c. 1792, married Aaron Cross after his first wife, Sally Lewis, died.

Eben married Susan B. Lowell of Hiram, the daughter of David and Louisa Brown Lowell. Eben left Hiram for eastern Maine.

Rachel, born 1794, married William Storer Jr. of Hiram. Late in life, Jonathan K. lived with him and his family.

Jonathan, born 1798, married Mary Howard of Hiram, daughter of Lemuel and Hannah Clemons Howard.

David married Louisa Brown Merrifield of Hiram (the widow of pauper Isaac Merrifield), and drowned in the Penobscot River about 1847.

Elizabeth (Betsey), born c. 1803, married Dr. Charles Wilson of Hiram.

A grandson of Moses and Rachel, of whom there is a photograph, was Charles C. Lowell, 1850–1911.

This photograph in the collection of Hiram Historical Society is labeled "Moses Lowell and Rachel Newcomb Lowell," but Moses died in 1847, before photography became widely known in Maine. The clothing also indicates a later date. Perhaps the photo is of the next generation. Does anyone know who they may be?

Charles was the rural mail carrier, whose route took him to Lemuel Cotton & Son store and Mt. Cutler House.[419] Charles married three times, first in 1873 to Mary Etta Lowell, 1854–1901, second to Lilla E. Poor, 1866–1904, third in 1906 to Anna L. Marston, 1863–?, yet had no children, only one stepdaughter, Helen G. Marston.

The ties with Gorham continued with Jonathan K.'s son Reuben's children, three of whom married residents of Gorham:

- Son Reuben married Abbie Watson of Gorham;
- Son Henry married Betsey Rice of Gorham;
- Daughter Rhoda married Joseph Cressey of Gorham.

---

419 Charles's parents were Samuel and Deborah D. Boston Lowell.

Charles C. Lowell, rural mail carrier, in front of Cotton's Store. Mt. Cutler House is in the background.

Reuben kept a large tavern owned by Jacob H. Clement, the father-in-law of Thomas A. Barker, formerly of Hiram. He succeeded Peleg Barker, formerly of Hiram.[420] While there, Reuben was active in the community, a charter member of the Gorham Grange, holding the office of gate keeper. The connection continued when George W. Lowell, a builder and contractor in Gorham, married Sarah J. Lowell of Hiram. Mary Ann and Rhoda, other grandchildren of Jonathan K. Lowell, also married Gorham men.

Town Offices Held

Fence Viewers
1821   Jonathan Lowell

Hog Reeves
1822   Jonathan Lowell
1823   Jonathan Lowell

Surveyors of Highways
1811   Jonathan Lowell [crossed out]
1817   Reuben Lowell

1827   Daniel Lowell (alias David Lowell)
1828   Thomas Lowell
1829   Thomas Lowell

The grave site of Jonathan K. Lowell, Revolutionary War soldier, on Hiram Hill Road is marked by a depression behind a stone wall and a veteran's flag. The graves of other Lowells are in the Spring Cemetery.

---

420   Hugh D. McLellan, *History of Gorham, Maine* (Somersworth: New England History Press, facsimile of the 1903 edition, 1980), 273, 318.

JOSIAH MABRY[421]
February 13, 1775–February 16, 1849
Married April 26, 1798
Rebecca Jordan, 1775–February 16, 1849

Josiah and his wife, Rebecca Jordan Mabry, struggled all their married life to make better lives for their children. They succeeded. Although one of the poorest in Hiram, the family was highly regarded. Josiah was a founder of the Baptist Society enacted by the Massachusetts Legislature on June 21, 1811. Their son, Thomas, became a deacon, deputy sheriff, and selectman in Hiram. Grandson Madison K. Mabry was a lieutenant in the Civil War and one of the longest-serving and most-loved teachers in Hiram.

Josiah and Rebecca came to Hiram from Windham, Maine, before 1800, perhaps soon after 1798, when they married. The census of 1800 lists them in Hiram with one male under ten. According to Hiram Historical Society records the child was a girl, Mary, born 1798, not a boy, as recorded in the 1800 census. Son Thomas followed in 1802, and Sumner in 1804. Sumner was an unlucky name. He died at two years of age in 1806. The next Sumner lasted one year. The third Sumner, born 1808, died in 1831, a bachelor. The last child, Worster, named after Josiah's mother, Mary Worster, was born in 1810 and also died a bachelor in 1830. Daughter Mary never married and lived to be sixty-five years old. The Mabry name was carried on by Thomas.

Josiah and Rebecca settled first near Hancock Pond,[422] which later was named Barker Pond. They lived in a log house for two years and minded Barker's mill, nearby on Hancock Brook, then part of Baldwin, and Barker's dam, built in 1807. They then succeeded the Tylers on Hiram Hill[423] and moved from there to the Denmark Road near Tear Cap,[424] where Thomas Mabry was still living in 1858. Thomas was responsible for laying out the present route of the Denmark Road (Route 117).

Josiah signed Cutler's petition of 1801 to incorporate Hiram as a town and was one of the few who

The old Mabry Place off Christian Hill Road, now called Bull Ring Road, on the old Tear Cap Road. The road is now called Fletcher Road, after Llewellyn Fletcher who lived there many years in the late nineteenth to early twentieth centuries. Present address is 166 Fletcher Road.

The Mabry place, 1993. Note the addition of a deck off the ell and gardens edged in field stones.

---

421 Other spellings are Mayberry, Mabury.

422 Ridlon, *Saco Valley Settlements and Families*, 149.

423 Subsequently the Ridlon farm, now 299 Hiram Hill Road.

424 Now called Fletcher Road.

did not change his mind and sign the counter petition of Charles L. Wadsworth.

Josiah, like most of the Hiram residents, always needed cash, as seen in this letter of 1806:

> Sq
> John Park Little
> Gorham
> Hiram August the 3 1806
> Sir I received your letter with Surprise for as for my Uncle John Chute who he and his partners hold of the note and i told him when i Could be free To part of the money & he said he Could weight. [sic: wait] I Do Expect that his partner has done this unbeknownst To my uncle and know of as it is Come upon me on a Suden and it is Difficult Season with me for my family is sick so that Cannot Leave them in no case What Ever and it is out of my power to make out The money at present as it is for me to make a new World. Sir your humble Servant Begs that your honour Would send a line to my uncle that Distress me being Difficulty Yours?? would non [?]
> Josiah Mayberry[425]

In 1809 his "rateables," upon which taxes were based, were one dwelling house, one barn, six tillable acres, two mowing acres, four pasturage acres, one hundred acres unimproved, one cow, one horse, and six swine.

In 1813, his real property was valued at $35, his personal property at $20, and his total tax was $4.38, as assessed by Aaron Richardson of Richardson Road, his neighbor on Hiram Hill. Aaron's own assessment was $235.66 real property and $112 personal property, much higher than Josiah's.

Josiah voted in 1809, 1810, 1811, 1813, 1814, and 1819, all the years for which there are records, except for 1812, during which he was probably serving in the War of 1812 as corporal under Captain Alpheus Spring of Hiram, with service in Portland.

In the bridge tax of 1815 his property value was $24, giving him a property tax of 32 cents and a total bridge tax of 90 cents. Only property owner William Woodsome paid less (67 cents). Woodsome's property was valued more, at $50, but he did not pay a poll tax of 58 cents, so his total tax bill was less than Josiah's.

The lack of cash drove some to use any means to provide for their families. Justice of the Peace Asa Osgood intervened on behalf of Josiah in 1813, when a tenant farmer cheated him of his share of crops. Samuel Jelerson agreed "to let Josiah Mayberry have 2/3 of corn and wheat and rye that he raises on said Mayberry's land & it is to be delivered to said Mayberry by the hand of Asa Osgood at his dwelling House in said Hiram. Also Mayberry is to have ½ potatoes. That is to be a final settlement of the whole. Attest Asa Osgood Jr. Witness Samuel Jelerson, his mark."[426]

In another case, Benjamin Swett accused Josiah of trading spoiled hay. Several witnesses made statements; most were damaging to Josiah. Benjamin said Josiah hauled in hay worth $10 per ton, but "it was not good" and his cattle refused to eat it. Asa Burbank said Josiah assured him the hay was of good quality, but Burbank thought it poor quality and worth only $6.66. John Bucknell said he helped load hay, but only nine hundred pounds of the ton. Ephraim Kimball, however, said he saw Benjamin Swett feeding his cattle hay worth $10 per ton. The outcome of this dispute is not known, but such discrepancies in witness accounts are familiar today.

Thomas's son Madison Mabry served in the Civil War and was one of the longest-serving and most-successful teachers in Hiram. See the chapter Schools.

Town Offices Held

Fence Viewers

1815	Josiah Mayberry
1826	Josiah Mayberry

---

425 Transcription of letter in collections of Hiram Historical Society was facilitated by Maine State Archives.
426 Maine Historical Society, Coll. 16, Box. 2, Folder 4, Vol. 2, 72.

Dea. Thomas Mabry

Dea. Thomas Mabry died Feb. 3, of lung fever, aged 83 years and 5 months. He was the son of Capt. Josiah Mabry, who lived in Hiram as early as 1805, and served in the war of 1812. The deceased was a man of intelligence, integrity and sterling character, and had always taken a deep interest in public affairs and the stirring reforms of the day. He served the public as deputy sheriff and selectman, and held prominent rank and position in the agricultural societies of the town and county. He has been a member of the Universalist church in Hiram for fifty years. We shall miss his tall, erect form and cheerful, genial presence from our midst, and remember his pure life and example. He leaves a wife and two sons. His funeral was attended on the 5th by Rev. G. W. Barber.

LLEWELLYN.

Llewellyn A. Wadsworth wrote the obituary of Deacon Thomas Mabry, son of Capt. Josiah Mabry.[427]

Field Drivers

1811	Josiah Mayberry
1816	Josiah Mayberry (voted at illegal meeting March 4 and not elected April 6)
1818	Josiah Mayberry

Hog Reeves

1815	Josiah Mayberry

Surveyors of Highways

1820	Josiah Mayberry
1830	Josiah Mabry, Thomas Mabry

Surveyors of Lumber

1830	Josiah Mabry

---

427   Llewellyn A. Wadsworth, Obituaries, Hiram Historical Society, Hiram, ME.

JOHN McLUCAS

c. 1744-March 27, 1813

Married December 22, 1775

Margaret Brown, dates unknown

John McLucas Sr., a drummer at the battle of Bunker Hill in the Revolutionary War, came to Hiram in 1787 and settled near General Wadsworth. He was a man of brute strength.

The following stories demonstrate how one interpretation can change the meaning for history. One story is that Gen. Peleg Wadsworth saw John pulling a plow by himself and exclaimed that "he would not have such a man in his field." This shortened version doesn't make much sense, but by putting together the next two versions, the essence of fear is revealed in the message. Llewellyn Wadsworth published this version:

> In 1787 John McLucas of Hollis, a revolutionary soldier, settled below Hiram Falls, near the lot of the old school-house. His five sons, John, James, Jacob, Jeremiah and Robert, served in the war of 1812. He was a man of giant frame and strength. One day Gen. Wadsworth, needing some labor, called on Mr. McLucas and found him in the field, and offered to let him his oxen a day in exchange for labor. "General," said he, "I don't need any oxen," and bidding one of his sons to guide the plow, he took the chain over his shoulder, and plowed a furrow rapidly. Gen. Wadsworth looked on in amazement, and exclaimed "Bless me, bless me, I wouldn't have such a man in my field.[428]

Finally the sense of the story is revealed. Gideon T. Ridlon, Sr. wrote in an undated, unnamed newspaper that:[429]

> ...it is related of him that while he was drawing a plow, held by one of his sons, with the chain over his shoulder, General Peleg Wadsworth (grandfather of the poet Longfellow) approached him. When he saw the doughty old general, for whom, by virtue of his military service he had profound esteem, he paused in his furrow. "Well, well" said the old officer, "This beats all, this beats all. Why, I came to hire you, but bless me! bless me! I should be afraid to have such a man on my farm.

A year later, John would die.

John married Margaret Brown in Buxton. They were both from Limerick. Their children were John Jr., born 1785; Jeremiah, 1786; Jacob, no birth date; Robert, 1796; James, 1797; Abraham, 1798; and Sally, 1803.

According to the family, John and Margaret's six sons all served in the War of 1812. There are records of five. Abraham, age sixteen, was a musician from July 4 to September 2, 1814, in Capt. E. Andrew's detached company, raised at Scarborough and vicinity for service at Portland. Jeremiah and Robert were privates. James was a musician from September 13 to 24, 1814, in Capt. Alpheus Spring's company, Major James Steele's battalion of artillery raised at Hiram, service in Portland.

Jacob died in the War of 1812, leaving a widow, Betsey Gray of Brownfield, whom he'd married in 1800, and six young children, the youngest born September 3, 1813. A third female noted in the U.S. census of 1790 is unknown.

Curiously, no official record of Jacob, who was mortally wounded at Plattsburg, New York, was found.

According to the *Eastern Argus* newspaper of February 18, 1813, Robert deserted from Fort Scammel, Portland Harbor, and a reward of $10 was offered for his return. He was described as five foot seven or eight, light complexion, light hair, and blue eyes. Whatever his fate as a deserter, the stigma did not prevent him from marrying Abby Emlin on May 16, 1818.

---

428   Llewellyn A. Wadsworth, *Centennial, Hiram, Main, 1814-1914*, 17.

429   Gideon T. Ridlon, Sr., unnamed, undated newspaper in the collection of Hiram Historical Society.

The family was proud that all sons served in the War of 1812. According to the family, John had taken five sons to Portland to enlist, excluding Jacob who had already done so. John died on March 27, 1813, age sixty-nine years,[430] in Portland, on his way back to Hiram.[431] If Robert was with his father when he enlisted, presumably before he deserted on February 10, John had a lengthy stay in Portland.

Regarding the family's service to the town, the only record of a McLucas serving as an officer of Hiram was son James, who was a hog reeve in 1820. John McLucas, however, was listed regularly as a voter and sent his children to school, even Elizabeth (Betsey), still unmarried, at the advanced age of twenty-five.[432]

For the 1811–1812 term, six of his children were registered in a list of Districts 5 and 6: Betsy, age c. twenty-five; Robert, fifteen; James, fourteen; Abraham, thirteen; Sally, eight.

John McLucas Jr., who had married Abigail Brown, daughter of Moody Brown, had two girls in school in 1811: Susanna and Ruth, no birth dates found. Brother Jacob had three: Timothy, age eleven; Seleny (Salina), age eight; and Mary, age five. Jeremiah had John Lambert (?) or John & Lambert (?) in school.

On the list of scholars for 1813 tallied on November 1, after John's death, widow McLucas had three children in school (they were not named). The widows McLucas and Hartford, who both had children in school, were not eligible to vote, but the men voted and chose Joseph Chadbourn to be the class master of the "low school.[433]

After John's death, his family fell into poverty and became paupers in the town. See the chapter Paupers.

A year after his death, in 1814, John's widow, Margaret, married Thomas Welch of Waterboro and filed for a pension for John McLucas's service in the Revolution. After her death in 1843 it was awarded to her children.

Ten Dollars Reward

DESERTED on the 10th inst. From Fort Scammel, Portland Harbor, a Soldier of the 21st Regt. of Maine by the name of ROBERT M'LUCAS: is about five feet, seven or eight inches high, of light complexion, light hair, blue eyes, by profession a farmer; when he left the Fort, he had on blue pantaloons with yellow welts & a uniform coat of the U.S. Infantry; over which he wore a brown surtoute.[434] He has been living for several years past in Hiram, in the County of Oxford. Whoever will apprehend said deserter and deliver him to this Post, or any Post or Garrison in the United States, or secure him in any Goal, so that he may be had in the United States service, shall receive ten dollars reward, and all necessary charges paid them.
GRL'ENL DEARBORN[435],
Lt 3rd Regt US Artillery, Commanding recruits at Fort Scammel Feb 15, 1813

The McLucas family had some "characters" that Gideon T. Ridlon Sr. pointed out in a manuscript[436] titled "Ironsided Old Family: McClucas is held to be a genuine Irish surname" quoted below.

---

430 John was baptized in Biddeford on August 26, 1750.

431 Death notice in newspaper *Eastern Argus*. April 1, 1813.

432 Parents hoped to marry daughters at age 18. Betsy married Nathaniel Lombard of Gorham on April 8, 1813, age 26 or 27.

433 Voting were Jacob Lord, Joseph Durgin, John Warren, John Fly, Stephen Tibbetts, John W. Chadbourn, John McLucas, Levi Lord, William Storer, Samuel Merrifield, and John Lord.

434 A man's long close-fitting overcoat of a style similar to a frock coat.

435 General Henry Dearborn.

436 Typed manuscript, no date, Hiram Historical Society, Hiram, Maine.

McLucas is a genuine Irish surname and no one need assume it is Scotch or English. But the character of a family determines its right to claim honor: it is merit that counts. The words of Burns the poet apply here:

The title's but the guinea's stamp,
The man's the man for a' that.

Let every family honor their native land and never shame themselves by being Irish or Scandinavians. The Scotchman can never imitate the Irish brogue, nor the Native Hibernian the broad Scotch of the Lowlands.

The McClucas, or McLucas, family came to New England as early as 1718, and several of them served in the Revolution. A branch of the clan settled in Narragansett No. 2, now Buxton, where they multiplied fruitfully, producing scions of unusual vigor which, when removed from the parent stock and engrafted into other towns, propagated their species until their posterity is now discoverable in many sections of New England.

John McLucas removed from Buxton to Hiram along with the Lewis family, the head of which, Abijah, whose grave may be found in the Spring burying ground beside that of Betsey Eldridge, his wife, was his companion in arms during the struggle for independence, and it is related of him… [here is written the story of General Peleg Wadsworth's encounter with John's brute strength told above]. We have heard the following:

Aaron McClucas, son of the preceding, built his castle on Hiram Hill, an elevation lifted high above the Saco Valley, where, childless, he and his old wife lived until far advanced in life. They were quiet and law-abiding, but poor. To save shoe leather, Aaron went barefoot in the warm seasons, and could often be seen on his way to the village with his small basket of eggs, making enormous human tracks in the sandy road. The old man could never tell his age. However, as he sat down to rest at a neighbor's door after climbing the long hill one summer day, he said, "Well, Josh, I have found out how old I am. I was born the same year as Bennett Pike." "What year was that?" asked Joshua. "I dunno," answered Aaron.

Royal McClucas was for many years a man who dissipated and while returning home with a neighbor, both intoxicated, with a scythe over his shoulder, he fell with his neck across the edge, and, seeing the blood flow, his companion seized the scythe thereof and pulled the keen edged blade out, cutting a fearful gash in the fallen man's neck. The wound was sewed up and his life was saved. He always wore a worsted "comforter" around his neck thereafter to hide the terrible scar. In relating the particulars of this casualty, Josh Ridlon always said that nothing but his windpipe was left by the sharp scythe, but Harrison Taylor went farther and assumed that Royal carried his head in his own hand when they hauled him home in a horse-cart, and it was "chawing tobacco" all the way. Fancy!

When well advanced in years "Royal" was converted and permanently reformed from his intemperate habits. Believing that such a man's influence would be salutary in the cause of temperance, some prominent ladies approached him with a pledge, earnestly soliciting his signature thereto; but they were met with a sharp rebuff in the following language: "No, I won't sign it. Why, I wish Saco River was full o' new rum 'n' Hancock Brook full o' molasses so everybody could drink all they wanted. Howsomever, I don't want any."

A neighbor was employed to dig a grave in the family lot for a daughter of "Royal" and received full directions from the old man. "Find the best grave, Josh, then get over two feet and dig there." But when the spade went down it struck another grave and the sexton "set over" two feet farther than he was requested to. The procession was already on the road and knowing the bad temper and trumpet voice of "Royal," and to avoid any hitch or unpleasant scene at the grace, Josh went forward to meet the mourners.

Approaching the carriage in which the old man and his wife were riding, he told quietly that in his attempt to dig where he had signified he had found a coffin, but had excavated two feet farther away. This roused the old man's anger and, raising his right arm, he shouted: "He's no bizness in there, I tell ye, he has no bizness in there."

Thinking "discretion was preferable to valor," Josh hastily withdrew and retired to a secluded spot until the company had left the graveyard, and then went forward and finished his work of burial.

Moody McClucas, brother of the two preceding, was like Royal, a soldier in the Civil War. He saw hard service, was several times wounded and, I believe, carries a bullet in his leg. He is still living, having passed his 90th birthday in September, a hale old man.[437]

Isaiah McClucas, an uncle of the brothers mentioned before, is now living in Waterboro and draws a pension for services in the Mexican War where he acquitted himself like a brave and faithful solder.

Remarkable for longevity, this ironsided family has been represented on the battlefield of every war since the settlement of the American colonies and as law-abiding citizens have contributed their part toward the population and progress of our beloved civilization. May their blood never decrease in the land. —G.T. Ridlon, Sr.

Town Offices Held

Hog Reeves

1820   James McLucas

---

437 Moody McLucas, July 5, 1822 to May 10, 1913.

MERRIFIELD FAMILY

Samuel Merrifield
1774–1838

First marriage 1791
Lydia Reed, dates unknown
Second marriage 1822
Lydia Welch, dates unknown

There is no genealogical information about Samuel at the Hiram Historical Society. Family stories of descendants, the U.S. census, property deeds, receipts in the Maine State Archives, and documents in the Massachusetts State Archives are the sources of information about his life.

Samuel Merrifield (Merryfield) may have been the first settler on the Waters Grant in South Hiram. Samuel was a yeoman in Wells, Maine, when he bought one hundred acres of land in 1798 for $150 from Josiah Waters, the original grantee. His lot was No. 4 in the tract in a gore with Hiram on one side and Great Ossipee and Saco rivers on the other side.[438]

In the 1800 U.S. census of Hiram, his household consisted of three boys under sixteen and two girls under ten, plus Samuel and his wife, who were between the ages of twenty-six and forty-five. He signed Cutler's petition for incorporation of Hiram in 1801, and also the counter petition of Charles Lee Wadsworth against it, as did other settlers in South Hiram.

Another child was born after 1800, increasing the family from five to six. Samuel sent his children to school. There were five in school in 1813. A combined list of students in Districts 5 and 6 named six Merrifield "scholars" for 1811–1812. The children named were:

> Isaac & Betsey
> Richard & Sally
> Simeon & Samuel

According to descendants, Isaac had two half brothers: Simeon Merrifield, born 1798 in Wells, Maine, and Samuel Merrifield Jr.

Samuel Merrifield sold lot No. 4 to Simeon Merrifield of Wells for $200 in 1809. This obviously was not Samuel's son Simeon, who was in school in 1812. This Simeon voted in 1809 and 1810, but was crossed out in 1811, indicating he was no longer in Hiram.

A Jesse Merrifield also voted in 1809, but there is no further record of him. Samuel, however, remained in Hiram for a while. He voted regularly—in 1810, 1811 (there is no record for 1812), 1813, and 1814. He paid his highway tax in 1806, received a tax deferral in 1808, and paid the bridge tax of 1815.

Samuel had bought lots No. 5 and No. 6, which consisted of 207 adjacent acres, from land speculator Church Trouant of Marshfield, Massachusetts, in 1812.[439] The price was $310, which he mortgaged

The Merrifields lived in this house at 753 Brownfield Road nearly one hundred years, but the original builder is yet to be identified. Was it Edmund Trafton, who owned the land 1818–1823, or a later owner?

---

438 Oxford County Registry of Deeds, Fryeburg, now Paris, September 28, 1798, Book 5, 112, recorded September 23, 1809.

439 Trouant had paid $420 for the land in 1800. In 1823 Trouant's remaining property of .08 acre was sold at auction for $5.01 to Joseph Farnham. The venue was Levi Morrill's store. Oxford County Registry of Deeds, Fryeburg, now Paris, Book 5, 595.

to Trouant at the same amount plus interest. Samuel sold one hundred acres of this to John McLucas for $300, a tidy profit. As soon as McLucas had paid off his mortgage, he sold it to George Storer, a cooper from Cornish. This land was adjacent to David Durgin and John McAllen. Finally, Samuel sold his remaining one hundred acres in 1817 for $300. The next year, 1818, Simeon Merrifield sold his hundred acres in Hiram.

Simeon Merrifield bought land in Porter and afterward removed to Denmark, where Samuel's son Richard Merrifield resided. In 1820, Samuel Merrifield was in Wells, and in 1830 in South Berwick, where the family says he died in 1838. Samuel's son Isaac was not so adept, and became a pauper in Hiram.

Read more in the chapter Paupers.

Andrew Merrifield
September 13, 1794–December 19, 1855
Married Jane Anderson Berry
February 14, 1796–December 19, 1855

Andrew Merrifield Sr. built his homestead in Porter, living there with his wife Jane Anderson Berry and nine children, and died there. Son Andrew Jr., however, had a propensity to purchase land along the Hiram/Porter border around the Clemons Ponds, Jaybird and Trafton, and made his home in Hiram, as did his brother John. The Merrifield name lives on in the Hiram maps of 1858 and 1880. The relationship with Samuel and Simeon is unknown.

ASA OSGOOD

1756–August 10, 1833

First marriage, name and dates unknown
Second marriage, intentions published
July 16, 1808
Hannah Powers, c. 1779–c. 1854

Asa Osgood served in both major wars that erupted in his lifetime. In his twenties he rose to sergeant major in the Continental Massachusetts Army. In his late fifties he enlisted as a private in Captain W. Wheeler's company, raised at Rumford, Maine, and served with fellow Hiram residents Lt. Asa Burbank, Sergeant Thomas B. Watson, and Corporal Josiah Mayberry (Mabry), with service in Portland. He served three terms as selectman before the War of 1812. Both before and after that war, he was respected enough to be elected to the office of tithingman.

Asa was a farmer and well off. Like his neighbor, John Watson, he settled in Brownfield and was re-assigned to Hiram in 1807. In 1810, he had a house and a barn, 128 acres, of which three were tilled, six were in mowing, and three were pasturage. He owned a couple of cows, four cattle, a horse and colt, and four swine. In accumulated wealth, measured by taxes paid, Asa was in the upper third. Asa was physically strong and he was elected hog reeve because of it, but life was not easy.

Asa realized the pain of the death of both a wife and his adult son, Asa Osgood Jr., but lived to see the birth of two grandsons.

Children by his first wife were Asa Jr. and James.

Like his father, Asa Osgood Jr., birth date unknown–1825, served in the War of 1812, but in a different militia: Alpheus Spring's battalion under Maj. James Steele.

On March 19, 1821, Asa Osgood Jr. married Hannah S. Wentworth, born April 14, 1803. He was married only four years before he died in 1825, leaving a widow, age 22, and a three-year-old son, Charles A. Osgood, born May 2, 1822.

A year later, on January 11, 1826, Hannah married John Bucknell. She became the mother of Andrew Bucknell.

Asa Osgood's second son, was James Osgood, March 3, 1800–January 19, 1879. James married

Betsey McDonald on June 16, 1822. They are buried in Hiram Village Cemetery.

Town Offices Held

Collectors of Taxes

1820	Asa Osgood Jr.

Committees on Accounts

1820	Asa Osgood Jr.

Field Drivers

1819	Asa Osgood

Hog Reeves

1816	Asa Osgood
1821	Asa Osgood Jr.

Pound Keepers

1819	Asa Osgood Jr.
1820	Asa Osgood Jr.

School Committees

1822	Asa Osgood Jr.

School Teachers

1822	Asa Osgood Jr., School District #2

Selectmen

1806	Asa Osgood
1807	Asa Osgood
1811	Asa Osgood

Surveyors of Highways

1811	Asa Osgood
1820	Asa Osgood Jr.

Tithingmen

1811	Asa Osgood
1815	Asa Osgood

JOHN PIERCE

May 26, 1764–September 21, 1838

Marriage date unknown

Rebecca Wilson, dates unknown

The fifth, sixth, seventh, eighth, ninth, and tenth children of John and Rebecca Pierce were born in Hiram between 1798 and 1807. Before that, John lived in Woburn, Massachusetts, and Baldwin, Maine. In Hiram, he settled around the intersection of Notch Road and Pequawket Trail. Soon after, he was elected and re-elected selectman for five consecutive years, beginning in 1803,[440] and became a trusted office-holder in Hiram. When the petition for incorporation was submitted to the Massachusetts Legislature in Boston in 1806, he was elected the agent to do it. When the Saco River bridge and the Hancock Brook bridge needed attention, he was a member of both committees and, in 1816, the Committee for a Plan for a Town House.

He was the second largest landholder in Hiram. In the 1815 bridge tax list, Pierce was charged for 1,118.66 acres, compared with 2,398.33 acres owned by Peleg Wadsworth. The next largest landowner was J. Osgood Jr. with 772.66. In Hiram the wealthy were active supporters in town governance, and John Pierce and his family were among them, holding offices of clerk, selectman, and highway surveyors, and serving as members of many committees, including the School Committee.

Children

John Jr., 1789–1871

Josiah, 1790–1864

Rebecca O., 1792–1860

Benjamin F., 1794–1880

William, 1796–1876

Timothy C., March 14, 1798–August 1, 1798

Timothy C., 1800–1876

Daniel, 1802–1891

Levi, 1804–1880

Ruth S., 1807–1877

The Pierce homestead on Pequawket Trail, built in Greek Revival style, burned in the wildfires of 1947. On the site, fifth-generation descendent Edward Clemons Pierce built a toy train museum that included a railroad caboose. The caboose is no longer there and the building, at present, is a private residence, 1996A Pequawket Trail.

---

440 This is the earliest Hiram record found.

The Pierce family continued to be prominent in Hiram for many years. When John Jr. died at age eighty-two, the obituary was short but effusive:

> One of our most venerable and respected citizens died Dec. 19, 1871, at his residence at Hiram Bridge, of paralysis, heart disease, and lung fever, after an illness of some 9 days. The deceased was a cousin to the late Judge Pierce of Gorham and was also related to President Pierce. He leaves a widow, 2 sons, and 3 daughters.[441]

In the third generation, John Pierce, Esq., became postmaster of Hiram in 1872 and was associated with his brother-in-law, Rev. A. P. Sanborn, in the merchandising firm of Pierce & Sanborn. Grandson Daniel donated the land to build the Hiram Congregational Church.

The family, however, was not immune from suffering. Son Levi was blind from birth. Josiah died from cancer near his ear. Grandson John died age two. Grandson Nathan died at age twenty-three. Granddaughter Harriet died at age twenty-four, after four years of marriage. Grandsons Arthur, Henry A., and William were Civil War casualties. Many families at the time suffered such losses.

Town Offices Held

Clerk
1806	John Pierce
1807	John Pierce
1811	John Pierce

Committee on Accounts
1814	John Pierce
1815	John Pierce
1818	John Pierce

Committees on Bridge Building and Repairs
1812	Saco River: Charles L. Wadsworth, Simeon Bucknell, John Pierce
1815	Saco River: Marshall Spring, Asa Burbank—to distribute subscription papers and obtain donations; John Pierce, Asa Burbank, Isaac Gray—to view and ascertain the best place to erect said Bridge; John Pierce, Asa Burbank, Marshall Spring—superintend the erecting of said Bridge
1816	Hancock Brook: Chose John Pierce, John Watson, Asa Burbank a Committee to Superintend building the Bridge

Committee on Incorporation
1806	Thomas Spring, John Pierce

Committee on a Plan for a Town House
1816	Peleg Wadsworth, John Pierce, John Warren

School Agents
1827	John Pierce Jr.

School Committee
1816	A committee of 3 was chosen instead of an additional school agent. Chose Peleg Wadsworth, Alpheus Spring, John Pierce

Selectmen
1803–1807	John Pierce
1811	John Pierce

Surveyors of Highways
1811	John Pierce
1816	John Pierce Jr. John Pierce Jr. was replaced by David Newcomb at meeting 6 April.
1818	John Pierce Jr.
1819	John Pierce Jr.
1820	John Pierce
1833	Daniel Pierce

---

441 Hubert W. Clemons, "The Pierce Family of Hiram, Maine," *Downeast Ancestry*, Vol. 12 No. 3, 107.

JOSEPH RANKIN

February 7, 1778–May 8, 1851
First marriage April 1, 1802
Jane Perry, May 10, 1778–April 13, 1828
Second marriage date unknown
Betsey Hunt, c. 1778–November 10, 1841

Joseph Rankin came from Buxton and by 1810 was settled in Baldwin on Ward's Hill near the Hiram line. According to Llewellyn A. Wadsworth, Joseph was a man of herculean frame and strength. He built a mill on Hancock Brook, "where the Rankin family maintained mills for many years, and where his great grandson, Gardiner H. Rankin, of the Hiram Lumber Co., conducts a lumber mill."[442]

The Rankin family also operated a sawmill, a carding mill, and a stave and shingle mill here in the second half of the nineteenth century. Early in the twentieth century, Gardiner Rankin attached a dynamo to his waterwheel and produced enough electricity to light his home a quarter-mile away."[443] James Rankin held the town office of surveyor of split lumber in 1830, the only office held by a Rankin within the scope of this book.

Joseph married Jane Perry of Parsonsfield, with whom he had eight children before she died, after which he married Betsy Hunt and had no more children. He was the father of Mehitable, James, Joseph, John, Enoch, Jane, Perley, and Susan. Before he died, the Rankins had intermarried with the Watsons, Wentworths, Kimballs, Hodgdons, Grays, and Richardsons.

So close to Hiram were the Rankins' properties that in 1820, Jesse Kimball and Ephraim Wentworth, who were Rankin families by marriage,[445] along with Thomas Day, petitioned the legislature and succeeded in 1822 in seceding from Baldwin in favor of Hiram.[446]

Town Offices Held

Surveyors of Split Lumber
1830   James Rankins

Rankin's Mill looking in the other direction.[444]

---

442 Llewellyn A. Wadsworth, *Centennial, Hiram, Maine, 1814-1914*, 20. This was the Scribner Mill.

443 Robert C. Jones, *Two Feet to the Lakes* (Edmonds, WA: Pacific Fast Mail, 1993), 46.

444 Robert C. Jones, 47.

445 Joseph Rankin Jr. married Lydia Wentworth, daughter of Ephraim Wentworth. Enoch Rankin married Hope Kimball, daughter of Jesse Kimball.

446 Maine State Archives, "An Act to Set off Part of Baldwin and Annex It to Hiram Year 1821," Type PS, Access 7–99.

The narrow gauge Bridgton & Saco River Railroad, 1883–1941, stopped at Rankin's Mill (center). The tracks on the right loop around the back of what became the home of Fred Stanton and, later, Jack and Diane Barnes, on Dearborn Road, off Sebago Road. This is a close-up from a glass negative photographed by John F. Haley of Sebago, c. 1890.

RICHARDSON FAMILY

Aaron Richardson
September 1, 1779–December 25, 1860
Married January 13, 1808
Mehitable Cummings, c. 1782–?

Edward Richardson
March 15, 1786–May 15, 1849
Married December 2, 1808
Mary W. (Burnell?)
February 9, 1793–July 11, 1882

Aaron and Edward Richardson were brothers, sons of Moses and Lydia Hall Richardson of Newton, Massachusetts. They came together from Standish to Hiram in 1810, after their marriages in 1808, and bought land adjacent to each other. Edward, seven years younger at age twenty-four, a cordwainer, wrote his deed first, on July 14, 1810, buying land on the east side of the Saco from the heirs of John Hancock, governor of Massachusetts, adjacent to land formerly owned by John and Stephen Burbank. Aaron Richardson was living in Hiram on October 30, 1810, when he paid $800 to John Burbank of Standish for 229 acres near John Watson's on the east side of the Saco River, land formerly owned by John and Stephen Burbank, "late of Hiram," on the Old County Road to Denmark.[447] This road is now called King Street.

Because someone processed a deed on a certain date doesn't mean that person moved or built in that location on or near that date, but in the case of Aaron and Edward Richardson, the evidence is in the 1810 inventory.

Aaron had a barn, but Edward did not. With no house and barn, this is a very convenient split if Edward was sharing a house and barn with Aaron. By the 1818 inventory, Edward had added a house and barn, two more acres in mowing and four in pasture, and a horse. Aaron had increased his pasturage and decreased his tillage and livestock, but his property

Capt. Artemas Richardson

Excerpt from the diary of Daniel Small, Saturday, June 15, 1844. "Capt. Artemas Richardson, buried in the P.M. Hung himself the 13 inst. Mr. Edgecomb preached."[448]

Much more graphic is the excerpt from Gideon T. Ridlon:

We saw the oaken beam among the debris of the barn frame where he, Capt. Richardson, closed his earthly career by self-strangulation. He seems to have been a man of violent temper, who demanded unquestioning obedience to all his wishes. Being habituated to command while upon the quarter-deck when a mariner, he carried the same rigid discipline into his family. It has been related that for some disregard of an unreasonable command by one of his daughters, he tied her up and whipped her until her flesh was cut into furrows, and to intensify her agony he washed her lacerated body in brine. For this inhuman act he was prosecuted, and the report reached far and wide until he could scarcely go abroad from his home without being shunned and reproached. It was supposed that his remorse for such cruelty to his child and the embarrassment caused by the public denunciation drove him to a self-made gallows. His body rests alone in a corner of his now forsaken farm, neglected and unvisited.[449]

He is buried in Hiram Village Cemetery.

---

447   Fryeburg Registry of Deeds, Book 6, 383.

448   Daniel Small, *Papers*, Maine Historical Society, Coll. 1449.

449   Ridlon, *Saco Valley Settlements and Families*, 184.

was valued slightly higher than Edward's in this and all tax documents studied. In one regard, however, Edward had more—he sired six children between 1809 and 1831 while Aaron fathered four between 1808 and 1818.

Except for Edward's stint as tax collector soon after he arrived in Hiram, the Richardsons held only neighborhood offices.

Artemas Richardson
February 17, 1780–June 13, 1844

First marriage November 23, 1801
Nancy Mills, October 8, 1782, died in childbirth
Second marriage May 23, 1804
Mary Thompson
October 4, 1779–October 23, 1864

Capt. Artemas Richardson of Baldwin was the son of Israel and Elizabeth Richardson of Templeton, Massachusetts. A retired seaman, he was forty-four in 1822 when he bought the homestead of John Clemons on what is now called Richardson Road, on the west side of the Saco River. John Clemons sold it when he left Hiram to go west to New York state in 1804. Eight of Richardson's nine children were born in Baldwin; he brought them to Hiram and amassed two hundred acres, farming extensively and living in a great house with wings and barns and large farm offices suitable for holding the abundant products of the estate. His daughters became expert wool and flax workers.[450] Unfortunately, he did not appreciate their work, and after flogging one daughter mercilessly, and being prosecuted and shunned for it, he committed suicide.

Town Offices Held

Collector of Taxes
1811   Edward Richardson

Some of the ruins of Artemas Richardson's farm near the top of Richardson Road.

---

450   Ridlon, *Saco Valley Settlements and Families*, 184.

Fence Viewers

1817	Aaron Richardson
1829	Artemas Richardson
1830	Artemas Richardson

Field Drivers

1811	Aaron Richardson

Hog Reeves

1811	Aaron Richardson

Surveyors of Highways

1813	Aaron Richardson
1816	Edward Richardson
1827	Artemas Richardson
1828	Artemas Richardson
1829	Edward Richardson
1830	Edward Richardson

SPRING FAMILY

Thomas Spring
September 16, 1756–July 27, 1842
Married December 17, 1780
Mary Osgood, August 29, 1759–July 7, 1832

The Springs were civic minded, no question. Five Springs—Thomas and sons John, Marshall, Alpheus, and grandson John H.—served in almost every office of Hiram in the early years.

Capt. Thomas Spring was born in Watertown, Massachusetts, and served in the Revolution: twenty-six months in the expedition against Quebec under Montgomery; under Washington at White Plains, Trenton, and Valley Forge. He came to Hiram from Grafton, New Hampshire, in 1791, after Benjamin Burbank deeded him the property on which Burbank was living. Family lore is that Thomas Spring built a log cabin near the present house, but he may not have, since Burbank had already built a house there. Clearly, it was Thomas Spring who built the Federal-style hip roof house that he opened as a tavern in 1796. It stands today.

The tavern served as a stage stop on the line from Bartlett, New Hampshire, to Portland, and, because it was twelve miles from Fryeburg,[451] horses running the "post" needed to be refreshed there. He received a license from the county court "to keep tavern and retail spiritous liquors" in 1809. The inn served as a guest house and tearoom as late as the early 1940s. Paul and Ada Wadsworth bought the property from the last Spring owner in 1948, after the Wadsworth's house off Hiram Hill was burned in the wildfires of 1947. The house that burned was built by Thomas Spring's son John, and was the home of Llewellyn A. Wadsworth after 1916, when Llewellyn's house, Mountain View Farm, burned. The house and barn, known as Old Homestead Farm, are occupied and farmed by Ruth Wadsworth Payne, daughter Christine, and Christine's partner, Melissa, who raise and sell prized organic beef.

Thomas Spring was entrepreneurial. In addition to being an innkeeper, he was one of the original investors in the Hancock Brook Canal, as was brother Seth Spring, a wealthy merchant in Biddeford, and

Thomas Spring built the Federal-style wing and operated it as a tavern and stage stop from 1796 to the early 1940s, 1912 Pequawket Trail.

---

451 The tavern is located between Ten Mile Brook and Thirteen Mile Brook, now called Red Mill Brook.

The sign commemorated Thomas Spring's tavern, opened in 1796. Collection of Hiram Historical Society.

Interior of the Spring Tavern prior to 1940. Collection of Hiram Historical Society.

son John. Permission to build was legislated on February 26, 1811, renewed on February 23, 1818, and extended to Denmark on January 24, 1820.

The Springs were proprietors in other canals: Seth Spring, Thomas Spring, and John Spring invested in Moose Brook, Brownfield, enacted February 24, 1807; Seth Spring, Thomas Spring, and John Spring invested under the name Buxton Proprietors of Canals, Locks, and Slips, on Saco River, passed June 22, 1811; Seth Spring invested on Ten Mile Brook, February 27, 1813.[452]

Read more about canals in the chapter Transportation.

Thomas Spring's wife, Mary Osgood, bore five children, all born in Bartlett, New Hampshire: daughter Jane Spring, born 1781, married James Steele of Brownfield, who raised a company of soldiers at Fryeburg in the War of 1812, and under whom several Hiram men served.

John Spring, born 1784, settled near his parents after he married Joanna Hancock in 1817. Her father, John Hancock (not the John Hancock in Boston who signed the Declaration of Independence and who did own land in Hiram and Brownfield), served in Capt. Daniel Lane's company in Col. Ichabod Alden's regiment in the Revolutionary War, and lived with John and Joanna Spring for some years. John was one of the most industrious and thrifty farmers in Hiram.[453] Their children, born between 1818 and

---

452 Ten Mile Brook ran from Clemons Pond, Hiram, to Saco River, Brownfield. Other proprietors included William Lane, Isaac Bradbury, Thomas Howard, and Joseph Howard Jr.

453 Llewellyn A. Wadsworth, "Hiram," *Oxford County Record*, May 10, 1884, reprinted in *Hiram Historical Society Newsletter*, Special Issue, Summer 1987, 5.

Right: home of Marshall Spring's son Marshall, and later his niece, Anne Spring, 1597 Pequawket Trail. Left: Universalist Church, donated by Susan Spring, daughter of Thomas Spring, on land of Marshall Spring, 1871. Photo by George French, 1944, Maine State Archives.

1829, were Thomas O., John H., Jane (died young), Marshall W., and Ebenezer H.

Col. Marshall, born 1786, married Dorcas W. Alexander late in life, in 1842, the year his father, Thomas, died. They had three children and two survived to adulthood—Mary O. and Marshall. Marshall Spring, was the last representative Hiram sent to the Massachusetts Legislature and the first representative from Hiram to the Maine Legislature, serving in 1822 and again in 1825. He was the delegate from Hiram to the convention that framed the Constitution of Maine.

Susan, born 1789, never married, and in 1871, near the end of her life, donated funds to build the Hiram Universalist Church, a Gothic Revival architectural treasure of Oxford County in Hiram.[454]

Capt. Alpheus, born 1791, married Sally C.

Goodenow in 1815 and had eight children between 1816 and 1835: Eliza W., Mary C., Daniel G., William G., James S. (who died young), James, Caroline, and Jane. Alpheus was captain in the militia and procured powder and bullets for the musters. As clerk of the district in 1812 he recorded births (two) and deaths (six), for which he charged the district 48 cents on November 25, 1812.

Alpheus Spring owned a mill on the lower part of Hancock Brook, which was part of Prescott's Grant. His partner in Hiram was Jonathan Haskell from Portland, who had owned a cabinet shop with his brother William N. Haskell on September 22, 1827, but this co-partnership was dissolved less than a year later on August 5, 1828. In Hiram in 1829 and 1830 Jonathan was elected surveyor of lumber. But the partnership with Alpheus Spring at

---

454 Randall H. Bennett, *Oxford County, Maine: A Guide to Its Architecture* (Bethel, ME: Oxford County Historic Resource Survey, 1984), 217–18.

the Spring & Haskell furniture factory did not last long either (not many did)—it was dissolved August 24, 1830[455]—and in 1831, Jonathan left Hiram and was back in Portland working in the Haskell Furniture Manufactory. Jonathan died in 1838 at the age of thirty-five.

This pair of Spring & Haskell chairs with yellow paint, painted bands and floral motif was sold for $35 at EBTH online auction in Cincinnati, Ohio, on December 3, 2017. If you know the whereabouts of these chairs, please let us know.

Child's rocking chair made in Hiram by Spring & Haskell, c. 1832. Collection of Hiram Historical Society.

The brand is burned into the bottom of the Spring & Haskell chair of Hiram Historical Society.

The Hiram furniture factory may have operated for a while longer, as reported in 1832:

> Hiram (168th town).... Here is a cabinet factory worked by water power, where ten or twelve men are employed, who "make annually 8 to 10,000 chairs; 4 to 600 bedsteads,—besides large quantities of other work." Hiram is the last residence of General Wadsworth who died there in 1830.[456] Ms. Let. from Hiram, and plan. [457]

This may be the mill on Hancock Brook that was behind Howard and Helen Forsythe's house at 25 Hancock Avenue. A wool-carding and cloth-dressing mill in that location on the 1858 map was run by Ephraim Kimball. The mill was refitted for a carpenter

---

455 Advertisement, the dissolution of co-partnership of Alpheus Spring and Jonathan Haskell, *Eastern Argus* (Portland, September 17, 1830), 4.

456 The general died November 12, 1829.

457 William D. Williamson, *History of the State of Maine from Its First Discovery, A.D. 1602 to its Separation in A.D. 1820, Inclusive* (Hallowell, ME: Glazier, Masters & Co., 1832), 608. The letter and plan mentioned were not found.

shop under Mr. Corson. Flint and Burnell purchased it about 1870. On the 1880 map it is identified as R. Flints S. M. (sawmill). In 1884, eighteen thousand axe helves and thirty thousand corn boxes for sweet corn were made there. It no longer exists.

A child's rocking chair made by Spring & Haskell, in the collection of the Hiram Historical Society, is a Windsor chair with a broad, deep inset slat and two lesser slats with tapered cylindrical spindles with ball turning. Unfortunately, little remains of the original paint, which probably consisted of a brick red ground embellished with yellow and white banding. A dark grained coat was applied later. Spring & Haskell also made roll-back side chairs painted yellow and decorated with a fruit and leaf motif.

Seth Spring
September 29, 1754–October 12, 1839

First marriage January 27, 1780
Sally McMillan (McMillen)
of Conway, New Hampshire, dates unknown
Second marriage May 12, 1804
Mrs. Mary Darbon
of Rochester, New Hampshire, dates unknown
Third marriage January 14, 1826
Lydia Hight of Hollis, Maine
c. 1771–October 19 1834, age 63

Capt. Thomas Spring's brother, Capt. Seth Spring, a Revolutionary War hero, who served at the Battle of Bunker Hill, was such a prominent man that the Marquis de Lafayette, the last surviving French general of the Revolution, a hero to all Americans, visited the captain at his imposing tavern home on Spring Island, Biddeford, on his triumphal farewell U.S. tour on June 25, 1825. Newspaper accounts of celebrations included a grand welcoming parade down Main Street, with much cheering and flag-waving; elegant receptions; a sumptuous banquet and a ball; a chance for two old soldiers to reminisce about

their exploits in their younger days; and concluding with an eloquent sermon on Sunday. The celebration was not without its highjinks—boys crept into the kitchen and ate food prepared for the general. There was plenty for all and the boys were not punished.[458] Most likely Seth's brother Thomas and wife Mary of Hiram were guests. If so, at ages 69 and 63, it may have been the most splendid event in their rural lives, one for which Mary may have ordered a special dress from tailoress Dinah Williams of Hiram!

A wealthy merchant, Seth speculated in property in the Hiram area. One of his early transactions in 1802 was a trade of property of Jonathan K. Lowell in Foster's Gore, Denmark, which allowed Lowell to relocate to Hiram on more fertile farmland. Spring also invested in new transportation modes, becoming a proprietor of the Fryeburg, Baldwin, and Portland Turnpike Corporation (1805), Moose Pond Brook Canal (1807), and Hancock Brook Canal (1811).

Seth T. Spring
June 16, 1791–March 22, 1844

Married November 4, 1821
Hannah Sellea, May 21, 1795–May 8, 1878

Seth T. Spring, nephew of brothers Seth and Thomas Spring, was born in Brownfield, son of Josiah and Anne Evans Spring of Fryeburg. He married Hannah Sellea in Boston; their children were Seth, born 1823; Thomas, born 1825; Lucy A., born 1826; Josiah, born 1827; Jonas, born 1829; John, born 1834; Peleg W., born 1836.

The Brownfield/Hiram Seth was a wealthy farmer, at least in 1831 when he owned one of the five "pleasure carriages" in Hiram.[459] Based on the 1831 tax list, he may have become an owner in Spring & Haskell after Alpheus Spring and Jonathan Haskell terminated their partnership. In that list, Seth was one of two noted to have $150 in stock in trade; the other was Mark Treadwell. But Seth did not follow the tradition of Springs for public service and never held office.

---

458 "Anniversary of Lafayette's visit Monday," *Biddeford Weekly Journal*, June 28, 1929, 3, http://biddeford.advantage-preservation.com/viewer/?k=lafayette&i=f&d=01011812-12311989&m=between&ord=k1&fn=biddeford_weekly_journal_usa_maine_biddeford_19290628_english_3&df=1&dt=10.

459 1831 inventory, Maine Historical Society, Coll. 146, Box 1/2. Peleg and Charles Lee Wadsworth owned one each, and Mark Treadwell owned two.

Town Offices Held

Clerk
1812, 1813	Alpheus Spring
1815, 1816	Alpheus Spring
1835	Alpheus Spring
1836	Alpheus Spring

Committee on Accounts
1806, 1807	Thomas Spring
1812	Marshall Spring
1814	Alpheus Spring

Committee on Incorporation
1805, 1806	Thomas Spring

Constables
1817	Townspeople voted to excuse John Pike and chose Alpheus Spring

Cullers of Hoops & Staves
1820	Alpheus Spring

Fence Viewers
1811	Thomas Spring, Esq.
1817	Thomas Spring

Hog Reeves
1818	John Spring

Jurors—Grand Jury
1810	Thomas Spring, Marshall Spring

Jurors
1813	Alpheus Spring, Thomas Spring

Justices of the Peace
1811, 1812	Thomas Spring

Money Clerk (this title was unique this year only)
1828	Alpheus Spring

Treasurer
1804-1809	Capt. Thomas Spring
1812	Capt. Thomas Spring

Selectmen
1808-1810	Thomas Spring
1812	Thomas Spring
1813, 1814	Alpheus Spring
1816	Col. Marshall Spring
1817	Alpheus Spring
1819	Capt. Alpheus Spring
1820	Capt. Alpheus Spring
1822	Alpheus Spring
1824, 1825	Alpheus Spring
1830–1832	Alpheus Spring

Surveyors of Highways
1807	Thomas Spring

Surveyors of Boards
1820	Marshall Spring

Surveyors of Boards and Logs
1819	Marshall Spring

Surveyors of Boards, Plank Timber, Slitworks, Clapboards & Shingles
1816	Marshall Spring

Surveyors of Shingles & Clapboards
1820	Marshall Spring

WILLIAM STANLEY
March 31, 1776–April 27, 1822

Married December 25, 1797

Susannah Morrison c. 1799–November 11, 1836

William and Susannah Stanley created a dynasty of Stanleys in South Hiram and Porter. Stanleys were mill owners and merchants, carpenters and farmers, and the family for whom Stanley Pond is named. The eighth generation resides in South Hiram today.

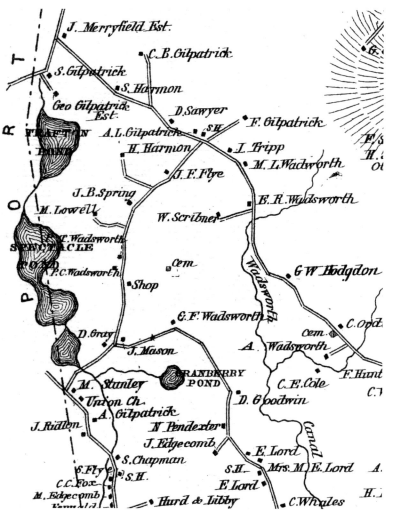

The shape of Stanley Pond is three-lobed and covers 137 acres. It is located in Hiram and Porter and is one of four ponds named for Hiram pioneers. The other ponds are Barker Pond, Clemons Ponds, and Trafton Pond, located entirely in Hiram. In this map, Stanley Pond is incorrectly labeled as Spectacle Pond.

The children of William and Susannah were: Esther, born 1798: Sally, c. 1799; Olive, 1801; Isaac, 1802; Jacob, 1806; Clarinda, 1809; Deborah, 1811; twins Joseph H., and William, 1814; John, 1816. All survived to adulthood, though Sally died at age 25 and eight months.

According to Hiram historian William Teg, William Stanley built two sawmills in Hiram, the first mill in 1810[460] at Stanley Pond at the outlet, now called Ridlon Brook, and the second mill in South Hiram Village, a few years later, near the mouth of Ridlon Brook, on the south side of South Hiram Road at the Porter line. Tax records refute this story.

There is no recorded deed or probated will to show how or when William acquired land to build either of the two mills in Hiram. Though William registered deeds for property in Porter, there is no primary document that William owned property or lived in Hiram before 1818. A deed for which he bought forfeited property in 1813 refers to him as living in Porter. A deed of 1814 records him being in Cornish.

Not locating deeds was an unexpected and disappointing revelation, because deeds could have pinpointed the dates and the boundaries of the properties.[461] The lack of a recorded deed, however, does not disprove the story—not everyone who possessed a deed registered it. Though William could have lived elsewhere and built mills in Hiram, he would have had to pay taxes on the mills. In no tax bills is he listed as a resident or nonresident of Hiram before 1818.

In a Hiram inventory of property for tax purposes conducted in May 1818, the earliest in which William Stanley is named, he and John Stanley are listed. However, the only mention of a mill is one belonging to Isaac Gray. In this document William was credited with one house, one barn, one hundred unimproved acres, two oxen and one swine, no outbuildings, and

---

460 Teg, *History of Hiram: Sesquicentennial Edition*, 36.

461 According to the Delorme map of Hiram grants, the Stanley Pond mill would have been built on part of the Wadsworth grant.

George French photographed Stanley Pond for the Maine Development Commission, before 1955. The dock is at Camp Hiawatha, now called Maine Teen Camp. A year-round population enjoys the pond. In summer, the replacement dam of Stanley Mills, on Tripptown Road at Brownfield Road (Route 160), is a popular swimming destination.

no cultivated acreage. The presence of a house, but no cultivated acreage, may imply that he recently acquired the property and had not yet cultivated crops that every family needed for survival.

William's tax on real property was $90, plus personal property tax of $74, a total of $164, which put his rank at fortieth out of 113. John Stanley had forty-eight acres plus two in mowing, but no buildings or livestock.[462] He paid $32 in real property tax, one of the lowest taxes owed, ranking ninety-eighth.

After 1818, William was active in Hiram town affairs. In 1819, he established a school district simply called "Stanley's" in town clerk records. The district was unnumbered, but it was the sixth school, and it attracted six students, called scholars, with funds of $4.56 out of an allocation of $200 for 263 students in the town.[463] William continued as school agent in 1821, and was possibly the school "master" or teacher. But he died in April 1822. By 1822, the school was labeled School District 8 with seventeen students under agent Samuel "Ridley" (Ridlon). The schoolhouse is now known as the Ridlon School. Other Stanleys who became school agents there were sons of William, John, and Isaac.

William was highly regarded as an upstanding Hiram citizen and was elected a tithingman in 1821. He voted in Hiram once, in 1822, the year he died at age forty-six.

462 With no house or livestock, was he living elsewhere and merely growing hay in Hiram? He is not listed as a nonresident, whose tax burden would have been much less.

463 Hiram Town Clerk records, March 1, 1819, 70; Maine State Archives, Hiram Box 14.

In 1819, William was elected a surveyor of boards and shingles, a fitting office for a millwright and a former sawmill owner. Before William built the Hiram mills, he gained significant experience in Porter. In 1803, William "Standley" (Stanley) of Sanford, Maine, arranged a deal with Caleb and William Emery of Sanford, in which Stanley would receive two hundred acres in Porter and $1,000 to occupy and improve a gristmill, at a date of his own choosing, and to pay back the money in two installments. The deed, written in 1803, was recorded in 1807. Caleb and William Emery also sold William's brother Joseph, of Shapleigh, one hundred acres in Porterfield in 1805.[464] William was a carpenter living in Porter in 1807 when he embarked on a joint venture in which he bought half ownership of a sawmill in Porter from Jesse Colcord of Arundel (Kennebunkport). Jesse and William were to use and improve the mill.[465] Colcord subsequently moved to Porter. William sold his share in 1809 to William Towle of Effingham, New Hampshire,[466] for $300, a substantial increase, on condition that the dam of the sawmill not be raised so high as to affect the flow to the gristmill. Thereafter, presumably, William pursued building his own mill in Hiram.[467]

When did he build the mills in Hiram? The Hiram town clerk recorded the William Stanley road on March 25, 1820. This road lead from the Porter line to "the Stanley House," fifty rods (825 feet) from the Porter/Hiram line on Main Street in South Hiram Village, and stretched four miles toward Cornish, but the record did not mention a mill.[468]

The earliest notation of a mill on Stanley Pond is a deed recording the purchase by sons Isaac and Jacob Stanley of one hundred acres situated between Spectacle Pond and Stanley Pond, which they bought

Owners of Stanley Mills

William Stanley, dates unknown
    Jacob Stanley, 1841 (one-quarter ownership)
    Peleg C. Wadsworth, 1847 (one-quarter)
    John Stanley II, 1853 (one-quarter)
    George Stanley, 1855 (one-quarter)
    Samuel Stanley, 1856 (half ownership from Isaac Stanley)
    Samuel Stanley, 1857 (half ownership from George Stanley)
    Moses Stanley, 1859
    Tobias Libby, 1859
    Randall Libby, 1867
    James R. Milliken 1867
    Joseph H. Stanley 1867
    George Stanley, 1868 (from William H. Stanley—not recorded)
    Joseph Stanley, 1870 (from William H. Stanley)
    Eugene F. and John S. Stanley, 1874
    George Stacey, 1875 (passed to Jordan Stacey)
    Eugene F. Stanley, 1884
    Allen Garner, 1901
    George Milliken, 1912

from Charles L. Wadsworth in 1834, in which the area around Stanley Pond was referred to as "Stanley Mills."[469]

While it is not known when the Stanley Pond mill was built, or how long it lasted, the mill in South Hiram Village was a stable business for over a century,

---

464 Joseph and William inherited property in Shapleigh from their father, William, of Kittery. Apparently Joseph moved to Shapleigh and William settled in Sanford.

465 Oxford County Registry of Deeds, December 21, 1807, Book 5, 57.

466 William Towle moved to Porter and ran a store at which forfeited property was auctioned. William was one who purchased such property.

467 There are no deeds recorded or wills probated to show how William acquired Hiram property. It is odd that deeds for Porter property were registered but not for Hiram property.

468 "Beginning at Porter line thence running S 65 E 50 rods to Stanleys House…," Hiram Town Clerk's Records, March 5, 1820, 93.

469 Fryeburg Registry of Deeds, December 22, 1834, Book 21, 359.

Stanley Mill showing the Allard house in the background. Photograph by George W. French, official photographer of the Maine Development Commission, 1936–1955.

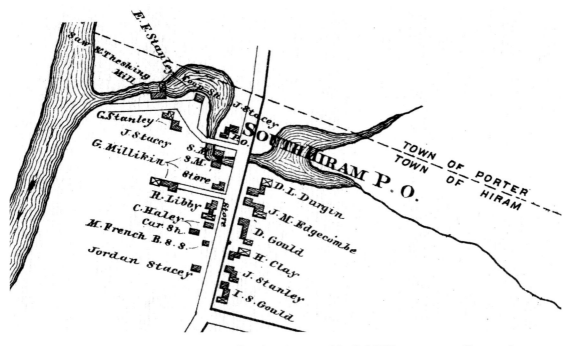

The 1880 map of South Hiram shows a sawmill and a store owned by G. Milliken, one sawmill across the brook owned by J. Stacey, one sawmill and threshing mill below, and a cooper shop owned by E. F. Stanley.

and helped earn the area the moniker "slab city" for its leading lumber industry.

It is rare to find a physical description of early settlers, but Ina N. (Stanley) Emery provided two in a talk given at a Stanley and Gould family reunion August 29, 1931. She relates that the Stanleys tended to produce tall people. She noted that Esther, the eldest of William's ten children with wife Susannah Morrison, was buxom and energetic, thus a perfect mate for her husband, Samuel Ridlon, whom she met while working at her father's mill in Cornish. Apparently Esther felt free of some gender restricted roles. "While her husband was at work 'piling' she would carry her baby to the 'rick' and assist him while burning logs and brushwood. She was as strong as her husband and never failed to carry her end of the log. When her father raised his barn by the broadside, help was scarce and his three daughters held the foot of the posts."[470]

Several sons remained in Hiram and Porter and succeeded William in the sawmill at South Hiram Village. Sons William and George operated Stanley mills in Cornish.

Three generations of William Stanley's family owned the mill in South Hiram Village—son Jacob, son Isaac, and Isaac's sons George, Samuel, and Moses. Moses sold it in 1859 to Tobias Libby of Porter. Tobias passed it on to his son, Randall Libby, who sold it in 1867 to James R. Milliken, who passed it in 1875 to his son, George.

The mill complex grew to three mills, two sawmills across the brook from each other and a threshing mill below, and ownership of parts of it bounced back and forth among Stanleys. In 1875, Joseph and John T. Stanley sold the stave and gristmill to George Stacy, who passed it to his son Jordan, who sold it to Eugene F. Stanley, son of George and Lydia Smith Stanley, in 1884. At that time, the property included

Earl Gould Stanley (1875–1912) was a merchant selling goods in his general store on South Hiram Road near the bridge over Ridlon (Stanley) Brook. Postcard image courtesy of Parsonsfield/Porter Historical Society.

---

470 Ina N. (Stanley) Emery and Florence (Stanley) Higgins, *Stanley-Gould Family Reunion* [Pamphlet], (s.l.: s.n.), 1932, 11. Collections of Parsonsfield/Porter Historical Society.

E. G. Stanley & Co. store and post office, South Hiram.

The former E. G. Stanley store and post office is now a residence, 25 South Hiram Road.

a cooper shop. Eugene held it until 1901, when he sold it to Allen Garner. Subsequent owners were Herbert Ridlon; the Oxford Land and Lumber Co., of which Ormand L. Stanley was treasurer; Frank E. Stearns; the Clark Lumber Co., of Hollis; and the Lewis Lumber Co., but after years of neglect it was dismantled and burned in 1964.[471]

More entrepreneurial Stanleys appeared in succeeding generations. Other mills in the area were operated by sons Isaac, William, and George. According to Raymond Cotton, these operations were sold to John Garner in 1868,[472] but the only registered deed is from Eugene F. Stanley to Allen Garner dated 1889.

Earl Gould Stanley, born in 1875 to parents Simon T. and Abigail F. Gould, owned a general store. Jacob Jr., son of Jacob and Betsey S. Thompson

---

471 H. E. Mitchell, B. V. Davis, and F. E. Daggett, *The Town Register: Brownfield, Denmark, Hiram and Porter* (Brunswick, Me: H.E. Mitchell Co., 1907), 92.

472 Raymond Cotton, *By the Toss of a Coin*, 3.

The G. C. Stanley General Store later housed Locklin's Pool Hall and South Hiram's first fire department. It was demolished c. 1970.

The middle building was Harold Burgess's store at the corner of Allard Circle and Main Street. In 2018, it, too, was leveled. Images courtesy of Parsonsfield/Porter Historical Society.

Stanley, ran an express courier company between Kezar Falls and Portland.

Other descendants of William Stanley also settled in Hiram and were merchants, including Grover C. Stanley, who owned the G. C. Stanley General Store, on the west corner of Allard Circle and Main Street. Jacob Stanley dealt in oysters, fish, and clams.

The Hiram Stanleys were followed by some of the children of Bartholomew Gould of Porter, several of whom married Stanleys. William's daughter Deborah F. married Daniel Gould. William's daughter Olive married George Gould and son Isaac married Susan Gould. Their daughter Lydia married Daniel Gould II—it was his second marriage.

Town Offices Held

Cullers of Hoops & Staves
    1823   John Stanley

School Agents
    1819   William Stanley District #6
    1821   William Stanley District #8
    1827   John Stanley. Voted to excuse from
            service, Isaac Stanley
    1828   Isaac Stanley
    1829   Isaac Stanley District #8

Surveyors of Highways
    1821   William Stanley
    1823   John Stanley
    1824   Isaac Stanley
    1826   Isaac Stanley
    1827   Isaac Stanley

Surveyors of Boards
    1824   Isaac Stanley

Surveyors of Boards, Clapboards and Shingles
    1819   William Stanley

Surveyors of Boards and Logs
    1819   William Stanley

Surveyors of Lumber
    1825   Isaac Stanley
    1827   Isaac Stanley
    1828   Isaac Stanley

Surveyors of Wood & Bark
    1827?   Samuel Stanley

Treasurers
    1819   Jacob Stanley

Tithingmen
    1819   William Stanley

STORER FAMILY

William Storer
1763–April 13, 1826
Married December 16, 1784
Sarah Chadbourne, 1766–January 4, 1855

Excerpted from an article in the newspaper *Oxford County Record*, Kezar Falls, December 25, 1886, by Lauriston Ward Small, a regular contributor.

William Storer and his brother Benjamin came to Cornish from Sandford [sic: Sanford], N.H. and built upon the Indian trail[473] a half mile south of the fording place in the Ossipee, where John Bradeen now lives. William Storer married a daughter of Joshua Chadbourne [of Cornish] and had the following children: William, Joseph, John, George, and Isaac, the last named who is now living; also Mrs. T. Storer,[474] Mrs. J. Fly,[475] Mrs. Benj. Wales,[476] Mrs. Ira Smith,[477] and perhaps others, howbeit that seems to be children enough for any man to buy shoes for. Now that I think of it, children did not have shoes in those days.

William moved over the river [from Cornish] to Hiram and lived and died in the house in which Dr. Tarr afterwards lived and perhaps died. That part of Hiram was then known as "pumpkin town."

According to Hiram Historical Society records, William Storer, Revolutionary War soldier, came from Wells, Maine, to Hiram in 1795, and settled near the Ossipee River. The location today is at the corner of Durgintown Road and River Road, across the street from the Tarr Cemetery. The Storer family lived in that area, near Humphrey Chadbourne and John Fly. Mary Tarr, wife of Seth Tarr, bought the house from John and George Storer in 1840.[478] There is barely any original part remaining in the present house.

William and Sarah's children were:
- John, 1786–1877, married Susan C. Gray of Hiram
- Susanna, 1787–1883, married John Fly of Hiram
- Mehitable, 1791–1875, married her cousin Thomas Storer of Cornish
- Joseph, 1793–1862, married Sarah (Sally) Lewis of Hiram. Joseph signed Cutler's petition of 1801 to incorporate Hiram as a town, and was one who didn't change his mind.
- William Jr., 1796–1865, married Rachel Lowell of Hiram
- George, 1798 or 1799–1867, married Mehitable Gray of Hiram
- Nancy, c. 1800–1883, married Benjamin Wales of Hiram
- Isaac M., 1805 or 1807–1898, married Mary Durgin of Hiram
- Sarah, c. 1810–1897, married Ira Smith of Limington

Jacob Storer
c. 1785–February 25, 1863
Married January 3, 1811
Mehitabel Meserve, 1800?–January 23, 1887

Jacob was William Storer's nephew, the son of Benjamin Storer of Cornish, who was the brother of William.

Jacob Storer lived in Cornish when the U.S. census of 1820 was compiled. He had bought land from David Durgin Jr. earlier that year, the northwesterly end of lot No. 3 in the first range of Wadsworth's

---

473 The original Pequawket Trail.
474 Daughter Mehitable Storer married cousin Thomas Storer.
475 Daughter Susanna Storer married John Fly.
476 Daughter Nancy Storer married Benjamin Wales.
477 Daughter Sarah Storer married Ira Smith.
478 Oxford County Registry of Deeds, Fryeburg, now Paris, May 1, 1840, Book 28, p442.

Grant.[479] Jacob voted in Hiram in 1822 and was in Hiram when the 1830 census was taken. The sons of William were yeoman. Jacob was a cordwainer. He was not in Hiram in 1850.

Town Offices Held

Cullers of Hoops & Staves
    1819   John Storer

Fence Viewers
    1822   William Storer
    1825   William Storer
    1830   Isaac M. Storer

Field Drivers
    1821   John Storer
    1822   William Storer

Pound Keepers
    1823   William Storer
    1824   William Storer
    1827   Isaac Storer
    1828   Excused Isaac Storer, chose George Storer
    1830   Isaac M. Storer

Surveyors of Highways
    1825   John Storer
    1827   Joseph Storer
    1830   John Storer

Surveyors of Split Lumber
    1830   John Storer

---

479 Oxford County Registry of Deeds, Fryeburg, now Paris, March 13, 1820, Book 9, 364.

TIBBETTS FAMILY

Stephen Tibbetts
1752–?

Married October 16, 1788
First marriage Mehitable Furbish
Second marriage dates unknown
to a Fabyan of Scarboro

Ephraim Tibbetts

Dates and marriage unknown

Timothy Tibbetts Sr.
September 17, 1782–June 9, 1856

Marriage date unknown
Sarah Flye, c. 1779–March 5, 1852

Much of what is known about the Tibbetts's lives was written by historian Gideon T. Ridlon in his article "Rambles About Durgintown."[480] He tells an amusing story about Stephen Tibbetts's Revolutionary War service.

Crossing the Warren farm we reached a small field where another soldier of the Revolution laid his hearthstone. Stephen Tibbetts, a son of Stephen and Alice Haines, was born in Rochester, N.H., in 1752. He was twice married; first, October 16, 1788, to Mehitable, daughter of Elijah and Hannah (Furbish) Tibbetts, second (tradition) to a Fabyan of Scarboro.

He was a drummer in the Colonial army and served the old militia in this musical capacity after his return from the army. He is marked on the muster roll as a "deserter" and when asked about "showing the white feather" said he was ordered to "beat a retreat" and as he was not commanded to halt he kept drumming and marching till he reached Rochester.

Not many years after the Revolution he moved from Saco to this mountainside, built a small, square house, cleared a field, and being a cordwinder by trade, he traveled far and wide by hill and valley with a leathern bag swung over his shoulder, which contained his tools to make the shoes for the families in several towns. We stood under the shade of some old half-decayed apple trees by the side of this foundation where his house once stood and found the little vale under the pines where his wife filled her buckets from the bubbling spring.

Near his house-place there is a large and singular stratified boulder where tradition says he would go at evening time to practice with his drum; and the dwellers in the valley heard the musical rattle of his reveille. He was an expert with the drumsticks and when playing his drum would throw them higher than his head and catch them as they came down without any break in the measure of his time.

When advanced in life his house was removed to the Hiram Bridge road; but with his son Timothy he removed to Rangeley plantation where he died a very old man. He was the father of no less than nine children: Abraham, Ezra, Nancy, Levi, Charlotte, Ellis, Stephen, Elijah and Timothy. Two of his sons—all were shoemakers and drummers— Stephen and Timothy, lived until almost one hundred years of age.

Timothy Tibbetts, Sr., son of Samuel and Hannah Haines, born in Scarboro, September 17, 1782; married Sarah Flye, daughter of James and his wife Jerusha Freeman, and settled on the Saco side of the mountain, not distant from Stephen, his uncle, each having half of a 100-acre lot of land on the "Waters grant." He served in the war of 1812; a cordwinder by trade, as nearly all of his name were.

The old house of Timothy Tibbetts was, like Stephen's far up on the hillside. It was a square "half-house" with but four rooms

---

480 G. T. Ridlon, Sr., "Rambles About Durgintown," *Biddeford Weekly Journal*, February 12, 1909.

and the chimney near the end. Some boards covered the hole in the floor by which the cellar was reached, and the corn was carried to the chamber on a ladder. He was childless and Henry Flye, a nephew of his wife, to whom he gave his farm for care in old age, moved the house to a lower terrace on the hillside and nearer the Hiram and Cornish road. He died June 9, 1856, aged 73 years and nine months, and a small stale stone, under bushes in the "Tarr burying ground," marks his grave. After the death of his wife, which occurred March 5, 1852, he was very disconsolate and would walk about his house sighing and saying "Oh, dear! Oh, dear, dear."

This old house on the mountainside was a favorite place for the old-time rustic rinktums and kitchen frolles and some old graybeards and their grave dames now living can tell with a significant twinkly in their eyes some racy and romantic stories touching adventures around that old house and the home-going with buxom lassies with crimson cheeks, dippled chins and freckled noses—???

Stephen was the son of Stephen and Alice Haines Tibbetts, as was Timothy Tibbetts Sr. Stephen and Timothy Sr. were brothers, but Stephen also had sons named Stephen and Timothy. Thus it is difficult to be certain of the correct Stephen and Timothy in official records.

Unfortunately, Ridlon did not mention Ephraim Tibbetts. U.S. census and Hiram records, such as property deeds, tax records, and voting lists, reveal facts but not age, marital status, or children during the time he lived in Hiram.

It appears that Ephraim joined Stephen in Hiram shortly after Stephen settled. Stephen incurred a highway tax in Hiram on May 27, 1813, in which he was credited with real property valued at $33.33 and no personal property.[481] The earliest highway tax Ephraim paid was 1814. Ephraim lived in Limerick, Maine, when in June 1813 he bought fifty acres of land from David Durgin, which was a lot adjacent to David Durgin's and joining Jacob Lord's.[482] There is no registered deed in Stephen's name, but Stephen sent three children to public school in 1813 in School District 5, which was in Durgintown.[483] Stephen would have been about age sixty-one at this time and it is likely that the children in school were by his second wife. Both Ephraim and Stephen are named on November 7, 1814, at the first Town Meeting after Hiram was incorporated as a legal town. At the meeting it was "Voted to accept of a private road laid out for the use of Stephen Tibbits [Tibbetts] and Ephraim Tibbits."[484]

Ephraim and Timothy were briefly engaged in neighborhood offices. It is unclear how long Ephraim was a resident of Hiram.

Town Offices Held

Hog Reeves
1821   Timothy Tibbets [Tibbetts]

School Agents
1822   Timothy Tibbets, School District 5
1825   Timothy Tibbets

Surveyors of Highways
1815   Ephraim Tibbets
1817   Ephraim Tibbets

---

481   List made November 27, 1813. The total tax incurred was $3.83, among the lowest. Maine State Archives, Hiram Box 8.

482   Oxford County Registry of Deeds, June 6, 1813, Book 6, 318. In the 1810 U.S. census of Limerick there were in his household three, male and female, ages twenty-six to forty-four and one female under ten years old.

483   List made November 27, 1813. Maine State Archives, Hiram Box 8.

484   Hiram Town Clerk Records, 4.

TREADWELL FAMILY

Mastress and Mary Little Treadwell were born and married in Wells, Maine. After fighting in the Revolution, Mastress relocated the family to Francisborough (Cornish), and in 1791 he signed the petition to incorporate separately from Limington. Mastress was then forty-one years old. Some of their eleven children chose to remain in Cornish. Son Jonathan led the way to Hiram.

Jonathan Treadwell
May 13, 1784–May 17, 1866

First marriage October 20, 1808
Ruth Stuart of Wells
November 24, 1791–April 22, 1817
Second marriage June 8, 1818
Lydia Hill of Cornish
September 7, 1784–May 28, 1866

Jonathan served three years in the War of 1812. With his first wife Ruth, he had seven children: Mark, born 1808; Nathan, 1809; and Jonathan, Ruth S., and Hannah J., birth dates unknown. His second wife, Lydia, bore Mary L., 1819; Mastress, 1821; Levi, 1823; Charles H., 1824; Enoch M., 1826; Eunice W., 1828; Albert, 1830; and "Little Orrin," who died an infant.

Son Mark married Mary Bucknell, daughter of Simeon and Hannah Burbank Bucknell. Their children died relatively young: Alphonzo at age twenty-one; Ethelinda (Etta) at age forty-one; Thomas, age nine months, ten days. Financially, Mark was successful: in the inventory of 1831, he was credited with $150 "stock in trade," as was Seth Spring (all other columns for Mark are blank). On Tuesday, September 13, 1831, the selectmen provided a one-year license for Mark Treadwell and Isaac Hamblin as retailers of strong liquors. The year 1850 found him in Lovell and 1860 in Standish. Mark died in Standish, Maine, on December 14, 1869, at age 61, and is buried with his wife, Mary, in Hiram Village Cemetery.

Jonathan's son Nathan C. Treadwell married Lucy Watson, daughter of Thomas B. and Mary Hill Watson of Hiram. Their son, Nathan C. Jr., served in the Civil War. Mary died at age forty-two in 1854, and the next year he married Olive D. Durgin. Nathan died in Naples, Maine, February 1, 1897, aged eighty-seven years. Olive died June 27, 1922.

Primary documents of the Treadwells in Hiram are scarce. The earliest record is Jonathan's county tax compiled August 28 1812, one of the lowest. He paid highway taxes in 1813 and 1814, but was not on the list of the 1815 bridge tax. He voted in 1813 and not again until 1831, when both he and son Mark voted. According to Llewellyn A. Wadsworth's journal, Jonathan settled in the house of Samuel Durgin.[485] In 1813, Jonathan enrolled two children in School District 5, Durgintown, but is not listed as having "scholars" before or after. There is no record that he was elected to any town office.

On March 4, 1813, he sold seventy acres of the easterly portion of Lot 3 on the Waters Grant to John Warren of Gorham. The property was adjacent to Levi Lord's and contained buildings, for which John Warren paid $625. In 1820, Jonathan lived in Cornish. He returned to Hiram by 1830 and remained until his death, at age eighty-two, in the road near Frank Huntress's.

Timothy Treadwell
June 14, 1796–October 10, 1884

Married March 26, 1823
Mary Berry, died soon after 1823

Jonathan's brother Timothy Treadwell served in the War of 1812. He suffered a tragedy in the loss of his wife that he chose not to soothe with another wife.

Susan M. Treadwell
March 26, 1786–November 29, 1875

Did not marry and lived with her brother Timothy

---

485 L. A. Wadsworth Journal, November 20, 1870.

Mary (Polly)
September 25, 1792–August 25, 1858

Johnathan's sister Polly had lockjaw for sixty-four of her sixty-six years and never married. In 1850 she lived with siblings Timothy and Susan M. She died in Hiram.

Lydia Treadwell
September 25, 1792–June 1847

Lydia, Polly's twin, lived at her brother Jonathan's and with others.

WARREN FAMILY

Major Nathaniel Warren
c. 1756–August 21, 1819

Married October 27, 1783
Margaret Haines, c. 1760–February 28, 1846

Aside from the Wadsworth family, is there any family more revered in Hiram's history than the Warrens? The Warren Bridge over the Ossipee River in South Hiram, named for the Major's son John, is a familiar reminder.

Major Warren was a veteran of the Revolutionary War. He and his wife, Margaret Haines, had only two children: John and Dorothy. Nathaniel and Margaret were a learned and cultural couple, so close that they ate off the same plate.[486] After the major died, widow Margaret lived in her own home in Hiram with a household of women.[487]

Col. John Warren
October 12, 1786–June 27, 1858

Married February 6, 1806
Susan Adams, November 6, 1798–January 3, 1876

Son John, born in Gorham, brought his parents to Buxton after he married Susan Adams there in 1806. Sometime between February 1812 and May 1813, he brought his parents, his wife, and six children to Hiram, settling in Durgintown. In March 1813, he bought the house and land of Jonathan Treadwell. Less than a year after he arrived, he was elected selectman. He was under thirty years old at the time.

By all accounts, John Warren led an exemplary life. Susan bore thirteen children between 1806 and 1826: Nathaniel, born 1806; Gen. William, 1807; Eliza, 1809; Margaret, 1810; Susan, 1811; John A. 1813; Rebecca, 1815;, Charles, 1816; Henry, 1820; George, infant, born and died 1822; George, 1822; Edward F., 1824; Joseph, 1826. Not only did the colonel send them to school, he taught school and was a school

agent, overseeing his neighborhood school, District 5, and, when it was split, District 7. He was elected to a town office or committee every year from 1814 to 1830, the years of this study, occasionally multiple offices or committees, working alongside Peleg Wadsworth for many of them.

Gideon T. Ridlon waxed eloquently about this man of prominence in civil, military, and business life, active in the lumber trade and keeping an inn on the banks of the Ossipee River.[488] He described him as a tall, erect man of commanding presence and military precision with courtly manners, efficient and attractive, popular with his regiment, and respected by the public. In addition he was kind and, not least, was fond of children.[489] Even after he was no longer selectman/assessor/overseer of the poor, he continued to provide services to the indigent.

Before he became a colonel in the militia, he wrote this letter that reveals his no-nonsense approach:

> 1821 Sept. 3rd To the Selectmen of the Town of Hiram. Gentlemen, you are hereby requested to furnish twenty pounds of Good Powder maid into Blank Cartridges for the use of Eighty membors on my Company roll and Deliver the Same at Fryburg on Fryday the fourteenth Day Sept ins[instant] in Front of John Bradleys Store at Six in the fore noon. Yours etc John Warren Capt.

As much as he valued education and would come to master the skills to build bridges and roads, he made mistakes in mathematics. In adding his highway tax list for 1816, he undercharged John Durgin $1, undercharged Jacob Lord 20 cents, and overcharged Stephen Tibbetts 55 cents. John Warren wasn't the only one to make mistakes. Most of the early tax statements contained such errors, including

---

486 Ridlon, *Saco Valley Settlements and Families*, 1202.

487 U.S. census 1820, Hiram.

488 Ridlon, *Saco Valley Settlements and Families*, 1202. The tavern was on the right side of the road leading from South Hiram to Cornish village, near the present Warren bridge at the west end.

489 Ridlon, *Saco Valley Settlements and Families*, 1202.

Homestead of John Warren, later owned and renovated by John William and Alice Bucknell Wadsworth, 495 River Road. Photo 1939, courtesy of Miss Alice Wadsworth.

495 River Road, under renovation, 2020.

one of Peleg Wadsworth's when he was treasurer, for which the town declined to reimburse him.

Town Offices Held

Agent to Defend Town vs. Bad Roads
1824   John Warren, Esq.

Agent to Work on the New County Road from Porter Line to the New Bridge over Ossipee River
1827   John Warren

Agent to Repair the New County Road
1830   John Warren

Committees on Bridge Building and Repairs
1818   Ossipee River bridge repair: John Warren agent

1823   Ossipee River repair: John Warren agent

1824   Ossipee River repair: John Warren

Committee on a Plan for a Town House
1816   John Warren

Constable
1829   John Warren, Esq.

1829   John Warren

Fence Viewers
1817   John Warren

1820   John Warren

1829   Nathaniel Warren

Field Drivers
1818   John Warren

1830   Nathaniel Warren

Justices of the Peace (incomplete list)
1827   John Warren

1828   John Warren

School Agents
1819   John Warren, School District #5

1821   John Warren, School District #7

1822   John Warren #7

1823   John Warren #7

1824   John Warren, Esq. #7

1825   John Warren

1828   John Warren, Esq.

1829   John Warren, Esq. #7

School Teachers
1819   John Warren, School District #5

1821   John Warren, School District #7

Selectmen
1814   John Warren

1815   John Warren

1818   John Warren

1820   John Warren

1823   Col. John Warren

1824   Col. John Warren

1826   John Warren

1827   John Warren, Esq. 1st

1828   John Warren, Esq.

Surveyors of Boards
1820   John Warren

1822   John Warren

Surveyors of Boards and Clapboards
1823   John Warren

Surveyors of Boards, Clapboards, and Shingles
1821   John Warren

Surveyors of Clapboards & Shingles
1821   John Warren

Surveyors of Lumber
1815   John Warren

Surveyors of Highways
1816   John Warren

1620   John Warren

1822   John Warren

1825   John Warren

1827   John Warren

Tithingmen
1823   John Warren

Homestead of John A. Warren, son of Col. John Warren, 322 River Road.
John A. Warren (1813–1867) married Sarah Rumery in 1836.

1816 Highway Tax: John Warren's List, July 29, 1816 (Durgintown)[490]

Names	Polls	Poll tax	Real property tax	Personal property tax	Total tax	Correct totals	Incorrect totals
Warren, John	1	1.08	3.51	3.33	7.92	7.92	
Warren, Nathaniel	1	1.08	1.71	2.50	5.29	5.29	
Durgin, Joseph	1	1.08	2.43	2.45	5.96	5.96	
Durgin, John	1	1.08	5.33	4.82	10.23	11.23	X
Durgin, Samuel	2	2.16	2.27	2.30	6.73	6.73	
Lord, Jacob	2	2.16	4.25	3.49	9.70	9.90	X
Durgin, David Jr.	1	1.08	0.00	0.27	1.35	1.35	
Tibbetts, Stephen Jr.	1	1.08	2.30	0.55	3.93	3.38	X
Tibbetts, Ephraim	1	1.08	1.16	0.32	2.56	2.56	
Tibbetts, Timothy	1	1.08	1.80	0.37	3.25	3.25	
Merrifield, Isaac	1	1.08	0.91	0.32	2.31	2.31	
Lord, Levi	1	1.08	0.91	0.83	2.82	2.82	
Roberts, Stephen	1	1.08	2.08	1.82	4.98	4.98	
Merrifield, Samuel	2	2.16	3.61	2.66	8.43	8.43	
McLucas, John	1	1.08	1.85	0.91	3.84	3.84	
Chadbourn, John W.	1	1.08	3.85	2.04	6.97	6.97	
Chadbourn, Humphrey A.	1	1.08	1.60	0.31	2.99	2.99	
Total					**89.26**	**89.91**	

490   Maine Historical Society, Coll. 146, Box 1/4.

WATSON FAMILY

John Watson
1750–July 19, 1827
Married
Lucy Bickford, 1758–June 26, 1829

John Watson, said to have come from England with a brother, served in the Revolutionary War and came to Hiram from Kennebunkport with his wife, Lucy Bickford, and baby son Thomas B. in 1778. Their next child, John Jr., was the first male born in Hiram, on February 7, 1780. Their third and last child was Mary, born April 14, 1787. From John Watson descended the Hiram family, including Cora Watson Clemons and her son Hubert Wentworth Clemons, a founder of Hiram Historical Society.

Because the deed to the property was lost, a new deed was written on December 15, 1781, by Henry Brown, who sold 102 acres in Brownfield, of which "so much land as is necessary" was reserved for roads through the lot. The lot was located on the east side of the Saco, "beginning at a white pine tree on the East bank of Saco River which tree is the N.W. corner of Thomas Veaseys lot."

Watson's first house was washed away in the great freshet of 1785, the same flood that took Benjamin Ingalls's house. John built a new house in 1785 in a style of architecture that mixed Georgian and Federal. When it was built, the house was located in Brownfield, but it was absorbed into Hiram in a population redistribution attempt by Hiram, Brownfield, and Porter acting in concert to gain incorporation as towns in 1806. The Massachusetts Legislature agreed to incorporate "Porterfield" as a town, but designated Hiram a plantation. It was not until 1814 that Hiram would be granted status as a town.

The Watson house at 287 King Street is the oldest intact house in Hiram—six generations of Watsons lived there—but it is not the oldest structure still

The couple pictured in front of the John Watson house is likely Francis L. Watson, March 28, 1837–November 2, 1915, and his wife, Charlotte Evans Watson, April 22, 1835–April 26, 1900. Photo courtesy of Maine Historic Preservation Commission.

standing.[491] The two-story Georgian-Federal house of John Watson that is today virtually the same as when built is indisputably more grand and handsome than the part of the smaller one-story Cape-style house built between September 1774 and April 1782, and was renovated and expanded in the late nineteenth century.

John Watson was a publicly spirited man, as were his sons John Jr. and Thomas B. As a citizen of Brown's Addition, John signed Timothy Cutler's petition to incorporate with Hiram as a town in 1801; he did not change his mind and sign the counter petition of Charles Lee Wadsworth as others did. He was surveyor of highways in 1807, selectman in 1808, 1809, and 1811, served on the Committee on Accounts in 1806, 1807, and 1814, and was a tithingman in 1827, the year he died at age seventy-seven. The following year, 1828, his elder son, Thomas B., took up the mantle of tithingman.

John Watson House was unchanged, except by exterior paint, when Francis M. O'Brien, antiquarian bookseller in Portland, purchased it in 1949. Photo by Roger Flint was taken in August 1964 during the sesquicentennial of Hiram's founding.

Watson house and Watson Cemetery, 287 King Street, 2014. Two wings with Palladian windows were added by Francis O'Brien after 1964. Iron rails surrounding the family cemetery were replaced by granite posts in 2012. Painting by artist Mary Barrett in 2014 for the Hiram in Art show during the bicentennial of Hiram's founding.

491   Part of the house at Brookside at 6 Hiram Hill Road was built between 1774 and 1781 by original surveyor John Curtis and sold to John Ayer in April 1782 "with house and barn."

Thomas B. Watson house. Standing in front are, from left, Phebe L. Chadbourne Watson, 1859–1935; Lizzie A. Watson, 1861–1923; and Benjamin S. Watson, 1852–1928, children of Thomas J. and Lydia C. Chadbourne Watson. Ella Butterfield Album, Collection of Hiram Historical Society.

At one time in the Watson family was a small pine box with a poem on the cover:

> John Watson is my name,
> New England is my nation,
> Brownfield is my dwelling place,
> And Christ is my salvation.[492]

John Watson Jr.
February 7, 1780–November 21, 1863
Married July 19, 1804
Abigail Foss, October 19, 1787–May 3, 1870

John Jr. and Abigail had twelve children between 1805 and 1835, all born in Hiram: Clarissa, Matilda A., Mary P., Walter F., Joseph B., Hannah F., Julia B., Abigail, Lucy B., John, George S., and Seviah C.

John Watson Jr. was a selectman in 1813, 1816, 1817, 1821, and 1822. It is likely the Watsons served in more years than listed, but because the early records are incomplete, it is not known.

John Jr., the second son, inherited the homestead at 287 King Street, and Thomas B., the elder son, the smaller house next door at 255 King Street.[493]

Thomas B. Watson
September 6, 1778–May 6, 1836
First marriage November 9, 1809
Mary Hill, 1789–March 4, 1825
Second marriage October 17, 1825
Mary B. Whitten, c. 1787–August 17, 1858

Thomas B. was the second child of John and Lucy. With Mary Hill, Thomas sired seven children between 1810 and 1822: Joanna, Lucy, Isabella, Royal, James J., Thomas J., and Mary J. His second wife, Mary Whitten, bore him two more children: Mary B. and Alfred H. All were born in Hiram.

Thomas B. was district clerk in 1808 and 1809, member of the Committee on Accounts in 1816 and 1819, surveyor of highways in 1827, tithingman in 1828, and a justice of the peace.

---

492   *Maine Historical and Genealogical Recorder* Vol. IX, No. 11, November 1898, 341.

493   Hubert W. Clemons speculated that a reason Thomas B., the elder son, did not inherit the homestead was that he had fathered a child with another woman prior to his marriage to Mary Hill. Conversation with Sally Williams, c. 2014.

Town Offices Held

Clerk

1808	Thomas B. Watson
1809	Thomas B. Watson

Committee on Accounts

1806	John Watson
1807	John Watson
1814	John Watson
1815	John Watson
1816	Thomas B. Watson
1819	Thomas B. Watson
1820	Thomas B. Watson
1821	Thomas B. Watson
1824	Thomas B. Watson
1827	Thomas B. Watson
1828	Thomas B. Watson

Committees on Bridge Building and Repairs

1815	Hancock Brook: Joseph Chadbourne, John Watson—to build bridge across Hancock Brook
1816	Hancock Brook: Chose John Pierce, John Watson, Asa Burbank a Committee to Superintend building the Bridge

Fence Viewers

1811	John Watson
1818	Thos B. Watson
1823	Thomas B. Watson

Justices of the Peace (incomplete list)

1830	Thomas B. Watson

School Committee

1821	Thomas B. Watson
1823	Thomas B. Watson
1828	Thomas B. Watson, Esq.

Selectmen

1808	John Watson
1809	John Watson
1811	Thomas B. Watson
1813	John Watson Jr.

Surveyors of Highways

1807	John Watson
1808	John Watson
1809	John Watson Jr.
1817	Thomas B. Watson
1819	John Watson Jr.
1827	Thomas B. Watson

Tithingmen

1816	Thomas B. Watson
1819	Thomas B. Watson
1820	John Watson
1821	Thomas B. Watson
1822	Thomas B. Watson
1823	Thomas B. Watson
1824	Thomas B. Watson
1825	John Watson
1826	John Watson
1827	John Watson
1828	Thomas B. Watson
1829	Thomas B. Watson
1830	Thomas B. Watson

Treasurers

1811	John Watson

Thomas B. Watson house, 255 King Street, 2018. Today the property supports Good Buddy Farm. Photo by Erin Barber.

NATHANIEL WILLIAMS
?–February 15, 1815
Married April 7, 1796
Dinah Davis, ?–June 8, 1849

Tailoress Dinah Williams had sufficient money to buy property from Simeon Merrifield in 1811 and was fortunate to have an occupation to provide income when she was widowed, as so many did not. She paid $220 for fifty acres located between Simeon Merrifield's property on the Waters Grant at the Ossipee River and that of James Fly Jr. It was unusual that the wife purchased the property, but because she did, her occupation, tailoress, was recorded, a rarity in researching women of this period.

Dinah came to Hiram before 1800, with her second husband, Nathaniel Williams.[494] In the U.S. census of 1800, they are listed as living in a household of five, three of whom were children, two boys and one girl, all under ten years old. Perhaps they had rented a farm earlier, because there is no record of activity before 1811, the year the deed was signed; that is, no property was assessed for taxes and no family made appearance on voting lists. Nathaniel voted for the first time in 1811.

Most likely they had farmed the land previously, because in the first year of ownership, 1811, they raised eighteen bushels of corn, two bushels of peas and beans, and four tons of English hay—less than most farmers produced in this sample of eighteen farmers' crops.[495] The full sample, in original order, appears in Appendix 6. In 1812, Nathaniel paid the lowest state tax of any in Hiram, 6 cents for personal property. For the county tax in 1812, he was rated $43 for real property (though purchased in Dinah's name) and $23 for personal property, for a total tax of $1.48—2 cents more than William Cotton and 1 cent less than David Durgin, ranking in the lower third of eighty settlers. For the 1812 highway tax, the Williamses' real property was valued at $50 and personal property $30, for which Nathaniel

paid $1.60. But he made improvements, and he had progressed to the upper half of taxpayers in 1815, the last year he was alive. His widow received a pension for his Revolutionary War service until she died.

The only known name of a child of Nathaniel and Dinah was Aaron Williams.[496] Aaron lived with his mother and in 1839 purchased property along the road to Porter. The land was described as the "Nursery lot," and was most likely used to grow apple trees. It was next to Eli Clements' (Clemons) property and adjacent to property of Joseph Williams—possibly Aaron's brother, but there is no conclusive information about him.

Aaron remained in Hiram and was elected school agent in 1826, 1828, and 1830, before he married Alicia Lane of Brownfield on November 29, 1830.[497] Aaron fathered seven children, the first of whom was Lucy, born December 18, 1831. Children following Lucy were Nathaniel D., born c. 1834; William Ancel (Ansel), 1835, who died at Ship Island, Mississippi in 1862; Alice (June?), 1839; Eli, 1841; Ruth, 1843; and Ella, 1850. Aaron died in Hiram, a widower, at age eighty-three in 1883, and is buried in the Spring Cemetery.

Town Offices Held

School Agents
1826, 1828, 1830	Aaron Williams

Surveyors of Highways
1824–1830	Aaron Williams

---

494 Dinah Davis married first Hezekiah Hildreth on October 7, 1790, in Tyngsboro, Massachusetts, the same town in which she later married Nathaniel Williams. Massachusetts Town and Vital Records, 1620–1988.

495 Maine Historical Society, Coll. 146, Box 1/4.

496 Maine Wills and Probate Records, 1584–1999.

497 Fryeburg Marriage Intentions.

Appendices

APPENDIX 1

1790 U.S. Census of "Hiram Town"

Names	Males over 16	Males under 16	Females	Total
Ayer, John	2	3	5	10
Barker, Thomas	2	0	2	4
Baston (Boston), Daniel	1	4	2	7
Bucknell, John	1	0	1	2
Bucknell, John Jr.	1	1	5	7
Bucknell, Simeon	1	2	3	6
Burbank, Benjamin	1	1	2	4
Clements (Clemons), John	1	1	1	3
Bickford, Dyer	1	1	1	3
Eastman, Solomon	1	3	1	5
Goald (Gould), Aaron	1	2	4	7
Haywood (Howard), Lemuel	1	0	0	1
Libby, John	2	0	2	4
Libby, Jonathan	1	0	2	3
Libby, Stephen	1	2	2	5
McLucas, John	1	3	3	7
Midget (Mudget), David	2	3	3	8
Ryan, Curtis	1	3	2	6
Total	22	29	41	92
18 families				

APPENDIX 2

1800 U.S. Census of "Hyram and Cutler's Grant," Brownfield Addition, Prescott's Grant

Names	Free white males					Free white females					Total
	to 10	to 16	to 26	to 45	45+	to 10	to 16	to 26	to 45	45+	
Hyram and Cutler's Grant											
Baston, Daniel		1	3		1					1	6
Baston, Benjamin	2			1				1			4
Brown, Moody		1		1		1	1		1		5
Bucknell, John				1						1	2
Bucknell, Simeon	3			1		2		1			7
Clements (Clemons), Eli	1		1	1						1	4
Clements (Clemons), John	3	2		1		1			1		8
Clements (Clemons), Jonathan				1		1				1	3
Cotton, William			1					1			2
Cutler, Timothy				1				1		1	3
Durgin, David	1		2	1				1		1	6
Durgin, Samuel	2			1		1			1		5
Eastman, James	3	1			1	2			1		8
Fly, James Jr.	2			1		1		1			5
Fly, James			1		1	1				1	4
Hartford, John	1			1		2	1		1		6
Hayward (Howard), Samuel			3		1	1	1			1	7
Hayward (Howard), Lemuel		1			1	1		2		1	6
Hickey, Daniel				1							1
Lewis, Abijah	3	1	1	1		4			1		11
Lord, Jacob	1		1					1			3
Mariner, John	1		1					1			3
Maybury (Mabry), Josiah	1		1					2			4
Merrifield, Samuel	2	1		1		2			1		7
McLucas, John	4	1			1	1	1		1		9
Pierce, John	4	1		1		1			1		8
Spring, Thomas	1	1	1	1		1	1	2	1		9
Strout, Eleazer			1						1		2
Storer, William	2	2		1		1	2		1		9
Tyler, David			1			3			1		5
Williams, Nathaniel	2			1		1			1		5
Wilson, Joshua		1				2		1			4
Wakefield, John	1		1			1		1			4
Wadsworth, Charles L.	3	1	1				1	1	1		8
Total persons Hiram	43	14	20	14	12	26	12	17	16	9	183
				Total males:	103			Total females:	80		
Total Hiram families											34

continued on next page

Appendix 2: *1800 U.S. Census of "Hyram and Cutler's Grant," Brownfield Addition, Prescott's Grant*

Names	Free white males					Free white females					Total
	to 10	to 16	to 26	to 45	45+	to 10	to 16	to 26	to 45	45+	
Brownfield Addition											
Burbank, Israel		1			1	2		2		1	7
Burbank, John	1	1		1		1	1		1		6
Lane, John					1	3			1		13
Lane, William					1	3	1				5
Osgood, Asa	3	1			1			1	1		7
Watson, John			2	1		1	3		1		12
Total persons Brownfield Addition	4	3	2	2	4	10	5	3	4	1	38
	Total males:			15			Total females:		23		
Total Brownfield families											6
Prescott's Grant											
Bucknall (Bucknell), John	2				1	2	2	1	1		9
Gilman (Gilmor), James	1			1		1			1		4
Sloper, Samuel	2			1		3			1		13
Total persons Prescott's Grant	5			2	1	6	2	1	3		20
	Total males:			8			Total females:		12		
Total Prescott's families											3
Grant totals											
Total persons											241
	Total males:			126			Total females:		115		
Total families											43

APPENDIX 3
1810 Hiram Voting List

Joseph Adams
Thomas Barker
Benjamin Baston
Loammi Baston
Royal Baston
Winthrop Baston
Moody Brown
John Bucknell
John Bucknell Jr.
Simeon Bucknell
Israel Burbank
Joseph Chadbourn
Eli Clemons
Jonathan Clemons
David Durgin Jr.
Joseph Durgin
Samuel Durgin
John Eames
James Eastman
James Fly Jr.
John Fly
James Gilmore
John Howard
Joseph Howard
Lemuel Howard
Ephraim Kimball
Daniel Lane
Abijah Lewis
Edward Lewis
Jacob Lord
Levi Lord

Jonathan Lowell
Moses Lowell
Josiah Mayberry
Benjamin McLellan
Jacob McLucas
John McLucas
John McLucas Jr.
Samuel Merrifield
Simeon Merrifield
Asa Osgood
John Pierce
John Pierce Jr.
Samuel Sloper
John Spring
Marshall Spring
Thomas Spring
William Storer
Peleg Wadsworth
Charles L. Wadsworth
John Watson
John Watson Jr.
Thomas B. Watson
William West

Total   53

"Peleg Wadsworth, Thomas Spring—Selectmen, will meet 9 a.m. day of TM 2 April to consider qualification of any inhabitant aggrieved by name omitted."

Source: Maine Historical Society, Coll. 146 Box 1/6.

APPENDIX 4

1810 Hiram Polls

N.B. The 1810 U.S. Census of Hiram was lost. This 1810 inventory was compiled by the District of Hiram for tax purposes. The full document also includes real and personal property taxes.

Names	Polls		Names	Polls
Adams, Joseph	1		Lewis, Marshal	1
Anderson, Nathaniel	1		Lord, Jacob	1
Barker, Thomas	1		Lord, Jacob	1
Baston, Benjamin	1		Lord, Levi	1
Baston, Loammi	1		Lowell, Jonathan	2
Baston, Royal	1		Lowell, Moses	1
Baston, Winthrop	1		Mayberry, Josiah	1
Bridges, John	1		McLellan, Benjamin	1
Brown, Moody	2		McLucas, Jacob	1
Bucknell, John	1		McLucas, John Jr.	1
Bucknell, John Jr.	1		McLucas, John Sr.	1
Bucknell, Simeon	2		Merrifield, Samuel	2
Burbank, Israel	2		Merrifield, Simeon	1
Chadbourn, John	1		Osgood, Asa	1
Chadbourn, Joseph	1		Pierce, John	2
Clemons, Eli	1		Pierce, John Jr.	1
Clemons, Jonathan	1		Rand, Aaron	1
Clemons, Widow Abigail	0		Richardson, Aaron	1
Cotton, William	1		Richardson, Edward	1
Cross, Aaron	1		Robbins, John	1
Durgin, David Jr.	1		Rowe, Daniel	1
Durgin, David Sr.	1		Sloper, Samuel	1
Durgin, John	1		Spring, John	1
Durgin, Joseph	1		Spring, Marshall	1
Durgin, Samuel	1		Spring, Thomas	2
Eastman, James	2		Storer, William	2
Fly, James Jr.	1		Wadsworth, Charles L.	1
Fly, John	1		Wadsworth, Peleg	2
Gilmore, James	1		Watson, John	1
Gray, William	1		Watson, John Jr.	1
Hartford, Simeon	1		Watson, Thomas B.	1
Howard, John	1		West, William	blank
Howard, Joseph	1		Total polls	80
Howard, Lemuel	1		Total households	70
Kimball, Ephraim	1			
Lane, Daniel	1		Source: Maine Historical Society, Coll. 146 Box 1/4.	
Lewis, Abijah	2			
Lewis, Edward	1			

APPENDIX 5
1810 Rateables

Names	Polls	Houses	Out-houses	Barns	Tillage	Mowing	Pasturage	Unimproved	Oxen	Cows	Cattle 3yr	Cattle 2yr	Cattle 1yr	Horses	Colts 3yr	Colts 1yr	Swine
Adams, Joseph	1	1		1	2	7	6	92.5	1	2	1	2	1	0.5			2
Anderson, Nathaniel	1									1							1
Barker, Thomas	1	1	1	2	10	20	20	75	6	3		3	3	2			3
Baston, Benjamin	1	1		1	3	20	25	152	4	4		2	2	1			2
Baston, Loammi	1	0.5		1	2.5	10	6	31.5	2	2		3	1	0.5			3
Baston, Royal	1	0.5		1	2	15	7	34	2	3			4	0.5			2
Baston, Winthrop	1	1		1	4	15	5	26	2	2			6	1			0.5
Bridges, John	1																
Brown, Moody	2	1		1	5			95		2							
Bucknell, John*	1	1		1				40		1	2			1			
Bucknell, John Jr.	1	0		0	2	5	0	0		1							1
Bucknell, Simeon	2	1		1	5	7	10	80	4	2		1	1	2			2
Burbank, Israel	2	1		1	2	5		143		1		1	2	1		1	1
Chadbourn, John	1							100									
Chadbourn, Joseph	1	1		1	5	8	1	90	2	4							2
Clemons, Eli	1	1			1.5	5	1	42.5		3						1	2
Clemons, Jonathan	1	1		1	2	8	8	112	2	3		2		1			2
Clemons, Widow Abigail	0	0		1	1.5	5	1	42.5		2		2	2				2
Cotton, William	1	1		1	2	2		46		2		1					1
Cross, Aaron	1	1			2	7	5	92	1	2				0.5			1
Durgin, David Jr.	1	0.5			2	2		36		1							1
Durgin, David Sr.	1	1		1	1	2		197		2				1			

* 1 gristmill, 3/4 sawmill

continued on next page

Appendix 5: *1810 Rateables*

Names	Polls	Houses	Outhouses	Barns	Tillage	Mowing	Pasturage	Unimproved	Oxen	Cows	Cattle 3yr	Cattle 2yr	Cattle 1yr	Horses	Colts 3yr	Colts 1yr	Swine
Durgin, John	1							100				2					1
Durgin, Joseph	1				2	3	4	91		1			1	1			1
Durgin, Samuel	1	1		1	2	4	2	92		2							1
Eastman, James	2	1		1	3	6	4	37		2		1	1	2		1	2
Fly, James Jr.**	1	1		1		2		45		2		1	3				2
Fly, John	1	1		1	6	6		188	2	2				1			2
Gilmore, James	1	1		1	1	6		73	2	3		3	2	1			2
Gray, William	1																
Hartford, Simeon	1																
Howard, John	1					8	6	36	4			1		1			
Howard, Joseph	1					0		70									
Howard, Lemuel	1	1		1	4	12	6	40	2	6		1	1	1		1	2
Kimball, Ephraim	1	blank		1	3			217	2	1							
Lane, Daniel	1	1			2	2		46		1			2				1
Lewis, Abijah	2	2		1	4	12	12	84	2	5		2	1	1			3
Lewis, Edward	1									1		2		1			1
Lewis, Marshal	1	1			1			49									
Lord, Jacob	1	1		1	3	6	2	39	0	1		1		1			3
Lord, Jacob Jr.	1	1			4	6		40		1		2		1			2
Lord, Levi	1							0		1						1	1
Lowell, Jonathan	2	1			4	8	5	43	2	1	2	1	2	1			2
Lowell, Moses	1	1				1		49		1			2				1
Mayberry, Josiah	1	0.5			1.5	3	3			1			3				3
McLellan, Benjamin	1																
McLucas, Jacob	1	1		1	5	10		145	2	1							1

** colts 2 years

Kimball, Ephraim has 217 acres unimproved of which 100 is poor

continued on next page

Appendix 5: *1810 Rateables*

Names	Polls	Houses	Out-houses	Barns	Tillage	Mowing	Pasturage	Unimproved	Oxen	Cows	Cattle 3yr	Cattle 2yr	Cattle 1yr	Horses	Colts 3yr	Colts 1yr	Swine
McLucas, John Jr.	1	1		1	3	6		91		1				1			1
McLucas, John Sr.	1	1			2	4		94		1							1
Merrifield, Samuel	2	1		1	3	3	8	86		1							2
Merrifield, Simeon	1	1			1.5	5	2	41.5		1	2						1
Osgood, Asa	1	1		1	3	6	3	116		2		2	2	1		1	4
Pierce, John	2	1	1	1	6	20	10	1214	2	4		2	4	2			4
Pierce, John Jr.	1							200	2								
Rand, Aaron	1	1		1	2			98									
Richardson, Aaron	1	1		1	4.5	5	6	105	4	3		3		1			
Richardson, Edward	1				2	2		96		2			1		1		1
Robbins, John	1													1			
Rowe, Daniel	1																
Sloper, Samuel	1	1			3			47		2			1				1
Spring, John	1	0.5		1.5	3	6	12	49	2	1		0	1		1		
Spring, Marshall	1		1	2	3	5	5	25				4	1	1	1		
Spring, Thomas	2	1		3	10	20	15	14	4	5	2		4	1		1	4
Storer, William	2	1		1	3	1		96	2	2							2
Wadsworth, Charles L. ***	1	1	1	1	10	20	40	1300	4	4		3	3	1			15
Wadsworth, Peleg – 1 mill	2	1	2	2	20	20	20	5200	2	6		4	4	4			2
Watson, John	1	0.5		0.75	4	5	2	71	2	2	2			1			1
Watson, John Jr.	1	0.5		0.75	4	5	2	69		2		5	2			1	1
Watson, Thomas B.	1	1		0.75	4	5	2	69	2	1				1			1
West, William	blank																
Total	79	46.5	6	43.75	191	376	265	12092.5	70	115	11	11	62	39	3	8	100.5

*** .25 mill
Spring, Marshall 1 Out-house is a Shop

Source: Maine Historical Society, Coll 146 Box 1/4.

APPENDIX 6

1811 Agricultural Produce

Names of Persons in Original Order	Bush-els of Wheat	Rye	Oats	Barley	Corn	Peas & Beans	Pounds of Hop	Tunnes of English Hay	Mea-dow Hay	Barrels of Cider
									none	none
Jonathan Lowell	8	10			50	3		12		
Abijah Lewis	12				20	3		5		
Moses Lowell	2	3	4		13	2		4		
Aaron Cross	10	3			15	1		5		
Marshall Lewis					4			0.5		
Lemuel Howard	7				40	3		5		
John Howard	2							5		
Jonathan Clemons	10				50			2		
Daniel Lane					10			4		
Eli Clemons	10	5			40	7		4		
Nathaniel Williams					18	2		4		
James Fly Jr.										
James Eastman	9	6	12		20	2		6		
Benjamin Baston	6				40	1		10		
Benjamin McLellan	6				40			10		
William Cotton	3				20	1		5		
Edward Lewis	6				60	1				
Noah Lewis	3				50	1				
Joseph Adams	3				60					
Total	97	27	16		550	27		81.5		

APPENDIX 7

1815 Bridge Tax

Names	Polls	Amount of Property	Poll Tax	Property Tax	Bridge Tax
Anderson, Nath.	1	15.00	0.58	0.20	0.78
Barker, Thomas, Jr.	2	246.33	1.16	12.98	13.94
Barnes, Henry W.	1	108.00	0.58	1.35	1.93
Baston, Benj.	2	110.33	1.16	1.48	2.64
Baston, Daniel	1	115.00	0.58	1.55	2.13
Baston, Loammi	1	254.66	0.58	3.43	4.01
Baston, Winthrop	1	240.33	0.58	2.94	3.52
Brown, Moody	1	170.00	0.58	2.49	3.07
Bucknell, Andrew R.	1		0.58		0.58
Bucknell, Benj.	1	96.33	0.58	1.00	1.58
Bucknell, John	1	65.00	0.58	0.87	1.45
Bucknell, Simeon	1	270.00	0.58	3.64	4.22
Burbank, Asa	1	223.00	0.58	3.13	3.61
Burbank, Israel	1	111.00	0.58	1.50	2.08
Chadbourn, John W.	1	177.00	0.58	2.39	2.97
Chadbourn, Joseph	2	253.00	1.16	3.95	5.11
Chase, Gideon	1	67.00	0.58	0.89	1.47
Clemons, Abigail		109.66		1.48	1.48
Clemons, Eli	1	172.00	0.58	2.32	2.90
Clemons, Jonathan	1	336.66	0.58	5.34	5.92
Cotton, Wm	1	107.00	0.58	1.44	2.02
Cram, Daniel	1	105.00	0.58	1.42	2.00
Cram, Weldon J.	1	56.33	0.58	1.29	1.87
Cross, Aaron	1	35.00	0.58	0.47	1.05
Durgin, David	1	139.00	0.58	1.87	2.45
Durgin, John	1	99.50	0.58	1.33	1.91
Durgin, Joseph	1	137.00	0.58	1.85	2.43
Durgin, Samuel	1	91.00	0.58	1.23	1.81
Eastman, James	1	143.33	0.58	2.01	2.57
Fly, James	1	188.00	0.58	2.54	3.12
Fly, John	1	239.00	0.58	3.22	3.80
Gray, Abraham	1	60.00	0.58	0.81	1.39
Gray, Isaac	1	266.33	0.58	3.43	4.01
Gray, Joseph	1	113.00	0.58	1.52	2.10
Gray, William	1		0.58		0.58
Hartford, Solomon	1		0.58		0.58
Howard, Lemuel	1	377.00	0.58	5.25	5.87
Kimball, Ephraim	1	217.66	0.58	2.84	3.42
Lane, Daniel	1	97.00	0.58	1.31	1.89

continued on next page

Appendix 7: *1815 Bridge Tax*

Names	Polls	Amount of Property	Poll Tax	Property Tax	Bridge Tax
Lewis, Abijah	1	174.00	0.58	2.35	2.93
Lewis, Edward	1	89.00	0.58	1.20	1.78
Lewis, Morgan	1	33.33	0.58	0.44	1.02
Lewis, Noah	1	162.66	0.58	2.19	2.77
Lord, Jacob	1	128.00	0.58	2.48	3.06
Lord, Levi	1	43.00	0.58	0.58	1.16
Lowell, Jonathan	2	158.00	1.16	2.13	3.23
Lowell, Moses	1	102.66	0.58	1.39	1.97
Lowell, Reuben	1	167.00	0.58	2.25	2.83
Maybury, Josiah	1	24.00	0.58	0.32	0.90
McLellan, Benj.	1	365.66	0.58	4.92	5.50
McLucas, Jeremiah		80.00		1.08	1.08
McLucas, John	1	66.66	0.58	0.88	1.46
Merrifield, Samuel	2	276.00	1.16	3.63	4.73
Newcomb, David	1	38.00	0.58	0.51	1.09
Osgood, Asa	2	222.33	1.16	3.00	4.16
Osgood, J., Jr.		772.66		10.43	10.43
Pierce, John	3	564.33	1.74	7.61	9.35
Pierce, John de Vendu (from Auction)		203.33		3.82	3.82
Pierce, John de Vendu (from Auction)		350.00		4.72	4.72
Pierce, John, Jr.	1	96.33	0.58	1.29	1.87
Pierce, Josiah	1	125.00	0.58	1.69	2.27
Rand, Aaron	1	97.00	0.58	1.28	1.86
Richardson, Aaron	1	330.00	0.58	4.45	5.03
Richardson, Edward	1	262.33	0.58	3.54	4.12
Robbins, John	2	414.33	1.16	2.54	3.12
Sloper, Samuel	1	95.00	0.58	1.28	1.86
Spring, Alpheus	1	193.83	0.58	2.50	3.08
Spring, John	1	263.00	0.58	3.55	4.13
Spring, Marshall	1	461.00	0.58	6.22	6.80
Spring, Thomas	1	436.00	0.58	5.88	6.46
Storer, Joseph	1	33.93	0.58	0.44	1.02
Storer, William	1	136.00	0.58	1.83	2.41
Storer, Wm, Jr.	1	81.00	0.58	1.09	1.67
Tibbetts, Ephraim	1	33.00	0.58	0.44	1.02
Tibbetts, Stephen	1	45.33	0.58	0.60	1.18
Trafton, Jeremiah	1	33.33	0.58	0.44	1.02
Wadsworth, Charles L.	1	1088.66	0.58	14.02	14.60
Wadsworth, Peleg	2	2398.33	1.16	36.06	37.22
Wadsworth, Peleg, 3rd	1		0.58		0.58
Warren, John	1	276.66	0.58	3.72	4.30
Watson, John	1	210.33	0.58	2.83	3.41
Watson, John, Jr.	1	222.33	0.58	3.00	3.58

continued on next page

Names	Polls	Amount of Property	Poll Tax	Property Tax	Bridge Tax
Watson, Thomas	1	200.00	0.58	2.70	3.28
Williams, Nathan	1	113.00	1.16	1.52	2.68
Woodsome, Wm		50.00		0.67	0.67
Total Polls	89			Subtotal	297.49

Nonresidents	No. of Acres	Taxable Acres			Bridge Tax
Osgood, Joshua B.	566	377.33			5.09
Cutler, Timothy lower grant	150	50.00			0.67
O'Dell, Richard Unknown	100	66.66			0.90
Lewis, Jeremiah Unknown	50	33.33			0.45
Cutts, Thomas	200	66.66			1.80
Total Nonresident	1066			Subtotal	8.91
				Total Tax	306.40

Source: Maine Historical Society, Coll 146 Box 1/6.

APPENDIX 8

Budgets for Support of Schools, Highways, and the Poor 1812, 1815–1831

Year	Schools	Highways	Poor
1812	100	N/A	N/A
1815	100	700	N/A
1816	200	800	N/A
1817	200	750	N/A
1818	150	1000	N/A
1819	200	1000	100
1820	300	1000	170
1821	300	1000	200
1822	250	1000	N/A
1823	300	1000	200
1824	350	1500	120
1825	350	1500	125
1826	350	1500	50
1827	350	1500	100
1828	350	2000	212
1829	350	2000	148.5
1830	350	2000	175
1831	410	2000	N/A

Source (1812) Maine State Archives, Hiram Box 8.
Source (1815–1831) Hiram Town Clerk Records.

APPENDIX 9

1820 U.S. Census of Hiram

Names	Free white males						Free white females					Persons engaged in agriculture	Persons engaged in manufacturing	Total
	under 10	10 under 16	16 under 18	18 under 26	26 under 45	45+	under 10	10 under 16	16 under 26	26 under 45	45+			
Allen, Daniel					1								1	1
Allen, Joseph	1				1		1		1			1		4
Barker, Thomas A.				1					1			1		2
Barnes, Henry W.	1				1	1	1		1			1		5
Baston, Benjamin	2			1		1	1	1		1		1		7
Baston, Daniel														0
Baston, Loammi	2	1			1	1	2	1	1	1		1		10
Baston, Royal	2				1			1	1	1		1		5
Baston, Winthrop	3	1			1		1	1	1			1		8
Boynton, Joseph D.		1			1		3	1		1		1		7
Boynton, Samuel				1			1	1	1				1	4
Brown, Jacob						1					1	1		2
Brown, Joseph						1					1	1		2
Brown, Moody		1		1			1				1	1		4
Bucknell, Benjamin					1		1	1	1			1		4
Bucknell, John														0
Bucknell, John Jr.				1					1			1		2
Bucknell, Simeon				1	2				1		1	4		6
Burbank, Asa	1				1		1			1			1	4
Burbank, Israel						1	1	1			1	1		4
Burbank, John		1				1	1	2		1		1		6
Chadbourn, Humphrey				1			3		1	1		1		6
Chadbourn, John	1				1	1	3	2		1	1	1		10

continued on next page

253

Appendix 9: *1820 U.S. Census of Hiram*

Names	Free white males						Free white females					Persons engaged in agriculture	Persons engaged in manufacturing	Total
	under 10	10 under 16	16 under 18	18 under 26	26 under 45	45+	under 10	10 under 16	16 under 26	26 under 45	45+			
Chadbourn, Joseph				1		1			3		2	2		7
Chadbourn, Samuel	1				1		2		1			1		5
Chadbourn, Simeon				1	1							1	1	2
Chase, Gideon	3	1			1		1	1		1		1		8
Clark, Morris				1			1		1			1		3
Clemons, Abigail				1		1			1		1			4
Clemons, Eli	3	2				1	3			1		3		10
Clemons, Jonathan	1	2	1			1	2			1		2		8
Cole, Tobias	3				1		2		1			1		7
Cotton, William		3	1			1	1	1	1	1		1		9
Cross, Aaron	2	1			1		1	1		1		1		7
Day, Thomas	2				1		2		1			1		6
Durgin, David Jr.	2		1		1		2	2	1	1		2		10
Durgin, John	2				1				1	1	1	1		6
Durgin, Joseph		1			1		4	1		1		1		8
Durgin, Joseph Jr.	1			1			2	1		1		1		6
Durgin, Samuel	1			2		1	1	2	1	2	1	3		11
Dyer, James	2				1				1	1		1		5
Eastman, James		1				1		1	1		1	1		5
Fly, James		1	1			1		1	3	1	1	1		9
Fly, John		2	1		1			1		1		1		6
Gilpatrick, John	1	1									1	1		3
Gilpatrick, John Jr.	1	1	1	1			1			1	1	3		7
Gilpatrick, Stephen	3				1					1		1		5
Gray, Abraham	3			1			2			1		1		7
Gray, Isaac	2			2			1	1	1	1		2	1	8
Gray, Joseph	1				1		3		1				1	6

continued on next page

Appendix 9: *1820 U.S. Census of Hiram*

Names	Free white males						Free white females					Persons engaged in agriculture	Persons engaged in manufacturing	Total
	under 10	10 under 16	16 under 18	18 under 26	26 under 45	45+	under 10	10 under 16	16 under 26	26 under 45	45+			
Gray, William	2				1		2	1		1		1		7
Hartford, John														
Hartford, Solomon	5				1	1	1	1		1	1	1		10
Hickey, Daniel														
Hodsdon, John	1	1			1		4			1		1		8
Howard, John	1		1		1		2			1		2		6
Howard, Joseph	2				1	1	1			1		1		6
Howard, Lemuel						1		1	1		1	1		4
Hubbard, Allen	1			1					1			1		3
Huntress, Robert	2	1	1	1		1	1	1	1		1	3		10
Hyde, Henry				2	1			1	1	1		1	2	6
Kimball, Ephraim	1	2			1		2			1		1		7
Kimball, John				1			1		1			1		3
Lewis, Abijah				1		1		1		1	1	2		5
Lewis, Abijah Jr.				1					1			1		2
Lewis, Edward	3				1		2	1		1		1		8
Lewis, Noah			1		1		1	1	1			1		5
Lord, Jacob	1	1				1	1	1	1		1	2		7
Lord, Jacob Jr.				1			1		1			1		3
Lord, Levi	2	2				1	1			1		1		7
Lowell, Jonathan			1	1		1			2		1	3		6
Lowell, Moses	3				1		2			1		1		7
Mayberry, Josiah	1	1	1	1		1			1		2	2		8
McLellan, Benjamin	2			1	1	1	1	1		1		1		8
McLucas, James				1	1					1		1		3
McLucas, John	1				1		1			1				4
Merrifield, Isaac	1				1		1		1			1		4

continued on next page

Appendix 9: *1820 U.S. Census of Hiram*

	Free white males						Free white females					Persons engaged in agriculture	Persons engaged in manufacturing	Total
Names	under 10	10 under 16	16 under 18	18 under 26	26 under 45	45+	under 10	10 under 16	16 under 26	26 under 45	45+			
Newcomb, David	1	1			1		2		1			1		6
Osgood, Asa	1			1	1	1	2				1	3		7
Osgood, Isaac	1			1					1			1		3
Paine, William				1			1		1			1		3
Palmer, Moses					1					1		1		2
Parker, Nathaniel	1				1		2		1				1	5
Pierce, John			1	2		1		2		1	1	2		8
Pierce, John Jr.	1				1		1	1				1		4
Rand, Aaron	3	1			1		2			1		1		8
Richardson, Aaron		1		1	1		3			1		2		7
Richardson, Edward	3			1	1		4	1		1		2		11
Ridley, Samuel	2			1					1			1		4
Robbins, John					1	1			1		1	2		4
Sloper, Samuel		1			1				1	1		1		3
Spring, Alpheus					1		2	1	1	1		1		6
Spring, John	3	1			1				1	1		2		7
Spring, Thomas	1			1	1	1		1	1	1	1	1	1	8
Stanley, William	3	2			1		2	1	1	1		3		11
Storer, Jacob	4								1	1		1		6
Storer, John				1					1			1		2
Storer, Joseph	2				1				1	1		1		5
Storer, William		1		1		1	1	1	1	1	1	2		8
Storer, William Jr.	1				1		2		1			1		5
Strout, Eleazer						1					1	1		2
Stuart, Aaron	2				1		2			1		1		6
Sutton, George				1					1	1		1		3
Sweat, Benjamin	1			1	2				1				3	5

continued on next page

Appendix 9: *1820 U.S. Census of Hiram*

Names	Free white males						Free white females					Persons engaged in agriculture	Persons engaged in manufacturing	Total
	under 10	10 under 16	16 under 18	18 under 26	26 under 45	45+	under 10	10 under 16	16 under 26	26 under 45	45+			
Thombs, Edmund				1				1		1		1		3
Tibbets, Stephen	1	2				1		1			1	1		6
Trafton, Jeremiah	1			1	1		1			1		1		5
Trafton, Simeon	2				1		1		1			1		5
Wadsworth, Charles L.	2	2		4		1			1	1	1	7		12
Wadsworth, Dura	1					1			2		1	2		5
Wadsworth, Peleg	2	1	1	3		1			4		1	5		13
Wadsworth, Peleg 3rd					1		2	1		1		1		5
Warren, John	2	2			1		2	1		1		1		9
Warren, Margaret							1			1	1			3
Watson, John						1		1		1	1			4
Watson, John Jr.		2			1		3	1		1		1		8
Watson, Samuel?	1				1		1		1			1		4
Watson, Thomas B.	3				1		2	1		1		1		8
Wentworth, John	2	1			1		2	1		1		1		8
Wentworth, Jonathan		1				1	2	2	1	1		2		8
Wentworth, Noah				1					1			1		2
Whale, John				3		1	1	2	2		1	4		10
Williams, Dinah				1			1	2	1	1	1	1		7
Wilson, Joshua														
Wood, Josiah					1					1		1		2
York, John		1				1	1		1		1	1		5
Total	122	51	13	57	70	41	124	56	70	66	39	156	13	709

APPENDIX 10

1830 U.S. Census of Hiram, Persons Under the Age of 40

Names	Free white males							Free white females							Total personss under 40	Total persons
	Under 5	5 under 10	10 under 15	15 under 20	20 under 30	30 under 40	Total males under 40	Under 5	5 under 10	10 under 15	15 under 20	20 under 30	30 under 40	Total females under 40		
Adams, Joseph		2	1	2			4	1				1		3	7	10
Alexander, Jeduthan				1			1			1	1	1		3	4	5
Allen, Hosea	2	2			1		5	1		1		1		3	8	8
Barker, Benjamin	1		1	1	2	2	7	2				1	1	4	11	12
Barnes, Henry W.	1	1		1			3			1	1		1	3	6	7
Baston, Benjamin			1				1							0	1	3
Baston, Rebeca		1					1		1			1		2	3	4
Baston, Winthrop			1	1			2				1			1	3	6
Brazier, James Jr.	3	2				1	6		2				1	3	9	9
Bridges, James	1				1		2		1			1		2	4	5
Brown, Jacob							0							0	0	2
Brown, Moody						1	1							0	1	3
Bucknell, John							0					1		1	1	2
Bucknell, John Jr	1		1			1	3		1			1	1	3	6	6
Bucknell, Simeon						1	1					1	2	3	4	6
Burbank, Asa	1	1		1			3		1	1				2	5	7
Burbank, Henry S.			1			1	2			1		1		2	4	4
Burbank, Isaac							0					1		1	1	1
Burbank, Stephen					1		1							0	1	3
Burbank, Wiliam G.					1		1	2				1		3	4	4
Butterfield, Edmund	1	1			1		3					1		1	4	4
Butterfield, Joseph	1				1		2			1		1		2	4	4

continued on next page

Appendix 10: *1830 U.S. Census of Hiram, Persons Under the Age of 40*

Names	Free white males							Free white females							Total persons under 40	Total persons
	Under 5	5 under 10	10 under 15	15 under 20	20 under 30	30 under 40	Total males under 40	Under 5	5 under 10	10 under 15	15 under 20	20 under 30	30 under 40	Total females under 40		
Chadbourn, Benjamin	1		1			1	3					1		1	4	4
Chadbourn, John		2					2			2	1			3	5	6
Chadbourn, Joseph							0				1			1	1	3
Chadbourn, Samuel	1		1			1	3	1			1		1	3	6	6
Chaney, Mary							0					1		1	1	1
Chase, Gideon			1	2			3	2	3	1	1		1	8	11	12
Clark, John						1	1		1			1		2	3	3
Clark, Morris	1					1	2	1	1	1			1	4	6	6
Clay, John R.							0		1					1	1	3
Clemons, Eli	1			1	1		3	1	1	1	2			5	8	10
Clemons, John L.					1		1							0	1	1
Clemons, John							0							0	0	3
Clemons, Jonathan	1		1		1		3		1		1			2	5	7
Clemons, Samuel					1		1	1				1		2	3	3
Cole, Tobias	1	2	1	1			5	1		1		1	1	4	9	10
Cotton John					1		1							0	1	1
Cotton, Lemuel			1		1		2				1			1	3	3
Cotton, William					2		2				1	1		2	4	6
Cross, Aaron							0	1					1	2	2	4
Durgin, David				2	1		3		1					1	4	6
Durgin, John		2	2			1	5	2	2				1	5	10	12
Durgin, Joseph					1	1	2				2	1		3	5	7
Eastman, John S.		1	1	1		1	4	1			1		1	3	7	7
Evans, James		2				1	3	1			1	1		3	6	7
Evans, Oliver						1	1	2				1		3	4	4
Farnham, Joseph			1	1	2		4	1	2	2		1		6	10	12
Fly, John				1	2		3	1						1	4	6

continued on next page

Appendix 10: *1830 U.S. Census of Hiram, Persons Under the Age of 40*

Names	Free white males							Free white females							Total personss under 40	Total persons
	Under 5	5 under 10	10 under 15	15 under 20	20 under 30	30 under 40	Total males under 40	Under 5	5 under 10	10 under 15	15 under 20	20 under 30	30 under 40	Total females under 40		
Flye, James					1		1	1						1	2	4
Gerrish, Obediah	1	1				1	3	1	2				1	4	7	8
Gilpatrick, Ammi L.					1		1				1			1	2	4
Gilpatrik, Stephen	1	1	2	1		1	6	1	1				1	3	9	10
Goodwin, Carll					1		1					1		1	2	2
Goodwin, Nathaniel C.?	1						1	1					1	2	3	3
Goodwin, Thomas 3d	1		2			1	4	1	2				1	4	8	8
Goodwin, Thomas Jr	2				1		3					1		1	4	6
Gowen, Moses	1				1		2				1	1		2	4	4
Gray, Abram	2	2	1				5		2					2	7	8
Gray, Joseph	2	1					3		2	1	1			4	7	9
Gray, William	1	1					2	1	1	1	1			4	6	8
Gubtill, James	1	1	1				3		1	2	2		1	6	9	10
Hamblen, Isaac	1					1	2	1				1	1	3	5	5
Hancock, John				1			1			1				1	2	4
Hannaford, Levi A.					1		1	1		1		1		3	4	4
Hanson, Oliver	1				1		2	1				1		2	4	4
Harmon, Samuel?	1				1		2		1			1		2	4	4
Hartford, Hannah							0							0	0	1
Hartford, James	3					1	4	2	1	1			1	5	9	9
Haskell, Jonathan	1			7			8							0	8	10
Heath, Abner	1	1				1	3					1	1	2	5	5
Heath, Richard	2					2	4		1			1	1	3	7	8
Hodgdon, James				1	1		2		1		1	1		3	5	7
Howard, Joseph	1	3	2				6			1				1	7	9
Hubbard, Allan	1	2				1	4	2			1	2		5	9	10

continued on next page

Appendix 10: *1830 U.S. Census of Hiram, Persons Under the Age of 40*

Names	Free white males Under 5	5 under 10	10 under 15	15 under 20	20 under 30	30 under 40	Total males under 40	Free white females Under 5	5 under 10	10 under 15	15 under 20	20 under 30	30 under 40	Total females under 40	Total persons under 40	Total persons
Huntress, John	1				1		2	1				1		2	4	4
Huntress, Robert				1	1		2				1			1	3	5
Huntress, Temple				1		1	2	2				1		3	5	5
Kimball, Ephraim	1	1	1		1		4				2			2	6	8
Kimball, Jesse				1			1		1	1				2	3	5
Kimball, John		1		1	2	1	5		1	1	1			3	8	9
Lewis, Abijah							0							0	0	2
Lewis, Alexander					1		1	2					1	3	4	4
Lewis, Noah	1	2	1			1	5			1	1		1	3	8	8
Lord, Hosea	1				1		2	1				1		2	4	4
Lord, Jacob							0	1		1				2	2	4
Lord, Jacob Jr	1	1				1	3		1	1		1		3	6	6
Lord, Thomas	2					1	3	1	1	1		1		3	6	6
Lowell, Jonathan		1				1	2	1	1				1	2	4	6
Lowell, Luther	1	1	1				3	2	1		1		1	5	8	9
Lowell, Moses		1	1	2			4		1	1	1			3	7	9
Lowell, Thomas			1		1		2	2	3			1	1	7	9	11
Mabry, Thomas		1			1		2	1				1	1	3	5	5
McDonald, Abner					1		1					1		1	2	2
McDonald, Benjamin	1	1	1	1			4	1		1	2			4	8	10
McDonald, John	1				1		2					1		1	3	3
McDonald, Noah	2				1		3					1		1	4	4
McLucas, John	1	2	1	1			5			1	1			2	7	9
McLucas, Robert		1				1	2	3	2					5	7	8
Meader, Timothy E.					1		1							0	1	1
Morrill, John	2						2	1	2	2			1	6	8	9
Osgood, Asa		1					1			1	1			2	3	5

continued on next page

Appendix 10: *1830 U.S. Census of Hiram, Persons Under the Age of 40*

Names	Free white males							Free white females							Total personss under 40	Total persons
	Under 5	5 under 10	10 under 15	15 under 20	20 under 30	30 under 40	Total males under 40	Under 5	5 under 10	10 under 15	15 under 20	20 under 30	30 under 40	Total females under 40		
Osgood, Benjamin	1	1		1			3			1	1	1		3	6	9
Osgood, Timothy	1	1					2	2				1		3	5	6
Palmer, Moses			1	1		1	3						1	1	4	4
Parker, Nathaniel	2	2	1			1	6	1		1			1	3	9	9
Peterson, Nicholas	2	2				1	5						1	1	6	6
Pierce, Calvin					1		1							0	1	1
Pierce, Daniel					1		1	1	1			1		3	4	4
Pierce, John			1		1		2					1		1	3	5
Pierce, John Jr.	2		1				3	2	1				1	4	7	8
Pierce, Timothy C.			1			1	2	2					1	3	5	5
Pierce, William	1					1	2	1	2	1			2	6	8	8
Pike, Noah	2					1	3						1	2	5	5
Pike, Samuel T.			1			1	2	1		1			1	2	4	4
Rand, Aaron		1	1				2	1	1		1			3	5	7
Rankins, James					3		3		1		1			2	5	5
Richardson, Aaron		1			1		2			1	2			3	5	7
Richardson, Artemas			2	1	1		4		2		1	3		6	10	12
Richardson, Edmund		1	2	1			4	1		1	1	1	1	5	9	10
Richardson, Genevieve		1	2	1			4			1				1	5	6
Ridlon, Samuel			2			1	3	2	1				1	4	7	7
Robins, Hannah							0				1		1	1	1	1
Robins, Joshua						1	1				1			1	2	3
Sloper, Samuel	1				1		2							0	2	4
Small, Daniel	1				1		2	1					1	2	4	4
Smith, ? L.	1					1	2	1			1	1		3	5	5
Smith, Ranson	2	1				1	4	1					1	1	5	5

continued on next page

Appendix 10: *1830 U.S. Census of Hiram, Persons Under the Age of 40*

Names	Free white males							Free white females							Total personss under 40	Total persons
	Under 5	5 under 10	10 under 15	15 under 20	20 under 30	30 under 40	Total males under 40	Under 5	5 under 10	10 under 15	15 under 20	20 under 30	30 under 40	Total females under 40		
Smith, Stephen						1	1	1				2		3	4	4
Spring, Thomas				1			1						1	1	2	6
Spring, Alpheus	2		1			1	4		1	2			1	4	8	10
Spring, John	1	2	1				4				1			1	5	7
Stanley, Jacob	2		1	1			4				1	2		3	7	8
Storer, Deacn?	1				1		2					1		1	3	3
Storer, George					1		1	2			1	1		4	5	5
Storer, Jacob		1	1				2	1						1	3	5
Storer, John	1					1	2		1	1		1		3	5	6
Storer, Joseph		2	1	1		1	5		1	1	1		1	4	9	9
Storer, Wiliam	2						2		1	2			1	4	6	7
Strout, Eleaser							0							0	0	2
Strout, George D.	1				1		2		1			1		2	4	4
Sutton, George		2				1	3	2	1				1	4	7	7
Tebbetts, Elijah	1				1		2		1			1		2	4	4
Tebbetts, Stephen				1			1					1		1	2	2
Tebbetts, Timothy		1					1							0	1	3
Thomb, Edmund					1	1	2	1					1	2	4	5
Trafton, Jeremiah	1		1				2		1			1		2	4	6
Trafton, Simon	1		1				2		1		1			2	4	6
Treadwell, Jonathan		2	1	1			4		1	2				3	7	9
Tripp, Richard	2					1	3	1	1			1		3	6	6
Tripp, Thomas				1	1		2		1	1				2	4	6
Tyler, Samuel						1	1							0	1	1
Wadsworth, Charles			1			1	2	2				1	1	4	6	6
Wadsworth, Charles L.			1	1	3		5							0	5	8
Wadsworth, John	3	1		1		1	6			1		1		2	8	8

continued on next page

Appendix 10: *1830 U.S. Census of Hiram, Persons Under the Age of 40*

Names	Free white males							Free white females							Total persons under 40	Total persons
	Under 5	5 under 10	10 under 15	15 under 20	20 under 30	30 under 40	Total males under 40	Under 5	5 under 10	10 under 15	15 under 20	20 under 30	30 under 40	Total females under 40		
Wadsworth, Peleg	1	1	1	2	2	1	8	2	1			2	1	6	14	17
Wadsworth, Peleg 2d		1				1	2	1		2			1	4	6	8
Wadsworth, Peleg C.	2	1					3	2	1				2	5	8	8
Wadsworth, Uriah	1				1		2	1			1			2	4	4
Warren, John	1	2	2	1	2		8				1	1		2	10	12
Warren, Nathaniel	1			1			2					1		1	3	3
Watson, John	2		1	1			4	1	2	1		2		6	10	14
Watson, Thomas B.	1	1	2				4				2			2	6	8
Wentworth, Charles		1	1		1		3	2			2			4	7	8
Wentworth, Ephraim		1	1			1	3						1	1	4	4
Wentworth, Jonathan		1					1			1	1	1		3	4	6
Wentworth, Louise							0	1			1			2	2	3
Wentworth, Moses E.			1			1	2	2	1			1		4	6	6
Wentworth, Stephen						1	1	1				1		2	3	3
Whale, Benjamin	1					1	2	1	1					2	4	6
Whale, John						1	1							0	1	1
Whale, Solomon	1				1		2	1				1		2	4	4
Whitney, William	1	1				1	3		1				1	2	5	5
Williams, Aaron	1				1		2					1		1	3	4
York, John					1		1					1		1	2	4
Total persons	97	79	66	52	76	62	432	100	71	56	56	79	57	419	848	1026
Total households 175																

APPENDIX 11
1830 U.S. Census of Hiram, Ages 40+

Appendix 11: *1830 U.S. Census of Hiram, Ages 40+*

Names	Free white males							Free white females							Total persons
	40 under 50	50 under 60	60 under 70	70 under 80	80 under 90	90 under 100	Total Males	40 under 50	50 under 60	60 under 70	70 under 80	80 under 90	90 under 100	Total Females	
Adams, Joseph		1					1	1		1				2	3
Alexander, Jeduthan	1						1							0	1
Allen, Hosea							0							0	0
Barker, Benjamin	1						1							0	1
Barnes, Henry W.	1						1							0	1
Baston, Benjamin		1					1		1					1	2
Baston, Rebeca							0	1						1	1
Baston, Winthrop		1					1	1			1			2	3
Brazier, James							0							0	0
Bridges, James							0	1						1	1
Brown, Jacob				1			1							0	1
Brown, Moody			1				1			1				1	2
Bucknell, John	1						1							0	1
Bucknell, John Jr							0							0	0
Bucknell, Simeon				1			1			1				1	2
Burbank, Asa	1						1	1						1	2
Burbank, Henry S.							0							0	0
Burbank, Isaac							0							0	0
Burbank, Stephen			1				1		1					1	2
Burbank, Wiliam G.							0							0	0
Butterfield, Edmund							0							0	0
Butterfield, Joseph							0							0	0

continued on next page

Appendix 11: *1830 U.S. Census of Hiram, Ages 40+*

Names	Free white males							Free white females							Total persons
	40 under 50	50 under 60	60 under 70	70 under 80	80 under 90	90 under 100	Total Males	40 under 50	50 under 60	60 under 70	70 under 80	80 under 90	90 under 100	Total Females	
Chadbourn, Benjamin							0							0	0
Chadbourn, John	1						1			1				1	2
Chadbourn, Joseph			1				1		1					1	2
Chadbourn, Samuel?							0							0	0
Chaney, Mary							0							0	0
Chase, Gideon	1						1							0	1
Clark, John							0							0	0
Clark, Moses							0							0	0
Clay, John R.		1					1	1						1	2
Clemons, Eli		1					1	1						1	2
Clemons, John L.							0							0	0
Clemons, John*			1				1			1				1	2
Clemons, Jonathan		1					1	1						1	2
Clemons, Samuel							0							0	0
Cole, Tobias	1						1							0	1
Cotton John							0							0	0
Cotton, Lemuel							0							0	0
Cotton, William		1					1	1						1	2
Cross, Aaron	1						1							0	1
Durgin, David		1					1		1					1	2
Durgin, John					1		1					1		1	2
Durgin, Joseph	1						1	1						1	2
Eastman, John S.?							0							0	0
Evans, James							0		1					1	1

continued on next page

* Clemons, John, 1 female age 100+

Appendix 11: *1830 U.S. Census of Hiram, Ages 40+*

Names	\	Free	white	males	\	\	Total Males	\	Free	white	females	\	\	Total Females	Total persons
	40 under 50	50 under 60	60 under 70	70 under 80	80 under 90	90 under 100		40 under 50	50 under 60	60 under 70	70 under 80	80 under 90	90 under 100		
Evans, Oliver							0							0	0
Farnham, Joseph	1						1							1	2
Fly, John	1						1							1	2
Flye, James		1					1		1					1	2
Gerrish, Obediah							0				1			1	1
Gilpatrick, Ammi L.		1					1		1					1	2
Gilpatrik, Stephen			1				1							0	1
Goodwin, Carl?							0							0	0
Goodwin, Nathaniel C.?							0							0	0
Goodwin, Thomas 3d							0							0	0
Goodwin, Thomas Jr		1					1		1					1	2
Gowen, Moses							0							0	0
Gray, Abram	1						1							0	1
Gray, Joseph	1						1		1					1	2
Gray, William	1						1		1					1	2
Gubtill, James	1						1							0	1
Hamblen, Isaac							0							0	0
Hancock, John				1			1			1				1	2
Hannaford, Levi A.							0							0	0
Hanson, Oliver							0							0	0
Harmon, Samuel?							0							0	0
Hartford, Hannah							0			1				1	1
Hartford, James							0							0	0
Haskell, Jonathan		1					1		1					1	2
Heath, Abner							0							0	0
Heath, Richard							0		1					1	1

continued on next page

267

Appendix 11: *1830 U.S. Census of Hiram, Ages 40+*

Names	Free white males 40 under 50	50 under 60	60 under 70	70 under 80	80 under 90	90 under 100	Total Males	Free white females 40 under 50	50 under 60	60 under 70	70 under 80	80 under 90	90 under 100	Total Females	Total persons
Hodgdon, James							0	1						1	1
Howard, Joseph	1						1	1						1	2
Hubbard, Allan							0			1				1	1
Huntress, John							0							0	0
Huntress, Robert		1					1		1					1	2
Huntress, Temple							0							0	0
Kimball, ?	1						1	1						1	2
Kimball, Jesse	1						1	1						1	2
Kimball, John							0	1						1	1
Lewis, Abijah				1			1				1			1	2
Lewis, Alexander							0							0	0
Lewis, Noah							0							0	0
Lord, Hosea							0							0	0
Lord, Jacob		1					1		1					1	2
Lord, Jacob Jr							0							0	0
Lord, Thomas?							0							0	0
Lowell, Jonathan				1			1				1			1	2
Lowell, Luther	1						1							0	1
Lowell, Moses	1						1	1						1	2
Lowell, Thomas				1			1			1				1	2
Mabry, Thomas							0							0	0
McDonald, Abner							0							0	0
McDonald, Benjamin	1				1		2	1						1	3
McDonald, John							0							0	0
McDonald, Noah							0							0	0

continued on next page

Appendix 11: *1830 U.S. Census of Hiram, Ages 40+*

Names	Free white males 40 under 50	50 under 60	60 under 70	70 under 80	80 under 90	90 under 100	Total Males	Free white females 40 under 50	50 under 60	60 under 70	70 under 80	80 under 90	90 under 100	Total Females	Total persons
McLucas, John	1						1	1						1	2
McLucas, Robert							0	1				1		2	2
Meader, Timothy E.							0							0	0
Morrill, John	1						1							0	1
Osgood, Asa				1			1		1					1	2
Osgood, Benjamin		1					1	1	1					2	3
Osgood, Timothy	1						1							0	1
Palmer, Moses							0							0	0
Parker, Nathaniel							0							0	0
Peterson, Nicholas							0							0	0
Pierce, Calvin							0							0	0
Pierce, Daniel							0							0	0
Pierce, John			1				1			1				1	2
Pierce, John Jr.	1						1							0	1
Pierce, Timothy C.							0							0	0
Pierce, William							0							0	0
Pike, Noah							0							0	0
Pike, Samuel T.							0							0	0
Rand, Aaron	1						1	1						1	2
Rankins, James							0							0	0
Richardson, Aaron		1					1	1						1	2
Richardson, Artemas		1					1		1					1	2
Richardson, Edmund	1						1							0	1
Richardson, Genevieve							0		1					1	1
Ridlon, Samuel							0							0	0
Robins, Hannah							0							0	0

continued on next page

Appendix 11: *1830 U.S. Census of Hiram, Ages 40+*

Names	Free white males							Free white females							Total persons
	40 under 50	50 under 60	60 under 70	70 under 80	80 under 90	90 under 100	Total Males	40 under 50	50 under 60	60 under 70	70 under 80	80 under 90	90 under 100	Total Females	
Robins, Joshua				1		1	2							0	2
Sloper, Samuel			1				1		1					1	2
Small, Daniel							0							0	0
Smith, ? L.							0							0	0
Smith, Ranson							0							0	0
Smith, Stephen							0							0	0
Spring, Thomas	1			1			2	1			1			2	4
Spring, Alpheus				1			1				1			1	2
Spring, John	1						1	1						1	2
Stanley, Jacob							0		1					1	1
Storer, Deacn?							0							0	0
Storer, George							0							0	0
Storer, Jacob	1						1	1						1	2
Storer, John							0			1				1	1
Storer, Joseph							0							0	0
Storer, Wiliam	1						1							0	1
Strout, Eleaser		1					1			1				1	2
Strout, George D.							0							0	0
Sutton, George							0							0	0
Tebbetts, Elijiah							0							0	0
Tebbetts, Stephen			1				1			1				1	2
Tebbetts, Timothy	1						1		1					1	2
Thomb, Edmund							0	1						1	1
Total households 175															
Trafton, Jeremiah	1						1	1						1	2

continued on next page

Appendix 11: *1830 U.S. Census of Hiram, Ages 40+*

Names	Free white males 40 under 50	50 under 60	60 under 70	70 under 80	80 under 90	90 under 100	Total Males	Free white females 40 under 50	50 under 60	60 under 70	70 under 80	80 under 90	90 under 100	Total Females	Total persons
Trafton, Simon	1						1	1						1	2
Treadwell, Jonathan	1						1	1						1	2
Tripp, Richard							0							0	0
Tripp, Thomas		1					1	1						1	2
Tyler, Samuel							0							0	0
Wadsworth, Charles							0							0	0
Wadsworth, Charles L.	1						1	1	1					2	3
Wadsworth, John							0							0	0
Wadsworth, Peleg	1		1				2			1				1	3
Wadsworth, Peleg 2d				1			1				1			1	2
Wadsworth, Peleg C.							0							0	0
Wadsworth, Uriah							0							0	0
Warren, John	1						1	1						1	2
Warren, Nathaniel							0							0	0
Watson, John		1					1	2		1				3	4
Watson, Thomas B.		1					1	1						1	2
Wentworth, Charles							0	1						1	1
Wentworth, Ephraim							0							0	0
Wentworth, Jonathan			1				1		1					1	2
Wentworth, Louise							0							0	0
Wentworth, Moses E.							0							0	0
Wentworth, Stephen							0							0	0
Whale, Benjamin			1				1		1					1	2
Whale, John							0							0	0
Whale, Solomon							0							0	0
Whitney, William							0							0	0

continued on next page

Appendix 11: *1830 U.S. Census of Hiram, Ages 40+*

Names	Free white males							Free white females							Total persons
	40 under 50	50 under 60	60 under 70	70 under 80	80 under 90	90 under 100	Total Males	40 under 50	50 under 60	60 under 70	70 under 80	80 under 90	90 under 100	Total Females	
Williams, Aaron							0		1					1	1
York, John		1					1		1					1	2
Total persons	39	22	11	11	2	1	86	39	25	15	7	2	0	88	174
Total households 175															

APPENDIX 12

Population of Hiram with Percent Increases

1774	5 families[498]		
1784	17 families[499] plus John Clemons family that settled on the Wadsworth grant		
1790 census	18 families [51 males, 41 females = 92]		
1800 census	34 families	184	100.0% [183? 103 males, 80 females]
1809	53 eligible voters, 74 polls[500]		
1810 census	336	82.6%[501]	
1810	53 eligible voters		
1814	72 eligible voters		
1815 bridge tax	89 polls		
1819	72 eligible voters		
1820 census	700	108.3 % [actual count 709[502]. 354 males, 355 females—103 families]	
1820 census	123 heads of households		
1822	152 eligible voters (149)		
1830 census	1026	46.6%	
1840 census	1233	20.2%	
1850 census	1210	-1.9%	
1860 census	1283	6.0%	
1870 census	1393	8.6%	
1880 census	1452	4.2%	
1890 census	1063	-26.8%	
1900 census	1015	-4.5%	
1910 census	945	-6.9%	
1920 census	921	-2/5%	
1930 census	813	-11.7%	
1940 census	787	-3.2%	
1950 census	804	2.2%	
1960 census	699	-13.1%	
1970 census	686	-1.9%	
1980 census	1067	55.5%	
1990 census	1260	18.1%	
2000 census	1423	12.9%	
2010 census	1620	13.8%	
2019 census	1753	8.2%	

---

498   Lieut. Benjamin Ingall's survey of 1774.

499   1788 petition of 17 settlers to regain their land from Cutler's Grant having settled before January 1, 1784.

500   1809 list of voters, Maine State Archives, Hiram Box 6.

501   Summary only. The 1810 census is not available.

502   Totals on several pages of the original 1820 census were added incorrectly.

APPENDIX 13

Marriage Intentions 1779 to 1827

Source: Town of Fryeburg.
N.B. In 1807 part of Brownfield became part of Hiram. These Brownfield people are included in this list.

1779 May 3 Marr. Intent. Lemuel Haywood and Hannah Clemens, both of Brownfield. Cert. granted June 3, 1779.

1782 Mar. 10 Marr. Intent. Mr. Simeon Bucknell of Fryeburg and Hannah Burbank of Brownfield. Cert. granted March 20, 1782. Mar. by the Rev. Mr. Wm. Fessenden Mar. 21, 1782.

1786 Nov. 5 Marr. Intent. Benjamin Burbank of Brownfield and Mary Richardson of Hiram. Cert. granted Nov. 25, 1786. Mar. Dec. 20, 1786 by Simon Frye, J.P.

1789 Mar. 22 Marr. Intent. Thomas Barker and Sally Ayeres [Ayer] of Hiram. Cert. granted July (?), 1789.

1790 Nov. 22 Mar. John Lane and Hannah Bean, both of Brownfield, by Simon Frye, Esq.

1790 Oct. 2 Marr. Intent. John Lane and Hannah Bean, both of Brownfield. Cert. granted Nov. 23, (1790).

1793 Aug. 18 Marr. Intent. Elias Heath of Prescott's Patent and Olive Eldridge of Brownfield. Cert. granted Sept. 2, 1793.

1793 Nov. 3 Marr. Intent. Daniel Hickey and Sophia Cole, both of Hiram. Cert. granted Nov. 17, 1793.

1794 April 20 Marr. Intent. Ephraim Westcoat and Rebecca Powers, both of Hiram. Cert. granted May 5, 1794.

1795 Mar. 29 Marr. Intent. John Burbank of Brownfield and Catherine Boston of Hiram. Cert. granted April 13, 1795. Mar. Apr. 16, 1795.

1795 Sept. 6 Marr. Intent. Charles Wadsworth and Ruth Clemons, both of Hiram. Cert. granted Sept. 21, 1795.

1797 June 18 Marr. Intent. Jonathan Clemons of Hiram and Abigail Kilgore of New Suncook. Cert. granted July 3, 1797. Mar. Sept 3, 1797 by Rev. William Fessenden.

1800 Feb. 8 Marr. Intent. John Burbank of Brownfield and Lois Boston of Hiram. Cert. granted Feb. 24, 1800.

1800 May 25 I joined in marriage Mr. William Cotton with Miss Hannah Howard, Joseph Howard, J.P., Brownfield.

1802 Oct. 24 Mar. Asa Mansfield of Brownfield and Jane Osgood of Hiram by Rev. William Fessenden.

1824 Apr. 15 Mar. Capt. Charles Wadsworth and Sally Lewis of Hiram by Judah Dana, J.P.

1825 Apr. 23 Marr. Intent. Mr. Daniel Small of Hiram and Miss Susan Abbott of Fryeburg. Cert. not entered. (Month in sequence, but posted within 1826.)

1827 Nov. 29 Mar. Mr. John Johnson of Cornish and Miss Ruth L. Pierce of Hiram by Carleton Hurd, Pastor of the first church in Fryeburg.

Marriage intentions 1808–1811

Source: Maine Historical Society, Coll. 16 Box 1.

1808 July 16 Asa Osgood and Hannah Powers, both of Hiram

1808 October 14 Moses Lowell of Hiram and Rachel Newcomb of Windham

1808 November 9 Aaron Cross and Mirriam Lewis both of Hiram

1809 February 9 Edward Lewis and Mehitable Baston both of Hiram

1809 March 1 Royal Baston and Sally Leathers both of Hiram

1809 April 15 John Eames and Louisa Burbank both of Hiram [signed] Thomas B. Watson, District Clerk

1809 June 4 William Gray and Peggy McLucas both of Hiram

1809 November 9 Thomas B. Watson and Polly Hill both of Hiram

1811 March 23 John W. Chadbourne of Hiram and Lydia Boynton of Cornish

Miscellaneous notes
1780 Clemons, Hannah and Lemuel Hood [Hayward, Howard], Hiram

1806 August 22, Clemons, John L. and Joanna H. Richardson, Hiram

1813 January 31 "I joined Henry W. Barnes & Betsey Wadsworth in marriage last Sunday January 31, 1813—Peleg Wadsworth."

Marriage Intentions Town of Porter 1829-1848
1830 March 1 John Cohrain and Mrs. Lucy B. Shute both of Hiram

1830 22 April John Fox Jr. of Porter and Clarina Standley [Stanley] of Hiram

1833 November 28 Daniel Gould of Porter and Deborah Stanley of Hiram

Early Marriage Records of Brownfield compiled by Ruth N. Peckham
1825 December 13 Frederick Howard of Brownfield and Ruth Cotton of Hiram 7 January 1826

Marriages Solemnized by Joseph Howard Esq.
1798 February 11 James Flye and Eunice Clements
1800 May 25 John Burbank and Lois Boston

1800 May 25 William Cotton and Hannah Howard

1803 January 27 Winthrop Boston and Huldah Robbins

1803 March 3 Jonathan Clements and Hannah Lane

1830 November 29 Aaron Williams of Hiram and Alicia Lane of Brownfield

APPENDIX 14
Officers of Hiram

Agent to Defend Town vs. Bad Roads

1815	Peleg Wadsworth
1824	John Warren, Esq.
1828	Benj Barker
1829	Benj Barker
1831	Artemas Richardson

Agent to Repair the New County Road

1830	Col John Warren

Clerk

1805	Charles Wadsworth
1806	John Pierce
1807	John Pierce
1808	Thomas B. Watson
1809	Thomas B. Watson
1811	John Pierce
1812	Alpheus Spring
1813	Alpheus Spring
1814	Benjamin Bucknell
1815	Benjamin Bucknell
1816	Alpheus Spring
1817–1819	Benjamin Bucknell, Esq.
1820–1821	John Bucknell
1822–1823	Benjamin Barker
1824–1826	John Bucknell
1827	Peleg Wadsworth Jr.
1828–1834	Dr. Levi A. Hannaford

Collectors of Taxes

1803	John Fly
1804	John Fly, Thomas Barker?[503]
1805	James Eastman, Israel Burbank
1806	James Eastman, Israel Burbank
1807	James Eastman agrees to collect taxes at 3 cents on the dollar. In 1811 Winthrop Baston received $9.75 for services as Collector in 1807
1808	Winthrop Baston

1808	Stephen Burbank, James Eastman
1809	John Fly
1811	Edward Richardson
1813	Asa Burbank
1814	John Bucknell
1815	Asa Burbank
1816	Voted to merge with Constable Asa Burbank
1817	John Pike Jr. (he is to have 3 ½%)
1818	Andrew R. Bucknell (he is to have 5%)
1819	Simeon Chadbourn
1820	Simeon Chadbourn (5 cents on a dollar)
1821	Simeon Chadbourn (5 ½ percent)
1822	Ephraim Kimball (4 ¾ percent)
1823	Benjamin Chadbourn (5 ½ percent)
1824	Benjamin Chadbourn
1825	Levi Morrell (5 ¾ percent)
1826	Benjamin Chadbourn (5 ¼ percent)
1827	Andrew R. Bucknell bid it off at 12 ½ dollars
1828	Voted that the Treasurer be Collector for the ensuing year
1829	Voted to connect Collectorship with Constable
1830	Peleg Wadsworth

Committee on Accounts

1806	Peleg Wadsworth, John Watson, Thomas Spring, Thomas Barker
1807	Peleg Wadsworth, John Watson, Thomas Spring
1812	Charles L. Wadsworth, Marshall Spring, Benjamin Bucknell
1813	Isaac Gray, Benjamin McLellan, Charles L. Wadsworth
1814	John Watson, Alpheus Spring, John Pierce
1815	John Watson, Alpheus Spring, John Pierce

---

503 Thomas Barker may have been Collector of Taxes, Constable, or Selectman per receipt for tasks of those offices (receipt for collecting taxes the year 1804 $4:41, taking the valuation & in voting & tending to get warrants set up & put up 1:82, to going to Brownfield .50, received $6:73 May 10, 1806).

1816	Charles L. Wadsworth, Thomas B. Watson, Ephraim Kimball
1817	Simeon Chadbourn, Benj. Bucknell, Charles L. Wadsworth
1818	Ephraim Kimball, John Pierce, Simeon Chadbourn
1819	Thomas B. Watson, Andrew R. Bucknell (deficient)
1820	Peleg Wadsworth, Esq., Thomas B. Watson, Asa Osgood Jr.
1821	Thomas B. Watson, Benjamin Bucknell, Joseph Howard
1824	Marshall Spring, Thomas B. Watson, Charles L. Wadsworth
1825	no record
1826	no record
1827	Thomas B. Watson, Simeon Chadbourn, Charles L. Wadsworth (voted to excuse C. L. Wadsworth), chose Alpheus Spring
1828	Alpheus Spring, Esq., Thomas B. Watson, Simeon Chadbourn
1829	no record
1830	no record of election to members. Voted to read and level the accounts of the Committee on Accounts

Committees on Bridge Building and Repairs

1812	Saco River: Charles L. Wadsworth, Simeon Bucknell, John Pierce
1814	Cornish Bridge: Joseph Durgin, Jacob Lord—to nail that part of Cornish Bridge belonging to Hiram and make any other necessary repairs, and to put up a fence to prevent passengers from falling into the gully made by the Freshet and immediately that their Labours thereon should be accounted for in their future Highway Taxes.
1815	Saco River: Marshall Spring, Asa Burbank—to distribute subscription papers and obtain donations; John Pierce, Asa Burbank, Isaac Gray—to view and ascertain the best place to erect said Bridge; John Pierce, Asa Burbank, Marshall Spring—superintend the erecting of said Bridge (work

to be paid at $1.25 per day up to July 15, 75 cents after).

1815	Hancock Brook: Joseph Chadbourne, John Watson—to build bridge across Hancock Brook; Joseph Chadbourn, agent
1816	Hancock Brook: Chose John Pierce, John Watson, Asa Burbank—a Committee to Superintend building the Bridge
1818	Ossipee River bridge repairs: Thomas Spring, Joseph Chadbourn, Simeon Bucknell; John Warren agent, raise $100. Sept 1818 raise $400
1820	Saco River repair: Marshall Spring agent; Ossipee River repair: Jacob Lord, $500 for both (work to be paid at 75 cents per day)
1821	Saco River repair: Isaac Gray agent (work to be paid at 75 cents per day). Sept 1821 voted to dismiss Gray as agent. Chose Marshall Spring, John Bucknell & Ephraim Kimball a committee to Superintend the Repair of the bridge
1822	Saco River repair: Charles L. Wadsworth agent
1823	Ossipee River repair: John Warren agent
1823 Sept	Ossipee River build: Charles L. Wadsworth, Peleg Wadsworth, Esq., Alpheus Spring, Esq., John Warren, Esq., Capt Ephraim Kimball
1824	Ossipee River repair: Charles L. Wadsworth, Alpheus Spring, John Warren
1824 Nov	Ossipee River rebuild: Chose Alpheus Spring, Samuel McDonald, Marshall Spring a committee to examine said Bridge. 1825 April voted not to rebuild.
1825	Saco River and Hancock Bridge repair: Benjamin McDonald agent to Superintend
1826	Saco River repair: Alpheus Spring agent
1826	All bridges: Peleg Wadsworth Jr. agent to view

1826	Ossipee River build: Alpheus Spring agent to Superintend the building Said bridge
1826	Saco River: voted to prosecute the Petition for a toll Bridge, voted that the Selectmen take charge of the Petition
1827	Saco River repair: Voted that Benjamin Barker be an agent to superintend the repair of the bridge across Saco river under the direction of the Selectmen. Voted not to excuse Mr. Barker as agent for the bridge, & Ephraim Kimball as one of the committee (being one of the Selectmen) to direct him
1828	Saco River new bridge: Simeon Chadbourne agent to see when the covering & boards are completed
1830	Sept. 13, Ossipee River: Voted to choose Ben Chadbourne an Agent to consult with Cornish respecting the repairs of the upper bridge

Committee on Incorporation

| 1805 | Thomas Spring |
| 1806 | Thomas Spring (1805? DSC 0163), John Pierce |

Committee on a Plan for a Town House

| 1816 | Peleg Wadsworth, John Pierce, John Warren |

Constables

1804	Thomas Barker ?[504]
1806	Jacob Lord Jr.
1807	Jacob Lord Jr., voted in March 24, resigned & replaced with Winthrop Baston
1809	John Fly
1810	John Fly
1811	James Eastman under the condition he finish collecting taxes
1812	John Burbank

1812	John Bucknell Jr.
1813	Asa Burbank, John Bucknell Jr.
1814	Asa Burbank
1815	Asa Burbank
1816	Voted to merge with Collector Asa Burbank
1817	Voted to excuse John Pike Jr. & chose Alpheus Spring
1818	Andrew R. Bucknell
1819	Simeon Chadbourn
1820	Simeon Chadbourn
1821	Simeon Chadbourn
1822	Ephraim Kimball
1823	Benjamin Chadbourn
1824	Benjamin Chadbourn
1825	Levi Morrell
1826	Benjamin Chadbourn
1827	Andrew R. Bucknell
1828	Benjamin Chadbourn?
1828	Andrew R. Bucknell bid at $30.50
1829	Samuel Harmon 3% could not produce bond, elected John Warren, Esq. at 3.5%
1830	John Fly at $14.00

Cullers of Hogs and Steeres

| 1828 | Joseph Butterfield, James Brazier Jr., Gideon Chase, Benj. Chadbourn, John Clark, Edmund Thombs, John Bucknell Jr. |

Cullers of Hoops and Staves

1816	Simon Chadbourne, Gideon Chase, Marshall Spring, Aaron Rand
1817	Aaron Rand, Gideon Chase
1818	Aaron Rand
1819	Gideon Chase, Alpheus Spring, James Brazier, John Storer
1820	Benj. Swett, Alpheus Spring, Joseph Chadbourn
1821	Joseph Chadbourn, Simeon Chadbourn
1822	Simeon Chadbourn, Benjamin Chadbourn

---

504 Thomas Barker may have been Collector of Taxes, Constable, or Selectman per receipt for tasks of those offices (receipt for collecting taxes the year 1804 $4:41, taking the valuation & in voting & tending to get warrants set up & put up 1:82, to going to Brownfield .50, received $6:73 May 10, 1806).

1823	Aaron Rand, Henry Hyde, James Brazier, Edmund Tombs, Benjamin Chadbourn, John Stanley, Morris Clark, John Hodgdon
1824	Aaron Rand, Benj. Chadbourn, Joseph Butterfield
1825	no record
1826	Edmund Thombs, Aaron Rand, Benjamin Chadbourn, John Bucknell Jr., James Brazier, Jeremiah Trafton
1827	Joseph Butterfield, Aaron Rand, James Brazier, Daniel Small, Benjamin Chadbourn, Edmund Thombs, John Bucknell Jr., Samuel Ridlon, Morris Clarke, Joseph Butterfield, James Brazier Jr., Gideon Chase, Daniel Small, Benjamin Chadbourne, John Clark, Edmund Thombs [first use of "h" in Tombs], John Bucknell Jr., Samuel Ridlon, Edmund Tombs [Thombs], John A. Fly, Stephen Smith, Morris Clark, John Bucknell Jr., Benja Chadbourne, Gideon Chase, James Brazier Jr., Edmund Butterfield, Daniel Small

Fence Viewers

1811	Thomas Spring, Esq., John Watson
1815	Thomas Spring, Joseph Chadbourn, Josiah Mayberry, John Fly
1816	Simeon Bucknell, Charles L. Wadsworth
1817	Thomas Spring, John Warren, Aaron Richardson
1818	Loami Baston, Thos B. Watson, John W. Chadbourn
1819	Thomas Spring, Ephraim Kimball, Aaron Cross?
1820	Thomas Spring, Esq., Ephraim Kimball, John Warren
1821	Thomas Spring, Esq., Jonathan Lowell, Ephraim Kimball
1822	William Storer, Thomas Spring, Ephraim Kimball, Aaron Cross
1823	Thomas B. Watson, Jacob Lord, Josiah Maybury

1824	Marshall Spring, Edmond Thombs, Ephraim Kimball
1825	Thomas Day, William Cotton, William Storer
1826	Josiah Mayberry, Samuel Hammon
1827	John Bucknell, Daniel Small, Edmund Thombs
1828	Peleg Wadsworth Jr., John Bucknell Jr., Aaron Cross, John Fly, Edmund Thombs
1829	Nathaniel Warren, Andrew R. Bucknell
1830	Isaac Hamblin, Artemas Richardson, William C. Burbank, Stephen Gilpatrick, Isaac M. Storer

Field Drivers

1811	Aaron Richardson, Josiah Mayberry, David Durgin
1815	Aaron Richardson, Loammi Baston, Joseph Durgin
1816	Ephraim Kimball, Joseph Allen. Asa Burbank, Joseph Chadbourn, Josiah Mayberry voted at illegal meeting March 4 and not elected April 6.
1817	Winthrop Baston, Edward Richardson, John Howard, John W. Chadbourn
1818	Henry Hyde, Josiah Mayberry, Benjamin Bucknell, Royal Baston, John Warren
1819	Andrew R. Bucknell, Asa Osgood
1820	Joseph Howard, Asa Burbank, Aaron Cross
1821	Noah Wentworth, Royal Baston, John Storer
1822	Noah Wentworth, Abijah Lewis Jr., Simeon Chadbourn, William Storer, Royal Baston
1823	James Evans, Simeon Bucknell Jr., Moses Palmer, Alpheus Lewis, Jacob Lord
1824	Noah Wentworth, Richard Tripp, Robert Huntress, Andrew R. Bucknell
1825	no record
1826	no record
1827	Simeon Bucknell Jr., Benjamin Barker, Simeon Chadbourn, Edmund Thombs, Levi Morrell, Artemas Richardson

1828	Dr. Levi A. Hannaford, Andrew R. Bucknell, Edmund Tombs (Thombs), Noah Lewis
1829	no record
1830	Samuel L.? Pike, Nathaniel Warren

Hog Reeves

1807	voted to let hogs run at large with sufficient yokes and rings
1811	Aaron Richardson, Peleg Wadsworth, Loammi Baston (Bastern)
1812	Benjamin Bucknell
1815	John Fly, Josiah Mayberry, James Eastman, Winthrop Baston, John Chadbourne
1816	Noah Lewis, Asa Osgood, John W. Chadbourne, James Fly Jr.
1817	Noah Lewis, John Howard, John Durgin
1818	John Kimball, John Spring, Joseph Durgin Jr., Benj. Swett
1819	voted to let hogs run at large but not horses
1820	James McLucas, Noah Wentworth, Abijah Lewis
1821	Timothy Tibbets, James Brazier, Asa Osgood Jr., James Evans, Aaron Cross
1821	Voted that Swine shall not run at Large being Yoked and Ringed
1822	Seth Wadsworth, John Clark, Daniel Durgin, Jonathan Lowell, Peleg C. Wadsworth, Richard Trippe
1823	Jonathan Swett, Royal Brown, Jonathan Lowell, Jacob Lord Jr., John Clark
1824	no record
1825	Benj. Barker, Simon Whitney, Noah Barker

Justices of the Peace (incomplete list)

1807	Joseph Howard
1809	Peleg Wadsworth
1810	Peleg Wadsworth
1811	Thomas Spring
1812	Thomas Spring, Alpheus Spring
1813 or 1814	Peleg Wadsworth
1815	Peleg Wadsworth

1816	Benjamin Bucknell
1821	Peleg Wadsworth
1822	Peleg Wadsworth, Benjamin Bucknell
1823	Benjamin Bucknell
1824	Peleg Wadsworth
1825	Peleg Wadsworth
1827	Peleg Wadsworth, John Warren, Alpheus Spring
1828	Peleg Wadsworth , Benjamin Bucknell, John Warren, Alpheus Spring
1830	Thomas B. Watson

Measurer of Wood and Bark

1817	Benjamin Barker
1827	Benjamin Barker
1828	Benjamin Barker

Measurer of Wood

1822	Benjamin Barker

Money Clerk [unique title this year only]

1828	Simeon Bucknell Jr., Alpheus Spring, Thomas Lord, Samuel Pike, Jesse Kimball

Pound Keepers

1811	Samuel Sloper
1815	Samuel Sloper
1816	Samuel Sloper
1817	Samuel Sloper
1818	Samuel Sloper
1819	Asa Osgood Jr.
1820	Asa Osgood Jr.
1821	Eleazer Strout
1822	no record
1823	William Storer
1824	William Storer
1825	Joseph Chadbourn
1827	Isaac Storer
1828	Excused Isaac Storer, chose George Storer
1830	Isaac M. Storer

Sealer of Leather

1827	Peleg Wadsworth 3rd
1828	Peleg Wadsworth 3rd

Selectmen and Assessors and Overseers of the Poor

1803   John Pierce, John Burbank, Daniel Baston (the earliest record Llewellyn Wadsworth found and noted in his journal)

1804   Daniel Baston, John Pierce, John Burbank, Thomas Barker?[505]

1805   John Burbank, Thomas Barker, Charles Wadsworth, Daniel Baston? (receipt), John Pierce

1806   Daniel Baston, John Pierce, Israel Burbank [John Pierce, Asa Osgood before Town Meeting 1807]

1807   John Pierce, Asa Osgood, Joseph Chadbourne

1808   Peleg Wadsworth, John Watson, Thomas Spring

1809   Peleg Wadsworth, John Watson, Thomas Spring

1810   Thomas Spring

1811   Thomas B. Watson, John Pierce, Asa Osgood

1812   Peleg Wadsworth, Ephraim Kimball, Thomas Spring

1813   Peleg Wadsworth, Alpheus Spring, John Watson Jr.

1814   Peleg Wadsworth, John Warren, Alpheus Spring

1815   Peleg Wadsworth, John Warren, Asa Burbank

1816   Col. Marshall Spring, John Watson Jr., Rev. John Pike

1817   Peleg Wadsworth, Esq., John Watson Jr., Alpheus Spring

1818   Peleg Wadsworth, Esq., Simeon Chadbourn, John Warren

1819   Capt. Alpheus Spring, Ephraim Kimball, Joseph Howard

1820   Capt. Alpheus Spring, Ephraim Kimball, John Warren

1821   Peleg Wadsworth Jr., Simeon Chadbourn, John Watson Jr.

1822   Alpheus Spring, John Watson Jr., Simeon Chadbourne

1823   Col. John Warren, Benj. Bucknell, Simeon Chadbourne

1824   Col. John Warren, Benj. Bucknell, Alpheus Spring

1825   Benj. Bucknell, Alpheus Spring, Ephraim Kimball

1826   Benj. Bucknell, John Warren, Ephraim Kimball

1827   John Warren, Esq.1st , Ephraim Kimball 2nd , Lieut. Benj. Barker 3rd

1828   John Warren, Esq., Ephraim Kimball, Benj. Barker

1829   Benj. Barker, Capt. James Evans, John Bucknell

1830   Benj. Barker, Alpheus Spring, Levi A. Hannaford, MD

Surveyors of Boards

1811   William West

1820   Isaac Gray, Asa Burbank, John Warren, Marshall Spring

1822   James Evans, Asa Burbank, Marshall Spring, John Warren

1824   Marshall Spring, Asa Burbank, Tobias Cole, Isaac Stanley, Lemuel Jordan

1826   Jesse Kimball, Abraham Gray, Alpheus Spring, James Evans

Surveyors of Boards and Clapboards

1823   James Evans, Tobias Cole, John Warren, Marshall Spring, Asa Burbank

Surveyors of Boards, Clapboards, and Shingles

1817   Asa Burbank &Charles L. Wadsworth

1819   Marshall Spring, Isaac Gray, William Stanley

1821   Asa Burbank, Ephraim Kimball, John Warren, James Evans

Surveyors of Boards and Logs

1818   Issac Gray, Asa Burbank

1819   Marshall Spring, Isaac Gray, William Stanley

---

505 Thomas Barker may have been Collector of Taxes, Constable, or Selectman per receipt for tasks of those offices (receipt for collecting taxes the year 1804 $4:41, taking the valuation & in voting & tending to get warrants set up & put up 1:82, to going to Brownfield .50, received $6:73 May 10, 1806).

Surveyors of Boards, Plank Timber, Slitworks Clapboards, and Shingles

1816 Asa Burbank, Marshall Spring

Surveyors of Clapboards

1819 Asa Burbank, Marshall Spring

Surveyors of Clapboards and Shingles

1820 Marshall Spring, Asa Burbank

1821 James Evans, Marshall Spring, John Warren

Surveyors of Lumber

1807 Charles L. Wadsworth

1811 William West

1815 Charles L. Wadsworth, Asa Burbank, Gideon Chase, John Warren

1825 Simeon Chadbourn, Joseph Butterfield, Jesse Kimball, Samuel Jordan, Benj. McDonald, Isaac Stanley, James Evans, Benj. Chadbourn, Joseph Farnum, Simeon Whitney, Morris Clark, James Brazier

1826 no record

1827 Asa Burbank, Levi Lord, Isaac Stanley, Edward March, Joseph Butterfield, Ephraim Kimball (voted to excuse), chose Jesse Kimball

1827? A.B. Hubbard

1828 Asa Burbank, Gideon Chase, Jesse Kimball, Joseph Butterfield, Isaac Stanley, Simeon Chadbourne [first use of "e" at end]

1829 James Evans, Jesse Kimball, Abram Gray, Jonathan Haskell

1830 James Evans, Tobias Cole, Jesse Kimball, Josiah Mabry, Jonathan Haskell, Benja Chadbourne, Stephen Smith, John Bucknell Jr., John Storer

Surveyors of Split Lumber

1830 James Rankins, Joseph Farnham, Simeon Chadbourne, Daniel Small, Morris Clark. Voted to excuse Joseph Farnham, Chose Edmund Tombs [Thombs]

Surveyors of Wood and Bark

1827? Samuel D. Wadsworth, Samuel Stanley, Albion B. Benton

Surveyors of Highways

1807 John Watson, Thomas Spring, Benjamin Baston, John Fly, Jacob Lord Jr., Charles L. Wadsworth

1808 John Watson, Charles L. Wadsworth

1809 John Watson Jr., Charles L. Wadsworth

1811 Jonathan Lowell (crossed out), John Pierce, Asa Osgood, John Fly, Benjamin Baston

1812 Edward Lewis, John Spring

1813 Daniel Lane, Charles L. Wadsworth, Israel Burbank, Joseph Chadbourn, Joseph W. Chadbourn, Aaron Richardson

1814 No record

1815 Marshall Spring, Isaac Gray, Charles L. Wadsworth, Henry Barns, Ephraim Tibbets, John Howard, David Newcomb

1816 Marshall Spring, Edward Richardson, John Howard, Joseph Chadbourn, John Warren, John Pierce Jr., Charles L. Wadsworth were voted at illegal meeting 4 March. John Pierce Jr. was replaced by David Newcomb at meeting 6 April.

1817 Alpheus Spring, Thomas B. Watson, Charles L. Wadsworth, Ephraim Tibbets, John W. Chadbourn, John Howard, Reuben Lowell, Ephraim Kimball

1818 Marshall Spring, Isaac Gray, Charles L. Wadsworth, Joseph Howard Jr., Jacob Lord, Benj. Baston, John Howard, Ephraim Kimball, John Pierce

1819 Marshall Spring, John Watson Jr., Ephraim Kimball, Charles L. Wadsworth, Joseph Howard, Jacob Lord, John Howard, John Pierce Jr., Stephen Gilpatrick, James Fly, William Cotton

1820 Marshall Spring, Asa Osgood Jr., Joseph Howard, Stephen Gilpatrick,

Peleg Wadsworth Jr., Jonathan Wentworth, John Warren, William Cotton, James Fly, John Pierce Jr., Josiah Mayberry

1821   Dura Wadsworth, Isaac Gray, Peleg Wadsworth Jr., John Howard, John Flye, Joseph Chadbourn, Joseph Mayberry, William Cotton, Jesse Kimball, James Eastman, William Stanley, Temple Huntress, Levi Lord, Edward Lewis

1822   Marshall Spring, Simeon Chadbourn, Jonathan Wentworth, John Howard, Peleg Wadsworth Jun., Ephraim Kimball, John Fly, John Warren, William Cotton, Edward Lewis, James Gubtill, Stephen Gilpatrick, Temple Huntress, Allen Hubbard, John Spring, James Fly

1823   Marshall Spring, Tobias Cole, Simeon Chadbourn, Edmund Tombs, John York, Peleg Wadsworth Jr., John Hodgdon, John Fly, Joseph D. Boynton, Odebiah Gerrish, John Howard, John Spring, Samuel Folsome, Stephen Gilpatrick, Edward Lewis, Temple Huntress, Levi Lord, John Stanley

1824   John Pierce, Simeon Chadbourn, Ephraim Wentworth, John Howard, Aaron Williams, Stephen Gillpatrick [Gilpatrick], Isaac Stanley, Timothy Tibbets, Benja Chadbourn, Edmund Thombs, William Cotton, Edward Lewis, Levi Lord, Temple Huntress, Royal Baston, Joseph D. Boynton, Peleg Wadsworth Jr., Henry W. Barnes, Ephraim Kimball

1825   Andrew R. Bucknell, Benj. McDonald, Allen Hubbard, Ephraim Kimball, John Kimball, Peleg Wadsworth Jr., Solomon Hartford, John Warren, Samuel Ridlon, John Howard, William Cotton, Edward Lewis, John Storer, Aaron Williams, Gideon Chase, Samuel Hammons, John Wadsworth

1826   Marshall Spring, Benj. McDonald, George Sutton, John Clark, Jonathan Wentworth, Peleg Wadsworth Jr., Stephen Gilpatrick, Benj. Whales, Ben Baston, Reuben Sewell, Ben Chadbourn, Solomon Hartford, Jos. Farnum, William Huntress, Isaac Stanley, Aaron Williams, Levi Lord, John Howard, John Wadsworth

1827   Simeon Bucknell Jr., Benjamin Barker, Thomas B. Watson, Allen Hubbard, Daniel Small, Henry S. Burbank, Jeremiah Trafton, Artemas Richardson, Joseph Storer, Benjamin Baston, Aaron Williams, Peleg Wadsworth Jr., John Fly, John Warren, George Gould, Stephen Gilpatrick, John Huntress, Benjamin Whale, Daniel Lowell (alias David Lowell), Obediah Gerrish, Isaac Stanley (chosen instead of George Goold [Gould] who moved out of town), Moses Palmer (voted to reconsider), John Wadsworth (voted to excuse).

1828   Artemas Richardson, Thomas Lowell, Benj. Chadbourne Jr., Lemuel Cotton, Aaron Williams, Peleg Wadsworth Jr., John Fly, Joseph Farnham, Charles Wadsworth, Temple Huntress, Gideon Chase, John McDonald

1829   Simeon Bucknell Jr., E Wentworth, Ben Barker, Peleg Wadsworth Jr., Eph. Kimball, Richard Heath, Joseph Durgin, John Fly, Stephen Gilpatrick, Lemuel Cotton, Artemas Richardson, John McDonald, Joseph Howard, Aaron Williams, John Clark, Edmund Tombs [Thombs], John Wadsworth, Thomas Lowell, Edmund Butterfield, Samuel Clemmons, Allen Hubbard, John Huntress, Peleg C. Wadsworth, Edward Richardson

1830   Timothy E. Meader, Daniel Pierce, Alpheus Spring, Peleg Wadsworth, Thomas Mabry, Thomas Goodwin Jr., John Storer, Living Cotton, Joshua Robins [Robbins], Jeduthan Alexander, Joseph Howard, Aaron Williams, Hosea Allen, Edmund Tombs [Thombs], Obediah Gerrish (excused, chose Peleg C. Wadsworth), Noah Lewis, Gideon Chase, Aaron Cross, George Sutton, Temple Huntress, Jacob Stanley excused, Edward Richardson, Stephen Wentworth, Richard Heath, Charles Wadsworth, John Wadsworth (excused, chose Noah Pike, voted to excuse, chose Obediah Gerrish), Joshua Robins

Tithingmen

1811	Peleg Wadsworth, Asa Osgood
1815	James Fly, Asa Osgood
1816	James Fly, Thomas B. Watson
1817	James Fly, Jeremiah Trafton
1818	Jeremiah Trafton, James Fly
1819	Thomas B. Watson, Royal
1820	John Watson, Loammi Baston
1821	William Stanley, John Hodgson, Thomas B. Watson, Benjamin Bucknell
1822	Thomas B. Watson, Robert Huntress
1823	Thomas B. Watson, John Warren
1824	Thomas Joseph, Thomas B. Watson
1825	John Watson, Dura Wadsworth, Henry W. Barnes
1826	Dura Wadsworth, John Watson

1827	John Watson, Simeon Chadbourne, Robert Huntress (voted not to excuse)
1828	Thomas Goodwin, Thomas B. Watson, Alpheus Spring
1829	Thomas B. Watson, James Evans
1830	Thomas Goodwin, Thomas B. Watson, Ben McDonald, John Fly

Treasurers

1804	Capt. Thomas Spring
1805	Capt. Thomas Spring
1806	Capt. Thomas Spring
1807	Capt. Thomas Spring
1808	Capt. Thomas Spring, Peleg Wadsworth
1809	Capt. Thomas Spring
1811	John Watson
1812	Capt. Thomas Spring, Peleg Wadsworth
1813	Peleg Wadsworth
1814	Peleg Wadsworth
1815	Peleg Wadsworth
1816	Peleg Wadsworth
1817	Peleg Wadsworth
1818	Peleg Wadsworth
1819	Jacob Stanley
1820	Marshall Spring
1821	1830 Peleg Wadsworth Jr.

APPENDIX 15
Student Scholar Numbers in Districts 5, 6, and 7, 1814, 1815, 1818

Amount unexpended by District 5 shared with 5, 6, 7
Number of scholars by household 1814 and 1818
N.B. This document dated December 29, 1821, retroactively distributes amounts not expended by District 5 based on the number of children for the years 1814, 1815, and 1818.
Source: Maine State Archives, Hiram Box 8.

1814 District No. 5		**No. 6**		**No. 7**	
Stephen Tibbets	3	Joseph Chadbourn	4	Jacob Lord	4
Moody Brown	4	Will Storer	5	Joseph Durgin	4
William Gray	1	J.W. Chadbourn	1	Samuel Durgin	7
Widow McLucas	3	John Fly	3	John Warren	3
Total	11	Total	13	Samuel Merrifield	4
Due Dist. No. 5 for 1814	$16.96			Levi Lord	2
Due 1815	19.87			John McLucas	3
Due 1818	38.47			Jonathan Treadwell	2
				David Durgin, Jr.	2
				Total	31

Due	for 1814	for 1815
Due No. 5	5.39	3.97
Due No. 6	6.37	4.70
Due No. 7	15.20	11.20

In 1818 the following persons composed Dist. No. 5 but are now divided into

District No. 5		**No. 6**		**No. 7**	
Joseph Gray	1	Joseph Chadbourn	4	Samuel Merrifield	4
Stephen Tibbets	4	Will Storer	4	John Warren	6
Moody Brown	3	J. W. Chadbourn	1	Joseph Durgin	5
Stephen Tibbets Jr.	3	Joseph Howard	1	Samuel Durgin	5
Total	11	John Fly	4	Jacob Lord	4
		John McLucas	3	Stephen Roberts	1
		Total	17	Ephraim Tibbets	2
				David Durgin Jr.	4
				Total	31

Due Dist. No. 5 for 1818	$7.17
Due Dist. No. 6	11.09
Due Dist. No. 7	20.21
Total	38.47

[dated] Hiram Dec. 29th, 1821, [signed] Peleg Wadsworth Jr., John Watson Jr., Selectmen & Assessors of Hiram

APPENDIX 16

Student Scholars by Household, 1810, 1813

1810 Number of Scholars by Household—District No. 1

Names	Number of Scholars
Mr. John Andres	1
Winthrop Baston	1
Abijah Lewis	5
Joseph Adams	2
Jonathan Lowell	5
John Pierce	7
Thomas Spring Esqr	3
Simeon Bucknell	2
Thomas Barker	7
Israel Burbank	3
Total	36

1810 Number of Scholars by Household—District No. 2

Mr. John Robbins	2
William Cotton	5
Benjamin Baston	6
James Eastman	4
James Fly Jr.	7
Nathaniel Williams	6
Eli Clemons	2
Daniel Lane	4
Jonathan Clemons	2
Lemuel Howard	1
Marshall Lewis	4
Total	43

1813 Number of Scholars by Household—District No. 3

7 January 1813

Charles L. Wadsworth	8
Peleg Wadsworth	5
Total	13

1813 Number of Scholars by Household—District No. 5

27 November 1813

Joseph Chadbourn Class Master	
Jacob Lord	4
Joseph Durgin	4
Joseph Chadbourn	5
William Storer	5
Stephen Tibbetts	3
Samuel Durgin	7
John Warren	3
Samuel Merrifield	5
Levi Lord	2
John McLucas	3
John Chadbourn	1
Moody Brown	5
Widow McLucas	3
Widow Hartford	5
John Fly	3
Jonathan Tredwell	2
Total	60

Signed [506]
Jacob Lord
Joseph Durgin
John Warren
John Fly
Stephen Tibbets
John W. Chadbourn
John McLucas
Levi Lord
William Storer
Samuel Merrifield
Joseph Lord

Source: Maine State Archives, Hiram Box 8.

---

506 Widow McLucas and Widow Hartford did not sign because they had no right to vote.

APPENDIX 17
School Teachers, School Agents, School Committees

[] refers to information inserted by the compiler
refers to the number of each school district

Class Masters and Mistresses
Source: Maine State Archives,
Hiram Box 8, (except as noted).

1778	John Burbank (perhaps the first teacher)[507]
1804	James Fly Jr., John Goodenow, John Burbank, John Bucknell #5
1811	William Storer #5 & 6
1819	Charles L. Wadsworth #3, William Cotton #4, John Warren #5
1820	William Cotton #4
1821	Miss Mary A. Merrill #1, Miss Mary Benton #5, Olive Johnson #6 (summer), John Warren #7
1822	Alpheus Spring #1 (3 months) Asa Osgood Jr. #2

School Agents
Source: Hiram Town Clerk Records. Agents were elected at town meetings. Names are spelled as they appear in the original records.

1819	Alpheus Spring #1, Ephraim Kimball #2, Charles L. Wadsworth #3, William Cotton #4, John Warren #5, William Stanley #6
1820	John Bucknell #1, Ephraim Kimball #2, Charles L. Wadsworth #3 [no record of Districts #4, #5, #6]
1821	John Bucknell #1, Ephraim Kimball #2, Charles L. Wadsworth #3, William Cotton #4, Henry Barnes #5, Humphrey A. Chadbourne #6, John Warren #7, William Stanley #8
1822	Alpheus Spring #1, Ephraim Kimball #2, Charles L. Wadsworth #3, James Fly #4, Timothy Tibbets #5, Humphrey A. Chadbourn #6, John Warren #7, Samuel Ridlon #8, Allen Hubbard #9

1823	John Bucknell #1, Benjamin McDonald #2, Peleg Wadsworth Jr. #3, James Fly #4, Henry W. Barrons [Barnes] #5, Humphrey A. Chadbourn #6, John Warren #7, Peleg Wadsworth #8, Joseph D. Boynton #9
1824	Royal Baston #1, Ephraim Kimball #2, Peleg Wadsworth Jr. #3, Stephen Gillpatrick #4, Solomon Hartford #5, Benj. Chadbourn #6, John Warren, Esq. #7, Peleg C. Wadsworth #8, Joseph D. Boynton #9
1825	John Bucknell, John Kimball, Peleg Wadsworth Jr., Moses Palmer, Timothy Tibbets, Benj. Chadbourn, John Warren, Peleg C. Wadsworth, Allen Hubbard, Jeremiah Trafton, Charles Wadsworth
1826	John Bucknell, Benj. Barker, Peleg Wadsworth Jr., Aaron Williams, John Storer Jr., Ben Chadbourn, Edmund Thombs, Peleg C. Wadsworth, Allen Hubbard, Morris Clark and Charles Wadsworth
1827	John Pierce Jr., Alpheus Spring, Peleg Wadsworth Jr., Artemas Richardson, John Stanley, Benj. Chadbourn [voted to excuse from service], Edmund Thombs, John Storer, Isaac Stanley, Allen Hubbard, John Wadsworth, Charles Wadsworth
1828	James Evans, John Kimball, Peleg Wadsworth Jr., Aaron Williams, Henry Barns [Henry W. Barnes], Benj. Chadbourne, John Warren, Esq., Isaac Stanley, George Sutton, Obediah Gerish [Gerrish], Richard Trippe, John Clark
1829	James Evans #1, Ben Barker #2, Peleg Wadsworth Jr. #3, Artemas Richardson #4, Henry W. Barnes #5, Samuel Chadbourne #6, John Warren, Esq. #7, Isaac Stanley #8, Allen Hubbard #9,

---

507 Gideon T. Ridlon, *Saco Valley Settlements and Families*, 147.

John Wadsworth #10, Richard Tripp #11, John Clark #12, Eph. Wentworth #13

1830   Simeon Bucknell Jr., Isaac Hamblin. Voted to reconsider the last two votes. Chose Peleg Wadsworth, Aaron Williams, Henry W. Barns, Ben Chadbourne, Edmund Tombs, Peleg C. Wadsworth, Thomas Lord, Obediah Gerrish, Stephen Gillpatrick, Hosea Allen. Voted to excuse H. Allen. Chose John Clark, Moses E. Wentworth.

School Committees

Source: Hiram Town Clerk Records.

1816	A committee of three was chosen instead of an additional school agent. Chose Peleg Wadsworth, Alpheus Spring, John Pierce.
1817	Selectmen
1818	Selectmen
1819	Selectmen
1820	Selectmen
1821	Thomas B. Watson, Alpheus Spring, Benj. Bucknell, Esq.
1822	Alpheus Spring, Benjamin Bucknell, Asa Osgood Jr.
1823	Peleg Wadsworth Jr., Thomas B. Watson, Levi Morrell
1824	Levi Morrell, Benj. Bucknell, Peleg Wadsworth Jr.
1825	Benj. Bucknell, Peleg Wadsworth Jr., Alpheus Spring
1826	Alpheus Spring, Peleg Wadsworth Jr., Levi A. Hannaford
1827	Alpheus Spring, Levi A. Hannaford, Peleg Wadsworth Jr.
1828	Alpheus Spring, Esq., Peleg Wadsworth Jr., Thomas B. Watson, Esq.
1829	Timothy E. Meader, Nathan Kimball, Peleg Wadsworth Jr.
1830	Peleg Wadsworth, Timothy E. Meader, Nathan Kimball

APPENDIX 18
School Teacher Rates of Pay

Source: Maine State Archives, Hiram Box 8.
Receipts are in original language.

1804 John Goodenow $42 for teaching school 12 weeks, rate of $3.50 per week

1821 Dist 1. Miss Mary A. Merrill has taught a school for the year 20 weeks 7 shillings per week, board 6 shilling per week = $43.33. John Bucknell, Agent. Dec. 21, 1821

1821 Dist 2. Last summer 12 weeks @ 7/6 per week & board of mistress 6 shilling per week = $27, $2.50 for Agent = $29.54. Ephraim Kimball, Agent. Dec. 21, 1821

1821 Dist 3. This may certify that a school was kept last spring 21 days @ $15 dollars per month = $14.32. Charles L. Wadsworth, Agent, Sept. 25, 1821

1821 Dist 5. Miss Mary Benton kept a school last summer 8 weeks @ $2 per week & boarded herself. Henry W. Barnes, Agent, Nov. 16, 1821

1821 Dist 6. Miss Olive Johnson has taught a school the term of 12 weeks $1 per week, board $.75 per week, $1.50 as compensation for agency = $22.50. Humphrey A. Chadbourn, Agent, Sept. 22, 1821

1821 Dist 7. 8 weeks in the fall $1 per week for the schooling, $1 per week boarding the school mistress = $16. John Warren, Agent, Dec. 24, 1821

1822 Dist 1. 16 weeks $1 per week for Mistress, $1 per week for boarding & $2 dollars for Agency. Alpheus Spring, Agent, Sept. 20, 1822

1822 Dist 1. Alpheus Spring Esq. has taught 3 months @$16 per month = $48. John Bucknell, Agent, April 1, 1822

1822 Dist 2. Term of 4 months @ $10 per month. Please to make order to Asa Osgood, Jr. Ephraim Kimball, Agent, Sept. 20, 1822

1822 Dist 5. 12 weeks $1 per week for the mistress & one dollar per week for her board & $3.50 for Agency. Timothy Tibbets, Agent, Sept. 9, 1822

1822 Dist 6. 12 weeks at the rate of $4 per week for the mistress, 5 shillings & six pence per week for board, 50 cents for Agency. Humphrey A. Chadbourn, Agent, Sept. 9, 1822.

1822 Dist 7. Two months $8 for instructor, $8 for board. John Warren, Agent, Nov. 12, 1822

1822 Dist 8. $4.50 per month for mistress & $4 per month for board & $2 for wood & $2 for agency = $29.50, Samuel Ridlon, Agent, Dec. 21, 1822

APPENDIX 19

Services Rendered to Paupers

Receipts for goods and services rendered to paupers and submitted for reimbursement[508]

Original spelling is preserved. Names of individuals requesting reimbursement for services are <u>underlined</u>.

Stephen Burbank

1813 April 12 <u>John Watson Jr.</u> 25 cents for going to Wadsworth's to consult the removal of Stephen Burbank

1816 March 4 at the Annual Town Meeting it was voted to authorize Peleg Wadsworth to complete collection of Stephen Burbank's rate bills (taxes).

1817 April 7 the Town was asked to come to the assistance of the Stephen Burbank family now in Porter. The Town voted one hundred dollars for the support of the Poor, and to dispose of the family "discressionaly."

1821 April 7 <u>Winthrop Baston</u> received $11.25 for expenses related to Stephen Burbank pauper.

1823 Feb 14 <u>Ben Thompson</u> visit & medicine & wife distance 8 miles $1.55

Feb 15 visit & medicine Burbank's wife $1.50
March 7 ditto $1.50
April 2 ditto $1.50=$6.05

1823 Feb 20 <u>Widow Lilla[?]</u> 1 week 2 days as nurse in family S. Burbank $1.25

1823 Feb 20 <u>Joseph Boynton</u> holling wood 4 feet[509] for Stephen Burbank $0.58, holling wood 1 cord $1.25, ½ bushel wheat $0.87

Feb 10 holling wood 4 feet $0.50
Feb 17 ½ bushel wheat $0.87
March holling wood 4 feet $0.50, holling wood 1 cord $1.25
March 22 2 cord wood $2.50, pills $0.10
April 1 1/2 bushel wheat $0.87
April 5 1 cord wood 7/6 $1.25=$11.79. The Committee on Accounts allowed the bill with a deduction of $3.92=$7.83

1823 March 8 <u>Simeon Chadbourne</u> for notifying Overseers of Cumberland that family of Stephen Burbank had become chargeable to town of Hiram and requesting their removal $1.25, time spent victualing S. Burbank $1.00=$2.25

1823 March <u>Benjamin Swett</u> 41 lb pork $5.12
April 5 boarding S. Burbank $0.88=$6.00

1823 April <u>Eleazer Strout</u>[510] digging grave for wife of S. Burbank $1.00

1823 April 8 <u>Henry L. Burbank</u> taking care of S. Burbank while crazy 20 days & 10 nights $20. Overseers allowed with deduction of $10=$10

1823 April 8 <u>Benjamin Barker</u> ~~3 yds cotton cloth for Miss Burbank $0.75~~
April 15 8 lb pork $1.04, 2 11/16 lb butter $0.38, 3/8 yd muslin $0.22, tape & thread $0.08, 2 qt ginn $0.50, 1 lb sugar $0.13, 17 candles/10=$2.45

1823 April 8 <u>Simeon Chadbourne</u> 1 day pauper bus[iness] $0.50, to Cumberland to settle with Overseers, S. Burbank family $2.50, paid Mr. Abbott for serving papers to Portland $0.25=$3.25

1823 March <u>Alpheus Spring</u> going to Bridge & making a notice to Overseers Cumberland $0.25, posting notice to persons holding accts against

---

508   Maine State Archives, Hiram Box 14, except as noted.

509   Fire wood cut 4 feet long.

510   Eleazer Strout was himself a pauper, U.S. census 1850.

Overseers on acct of Burbank family $1.00
April 5 1 day on said accounts $1.00=$2.25

1823 April 8 John Warren visiting S.
Burbank family & settling accts for supplies 1 day $1.00
April 14 ½ day paupers accts making orders $0.50
May 14 ditto $0.50=$2.00

1823 April 17 George Sutton cloths to lay out Mrs.
Burbank $1.50, Dorcas Hubbard care of S. Burbank
1 week $1.00=$2.50

1823 July 16 Israel Burbank rec'd $1.00 for 8 lb pork
delivered to Stephen Burbank family in April last

1823 April 8 Benj Bucknell 1 day visiting family S.
Burbank $1.00
April 14 ½ day Pauper business drawing orders $0.50,
1 pr pantaloons for S. Burbank $1.50
May 14 ½ day settling paupers with Boynton et al
$0.50=$3.50

1823 June 12 Overseers of Poor, Cumberland.

"Cumberland June 12, 1823. Gentlemen, your letter of the 10th instant in this day rec'd. In answer we say we are now, and ever have been ready to pay to the town of Hiram all reasonable expenses of Stephen Burbank and his wife since they became inhabitants of this town, but did expect you to furnish us with your account of what expense has arisen to you, on their account, in order that we might settle with you for the same, which we have not received. Your letter notifying us that they had become chargeable, nor the one we have just rec'd furnishes us no account whatever, what the expenses have been to you, and your charge against us. You will please to forward us your bill and also have the goodness to inform us what is the situation of the two paupers. Please to write by mail, if an opportunity should not present of writing to us sooner.

Yours Respectfully David Prince, Moody Buxton—Oversees of Poor, Cumberland"

1823 May 15 James Burbank requested $6.50 for support S. Burbank wife 1 week & half.
The Overseers denied the request. "We think he ought not have anything as he was not engaged by the Overseers."

1823 June 30 Overseers Cumberland $89.10 paid in full for all supplies & support of S. Burbank family from 7 Feb 1823 to 30 June 1823 including funeral expenses of Mrs. Burbank

1850

"I Nathan Kimball of Hiram depose & say that I was well acquainted with Stephen Burbank late of this town, deceased. Said Burbank became a town charge in the Spring of 1850 leaving neither widow nor minor children. I was town agent in 1850 and in that capacity paid the last board bill of said Burbank in May 1850. It also appears by the town books that the bills for the funeral expense were paid by me Sept. 9, 1850. I have no interest in the subject matter of this affidavit. Appeared before me Nathan Kimball whom I certify is a man of truth & veracity [signed] Justice of the Peace."

Daniel Hickey[511]

1809 March 4. Hiram for boarding and clothing to 31 December 1808 $54.75

1810 March 8. Hiram for boarding and clothing and doctoring to 22 Jan. 1810 $67.20

1811 February 27. Baldwin for boarding to 1 January 1811 $36.30

1812 June. Baldwin for boarding and clothing to 1 May 1812 $89.23

1813 June. Baldwin for boarding and clothing to 1 May 1813 $21.25
1814 January. Baldwin for board to 1 January 1814 $45.15

---

511 Massachusetts. General Court. Acts and Resolves. Pauper Accounts.

1815 January. <u>Baldwin</u> for boarding and clothing to 1 January 1815 $67.20

1816 January. <u>Baldwin</u> for boarding and clothing to 1 Jan. 1816 $67.20

1816 June. <u>Baldwin</u> for support to 1 May 1816 $22.35

1816 November. <u>Baldwin</u> for board and clothing to 1 November 1816 $33.60

1817 June. <u>Baldwin</u> for board and clothing to 1 May 1817 $19.00

1818 June. <u>Baldwin</u> for board and clothing to 1 May 1818 $37.96

1819 June. <u>Baldwin</u> for board, clothing, doctoring, and nursing to 1 May 1819 $37.96

Jeremiah McLucas

"1821 Jan 26 Portland. Jeremiah McLucas an inhabitant of your town has become chargeable in this town as a Pauper. We conceive it necessary to give you this information that you may order his removal or otherwise provide for him as you may judge expedient. We have charged the expense of his support which has already arisen to your town and shall continue to do so, so long as we are obliged to furnish him with supplies. He is in our gaol at an expense of two dollars per week. We, gentlemen, with much respect, your most obedient and humble servants."

1821 Jan 26–Feb 1 Portland for support of Jeremiah McLucas 5 days $1.43, wood $0.35=$1.48

John McLucas family

1819 Mar 4 <u>Joseph Howard</u> visiting John McLucas family & employing a team to hol him wood & supplying provisions $2.25

1819 March <u>J Durgin's</u> account $10.25:
March 11 <u>Joseph & John Durgin</u> holling wood for

John McLucas, braking road, wood holling 2 hands 4 oxen 1 day $3.00
March 15 cutting & holling wood $1.50
March 19 cutting & holling wood 4 oxen 3 hands $5.00
March 20 cutting & holling wood to the Poor 1 day. $075=10.25

1819 March 15 <u>Alpheus Spring</u> account 1 day arrange business relative to John McLucas family $1.50

1819 April–July <u>Joseph Howard</u> acct April 6 team to hol wood for John McLucas 3/0 1 day spent purchase provision $1.50, boarding Eliza McLucas 3 weeks at 2/0 per week $1.00, keeping 5 days longer & moving to & from hoam $1.00
May 20 going for the doctor for John McLucas $0.75
July 20 going with Mr. Pierce for John McLucas $0.75, boarding Ruth McLucas 4 weeks 3/ per week $2.00, 1 gown for Ruth McLucas $1.25=$8.25

1819 March–Sept <u>John Warren's</u> account March 19 ½ bushel potatoes delivered to J McLucas $0.25, 11 lbs fish @ .05 per pound. $0.54
March 26 half barrel of potatoes 1/6 $0.25
April 6 carrying provisions to McLucas $0.40
April 7 hauling wood for J McLucas ½ day with oxen & horse 4/6 per day $0.12
April 28 cutting wood 1 day 4/6 $0.74, cutting ditto at Gore 1/6 $0.24, carrying John McLucas to Town meeting $0.17
May 3 to Cornish for McLucas $0.17
Sept 1 carrying home from Porter line to the road near John W. Chadbourne $1.00, pay 4 bushell apples 1/6 per bushel 1.00=$4.88

1819 Apr 6–July 20 <u>Joseph Howard</u> account April 6 team to hol wood for John McLucas 3/0 1 day spent purchase provision $1.50, boarding Eliza McLucas 3 weeks at 2/0 per week $1.00, keeping 5 days longer & moving to & from hoam $1.00
May 20 going for the doctor for John McLucas $0.75
July 20 going with Mr. Pierce ditto $0.75, boarding Ruth McLucas 4 weeks 3/ per week $2.00, 1 gown for Ruth McLucas $1.25=$9.50
1819 July 5 town meeting voted to set up John McLucas & family at vendue to go to the persons

who will take him the lowest & his wife & youngest Child to go with him if they Please. Struck off to Mr. John Pierce at nine dollars & ninety Cents per month.

1819 July 31 Ephraim Kimball board of John McLucas a town pauper from July 31, 1819 to Sept 18, 1819 at 5 shillings per week $5.75

1819 Sept 20 town meeting voted property of John McLucas to be rented, Winthrop Baston bid John McLucas Jr. at 55 cents per week to board, Winthrop Baston to take John McLucas & child $6, provide a plan for McLucas boy, voted $150 for poor, to sell land formerly of John McLucas to John Clark $58 Town Clerk Records Vol 1 p95

1820 April 1 Winthrop Baston approved keeping John McLucas for 17 weeks at $0.55 per week $9.35, 2 yards of cotton & wool cloath for jacot & trowsers & making them up making 2 $1.33, 3 yard of shirten at $0.30 yd=$0.90, making pair f[?] shirts $0.33=$11.01

1820 April 3 Winthrop Baston to take on John McLucas & one Child for Six Dollars per

Month. Voted that the Selectmen provide a plan for McLucas Boy.

1820 April 14 Alpheus Spring making indenture for John McLucas Jr. $0.25
April 15 ½ day settling with Treasurer & executing indenture $0.50=$0.75

1820 April 15, voted at town meeting to sell land of John McLucas

1820 Aug 22 Winthrop Baston rec'd $8.00 in part for keeping McLucas the present year by order of Treasurer

1820 April 20 Moses C. Buswell vs. Town of Hiram absinth for John McLucas $1.00

1820 Apr 1–March 31, 1821 Ephraim Kimball paid Winthrop Baston for boarding & clothing John McLucas & child $66.80.

1821 Jan Dr. Joseph Benton acct allowed

1822 March 30 visit for McLucas $0.34, $1.00, $0.87. $1.00, $0.87, $0.75,$0 .75,$0.87, McLucas child $0.25=$7.25.

1821 March 28 Winthrop Baston interest on several months keeping 1 home maid $1.50, 12 yd & ½ of shirten $5.25, 1 yd woolen cloath $0.50, making a pair of shirts & trowsers $0.75, ditto making little shirts $0.25, mending his coats out of season $0.75=$9.00, boarding McLucas & child $72.00 Committee on Accounts allows $66.00

1821 March 28 funeral charges, the Trubble of sick child 4 weeks $4.00, going after Hadley & Benton $0.51, digging grave $0.50, making coffin $1.17, John Spring horse & slay to the grave $0.25 Committee allows $2.00

1821 April 2 John Spring rec'd $20 of Overseers Hiram in full for taking John McLucas Jr. for indenture

1821 April 14 Cotton Lincoln gall molasses $0.40 to McLucas

1821 Winthrop Baston account for funeral expenses was accepted at Town Meeting 16 April 1821, *Town Clerk Records*, p.117

1821 Mar–Dec Peleg Wadsworth Jr. Mar 29 1 ½ yd coarse woolen cloth for McLucas child $0.50, sundries allowed Mr. Strout for keeping McLucas $2.52, sundries for support of Mr. John Whale's grandson $4.21
April 19 2/3 day of John Cotton 1 yoke oxen & cart moving John McLucas & family from William Gray's to Mr. Strout's $1.00
Dec 17 getting a place for McLucas & family & attending their moving $0.50=$8.73

1821 June 4–7 Dec Peleg Wadsworth account supplies at $0.32 per week 28 weeks $36.86
Oct hauling load of wood $0.25, ditto 3 loads partly green $2.00, ditto 1 load old wood $0.25
Nov. ditto 1 load green $0.58, paid Wm Pierce of

hauling 3 ½ cord wood & cutting up $5.00, 1 ½ yds flannel homespun at 4p for McLucas $1.00, 7 ½ yd cotton $2.25 & 3 ¼ flannel $2.00=$4.33, moving McLucas family & household stuff from Strouts to my house last June $0.75=52.02, second hand coat 12f ditto trowsers 6 McLucas $3.00=$55.02, deduct as charged by P. W. Jr. $1.00=$54.02

1821 June 6 Cotton Lincoln accnt paid John McLucas $2.00

1821 Dec 17 agreement of Solomon Hartford to support John McLucas and 2 children

"…promises and agrees to supply John McLucas and his two youngest children with good food, house room, fire, lodging at his own dwelling house, from this time until the third Monday in April next at the rate of two dollars & twenty five cents per week for all the time he shall so supply & the said Hartford also agrees to transport said McLucas, his family & furniture from the house where they now live to his own house at his own expense. And said Overseers on their part agree to furnish said Hartford with an order from the Selectmen of Hiram on the Treasurer of said Hiram for whatever their supplies shall amount to at the above rate; said order to be given on the said third Monday of April next. The wife of said McLucas is to have the privilege of making her home at said Hartfords so long as she behaves & they can agree." Peleg Wadsworth Jr., John Watson, Overseers

1821 Simeon Chadbourne paid John McLucas $1.33 Paid Eleazer Strout for keeping John McLucas & 2 children 48 days at 49.00 per month=$13.02 Paid Strout for frock & trowsers for McLucas $2.75, for pair of stent[?] Stockings $0.25, for helping move McLucas & making gown $0.63 1 pt rum for McLucas $0.17 1 pt W rum paid Strout for McLucas $0.09, 1 ½ pints W Rum $0.25, 1 ½ W rum del'd McLucas $0.14, 1 pt W rum $0.09, 1 pair shoes $1.75=$22.48 (less Grace Merrifield) Paid Abijah Lewis for making coffin $2.00, P. W. Jr. by paid Strout deduct $2.59=$21.96

1822 Mar 9 Eleazer Strout rec'd in full for keeping John McLucas & family April 19, 1821 to June 4 6 weeks 4 days $25.29

1822 April 18 Stephen Gilpatrick I have given Mr. John McLucas up my bid he will keep the child himself for the same that I was to have.

1822 April 20 Solomon Hartford rec'd $38.00 in full for support John McLucas & family 17 Dec to April 15, 1822

1822 Simeon Chadbourne for supplies delivered to John McLucas, paid Cotton Lincoln 12/ $2.00, cash paid for goods 6/ $1.00, cloth for a pare of trowsers 12/ $3.00, 1 pare of shoes 9/ $1.50, 5 yds cotton cloth=$10.75 1822 supplies for John McLucas & family 30 lb beef at 6 cts $1.80, ½ bushel corn $0.50, transporting same $0.30=$2.60

1823 March 15 John Warren $7.55 for supplies John McLucas

1823 April 5 Jacob Lord supporting Abigail McLucas [wife of John McLucas Jr.] 48 weeks food $0.33=$15.84, pair of shirts $0.63, 1 gown $0.63, 1 shift $0.34, cloth going down for gown $0.62=$18.06

1823 April 8 Simeon Chadbourne Pauper business & getting a place for Mrs. McLucas & moving her to Joseph Gray $2.00, 1 sheep with John McLucas the fall of 1822 $2.00 March 25 ½ day pauper business $0.50=$4.50

1823 Dec Benjamin Bucknell Dec 2 ½ day attending McLucas family $0.50 ¼ lb tea 21 cts 1 qt molasses 13 cts=$0.34 Dec 9 4 qts meal 13, 1 qt salt 6=$0.19 Dec 11 moving Mrs. McLucas & goods $1.50 Dec 19 2 qts molasses $0.25, ½ lb ea $0.38=$0.63,½ bushel meal $0.50, 1 lb beef $0.50, 1 day repairing chimney & getting wood hauled $1.00=$5.16, 2 days at Eastman & making deed $2.50, sending letter of notice to Portland accnt $0.50, 1 qt molasses del'd John McLucas by Cotton Lincoln $0.50, ½ day Pauper business=$8.66

1823 Dec Brownfield <u>William Lane</u> getting wood Abigail McLucas $1.75, 1 peck corn $0.21, year 1824:
1 peck corn $0.21
Jan 20 4 ½ lb pork ¾, 1 qt molasses $0.73
Jan 22 1 peck potatoes $0.12
Jan 24 ½ peck of rye 2/3, 1 peck wheat 2/ $0.82
Jan 30 1 peck potatoes $0.22
Feb 2 1 ½ peck corn $0.32, providing wood 3 weeks $4.00=$8.28

1824 June 2 <u>John Warren</u> use of a cow for John McLucas $6.50

1824 <u>Joseph Gray</u> 9 weeks board Mrs. McLucas & children at $3.00=$27.00, ditto Esther Gray for week work $1.00=$28.00

1853 May 9 Brownfield. John McLucas is in distress. Dr says in all probability the old gentleman will not recover.

Mrs. Robert McLucas

1823 Nov 4 Brownfield. Mrs. Robert McLucas has applied to us for assistance to support herself & children who is a inhabitant in your town. Supplied & charged to Hiram. Notice that you may remove her.

1823 Dec 2 <u>John Warren</u> 1 day Brownfield of Robert McLucas family 6/ $1.00

Royal McLucas

1858 Aug 16
> "To the Overseers of the town of Brownfield
> Gentlemen
>   Your letter of the 12th inst. stating that Royal McLucas & family had fallen into distress and been furnished relief by your town at the charge of the town of Hiram, was duly received. Upon inquiry we are satisfied this town is not the place of the lawful settlement of the paupers. We cannot therefore cause his removal, nor contribute to his support.

> Dated at Hiram Aug. A.D. 1858
> John P. Hubbard—Overseer of the Poor"

Isaac Merrifield

1820 <u>John Warren</u> account.
Sept 20 ½ day concerning Isaac Merrifield $0.50
Oct 14 boarding Merryfield's child 1 week & half week $1.00
Six dollars for Merryfield at Lem[512] Cotton's Store $6.00

1820 Nov 13 <u>Alpheus Spring</u> ½ day disposing of Isaac Merrifield Jr. $0.50
1820 Nov 13 to April 3, 1821 <u>Winthrop Baston</u> keeping Isaac Merrifield & child from Nov. 13, 1820 to April 3, 1821 at $2 week $40. Rec'd pay in full for keeping Merrifield & child after the 3rd of April & all other charges

1820 Nov 3 <u>Moody Brown</u> accnt for support of Isaac Merrifield & family—

> "I boarded Isaac M's wife Dec to July with her child, from this to the month of June she was at Wells. I made a journey to Wells for the express purpose of bringing her up she was sick at my house & recovered there took her & infant to Wells but finding she must suffer there I brought her back to my house where she has remained till within 3 weeks & I am further responsible for the Doctor's bill for her sickness."

1821 Jan <u>Dr. Joseph Benton</u>[513] acct account allowed March 30, 1822 with Merrifield child $1.00, $0.75=$1.75

1821 Jan <u>Dr Joseph Benton</u> acct visit & medicine for Merrifield child $1.00, $0.75=1.75

1821 Extraordinary Committee Account, <u>Winthrop Baston's</u> escrow acct for Merrifield $4.97, ditto funeral charges of his child $2.00

---

512   Lemuel Cotton born 1801, not Lemuel Cotton 2d who purchased Hubbards' store in 1875
513   Dr. Benton, of Baldwin, also attended General Peleg Wadsworth in 1829.

1821 March 28 <u>Winthrop Baston</u> 1 shirt for Mrs. Merrifield $1.09, pair of shirts for the child $0.75, 2 qt rum $0.80, medicine of Doc Bridges $0.50, 3 yds all wool cloath $1.50, tobacco for Merrifield $0.33=$4.97

1821 May <u>Winthrop Baston</u> articles for Isaac Merrifield & funeral 1 viewing sheet $1.00, shirt $0.58, handkerchief $0.33
1 pillercase $0.25, digging grave $0.50, 2 qts wine $1.00, 2 pound of plumbs $0.30, going to Cornish for articles $0.33=$4.32, getting matches & finding the victual & drink for term of 3 weeks & candles & firewood & keeping the child afterward $6.50, keeping him & child $4.29, 7 weeks & 2 days $14.50=$25.29

1821 Nov <u>Moody Brown's</u> accnt for keeping Mrs. Merrifield child 23 weeks from June 18-Nov 26 at $0.25 per week $5.75

1822 Feb 25 <u>Abijah Lewis</u> for making a coffin for Isaac Merrifield town pauper $2.00 Abijah Lewis his mark

Louisa was remarried in 1825 to David Lowell, born c. 1794. David died in 1847 but Louisa lived 42 years more. Their children were: David Lowell II, born 1827; Willoughby, born 1831 and drowned in Hiram in 1888; Susan B. who married Ebenezer Lowell; Lizzie S. (Louisa?) who died at age 19; Lida (Lydia?) Jane who married James Day Jr. of Brownfield.

William West

1812 March <u>John Watson</u> going to Fryeburg upon Lord & Durgin accnt $1.50, paid to William West for service on David Durgin Jr. and Levi Lord $1.48

1812 Apr-Oct <u>Peleg Wadsworth</u> account $31.29
1812 April 10 load wood cut up and hauled $1.00, peck Indian meal, 6 molasses, 1/ brandy $0.66, ½ bushel potatoes, 2 ½ lbs pork $0.66, ¼ lb Souchang Tea $0.25
April 13 small load wood cut up & hauled $0.75, ½ day take care of Mrs. William West $0.33

June keeping Mrs. West from 1st to 21st & 2 of her children 3 weeks at 15/ $7.50
July 10-26 ditto both 2 weeks & 2 day at 15/ $5.66, moving her & children to <u>Eastmans</u> $0.50
July 27 1 bushel Ind. Meal 6/ 10 lb beef 5/ 2 ½ lb pork 2/6 $2.25, ½ bushel potatoes 1/, ½ peck beans 2/ $0.50, ¼ Tea 2/, 1 lb butter 9d, sugar 9d $0.58
Aug 9 ½ lb pork 3/6, ¼ tea 2/ 1/4h lb mutton, 1 ½ peck meal $4.84
Aug 15 7 ½ lb pork 7/6 1 bushel meal 7/6, ½ peck beans 2/ $2.84, 3 lb lamb ½, ½ bushel potatoes, tobacco & sugar $0.65
August 17 ½ lb butter 6d ½ lb hogs fat [feet?] $0.17
Aug 19 ¼ tea 2/, 2 ½ pork 2/6 5 lb lamb 2/6 $1.17, 1 peck rye meal 2/3, rice & molasses 1/ $0.70
Sept 2 ¼ tea 2/, 3 lb mutton $0.50
Oct 7 3 ½ lb mutton ½, ½ peck meal 1/ $0.39

1812 Sept <u>John W. Chadbourn</u> Mary West $5.22, 9 weeks at 58 cents $1.24. $4 allowed April 3, 1813

1812 Aug 19 town meeting Article 4. To see what the town will do respecting support of the family of William West.

1812 Sept <u>John Chadbourne</u> account for Mrs. West (Mary) $4 allowed of claim for $6.46, 9 weeks board @$0.58=$5.22

1812 Sept 15 <u>Lemuel Howard</u> allowed $2 for board of Mrs. West 4 weeks @3/

1813 April 2 <u>Ephraim Kimball</u> account For going to Esq J Spring to agree what should be done with Mrs. West & children $0.25, one day moving Mrs. West and effects $0.67, half bushel of meal $0.50, half bushel of potatoes $0.20, 3 lbs butter $0.36, paid <u>James Gilmore</u> for carrying the same to Mrs. West $0.34, paid for men moving said family $0.50=$2.82

1813 April 3 <u>Benjamin McLellan</u> $2.50 paying <u>William Cotton</u> for going after Dr. Benton for Mrs. West $0.75, paying <u>Aaron Cross</u> for going after <u>Dr. Ritcheson</u> for Mr. West $0.50, 2 hands & yoak of oxen half day moving Mr. West's family $1.00=$2.25, plus ½ day on Committee of Accounts $0.33

1813 April 12 <u>John Watson Jr.</u> to <u>Wadsworths</u> to consult on removal of Stephen Burbank $0.25, attending Esq. Spring to hear his dispositions of Mr. West. Alpheus Spring $0.25

1813 April <u>John Watson Jr.</u> carrying provisions to West & family $0.75 5 ½ lbs beef $0.50, 4 bushell potatoes $0.25

Oct 26 3 peck Ind. Meal 6/, 10 ½ lb mutton 3/6 $1.58, 2 bushel potatoes, delivered <u>Eastman</u> in Jan 7, 1813 for a like quantity shirt he let Mrs. West have in Oct $1.00=$30.66, postage of letters respecting Mary West $0.66=$31.29

1813 May to Aug <u>Peleg Wadsworth</u> allowed $14.33
1/2 day attending Wm West family $0.34
June 21 ½ day ditto 2/, June 22 ½ day ditto 2 $0.67
Mr & Mrs. <u>Eastman</u> for support of West viz
June 23 ½ bushel potatoes 2/, 5 ¼ lb beef 2/7, 1 peck meal 3/ $1.27, honey 9d rice 4d blue Stone 6d pepper & tea 6d $0.40, Diacnicum 1/28th,[514] ½ bushel potatoes 2/, 1 peck meal 3 $1.00
June 28 8 ¼ lb beef 4/, 1 ½ beans & tea 9d, ½ bb raisins $1.31, 1 oz cinnamon 9d, 1 doz biscuits 9d $0.25, 1 bottle wine 4/6, ½ day attendance 2/ tea 9d $1.20
July 2 ½ day removing West family from Eastman $0.34, tea & biscuit 9d, 1 peck Ind[ian] meal del'd by <u>T Spring</u> for me 3/ $0.62, Capt to buy rum 9d, tea d $0,67
July 19 ½ bushel potatoes 1/6, 1 peck meal 3/, ½ peck beans $1.25, sugar & tea, Brandy, bisquit & vitriol, bread, rice $0.45
July 26 1 peck Ind[ian] meal 3/, ½ peck beans 3/ ½ peck potatoes $1.06
Aug 28 my horse for West use, 4 weeks to this day he being lame & unable to walk to save his Board $4.00=$14.33

1813 Aug 13–Sept 17 <u>Daniel Lane</u> account allowed $6 for 2 weeks board of 2 West children & 8 weeks of 1 child of claim of $12, allow 3/ per week each child

1813 June & July <u>Jonathan Clemons</u> allowed $2.17 for 11 gallons milk $0.92 & 7 ½ gal raw milk @1/ $1.25=$2.17
1813 July <u>Asa Burbank</u> allowed $2 of $3 claimed for making coffin for Mrs. West

1813 Sept <u>James Eastman</u> allowed $2.50 for taking care of child Abigail West 5 weeks @3/

John Whales grandson <u>Peleg Wadsworth Jr.</u>
1821 Mar 29 sundries for support of Mr. John Whale's grandson $4.21
1824 June 2 <u>John Warren</u> going to see John Whales Jr. & family, making provision for them $1.00

---

514 Diacnicum or syrup of carthamus: seeds of bastard saffron thistle, safflower, or dyer's saffron, *Carthamus tintorus*. Diaphoretic and cathartic. (*Dictionary of Protopharmacology: therapeutic practices, 1700–1850*, J. Worth Estes, 1990)

APPENDIX 20

Diary of Medical Treatment
of General Peleg Wadsworth Before
His Death on 12 November 1829

23 October to 11 November 1829 Diary[515]

Friday Oct. 23, 1829 morning
took Dover Powder about   9:40
Ditto pills (powdered)   10:40
Give Ammoniac & Liquorice   11:30
Ditto Dover Powder   1:30
Injection if necessary at 3
Ammoniac & Liquorice 3:30
Dover Powders   5:30
Ammoniac & Liquorice 7:30
Dover Powders   9:30
Pills   11:00
Ammoniac & Liquorice 11:30

Saturday
D. Powders   1:30
AM & L   3:30
D Powders   5:30
AM & L   7:30
D. Powders   9:30
Blister on left arm about 11
Ammoniac & Liquorice 11:30
Dover Powders   1:30
Calomel every 6 or 7 hours
Injection if necessary at 3 or 4
AM & L   3:30
D P   6:30
AM & L   7:30
Dover Powders & Red Pepper   9:40
10:30   Molasses water
10:45   Red Pepper in jelley
11:25   Ammoniac & L & Red Pepper
Hickups for an hour after 10:30
2:10   D. Powders & Red Pepper
      Sleep
5   Pills & Columbo
5:45   Ammoniac Liquorice
6   Gruel
7:15   D. Powders & Red Pepper
About 8   Cup of coffee & ¾ cracker

9:50   AM & Liq. & R.P.
11:20   Gruel
11:45   Columbo
12:45   D.P. & R.P.
2   Wine & water sweetened
      Broth
3   AM & Liq.
3:30   tea spoons wine & water
      Injection
4   Columbo & Wine & Water
6 ¼   Calomel
7   Ammoniac & Liquorice
8 ¼   Columbo & wine
9   D.P.
10   Dovers Powders
11   Ammoniac & Liquorice
12   Columbo & wine
Rhubarb & Salts of Wormwood
1 ¼   Calomel
2:30   Ammoniac & Liquorice
4   Columbo & wine
5 ¼   Dover powders
6–7 6 ½ Ammoniac & Liquorice
8   Columbo & wine
      ~~Dover Powders~~
9   Broth
11:30   Broth
12   Ammoniac & Liq
12:30   Wine & water
Hickups for some time stopped 2:35
asleep until 3:40
Tuesday
9   Ammoniac & Liquorice
11:15   Rheubarb & Salts of Wormwood
1:40   Dovers Powders
2:20   Ammoniac & Liquorice
      Tea 2 cups
4:15   Columbo & wine
5   Rheubarb & Salts of Wormwood
6   Suppository

---

515   Diary was kept by his daughters. Maine Historical Society, Coll 16 1/10.

Appendix 20: *Diary of Medical Treatment of General Peleg Wadsworth Before His Death on 12 November 1829*

6:30	D. Powders
7:55	Ammoniac & Liquorice
9:30	Columbo & wine
11	Rheubarb & Salts of Wormwood
12	Calomel

Wednesday 28th Oct

1:30	Dovers Powders
3	Ammoniac & Liquorice
4	~~Columbo & wine & water~~
5:30	Rheubarb & Salts of Wormwood
6	Columbo & wine & water
6:25	Calomel
8:30-3	
8:45	Wine & water
9:40	Arrow root tea
11:20	Wine & water
	Arrow root tea

p.m.

2:10	Rheubarb & Salts of Wormwood
3:00	Arrow root tea
4:15	Wine & water
8	Arrow root tea
9:15	Dovers Powders
12	Rheubarb & Salts of Wormwood
1	Gruel
3:25	Dovers Powders
6:30	Rheubarb & Salts of Wormwood

Thursday 29th

11:25	6 drops of Balsome Peru every 4 hours may increase to 8–10 or 12 drops if necessary
12	Rheubarb & Salts of Wormwood
4:30	Balsam Peru 7 or 8 drops
9	Dovers Powders
11	Balsam Peru 9 drops
12	Rheubarb & Salts of Wormwood
12:30	Gruel
3	Gruel
3	Ammoniac & Liquorice
4:40	Wine & water
5:20	Gruel
6:45	Rheubarb & Salts of Wormwood

Friday 30th Oct.

12:20	Dovers Powders
	Broth
2:15	Rheubarb & Salts of Wormwood
2:25	Balsom Peru 12 drops
4:20	Ammoniac & Liquorice

10:15	Ammoniac & Liquorice
12	Dovers Powders
2	Rheubarb & Salts of Wormwood
4	~~Ammoniac & Liquorice 6~~
7:30	Dovers Powders
12.5	Calomel

P.M.

2:15	Rheubarb & Salts of Wormwood
4:45	Ammoniac & Liquorice
	Evacuation
6:15	Ammoniac & Liquorice
8:30	Rheubarb & Salts of Wormwood
9:10	Arrow root tea
10:30	Ammoniac & Liquorice
4:10	Rheubarb & Salts of Wormwood
	Evacuation
6:40	Do
6:45	Ammoniac & Liquorice
7: 5	Balsom Peru 6 drops
9:45	Rheubarb etc.
10:15	Evac
10:30	Wine & water
11:30	Ammoniac & Liquorice

Sunday Nov. 1st

Balsom Peru once in 6 hours
Peruvian balsom Ditto
Rheubarb & Salts of Wormwood & ???
Ammoniac & Liquorice

P.M.

1	Balsom Peru 6 drops
4	Bark spoonful with little wine
5:15	Ammoniac & Liquorice
6:20	Rheubarb & Salts of Wormwood
7	~~Balsom Peru~~
	~~Ammoniac~~
10	Bark without wine
12	Ammoniac & Liquorice
1	Balsom Peru
4	Bark & wine
5	Ammoniac & Liquorice
6	Rheubarb & etc.
7:30	Balsom Peru

Monday Nov. 2 a.m.

10	Arrow root
	Bark
1:25	Balsom Peru
2:45	Wine & water

Appendix 20: *Diary of Medical Treatment of General Peleg Wadsworth Before His Death on 12 November 1829*

4	Bark & wine
5	~~Ammoniac & Liquorice~~
6	Rheubarb & Salts W
8:15	Balsom Peru
10	Bark
11:30	Ammoniac & Liquorice
1	~~Balsom Peru~~
4	Bark & wine
5:30	Ammoniac & Liquorice
7	Rheubarb & Sts. W-
8:25	Balsom Peru
10	Bark

Tuesday p.m.

2	Balsom Peru
4	Bark & wine
5	Ammoniac & Liquorice
7:30	Rheubarb & Salts of Wormwood
7	~~Balsom Peru~~
8:40	Dovers Powders
9	Arrow root
10	Bark
11:30	Ammoniac & Liquorice
2	Balsom Peru 6 drops
4	~~Bark & wine~~
5	Ammoniac & Liquorice
6:30	Rheubarb & Salts of W.
7	~~Balsom Peru~~
8:30	Bark & wine

Wednesday a.m.

9	Balsom Peru
12	Arrow
	Balsom once a day
	Bark 3 times
3	Bark & wine
5	~~Arrow~~

7 P.M.

7:50	Balsom Peru
9	Ammoniac & Liquorice
11:25	Arrow
4:50	Arrow
7:20	Arrow

Thursday p.m.

10:25	Am & Lq
11:30	Ether 30 drops
3:30	Balsom Peru
4:45	Am & Liq
6:25	Rheubarb & Sts. W.

Friday Nov. 6th

7:30	Rheubarb &
11	Wine & water
1:30	???
1:45	Arrow
4:30	Balsom Peru
6	Calomel
10:15	Evac
10:25	Sena
	Bark
	Sena
7:30	Evac
9:35	Bark
12	Evac

Sat. p.m.

1:15	Ammoniac & Liquorice
5:30	Ammoniac & Liquorice
5:50	Dovers Powders
7:00	ill tr???
10:25	Snakeroot & Saffron a little
11:45	Gruel
1:20	Snakeroot & Saffron
5:10	Gruel
7:30	Snakeroot & Saffron

Sunday p.m.

10:30	Arrow
12:10	Brandy & water
1:10	Arrow & Brandy
2:45	Port
3:20	Cordial every 6 hours

Sunday p.m. Nov. 8th

6	Arrow & Brandy
7:30	Brandy & water
8:35	Water & Brandy & water
9:15	Syrup of Saffron or Cordial
10	Arrow & a little wine

Monday p.m.

2	Snakeroot & Saffron
3:15	Syrup of Saffron
	Arrow 2 c Water
8:30	Brandy & water 1 swallow Water
12	Sena ½ glass
12:55	Arrow
2: 5	Sena
3:30	Syrup of Saffron water, Arrow, Snakeroot

Appendix 20: *Diary of Medical Treatment of General Peleg Wadsworth Before His Death on 12 November 1829*

	Arrow
9:20	Syrup of Saffron
	sound asleep
11:30	Snakeroot tea
11:53	Water
	Water
2:45	Arrow & wine
3:30	Syrup of Saffron

Tuesday 10th

6 AM Arrow

10:30	Sena
11:30	Water up in chair 1 hour
11:40	Arrow & little wine
1:25	Sena sat up
1:55	Wine & water
2:45	Brandy & water
3:20	Syrup of Saffron
3:45	Hiccoughs 15 minutes
4:00	Wine & water
	Arrow & water

6:30	Balsom John water
7:30	Water
7:40	Rheubarb & Salts Wormwood
9	Wine & water
9:45	Syrup of Saffron
10:20	Arrow
12:20	Balsom John. Evac
3:30	Syrup of Saffron
3:35	Arrow a few teaspoonsfull
6:25	Wine & water
6:20	Arrow & wine very little. Evac
9	Saffron Syrup

Wednesday 11th Nov. 1829 p.m.

1:15	Arrow very little

Nov. 12th, 1829

a.m.

6:45   Died easy

APPENDIX 21

Properties of Medicines Prescribed
to General Peleg Wadsworth

Ammoniac is the aromatic gum resin of a southwest Asian herb of the carrot family used as a cough medicine as it is an expectorant. It is not clear why it was combined with licorice.

Arrowroot tea is chiefly valuable as an easily digested, nourishing diet for convalescents, especially in bowel complaints.

Balsam of Peru is an essential oil from a tree grown in Central and South America. It was used for coughs but is highly allergenic and can cause redness, swelling, itching, and blisters.

Bark is an emetic, usually taken toward the approach of a paroxysm.

Calomel is mercurous chloride, a tasteless white compound. Medical uses for calomel were common well into the nineteenth century. It acts as a purgative and kills bacteria (and also does irreversible damage to humans). Some treatments are of historical interest. The three physicians attending General Washington's final hours administered calomel to the dying president. Lewis and Clark carried it on their expedition and used it to treat their men's STDs. Louisa May Alcott (author of *Little Women*) suffered from its effects. (Source: Loyola University)

Columbo is a native American botanical herb also known as elkweed, green gentian, and maidenhair fern. The root is cathartic, emetic, stimulant, and tonic.

Dover's powder was a traditional medicine against cold and fever developed by Thomas Dover, an English physician of the eighteenth century. The powder was a preparation of ipecac and opium and potassium sulfate. It was used to induce perspiration, to defeat the advance of a cold and at the beginning of any attack of fever. It was recommended that copious drafts of warm drink be ingested after taking the powder, accompanied by calomel, moderate use of port wine and a light farinaceous diet.

Red pepper. In traditional Chinese medicine and Ayurveda, red peppers have been used to treat digestive problems, circulatory problems, infections, and arthritis.

Rhubarb root, in traditional Chinese medicine, is a mild cathartic for weakness of the stomach, indigestion, laxity of the intestines, diarrhea, bilious disorders, cholic, and other similar complaints. A peculiar excellence in rhubarb is its evacuating viscid bile when lodged in the bile ducts. It was often used with bark.

Saffron has many therapeutic applications in many traditional medicines as antiseptic, antidepressant, antioxidant, digestive, and anticonvulsant. In hot drinks it soothes coughs and relieves colds.

Salt of wormwood is used to attenuate the blood and humors. It converts acidities into a mild aperient salt, and thus removes a cause of many chronic diseases. It resolves viscid and glutinous humors, by which, and its gentle stimulus, obstructions are removed, and wherever it passes secretions are promoted.

Snakeroot is an herb native to the East Coast of the United States and is said to promote blood circulation and alleviate fever, stomach ache, smallpox, scarlet fever, pneumonia, croup, and flatulence. A tea prepared with the herb may be used as a gargle to treat sore throats. However, when ingested in excess amounts, the herb is likely to result in vomiting, vertigo, and acute riveting pains. The root contains an alkaloid, which when ingested in excess amounts, may cause acute internal injuries, such as paralysis, and result in coma and death.

Senna is used to combat constipation. It is made from the dried leaves of *Senna alexandrina*.

APPENDIX 22
*General Peleg Wadsworth's Will
and Inventory of his Estate*

Though ill, Peleg Wadsworth signed his will on 11 November 1829, the day before he died.

He bequeathed the house in Portland that the Longfellows occupied to Zilpah Wadsworth Longfellow and her sister Lucia, who did not marry and lived with the Longfellows, "with all the privileges & appurtenances thereunto belonging in common & undivided, with the rent that is unpaid." To son Alexander Scammel he left a house lot in Portland that he had purchased from William Vaughan. Another house lot in Portland, bought of William Gorham, was left to the sons of his son Samuel B. Wadsworth. Samuel operated a store in Eastport, and wrote regularly to Peleg, but was not included.[516]

To Peleg Jr., he left "the home farm with all the stock, household furniture, & everything appertaining thereto including builds, etc." and some additional land adjoining the farm and land of Joshua Robbins, John Cotton, Charles Lee Wadsworth, and land on which Henry W. Barnes lived, and along the Saco River (Fall Meadow Brook, so called). He also bequeathed to Peleg Jr. "my lot of land called the Bucknell lot, except that part sold to the Town of Hiram where the Town House stands."

To son Charles Lee, Peleg left a tract of land by his southwest line, which ran from the Saco to the Ossipee River and to the corner of a lot of land he formerly sold to Jacob Lord to the corner of Lot No. 1 of Cutler's Grant and bounded on the northeast by Charles Lee's land. Frank Wadsworth, grandson of Charles Lee, received "Lot No. 3 of the fourth range, excepting the Pine timber thereon."

"My mills in Brownfield with the privileges, falls, mill lot & all my right thereunto with the Pine timber cut & hauled in the Ponds & Brook above the mill, I give to my five sons viz Charles Lee, John, Alexander Scammel, Samuel Bartlett (or rather I give what will have been Samuel Bartlett's part) to the children

of Samuel Bartlett Wadsworth, & Peleg." The same beneficiaries received "the lot of Pine timber between Porter line, the West Branch, the Joseph Howard lot, Clemons Pond, Eli Clemons' land & the road that leads from Eli Clemons through the Notch & a line from the North to the Joseph Williams lot." Alexander Scammel and the children of Samuel Bartlett received half of the remainder of his land in Hiram & Brownfield that was part of the Wadsworth Grant.

Inventory of the Portland property

An inventory of the Portland property signed 22 April 1830 valued the Longfellow house at $5,000, Alexander's lot at $50, the children of Samuel Wadsworth's lot on Washington Street at $100, for a total of $5,150.[517]

Inventory of the Hiram estate

A committee to appraise the inventory of the Hiram estate was appointed on 19 May 1830 and completed 22 May. On the committee were Benjamin Barker, Ephraim Kimball, and John Bucknell, all of Hiram. The inventory consisted of three parts: Real Estate; Personal Estate and Notes, Cash on Hand; and Additions to the above demands.

Real Property

Peleg's real property consisted of 1100 acres including "the Bucknell lot (so called) in Cutler's Grant valued at $2200, two lots No. 4 & 6 in Cutler's Grant $500[518], two fifty acre lots situated on or near the borders of the Middle Pond (so called) $200, one other tract or parcel of land situated in Brownfield containing three hundred and fifty acres being a part of the first described tract in Hiram." $350.

"Also the saw and grist mills on the Ten Mile

---

516 Not including son Samuel was unusual. Letters in the Longfellow House-Washington's Headquarters NHS may explain the reason.

517 Maine Historical Society, Coll. 16 Box 2/4

518 The Wiswall heirs sought Peleg's help in securing lots no. 4 and ½ of no. 5. He purchased them in 1812.

brook (so called) together with the privilege containing about twenty five acres of land." $525.

The worth of the combined properties was $3775.

Personal estate

1 horse & chaise	$100
31536 feet of boards 2 $3 per M	94.60
2600 R.O. Hhhd Stves 2 $4 per M	10.40
17 ¾ yds of mill cloth @ 3/	8.87
3 ½ Hs soaleather @ 1/	0.58
300 of white & hard pine logs in the Ten Mile Brook	150.00
A small lot of oak planks	1.00"
[The total was	$365.45]

Peleg held forty notes worth $3474.77 in amounts ranging from $1.72 to$557 dated between 1822 and September 1829, just two months before he died. Forty percent of the total value of the estate of $7,885.20 was money loaned. Most of the borrowers were Hiram men.

Appendix 22: *General Peleg Wadsworth's Will and Inventory of his Estate*

Promissory notes

Names	Date	Amount
Spalding & Tucker	25 May 1826	287.99
Ellis B. Archer	26 May 1829	339.68
A. Woodman	19 May1829	31.94
Moses Davis	18 April 1828	548.78
Isaac Davis & John Woodman order	6 June 1826	25.00
Jacob Graffam & James Edgcomb	15 June 1822	143.17
Jacob Graffam & James Edgcomb	15 June 1822	42.71
Gideon Chase	27 Dec 1825 & 27 July 1827	96.25
John Cotton	31 March 1828	63.04
Joseph & Aaron Williams	11 July 1827	29.66
Lemuel Cotton	1 Dec 1827	33.83
Joshua Robbins	30 April 1828	30.56
Peleg C. Wadsworth	15 Sept 1829	234.30
Timothy C. & Daniel Pierce	20 Nov 1826	65.00
John Huntress	9 July 1829	1.72
Thomas Trippe	13 May 1823	75.60
Edmund Butterfield		295.00
Charles Wadsworth	[Estimate based on subtraction from total]	296.98
William Ingalls		4.73
Royal Stanton		37.56
James Fly Jr.		50.00
Josiah Mabry		557.00
William Baston		12.00
Jacob Lord		8.55
Samuel S. Hadley		4.00
Winthrop Baston		7.18
John Wentworth		4.86
John C. Gilpatrick		1.44
Alexander Lewis		2.50
Samuel Harmon		1.75
Richard Trippe		1.17
Thomas Trippe		3.50
Solomon H. Gilpatric		2.50
Aaron Cross		20.00
Samuel Tappen		2.44
Cotton Lincoln due bill		23.80
Moses Richardson		16.74
John Thompson		15.24
Joshua Snow		9.18
Solomon H. Gilpatric		7.42
Charles Wadsworth	70 valued at 1/2	35.00
Stephen Gilpatrick	10 valued at 1/2	5.00
		3474.77
Cash on hand in bills & change		267.98

APPENDIX 23
Documents of Incorporation

Timothy Cutler's Petition to Incorporate in 1801

To the Honourable Senate and the Honourable House of Representatives of the Commonwealth of Massachusetts in General Court assembled at January Sessions at 1801.

The Petition of the Subscribers humbly, showeth that your petitioners Inhabitants of the plantation now called Hiram in the in County of York together with the Inhabitants of a Trial of Law on the eastern side of Saco River—and adjacent to Brownfield commonly called Browns addition and also Prescotts Grant humbly Showeth that your petitioner labours under various grievances in consequence of our present unincorporative situation and whereas the said tracts of Land are so situated that the inhabitants thereon can never be any better accommodated than to become one Incorporation, the Inhabitants of Brownfieldton one situated so remote from the majority of the Inhabitants of Brownfield which renders it inconvenient for the former to stand in connection with the latter as the travel to public meetings by the nearest routs will be as much as six miles and then who may hereafter settle on said tract which doubtless have to travel ten or twelve miles on every public occasion which together with the lowness of the Routs renders the Grievances grate both Laborious and expensive The plantation of Hiram being small is insufficient for a town of it self and there being no other tract of land except the aforesaid addition which can be added thereunto with conveniences as the principal Inhabitants there of an situated by the side of Saco River as is also the situation of the Inhabitants of the addition, and that considerably compacted—The plans herewith presented will be more fully Descriptive of the premises.

We therefore pray your Honours that an Act may pass the Legislature to Incorporate the aforesaid tracts of land together with the Inhabitants thereon into a Town by the name of [blank] with all the immunities and privileges which other Towns enjoy by law, and as in Duty bound your petitioners Shall ever pray.

Timothy Cutler
John Bucknell
Jonathan Clemons
John Pierce
Thomas Spring
John Wales
Jacob McLucas
Elezer Stout [Eleazer Strout]
Joseph Chadbourne
Joseph Storer
Samuel Merrifield
Samuel Durgin
Jacob Lord
David Durgin Jr.
Lemuel Howard
William Cotton
John Clemons
John E. Mariner
Samuel Hogsand
Simeon Bucknel
Daniel Baston
James Eastman
Joshua Wilson
Josiah Mabre [Mabry]
Inhabitance of Brownfield Additions
    & Prescots Grant
Asa Osgood
Stephen Burbank
Benja. Burbank
John Burbank
John Watson Jr.
John Watson
Thos. B. Watson
Seth Spring
Thos. Barker Jr.
Israel Burbank Jr.

Charles L. Wadsworth's Counter Petition Against Incorporation in 1801

Note that it was signed by some of the same men who signed Cutler's Petition for Incorporation.

In the House of Representatives Feby. 19, 1801 heard a committee to the standing committee on applications for incorporations of town & to consider a report.

Sent up for concurrence
Edw. W. Robbins Speaker
In Senate, Febry. 23rd, 1801
Read and concurred
Saml. Phillips, Prsdt.

To the Honorable Senate & honorable House of Representatives of the Commonwealth of Massachusetts in General Court assembled.

The Subscribers, Inhabitants of a place sometimes called Hiram, more commonly, Great Osappee, in the County of York, agreeably to an Order of the General Court published in Jenks' Portland Gazette of 6th April last on the Petition of Timothy Cutler & others praying for an Incorporation of Hiram, in part of Parsonfield & Prescotts Grant into One Town (if they the Subscribers are considered as coming within the premises) beg leave very respectfully to State as an Objection to the Measure the Smallness of the Number of the Inhabitants & their Inadequacy to bear the Expense of a Town, at this time.

The whole Number of Land holders on the premises do not exceed twenty-six of the whole number of Families are short of forty a considerable proportion of the Settlers could contribute to the Support of the Town but in a very slight degree, others would not be legal voters in the town.

Manner…[The next words, which are at the bottom of the page in the original are covered with paper and cannot be read.]…transient persons as several of the Petitioners for the Incorporation have already removed without the Limits of the proper Town.

The Subscribers therefore pray that the said Incorporation may not take place till the Inhabitants are become more numerous & better able to bear the Expenses of a Town.

Charles L. Wadsworth
James Flye (his mark)
John McLucas
Jacob McLucas
William Hartford
Samuel Merrifield
David Durgin
John Fly

Jacob Lord
David Durgin Jr.
Joseph Durgin
Samuel Durgin
Daniel Lane
John E Mariner
James Fly Junr.
Lemuel Hayward [Howard]
Eli Clemons
James Eastman
John Bucknell
Abijah Lewis
Moody Brown (his mark)"

Committee on Incorporation 1805

Peleg Wadsworth and John Watson, serving on the Committee on Accounts, approved the following receipts for reimbursements and bill for services.

Thomas Spring's demand for services for the Plantation in 1805
Services as Treasurer $1.33
As Committee on Accounts 0.67
As Committee for incorporation
1.00 = $3.00

Hiram May 10th, 1806 received the above account in full on the order of the Collector

Nathaniel Merrill, Esq. 1807 June 10
1805 to making a plan for incorporation $2.00
1807 to copying the same $0.50= $2.50 [the same as billed to Porter]
Thomas Spring Jany. 10, 1806

The District of Hiram to Thomas Spring to my services as Committee man to meet with the other Committees at Brownfield 0.75
To my services as treasurer 1.50 = $2.25
The above Acct. appears reasonable & ought to be allowed in the opinion of P. Wadsworth, John Watson—Committee on Accts.

Joseph L. Howard March 1, 1806
Accnt. of Joseph L. Howard against the Plantation of Hiram for attending the General Court at

Boston 1806. To the Plantation of Hiram to Joseph L. Howard agent for the purpose of applying to the General Court for incorporation 60/ $10.00

Petition to Incorporate Three Towns 1806

To the Honourable Senate and Honourable House of Representatives of the Commonwealth of Massachusetts, in General Court assembled, on the third Wednesday of January current. The Petition of the subscribers, agents from the town of Brownfield & the plantations of Hiram and Porterfield, and the Academy Grants and Foster's Gore, humbly shews, that the aforesaid Plantations and Grants of Land, with the town of Brownfield, all in the fourth part of the County of Oxford, are sufficiently large and commodiously situated to form Four Townships That the inhabitants of said town, plantations and grants, have by their committees, duly appointed at legal meetings, called for that purpose, mutually agreed to divide said town, plantations and grants, and to have said plantations and grants incorporated with a part of said Brownfield into three towns, and Brownfield aforesaid, to remain a town with a part of Porterfield aforesaid, instead of that part of Brownfield, which is to be incorporated with said grants and Hiram, agreeable to the plan & description of the town, plantations and grants aforesaid, herewith exhibited. Your petitioners further state, that they cannot enjoy in their present situation privileges, which are incident to and enjoyed by their fellow-citizens, in towns corporate;—that the situation of the inhabitants in said plantations and grants, would be ameliorated by being incorporated, with town privileges in manner aforesaid;—that the town of Brownfield has consented to said agreement;—that the said Brownfield and Porterfield have agreed that each shall retain the public lands in proportion to other lands each shall retain. Your petitioners therefore pray that the Honorable General Court would incorporate said town, plantations and grants, agreeable to the plan and description accompanying this petition. And as in duty bound will ever pray.

JOHN PIERCE, Agent appointed for Hiram

DAVID MOULTON, Agents appointed for NATH MERRILL, Porterfield

ELIAS BERRY, Agent appointed for Acad'y

Grants & Foster's Gore

JOSEPH HOWARD, Agent appointed by Brownfield

January 8, 1806.

COMMONWEALTH OF MASSACHUSETTS.

In SENATE, Feb. 5, 1806.

On the petition of JOHN PEIRCE & others, Agents for the Plantations of Hiram and Porterfield, and the Academy Grants and Foster's Gore, and the town of Brownfield, in the County of Oxford, praying that they may be incorporated into Four Towns, agreeable to a Plan by them exhibited. Ordered, That the petitioners cause an attested copy of their petition, with this Order thereon, to be published in the Eastern Argus, printed at Portland, three weeks successively, the last publication to be made twenty days at least before the second Wednesday of the next General Court, that all persons interested may then appear, and shew cause, if any they have, why the prayer of said Petition should not be granted.

Sent down for concurrence, H. G. OTIS, President. In the House of Representatives, Feb. 7, 1806. Read and concurred, T. Bigelow, Speaker. True Copy—Attest, W. DAVIS, Clerk of Senate"

An Act to Incorporate the Plantation of Hiram into a District By the Name of Hiram, in the County of Oxford. Approved Feb. 27, 1807

Section 1st Be it enacted by the Senate and House of Representatives in General Court assembled and by the authority of the Same, that the Territory described within the following bounds viz Beginning at a basswood tree on the bank of Ossipee River, the corner of the Plantation of Porterfield and running northwardly by the line of said Plantation seventeen hundred and seventy rods to a Stake and Stones, thence south eighty three degrees east two hundred and thirty rods to a Stake and Stones, a corner of Brownfield, thence north sixty degrees east four hundred and eighty rods to Saco River, thence across the said river south eighty seven degrees east one thousand sic hundred and ten rods to a hemlock tree marked on Baldwin line, thence south sixty degrees west by Baldwin line nine hundred and thirty rods to the corner of Prescott's Grant, thence south thirty degrees east three hundred and fifty one rods to a tree marked thus—HP—thence south sixty degrees west five hundred and fifty one rods to Saco River, thence down in the middle of Saco River to great Ossipee River with the Inhabitants thereon, be and hereby are incorporated into a District by the name of Hiram is hereby vested with all the powers, privileges and immunities which towns in this Commonwealth do or may enjoy, excepting the privilege of sending a Representative to the General Court and the Inhabitants of said District shall have liberty to join with the Inhabitants of Brownfield aforesaid in choosing a Representative, and shall be notified of the time and place of election, by a warrant from the Selectmen of said Brownfield directed to a constable of said District requiring him to warn the Inhabitants of said District to attend the meeting at the time and place appointed which warrant shall be duly turned by said Constable, and the Representative chosen from the said Town of District—the pay or expense to be borne by the Town or District in proportion as they shall from time to time pay to the State Tax.

Section 2d And be it further enacted by the authority aforesaid that any Justice of the Peace for said County of Oxford, upon application therefor, is hereby inpowered to issue his warrant directed to some suitable Inhabitant of Said District of Hiram requiring him to notify and warn the Inhabitants thereof qualified to vote in town affairs, to meet at such time and place as shall be expressed in said Warrant, to choose all such Officers as Towns are by Law required to choose at their annual Town Meetings.

Resolve Confirming the Doings of the Inhabitants of the Plantation of Hiram in Raising and Levying Taxes. Approved June 16, 1807.

To Honorable the Senate and the Honorable hous of Representatives of the Commonwealth of Massachusetts in General Court assembled at Boston January Sessions A.D. 1807 the petition of the subscribers Inhabitants of the Plantation of Hiram humbly shew that your petitioners labor under a greate disadvantage in regard to doing the Business of their Plantation meetings on the account of the qualification of

voters for a man must pay to one single tax besides the poll or polls a sum equal to two thirds of a single poll tax to make him a legal voter in town affairs but the tenor of the tax act has been such that the polls have paid all the taxes in said Plantation, till the Amendment was made to the tax act in March A.D. 1806 and by reason of the operation of the aforesaid act we had not one legal voter in town affairs but yet we are laid under all the restrictions of Incorporated town in regard to highways but are Considered ourselves unable legally to vote and Assess money for the Support of highways, Schools and other necessary Charges but there has bin a Complaint made to the Court of Sessions against said Plantation for not keeping their highways good, and that did put us under necessity of doing something therefore we did Call a meeting of the Inhabitants and took the list of legal voters for state offices and did allow them to vote in town affairs and then and by and we voted two hundred and fifty Dollars to be expended on the highways and one hundred and fifty Dollars for the purpose of paying our necessary Charges, and the remainder to be for the support of a School on the aforesaid Sums was Assessed as also the State and County taxes, and apportioned as the law directs, and bills them as was Commited to the Surveyors of highways and to the Collector of taxes for said Plantation but some of our prinsiple land holders do refuse to pay their proportion of said taxes on account of the Moneys being voted by Elegal voters in town affairs these five years. Petitioners would pray the Honorable legislators to enable them to Collect their taxes by Establishing the proceedings of their meetings to be good to the present time and as in duty bound will ever pray. Vote at a meeting of the Inhabitants of said plantation it was voted that the Clerk and Assessors and moderator of said meeting sign the foregoing petition in behalf of said plantation.

John Pierce plantation Clerk
Daniel Baston, Israel Burbank—Assessors
Thomas Spring moderator

Act to repeal in part an Act entitled "An Act to incorporate the Plantation of Hiram into a District by the name of Hiram," in the County of Oxford and for other purposes. Approved June 14, 1814.

In order to change the status of Hiram from District to Town, the act to incorporate Hiram as a District and unite with Brownfield in choosing a representative had to be repealed. When that was accomplished, the act to incorporate Hiram as a town could proceed, if the town of Brownfield approved. Brownfield remonstrated and laid down its requirement for Hiram to incorporate as a town.

At a Legal meeting of the Inhabitants of the Town of Brownfield held on the 23rd day of May 1814 they voted that James Steele, Ichabod Ricker & Timothy Gibson be a Committee to Remonstrate against the petition of the District of Hiram. Attest James Steele, Clerk of the Town of Brownfield.

…a Committee of the Town of Brownfield in the County of Oxford beg leave to Remonstrate against the granting of the prayers of the Petition of the District of Hiram in said County praying to be Separated from Brownfield aforesaid & incorporate into a Town & for Reasons beg leave to assign the following against the granting the prayers of the said petition of Hiram viz that if the Land which belonged to said Brownfield before it was incorporated with said Hiram for the purpose of sending a Representative was still connected with it, the said Town would be able to send a Representative without the assistance of said Hiram. That the Inhabitants of said Brownfield would never have consented to have given up a part of its territory to Fryburgh, Denmark & Hiram & been incorporated with Hiram for the purpose of sending a Representative if they not have supposed that said Hiram would have petitioned to be incorporated into a Town & thereby deprive said Brownfield of the privilege of Representation if they not have supported it even in the power of the Legislature to rescind a vested right so as to Deprive them of the same privilege. The Inhabitants of said Town of Brownfield have no objections to the incorporation of Hiram into a Town provided the Right of Representation is not thereby taken away from said Town of Brownfield.

As in Duty bound will ever pray by their Committee
James Steele
Ichabod Ricker
Timothy Gibson"

Brownfield was assured that its Right of Representation was guaranteed and the legislature proceeded with Section 2: "Be it further enacted that the district of Hiram in the county of Oxford, be and hereby is incorporated into a Town by the name of Hiram, and vested with all the powers and priviledges, and immunities which other towns in this commonwealth do or may enjoy. In Senate June 11, 1814. In the House of Representatives June 13, 1814. Approved June 14, 1814."

APPENDIX 24
1806 Map of Settlements on the
West Side of Saco River

Note: This map is a recollection of the 1806 settlement drawn after 1942, most likely by Eli C. Wadsworth (1871—1957).

Names on the map (map follows, next page).
Not all men listed had settled by 1806.
John Ayer, Mill 1785
Thomas Barker
H. [Henry] W. Barnes
Benj [Benjamin]. Baston
Daniel Baston 1783
Royal Baston
Winthrop Baston
Moody Brown
Simon Brown
Wm. [William] Brown
John Bucknell
Cellar, Marshall "B", Sudrick & Samuel Clemons' wives there gave birth to a boy each on the same night about 1835.
Cellar of Rosebush, unknown
Chase homestead (? Wm. [William] Huntress)
Clemons Ponds
Caleb C. Clemons
Caleb C. Clemons [1808-1894 succeeded John Ayer, Thomas Barker]
Eli P. Clemons
John Clemons 1780
Sam Clemons, A child born here [Samuel C. Clemons, March 1803-December 11, 1840?, Succeeded Andrew R. Bucknell]
Sudrick Clemons
Lem [Lemuel] Cotton
Daniel Cross
James Dyer
James Eastman

Eld [Elder] James Fly
John Fly
Dan [Daniel] Foster
Moses and Aaron Gould
Wm [William] Gray
Richard Heath
Daniel Hickey
Geo[George] Hodgdon
Fred Howard
Joseph Howard
Lieut. Benj [Benjamin] Ingalls
John Lane, Cellar washed away
Darius Lewis [1834-1895]
Marshall Lewis, Killed in 1812
James Lowell
Jonathan K. Lowell
Mial Lowell [1814-1893]
[John] Marriner [Mariner]
John McLucas
McLucas Settlement
Morey, Wm. [William] Riley [unknown]
[David] Newcomb
John Pierce
Wm. [William] Pierce
Aaron Rand
Artemas Richardson
John Ridlon
Abel Robbins
Joshua Robbins
Capt. Edmund Skillings
M. [Marshall] Spring [succeeded Thomas Spring]
Spring School House
John & David Tyler
General [Peleg] Wadsworth
Capt. Samuel Wadsworth [1815-1887]
Nath'l [Nathaniel] Williams

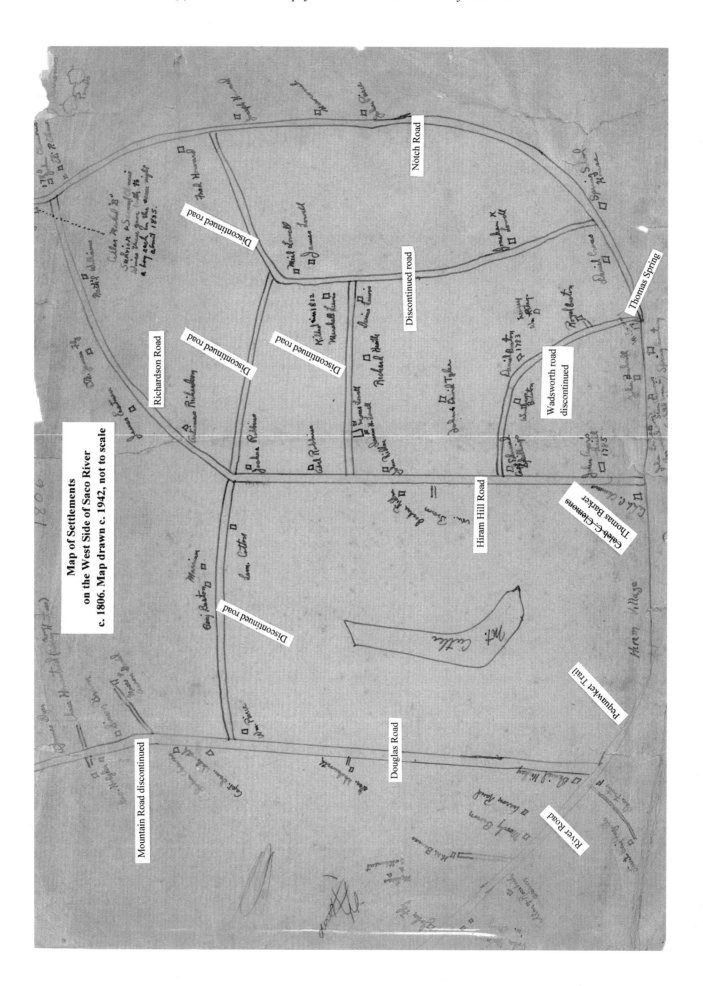

Map of Settlements
on the West Side of Saco River
c. 1806. Map drawn c. 1942, not to scale

APPENDIX 25

1858 Map of Hiram

APPENDIX 26

1858 Map of Hiram Bridge

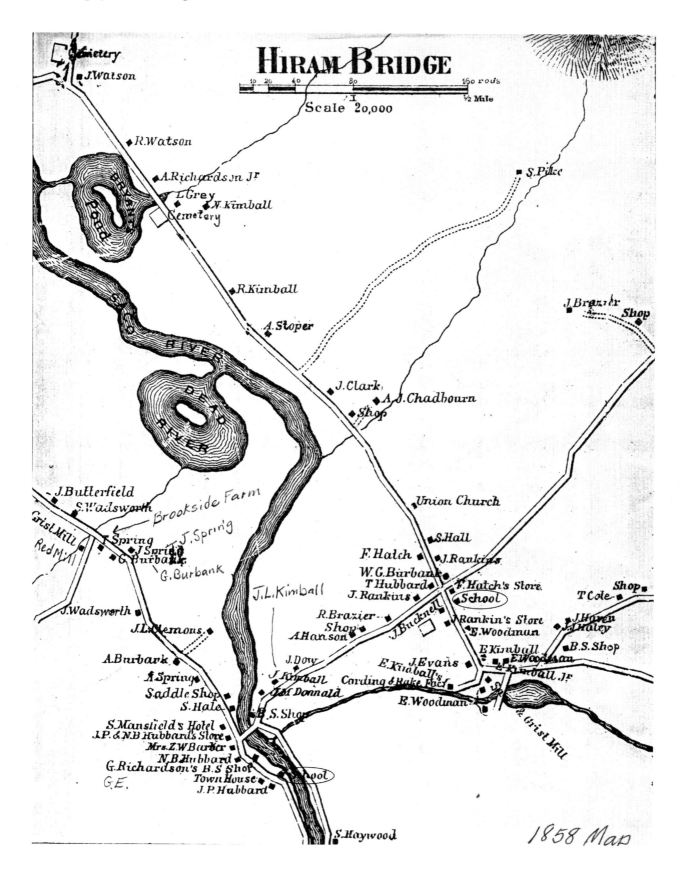

Resources

Anderson, Hayden L. V. *Canals and Inland Waterways of Maine*. Portland: Maine Historical Society, 1982.

Attwood, Stanley Bearce. *The Length and Breadth of Maine*. Orono: University of Maine Press, 2004.

Bacon, Elizabeth Chadbourne. *The Chadboune Family in America: A Genealogy*. Camden, Me: Picton Press, 1994.

Banks, Ronald F. *Maine Becomes a State*. Somersworth, NH: New Hampshire Publishing Co. & Maine Historical Society, 1973.

Bardwell, John D. *York Militia Company, 1642–1972*. York, ME: the author, 1972.

Barnes, Diane and Jack. *Images of America: Upper Saco River Valley—Fryeburg, Lovell, Brownfield, Denmark, and Hiram*. Charleston, SC: Arcadia Publishing, 2002.

Barry, Phillips, Fannie Hardy Eckstorm and Mary Winslow Symth. *British Ballads from Maine*. New Haven, CT: Yale University Press, 1929.

Bolton, Ethel Stanwood, and Eva Johnston Coe. *American Samplers*. Boston: Society of the Colonial Dames of America, 1921.

Bourque, Bruce. *Twelve Thousand Years: American Indians in Maine*. Lincoln, NE: University of Nebraska Press, 2001.

Butler, Joyce. "The Wadsworths: A Portland Family," in *Longfellow's Portland and Portland's Longfellow*. Portland: Maine Historical Society, 1987.

Butterfield Auction Galleries. *Catalog*. San Francisco: Butterfield, 2000.

Clemons, Hubert W. *A Bicentennial History of Hiram, Maine, 1776–1976*. Hiram, ME: Hiram Bicentennial Committee, 1976.

Clemons, Hubert W. *History of the First Universalist Church, Hiram, Maine, 1834–1979* Hiram, ME: The First Universalist Church, 1979.

Coleman, Emma Lewis. *New England Captives Carried to Canada: Between 1677 and 1760 During the French and Indian Wars*, Volume 2. Portland: The Southworth Press, 1925.

Conwill, Joseph D. *Maine's Covered Bridges*. Charleston, SC: Arcadia Publishing, 2004.

Cotton, Raymond C. *By the Toss of a Coin: An Abridged and Updated History of the Town of Hiram*. Hiram, ME: Hiram Historical Society, 1983.

Cotton, Raymond C. *Hog Reaves, Field Drivers, and Tything Men: The Birth Pains of the Town of Hiram*. Hiram, ME: Hiram Historical Society, 1983.

Cotton, Raymond C. *Split, Rive and Whittle: The Story of Lemuel Cotton's Axe Handle Factory*. Hiram, ME: Hiram Historical Society, 1989.

Cutter, William Richard, editor. *New England Families Genealogical and Memorial: A Record of Achievements of Her People in the Making of Commonwealths and the Founding of a Nation*. New York: Lewis Historical Publishing, 1913.

Day, Clarence Albert. *A History of Maine Agriculture, 1604–1860*. Orono, ME: University Press, 1954.

Drake, Samuel H. G. *The Book of the Indians; or, Biography and History of the Indians of North America from its First Discovery to the Year 1841*, ninth edition. Boston: Benjamin B. Mussey, 1845.

Dunbar, Michael. *Windsor Chairmaking*. New York: Hastings House, 1976.

Edwards, George Thornton. *Music and Musicians of Maine*. Portland: The Southworth Press, 1928.

Ellis, Leola C., and Kera C. Millard. *Early Cornish (1666–1916)*. Cornish, ME: 1972.

Emery, Ina N. (Stanley) and Florence (Stanley) Higgins, *Stanley-Gould Family Reunion*, [Pamphlet] (s.l.: s.n}, 1932.

Emery, William Morrell. *Chadbourne-Chadbourn Genealogy*. Fall River, MA: 1904.

Evans, Benjamin D., and June R. Evans. *New England's Covered Bridges*. Lebanon, NH: University Press of New England, 2004.

Evans, Nancy Goyne. *American Windsor Furniture: Specialized Forms*. New York: Hudson Hills Press/Henry Francis du Pont Winterthur Museum, 1996.

Freeman, Samuel. *The Town Officer*, seventh edition. Boston: Thomas & Andrews, facsimile of the 1808 edition, 2016.

Glatz, Larry. *Maine's Black Population in the Censuses of 1790 and 1800*. South Portland, ME: 2014.

Goold, Nathan, *Wadsworth-Longfellow House: Its History and Its Occupants*. Sanford, ME: Averill Press, 1927.

Greene, Evarts Boutell. *American Population Before the Federal Census of 1790*. New York: Columbia University Press, 1932.

Hamlin, Charles Eugene. *The Life and Times of Hannibal Hamlin*, Cambridge, MA: Riverside Press, 1899.

Hammond, Donna M. *Hiram—Lest We Forget: A Pictorial History*. Hiram, ME: Hiram Historical Society, 2001.

Haskell, Wayne, compiler. *Baldwin: The History of a Maine Town as Told by Its Citizens*. Baldwin, ME: Baldwin Historical Society, 2001.

Higgins, Pat. "Peleg Wadsworth," www.Mainestory.com, 2014.

Jernegan, Marcus Wilson. *Laboring and Dependent Classes in Colonial America: 1607–1783*. Social Service Monographs, Number Seventeen. Chicago, IL: University of Chicago Press, 1960.

Judd, Richard H., Edwin A. Churchill, and Joel W. Eastman, editors. *Maine: The Pine Tree State from Prehistory to the Present*. Orono: University of Maine Press, 1995.

Lane Genealogies, Volume 1. Exeter, NH: The Newsletter Press, 1891.

Lapham, William B. *History of the Town of Bethel, Maine*. Facsimile of the 1891 edition. Somersworth, NH: New England History Press/Bethel Historical Society, 1981.

Larkin, Jack. *The Reshaping of Everyday Life, 1790–1840*. New York: Harper & Row, 1988.

Little, George Thomas. *Genealogical and Family History of the State of Maine*. New York: Lewis Historical Publishing Company, 1909.

Maine Genealogical Society. *Maine Families in 1790*. Camden, ME: Picton Press, 1990.

MacMahon, Hugh G. E. *Progress, Stability and the Struggle for Equality*. Portland, ME: Drummond Woodsum & MacMahon, 2009.

Massachusetts Adjutant General's Office. *Records of the Massachusetts Volunteer Militia Called out by the Governor of Massachusetts to Suppress a Threatened Invasion During the War of 1812-14*. Boston: Wright & Potter, 1913.

Massachusetts Office of the Secretary of State. *Massachusetts Soldiers and Sailors of the Revolutionary War: A Compilation from the Archives, Prepared and Published by the Secretary of the Commonwealth in Accordance with Chapter 100, Resolves of 1891*. Boston: The Office, 1896–1908.

McLellan, Hugh D. *History of Gorham, Maine*. Somersworth, NH: New England History Press, facsimile of the 1903 edition, 1980.

Mitchell, Harry Edward, compiler. *The Town Register, 1907: Brownfield, Denmark, Hiram and Porter*, Brunswick, ME: H. E. Mitchell Co., 1907.

Mitchell, Harry Edward, compiler. *The Town Register, 1907: Fryeburg, Lovell, Sweden, Stowe and Chatham.* Brunswick, ME: H. E. Mitchell Co., 1907.

Morrison, Leonard Allison, and Stephen Paschall Sharples. *History of the Kimball Family in America from 1634 to 1807.* Rutland, VT: Charles E. Tuttle Company, 1971.

Moulton, Thomas. *Porter as a Portion of Maine: Its Settlement, Etc.* Portland, ME: Hoyt, Fogg & Donham, 1879.

Palmer, Joseph. *Necrology of Alumni of Harvard College, 1851–2 to 1861–2,* Boston: B. Wilson and Son, 1864.

Pearson, Edmund, editor. *The Autobiography of a Criminal: Henry Tufts.* New York City: Duffield and Company, 1930. Original edition, *A Narrative of the Life, Adventures, Travels and Sufferings of Henry Tufts,* now residing at Lemington, in the District of Maine (Dover, NH: Printed by Samuel Bragg Jr., 1807).

Portland City Directory and Register, Portland, ME: 1823–.

Price, H. H., and Gerald E. Talbot. *Maine's Visible Black History.* Gardiner, ME: Tilbury House, 2006.

Ridlon, Gideon Tibbetts. *Saco Valley Settlements and Families.* Portland, ME: G. T. Ridlon, facsimile of the 1895 edition, 1984.

Ring, Elizabeth. *Maine in the Making of a Nation.* Camden, ME: Picton Press, 1966.

"Saltmarsh Genealogy in North America." https://wc.rootsweb.ancestry.com/cgi-bin/igm.cgi?op=GET&db=saltyfail&id=I0079.

Small, Daniel. *Papers.* Maine Historical Society, Coll. 1449.

Sprague, Laura Fecych, editor. *The Mirror of Maine: One Hundred Distinguished Books that Reveal the History of the State and the Life of Its People.* Orono and Portland, ME: University of Maine Press and the Baxter Society, 2000.

Stakeman, Randolph. *A Black Census of Maine: 1800–1910.* Draft, Maine Historical Society Research Library, June 1997.

Taylor, Robert L. *Early Families of Cornish, Maine.* Camden, ME: Picton Press, 1993.

Taylor, Robert L. *Early Families of Limerick, Maine.* Camden, ME: Picton Press, 1993.

Taylor, Robert L. *History of Limington, Maine.* Norway, ME: Oxford Hills Press, 1975.

Teg, William. *Hiram,* Cornish, ME: Carbrook Press, 1941.

Teg, William. *History of Brownfield, Maine.* Cornish, ME: Carbrook Press, 1966.

Teg, William. *History of Hiram, Maine, Sesquicentennial Edition.* Cornish, ME: Carbrook Press, 1964.

Teg, William. *History of Porter.* Kezar Falls, ME: Parsonsfield/Porter Historical Society, 1957.

Thacher, James. *Military Journal.* Hartford: Silas Andrus and Son, 1854 edition.

True, Dr. Nathaniel Tuckerman. *The History of Bethel, Maine,* edited with an introduction by Randall H. Bennett. Bowie, MD: Heritage Books, Inc., 1994.

Underhill, Lora Altine Woodbury. *Descendants of Edward Small of New England and the Allied Families, with Tracings of English Ancestry,* Vol. 1. Cambridge: Riverside Press, 1910.

U.S. Federal Censuses.

Wadsworth, Llewellyn A. *Centennial: Hiram, Maine: Official Program.* Hiram, ME: 1914.

Wadsworth, Llewellyn A. *Journal.* Hiram Historical Society, January 30, 1876.

Wadsworth Family Letters. Maine Historical Society, Coll. 16.

Wells, Walter. *The Water-Power of Maine.* Augusta, ME: Sprague, Owen & Nash, 1868.

White, Virgil D. *Index to War of 1812 Pension Files.* Waynesboro, TE: National Historical Publishing Co., 1989.

Williamson, Joseph. *A Bibliography of the State of Maine: From the Earliest Period to 1891.* Portland, ME: The Thurston Print, 1896.

Williamson, William D. *History of the State of Maine, Volume 2.* Hallowell, ME: Glazier, Masters & Co., 1832.

Periodicals

Americana, 14 (1920), 379.

"Anniversary of Lafayette's visit on Monday," *Biddeford Weekly Journal*, June 28, 1929, 3, http://biddeford.advantage-preservation.com/viewer/?k=lafayette&i=f&d=01011812-12311989&m=between&ord=k1&fn=biddeford_weekly_journal_usa_maine_biddeford_19290628_english_3&df=1&dt=10

Bridges, Mary Eastman. "Timothy Eastman, M.D.," *Michigan Historical Collections*, 39 (1915), 420.

Clemons, Hubert W. "An Account of the 'Lord's Doings in Hiram.'" *Downeast Ancestry*, 3:22–23.

Clemons, Hubert W. "Deserted Burial Grounds in Hiram, Maine." *Downeast Ancestry*, 5:107–108.

Clemons, Hubert W. "Pilgrim Ancestry of Maine's Wadsworth Family." *Downeast Ancestry*, 1:19.

Clemons, Hubert W. "Some Descendants of Gen. Peleg Wadsworth, Patriarch of Hiram, Maine." *Downeast Ancestry*, 6:58–60.

Clemons, Hubert W. "Some Notes on Churches of Hiram, Maine." *Downeast Ancestry*, 8:76–78.

Clemons, Hubert W. "Some Wentworths of Hiram, Maine." *Downeast Ancestry*, 14:12–14.

Clemons, Hubert W. "The Adams Family of South Hiram, Maine." *Downeast Ancestry*, 8:156–157.

Clemons, Hubert W. "The Barker Families of Hiram and Cornish." *Downeast Ancestry*, 10:67–68.

Clemons, Hubert W. "The Bucknells: An early Hiram, Maine Family." *Downeast Ancestry*, 13:69–71.

Clemons, Hubert W. "The Burbank Family of Hiram, Maine." *Downeast Ancestry*, 6:141–142.

Clemons, Hubert W. "The Clemons Family of Hiram, Maine." *Downeast Ancestry*, 2:24.

Clemons, Hubert W. "The Cotton Family of Hiram, Maine." *Downeast Ancestry*, 7:62–63.

Clemons, Hubert W. "The Fly/Flye Family of Oxford County, Maine." *Downeast Ancestry*, 4:13–14.

Clemons, Hubert W. "The Gilpatrick Family of Hiram, Maine." *Downeast Ancestry*, 15:127–132.

Clemons, Hubert W. "The Gould Family of South Hiram, Maine." *Downeast Ancestry*, 7:17–20.

Clemons, Hubert W. "The Hartfords of Hiram, Denmark, and Brownfield Maine." *Downeast Ancestry*, 12:62.

Clemons, Hubert W. "The Howards of Hiram and the Warrens of South Hiram, Maine." *Downeast Ancestry*, 12:178–181.

Clemons, Hubert W. "The Huntress Family of Hiram, Maine." *Forebears in Your Maine Family Tree,* 3:3 (Fall 1997), 108–111.

Clemons, Hubert W. "The John Watson Family of Hiram, Maine." *Downeast Ancestry,* 1:33.

Clemons, Hubert W. "The Kimball Family of Hiram, Maine." *Downeast Ancestry,* 8:23–26.

Clemons, Hubert W. "The Lowell Family of Hiram, Maine." *Downeast Ancestry,* 15:111–114.

Clemons, Hubert W. "The Mabry Family of Hiram, Maine." *Downeast Ancestry,* 13:153–154.

Clemons, Hubert W. "The Pierce Family of Hiram, Maine." *Downeast Ancestry,* 12:107.

Clemons, Hubert W. "The Rankin Family of Hiram, Maine." *Downeast Ancestry,* 14:159–165.

Clemons, Hubert W. "The Spring Family of Hiram and Brownfield, Maine." *Downeast Ancestry,* 15:21–25.

Clemons, Hubert W. "The Stanley Family of Hiram & Vicinity." *Forebears in Your Maine Family Tree,* 1:13–17.

Clemons, Hubert W. "The Watson Family of Kennebunkport and Hiram, Maine." *Downeast Ancestry,* 5:19–23.

Clemons, Hubert W. "Tripp and Robbins Families from Hiram, ME Area." *Downeast Ancestry,* 16:22–24.

Ridlon, G. T. Sr. [*William Chadbourne…*]. *Portland Sunday Telegram.* Portland, ME: January 15, 1911), Hiram Historical Society.

Wadsworth, Llewellyn A. "First Settlement of Hiram, ME." *Maine Genealogist and Biographer,* 2:1 (September 1876), 94–96.

Wadsworth, Llewellyn A. *Oxford County Advertiser.* Norway and Paris, ME, February 11, 1888.

Wadsworth, Llewellyn A. *Oxford County Record.* Kezar Falls, ME, June 28, 1884.

Zimmerman, Sally. *Historic New England,* Winter 2015, 7.

Property Deeds and Probate Courts

Cumberland County Registry of Deeds (Portland, Maine)

Oxford County Registry of Deeds (Fryeburg and South Paris, Maine)

York County Registry of Deeds (Alfred, Maine)

Index